The

# *Quick* Resume
# &Cover Letter Book

## WRITE AND USE AN EFFECTIVE RESUME IN ONLY ONE DAY

*Fourth Edition*

**Michael Farr**

JIST
Works
America's Career Publisher

# The Quick Resume & Cover Letter Book, Fourth Edition

© 2008 by JIST Publishing

Published by JIST Works, an imprint of JIST Publishing
7321 Shadeland Station, Suite 200
Indianapolis, IN 46256-3923
Phone: 800-648-JIST    Fax: 877-454-7839    E-mail: info@jist.com

Visit our Web site at www.jist.com for information on JIST, free job search tips, book chapters, and ordering instructions for our many products!

Quantity discounts are available for JIST books. Please call our Sales Department at 800-648-5478 for a free catalog and more information. Have future editions of JIST books automatically delivered to you on publication through our convenient standing order program. Please call our Sales Department at 800-648-5478 for a free catalog and more information.

Trade Product Manager: Lori Cates Hand
Interior Design: Aleata Halbig
Interior Layout: Toi Davis
Cover Design: Amy Peppler Adams
Cover Photo: Photodisc Green/Getty Images
Proofreaders: Linda Seifert, Jeanne Clark
Indexer: Kelly Henthorne

Printed in the United States of America
13  12  11  10  09  08  07        9  8  7  6  5  4  3  2  1

Library of Congress Cataloging-in-Publication Data

Farr, J. Michael.
    The quick resume & cover letter book : write and use an effective resume in only one day /
    Michael Farr. -- 4th ed.
            p. cm.
    Includes bibliographical references and index.
    ISBN 978-1-59357-517-5 (alk. paper)
  1.  Résumés (Employment) 2.  Cover letters.  I. Title. II. Title: Quick resume and cover letter book.
    HF5383.F32 2008
    650.14'2--dc22

                                    2007038395

ISBN 978-1-59357-517-5

# You Don't Have to Read This Whole Book!

## *Read Just the First Part and Get a Resume Today!*

This is a big book, but you really don't have to read it all. Writing a resume doesn't have to be difficult. You can create a simple one in about an hour, and a few more hours will give you an even better resume. That's what part 1 is about: finishing an acceptable resume quickly. And that might be all the resume information you need.

Part 1 includes essential resume-writing information, along with some job search tips. The point is to help you get your resume done today, so that you can get started on your job search tomorrow—or this afternoon. After all, your goal is not to write a perfect resume—it's to get a good job.

But this book offers a lot more than resume-writing tips. After you've finished your resume, read the job search tips in part 5. These chapters give you brief but solid advice that can dramatically reduce the time it takes to get a good job.

Other sections provide lots of sample resumes (including electronic resumes) plus information on writing a superior resume, defining your perfect job, and much more. Review the Table of Contents to see what's inside, and read only those things that interest you.

So, yes, this is a pretty big book, but it can still help you find a job quickly. Good luck in your search!

## *Where the Sample Resumes Come From*

I want to thank the many professional resume writers who contributed samples for this book. I've always believed that there is no one right way to develop a resume, so presenting resumes with different design and writing styles is the best way to give you examples for writing your own, in your own way, with confidence.

These people make their livings writing resumes and, more importantly, helping people with their job searches. The sample resumes reflect many approaches to "accentuating the positive" for all sorts of real people. The contributions make this book better. I've included the contributors' names on the sample resumes and their contact information in appendix B. I encourage you to contact them if you want professional assistance in writing your resume. Most of them are very comfortable working over the phone and e-mail, so don't hesitate to contact someone who lives in a different place than you do.

# Contents

## Part 1: Write and Send a Resume in a Day

### Chapter 1: Quick Tips for Creating and Using a Resume ..............................3
What Is a Resume? ........................................................................3

Some People Say You Don't Need a Resume...............................4

Some Good Reasons to Have a Resume ......................................5

Everyone Thinks They're a Resume Expert...................................6

Resume Basics—for Print and Electronic Formats .......................6

Three Types of Resumes ............................................................10

"Send Your Resume to Lots of Strangers and, If It Is Good Enough, You Will Get Job Offers" and Other Fairytales ..............12

### Chapter 2: Write a Simple Resume in About an Hour ...................................15
Two Chronological Resume Samples ..........................................16

The Major Sections of a Chronological Resume...........................19

The Final Draft............................................................................29

### Chapter 3: Write a Skills Resume in Just a Few Hours .................................37
A Sample Skills Resume...............................................................38

Writing a Skills Resume...............................................................40

Tips for Editing Your Draft Resume into Final Form ....................46

More Sample Skills Resumes (and JIST Cards) ............................47

### Chapter 4: Develop an Electronic Resume in Less Than an Hour ..............61
Applying Directly on Employer Web Sites ....................................62

A Sample Text-Only Resume, with All Graphics and Formatting Removed ....................................................................63

Adapting Your Resume for Electronic Use ...................................66

The Importance of Keywords ...................................................67

Using the Internet to Go Beyond the Resume ...........................69

# Part 2: A More Thorough Approach to Resume Writing and Career Planning

**Chapter 5: Develop a Powerful New Skills Language** ...................**77**

Three Major Types of Skills ....................................................78

Identify Your Skills .............................................................79

**Chapter 6: Document the Many Details of Your Work and Life Experience** .........................................................**87**

Quick Tips for Completing the Forms ......................................87

The Worksheets ..................................................................88

**Chapter 7: Identify Your Perfect Job and Industry** .....................**105**

Why Your Resume Needs a Job Objective...............................105

Consider Jobs Within Groups of Related Occupations .............106

The U.S. Department of Labor's *Occupational Outlook Handbook* ........................................................................107

Other Important Sources of Occupational Information.............115

Also Consider Industries in Your Job Search .........................121

Values, Preferences, and Other Factors to Consider in Defining Your Job Objective ..............................................123

Write Your Resume's Job Objective.......................................128

Finalize Your Resume's Job Objective Statement ...................131

**Chapter 8: Highlight Your Strengths and Overcome "Problems" on Your Resume** ................................................**133**

Never Highlight a Negative..................................................133

General Guidelines for Handling "Problems" .........................135

Other Items to Include—or Not Include—on Your Resume ......147

A Final Few Words on Handling Problems..............................152

**Chapter 9: Write a Better Resume Now**..................................................**153**

If You Aren't Good at Writing a Resume, Get Some Help ..........153

What Sort of Resume Will Work Best for You?............................157

Gather Information and Emphasize Accomplishments,
Skills, and Results ........................................................................161

More Quick Resume-Writing Tips .............................................173

More Tips to Improve Your Resume's Design .............................177

# Part 3: A Stupendous Collection of Professionally Written and Designed Resumes

**Chapter 10: Sample Chronological Resumes** .............................................**183**

**Chapter 11: Sample Skills-Based and Combination Resumes** ................**225**

**Chapter 12: Sample Electronic Resumes** ...................................................**267**

# Part 4: Quick Cover Letters, Thank-You Notes, JIST Cards, and Other Job Search Correspondence

**Chapter 13: The Quick Cover Letter and How to Use It** ...........................**291**

Only Two Groups of People Will Receive Your
Cover Letters ...............................................................................292

Seven Quick Tips for Writing a Superior Cover Letter in
15 Minutes...................................................................................292

Writing Cover Letters to People You Know ...............................294

Writing Cover Letters to People You Don't Know .....................301

Additional Sample Cover Letters.................................................304

**Chapter 14: Thank-You Letters and JIST Cards** .........................................**315**

The Importance of Thank-You Letters .......................................315

JIST Cards®—A Mini-Resume and a Powerful Job Search
Tool ............................................................................................326

Other Job Search Correspondence ............................................332

# Part 5:  How to Find a Job Fast

**Chapter 15:  Get a Good Job in Less Time** .................................................**337**

Career Planning and Job Search Advice .....................................337

Changing Jobs and Careers Is Often Healthy.............................339

Seven Steps for a Quick and Successful Job Search  ...................340

The Quick Job Search Review .....................................................362

**Chapter 16:  Quick Tips for Using the Internet in Your Job Search** .........**365**

The Internet as a Tool for Your Job Search .................................365

Eight Quick Tips to Increase Your Job Search Effectiveness
on the Internet  .........................................................................369

The Most Useful Internet Sites ...................................................371

Closing Thoughts: Remember Your Main Purpose......................375

**Appendix A:  Sample Job Description from the *Occupational
Outlook  Handbook*** .................................................................**377**

**Appendix B:  How to Contact the Professional Resume Writers
Who Contributed to This Book**  .............................................**389**

**Index**  ................................................................................................**395**

# Quick Tips on How to Use This Book

I don't expect you to read this book in order from cover to cover. Instead, I suggest you skip around and use only those sections you need most or that interest you. Here are suggestions on the best way to use this book to write your resume and find a good job:

1. **Read the table of contents.** This introduces you to the content of the book and its chapters so that you can start to select the parts most relevant to your needs.

2. **Complete a basic resume as described in part 1.** This section shows you how to put together a resume that's fine for most situations—and helps you do this in just a few hours. You might also want to review the sample resumes in part 3 for examples to follow for your own resume.

3. **Begin looking for a job.** Once you have a basic resume, read part 5 for a quick review of self-directed job search techniques. These techniques can reduce the time it takes to find a job because they are active rather than passive. Then go out looking for your next job.

4. **Complete the activities in part 2.** Besides being helpful in writing a good resume, part 2 provides activities and tips that will help you plan your career, handle interviews, and get a better job than you might otherwise.

5. **If you really need to, and as time permits, write a great resume.** Although it will take more time, you may want to revise your resume and create one that is even better. This book provides lots of good information and sample resumes to help you do this. But keep in mind that your priority is to get a good job and *not* to stay home working on your resume.

This book will help you get over the resume hurdle, get a resume done quickly, and go about the more important task of getting a job.

# Preface

A mazon.com lists 741 books about writing resumes, so you might ask why yet another is needed. The answer is that most resume books misrepresent themselves. They typically argue that the way to get a good job is to do the following:

1. Create an outstanding resume.

2. Put it in front of lots of people who have job openings.

But, if you take that advice (which seems reasonable enough), you will probably be making a big mistake.

The reason is that the logic is flawed. Those authors assume that you should conduct your job search in the traditional way by sending out lots of resumes to human resource (HR) offices, search firms, or hiring managers, in response to an available opening. And they assume that the resume, if it's done well enough, will help you stand out from the pile of resumes that employers get. It all seems to make sense, *but most of the labor market does not work this way anymore!*

The fact is that most jobs are filled by people employers know before a job is ever advertised. For the relatively few jobs that are advertised (and the research indicates that only about 15 to 25 percent are), half of these jobs are filled by people who never read the ads.

So, if you believe that the way to get a job is to send in your resume for an available job opening or to post it on an Internet job board, you are missing out on most job opportunities. Sending your "dyna-mite" resume in the conventional way or over the Internet will cause you to miss about 75 percent of the jobs—the ones that are never advertised at all.

You could, of course, send your resume to lots of employers and hope for the best—and this has worked for some people. Or you could put it on a couple of the popular Internet job boards and wait. But you might be waiting a long time. There is a better way and that's what this book is about. Because you think you need a resume (and you probably do), the thing to do is to get one together quickly. This approach avoids the all-too-common problem of taking a week or more to work on your resume before getting started on your job search. Then, as time permits, you can work on writing a better resume.

That's how this book is arranged. Part 1 includes directions for creating and using a resume in a few hours, including an electronic version of your resume for posting or sending online. Part 2 provides a more detailed approach that will help you sort out your skills, job objective, and other details and provides a form of "career counseling in a book." This part, of course, teaches you much more about writing a good resume. Part 3 provides sample resumes written by resume-writing professionals. Part 4 gives you information and examples for other job search correspondence such as cover letters and thank-you notes. Finally, part 5 offers a quick review of job search methods that have been proven to cut the time it takes to get a job as well as tips on online job seeking.

This thoroughly updated fourth edition retains the successful approach of the preceding editions. Among its many changes and enhancements are the following:

- All new (over 80!) sample resumes from professional resume writers.

- Up-to-date information on using the Internet in your job search, reflecting the latest technology issues and hiring trends.

- Updated information on print and online resources for choosing a career direction and finding your ideal job.

But the real difference in this resume book is that I have spent more than 25 years studying, teaching, and writing about job-seeking skills, with an emphasis on techniques that work. For this reason, this book does something that few resume books do: It provides the facts about what a resume can and can't do. These facts are the following:

- A resume will not get you a job—an interview can.

- A resume is not a particularly good tool for getting interviews. Direct contacts and leads given to you by those you know—or can come to know—are far more important.

- A good resume can help you in your job search, but many people get good jobs without using a resume at all.

- A simple, error-free resume is a far more effective job search tool than an elegant one that you are working on while you should be out getting interviews.

I hope you like the book and, more importantly, that it helps you get the job you want.

Best of "luck" in your job search and your life.

Mike Farr

# Part 1

# Write and Send a Resume in a Day

This might be the only part of the book you'll need. It presents quick ways to create a good resume, along with tips on how to best use it to get a job in less time.

**Chapter 1: Quick Tips for Creating and Using a Resume   3**

**Chapter 2: Write a Simple Resume in About an Hour   15**

**Chapter 3: Write a Skills Resume in Just a Few Hours   37**

**Chapter 4: Develop an Electronic Resume in Less Than a Hour   61**

# CHAPTER 1

# Quick Tips for Creating and Using a Resume

This chapter provides basic information on how to write and use a resume. It gives an overview of resumes and how to use them during your search. Additional information on career planning, job-seeking skills, Internet resumes, and related topics is included in other chapters.

This book's objective is to help you get a good job in less time. Creating a superior resume, however, will not get you a job. No matter how good your resume is, you still have to get interviews and do well in them before getting a job offer.

So, a legitimate question might be "Why have a resume at all?" This chapter answers that question by presenting both sides of the argument as well as my own conclusions. I also give you an overview of guidelines for writing your resume and tips on how to use it.

All topics in this chapter are covered in more detail later. This chapter is an introduction that will help you understand the basics of writing and using a resume as one tool in your search for a new job.

## What Is a Resume?

As a first step in creating a resume, examine what a resume is and consider what it can and cannot do. The word "resume" describes a one- or two-page summary of your skills, training, and employment history. Although resumes are traditionally submitted on paper, they are increasingly sent in electronic form over the Internet. Whatever a resume's form, the idea is to highlight specific parts of your past that demonstrate that you can do a particular job well.

A resume presents you to prospective employers who—based on their response to the resume—may or may not grant you an interview. Along with the application form, the resume is the tool employers use most to screen job seekers.

So, a resume is clearly a tool to use in getting a job, right? The answer to this is both yes and no.

# Some People Say You Don't Need a Resume

For a variety of reasons, many career professionals suggest that resumes aren't needed at all. (Jeffrey Fox even wrote a book called *Don't Send a Resume*.) Some of these reasons make a lot of sense and are detailed in the following sections.

## Resumes Aren't Good Job Search Tools

It's true: Resumes don't do a good job of getting you an interview. Other methods (such as networking) do a better job. When you use your resume in the traditional way, it's more likely to get you screened out than screened in.

## Some Jobs Don't Require Resumes

Employers seeking to fill office, managerial, professional, and technical positions often want the details provided in a resume. But for many jobs, particularly some entry-level, trade, or unskilled positions, resumes typically aren't required. Often, completing an application is all that's required. For example, one recent high school graduate called to check on her application at a mall store and the manager said "Oh yeah—you were the one who included a resume!"

## Some Job Search Methods Don't Require Resumes

Many people get jobs without using a resume at all. In most cases, these people get interviews because they are known to the employer or are referred by someone the employer knows. In these situations, a resume might help; but the employer might not even ask for it.

### Some Resume Experts Call a Resume by Another Name

Many other names are used in place of the word "resume," including "professional profile," "curriculum vitae or CV," "employment proposal," and other terms. One resume book author, for example, advises you not to use a resume. Instead, he advises you to use a "qualifications brief." In all their forms, however, they are really various types of resumes.

## Some Good Reasons to Have a Resume

Although there are some legitimate arguments for why a resume isn't all that important, the reality is that most job seekers need to have a resume. In my opinion, there are several good reasons why.

### Employers Usually Ask for Resumes

If an employer asks for a resume, why make excuses? If you can't provide a resume, there are plenty of other applicants who can and will. This alone is reason enough to have one.

### Resumes Help Structure Your Communications

A good resume requires you to clarify your job objective; select related skills, education, work, or other experiences; and list accomplishments—and present all this in a short format. Doing this is an essential step in your job search, even if you don't give the resume to anyone. If you've put some effort into writing your resume, you'll find that you're much better prepared to speak about yourself in networking situations and interviews.

### If Used Properly, a Resume Can Be an Effective Job Search Tool

A well-done resume presents details of your experiences efficiently so that an employer can refer to them as needed. You can also use it as a tool to present the skills you have to support your job objective and to present details that are often not solicited in a preliminary interview. In other words, the resume helps you tell the employer what you want them to know about you, and often provides the employer with a starting point for interview discussions.

# Everyone Thinks They're a Resume Expert

A resume is one of those things that almost everyone seems to know more about than you do. If you were to show your resume to any three people, you would probably get three different opinions on how to improve it. And they will probably contradict one another.

One person might tell you that you really should have only a one-page resume ("And how come no references are listed?"). Another will tell you that you should list all your hobbies plus your spelling-bee victory from the sixth grade. The third may tell you that your resume is boring and that you should hand print it in red ink on a brown paper bag to get attention.

Few experts agree on the best way to prepare your resume. This means that *you* will have to become your own expert and make some decisions on how to present your qualifications.

**QUICK TIP**

Although the example of the brown-bag resume is a bit extreme, some professions (such as arts and design) allow for a bit more creativity in presenting your qualifications. Chapter 11 gives some examples of creative resumes that aren't too far out in left field.

# Resume Basics—for Print and Electronic Formats

I've developed some basic guidelines for you to consider as you develop your resume. Although these aren't hard-and-fast rules, they are based on many years of experience and common sense.

Many of these guidelines assume a traditional, printed-on-paper format rather than a resume submitted electronically (you can read more on resumes for the Internet and other electronic uses in chapter 4). But you will likely need a paper resume *and* an electronic resume, and this advice will help in either case.

## Length: Make Every Word Count

Opinions differ on length, but one to two pages are usually enough. If you are seeking a managerial, professional, or technical position and have at least 10 years of experience, if not more, two pages is the norm. In most cases, a busy hiring manager will not read all of a resume that is longer than two or three pages. Shorter resumes are often more difficult to write than longer ones; but when you do them properly, they can pay off.

If you can't get everything on one page without crowding, you are better off going onto a second page. Just be sure that you fill at least two-thirds of the second page. You can use a bigger point size, narrower margins, and more spacing between sections to expand your text to fill the second page.

## QUICK NOTE

Surveys have consistently shown that most employers and recruiters read resumes in only 10 to 30 seconds. That's all! The more unnecessary words you include in your resume, the more likely it is that the important information won't get read at all. So, keep your resume short and concise.

Write a long rough draft and then edit, edit, edit. If a word or phrase does not support your job objective, consider dropping it. Force yourself to shorten your resume to include only those words that build a case for why you should get an interview. You can start by putting down too much information to make sure you're not leaving anything out or shortchanging yourself. But then you need to boil it all down to the essential information.

### HONESTY IS THE BEST POLICY

Some people lie on their resumes and claim credentials that they don't have, hoping that no one will find out. Many organizations now verify this information, sometimes long after a person is hired. There have been many high-profile cases of people losing their jobs over such lies, such as the dean of admissions at MIT. So never lie on your resume.

But that doesn't mean that you have to present negative information! Make sure that everything you put in your resume is positive and supports your job objective in some direct way. If you really can do the job you are seeking, someone will hire you. You will sleep better, too.

## *Eliminate Errors*

I am amazed how often an otherwise good resume has typographical, grammatical, or punctuation errors. Employers who notice will not think highly of you and your lack of attention to detail.

Even if you are good at proofreading, find someone else who is good at proofreading and ask this person to review your resume. Carefully. If possible, wait at least one day (or longer, if you can) before reading your draft again to approach it with fresh eyes. A day's delay will allow you to notice what your resume says, rather than what you think it says.

### QUICK TIP

An old proofreading trick is to read your resume backwards, starting from the end. You will notice misspelled words more easily when you're not distracted by the way the sentence flows.

Then, after you've read your resume, read it again to make sure you catch the errors. Then go over it again. Remember that spell-check can find misspelled words, but it won't find words that you've used incorrectly.

## *Use Action Words and Stress Accomplishments*

Most resumes are boring. So don't simply list what your duties were; emphasize what you got done! Employers want to know what you can do for them—how you can help them solve their problems, reach their goals, save money, make money, and edge out the competition. If you only tell them your basic past duties, you aren't distinguishing yourself from other job seekers. All resumes can start to sound alike. But, if you highlight accomplishments, you will set yourself apart from your competition by showing employers how you can add value. Like an interview, your resume is no place to be humble. If you don't communicate what you can do, who will?

### QUICK TIP

Make sure that you mention specific skills you have to do the job, as well as any accomplishments and credentials. Even a resume put together quickly can include some of these elements.

The list entitled "Use Action Words and Phrases" in chapter 2 gives ideas on how to word your accomplishments, as do the sample resumes in part 3 and throughout the book.

## Write It Yourself

Although I expect you to use ideas and even words or phrases you like from the sample resumes in this book, it is most important that your resume represent *you* and not someone else. Present your own skills and experience, and support them with your own accomplishments.

If you do not have good written communication skills, get help from someone who does, such as a professional resume writer. Just make sure that your resume ends up sounding like you wrote it.

## Make It Look Good

Your resume's overall appearance will affect an employer's opinion of you. In a matter of seconds, the employer will form either a positive or a negative opinion. Is your resume well laid out? Is it crisp and professional looking? Is it easy to read?

### Photocopy and Print with Quality

Almost all printed resumes are produced on high-quality laser printers with word-processing software such as Microsoft Word. If you don't have a computer and printer that can produce high-quality print, have someone else print it for you. Your resume *must* be of the highest quality, so don't even consider using an old printer that does not produce excellent print.

When you're satisfied with your resume, you may want to print larger quantities than one-by-one on your computer printer. In that case, consider having a print shop make good-quality photocopies of your resume from a laser-printed original or your word-processing file. Most quick-print shops, including the national chains such as FedEx Kinko's and PIP Printing, will do the word processing and printing for a modest fee, or you can pay an hourly rental fee to do it yourself on their equipment. Ask to see samples of their work and fees—and be willing to go to a few places to get the quality you want.

## QUICK ALERT

Don't print too many copies of your resume at one time. Start with about 25 because you'll probably want to customize it for different jobs. You might be tempted to make hundreds of copies to do a large mailing, but resist that temptation. Mass mailings are usually not an effective job search method. It's better to target your resume to each specific position and employer you are interested in.

## Use Good Paper

Never print your resume on cheap, thin paper like that typically used for photocopies. Papers come in different qualities, and employers can see the difference. Papers that include cotton fibers have a richer texture and feel that is appropriate for a professional-looking resume. Most stationery and office-supply stores carry better papers, as do quick-print shops. The leading resume-paper brand is Southworth (www.southworth.com), and you can see examples of its papers in *Gallery of Best Resumes,* Fourth Edition, by Dr. David Noble.

Although most resumes are printed on white, off-white, bone, or ivory colored paper, you can also use other very light colors in shades of tan or gray, but I do not recommend red, pink, or green tints. Also avoid heavily textured, dark papers; they will not produce clean photocopies and will not show up well if your resume is scanned.

Once you've selected your paper, get matching envelopes. You may also find matching Monarch-size papers and envelopes. This smaller-sized paper, when folded once, makes for an inexpensive and perfectly acceptable thank-you note.

## *Don't Waste Valuable Time Fretting Over Your Resume*

Making contacts and getting interviews is far more important than having a "perfect" resume. So your task is to create a simple but acceptable resume quickly—then use it in an active job search. You can create a better resume later but use your simple one to get started on your job search without delay.

## Three Types of Resumes

To keep this simple, I'm going to discuss only three types of resumes. There are other, more specialized types, but these are generally the most useful: the chronological resume, the skills resume, and the combination resume.

## The Chronological Resume

The word "chronology" refers to a sequence of events in time, and the primary feature of this type of resume is the listing of jobs you've held from the most recent to the least recent. This is the simplest of resumes and can be an effective format if you use it properly. Many employers prefer it to other formats. Chapter 2 shows you how to create this basic type of resume.

## The Skills, or Functional, Resume

Instead of listing your experience under each job, this resume style clusters your experiences under major skill areas. For example, if you are strong in "communication skills," you could list a variety of work and other experiences under that heading. You would also include listings for several of your other major skill areas.

This format makes little sense, of course, unless your job objective *requires* these skills. For this reason and others, a skills resume is often more difficult to write than a simple chronological resume. But if you have limited paid work experience, are changing careers, or have not worked for a while, a skills resume may be a superior way to present your strengths and avoid displaying your weaknesses.

## Combination and Creative Resumes

You can combine elements of both the chronological and skills formats in various ways to improve the clarity or presentation of your resume. You can start the resume with skills categories and end with a listing of your jobs and the dates you worked there.

There are also creative formats that defy categorization but that are clever and have worked for some people. I've seen handwritten resumes (usually *not* a good idea); unusual paper colors, sizes, and shapes; resumes with tasteful drawings and borders; and lots of other ideas. Some of these resumes were well done and well received; others were not.

## WEIRD RESUME FORMATS

For your entertainment, here are some resume formats and presentations that I have seen or know of. Please, if you ever credit me for this list, be sure to mention that I thought many of these were bad ideas. But, then again, some of them did work.

- A cluster of helium-filled balloons, each with a copy of the same resume attached and a note saying, "Please hire me!"

- A small gift bag containing a handwritten resume and a stuffed bear. The bear was holding the candidate's JIST Card (which you will learn about in chapter 3).

- A box of candy with a resume inside.

- A 24-x-24-inch box, shipped overnight, with a balloon and confetti inside. As the recipient opened the box, the balloon floated up and spread confetti around. This, of course, was intended to surprise and delight. The balloon had a resume attached to a string. This one got some laughs but no job, other than cleaning up the confetti.

- And, yes, I really have seen a resume handwritten on a melon that was painted white.

I could keep going, but I don't want to encourage these types of resumes. They certainly get attention, and some people insist that they helped them land jobs. Such resumes might even make some sense in certain creative jobs such as marketing, graphic design, or sales—or in creative industries and organizations. But, for most situations, my advice is to stick to less outrageous approaches.

# "Send Your Resume to Lots of Strangers and, If It Is Good Enough, You Will Get Job Offers" and Other Fairytales

You've probably gotten the message loud and clear by now that your resume is only as good as how you use it. That is why I suggest doing a simple resume early in your job search—one you can create in a few hours. This approach allows you to get on with actively getting interviews instead of sitting at home working on a better resume. Later, you can develop an improved one.

## Resumes Don't Get Jobs

Contrary to the advice of many people who write resume books, writing a "dynamite" or "perfect" (or whatever) resume will rarely get you the job you want. That will happen only following an interview, with just a few odd exceptions. So the task in the job search is to get interviews and to do well in them. Sending out lots of resumes to people you don't know—and most other traditional resume advice—is a lot of baloney.

## Tips on the Right Way to Find a Job

Although I can't teach you all there is to know about getting a job in this book, part 5 includes information that will help. If you are particularly anxious to get on with your job search without delay, following are some basic tips on getting a good job that I have learned over many years.

1. **Know your skills and their value.** If you don't know what you are good at and what difference you can make to an employer, how can you expect anyone else to figure it out? One employer survey found that about 80 percent of those who made it to the interview did not do a good job presenting the skills they had to do the job. If you don't know your skills and accomplishments and how they relate to a particular job, you can't write a good resume or perform well in an interview, and are unlikely to get a good job.

2. **Have a clear job objective.** If you don't know where you want to go, it will be most difficult to get there. You can write a resume without having a job objective, but it won't be a good one. Part 2 helps you with this issue.

3. **Know where and how to look.** Because three out of four jobs are not advertised, you will have to use other job search techniques to find them. Part 5 provides additional information on the techniques I recommend you use in your search for a job.

4. **Spend at least 30 to 40 hours a week looking if you're unemployed and about 10 to 15 hours a week if you're currently employed.** Most job seekers spend far less time than this. As a result, they take much longer to find a new job than they need

to. So, if you want to get a better job in less time, plan on spending more time on your job search.

5. **Get two interviews a day.** It sounds impossible, but this *can* be done once you redefine what counts as an interview. Part 5 helps you do this and get those two interviews a day. Compare getting two interviews a day to the average job seeker's activity level of four or five interviews a *month,* and you see how it can make a big difference.

6. **Do well in interviews.** You are unlikely to get a job offer if you don't do well in this critical situation. I've reviewed the research on what it takes to do well in an interview and found, happily, that you can improve your interview performance relatively easily. Knowing what skills you have and being able to support them with examples is a good start. Part 2 includes a chapter on identifying your key skills and helps to prepare you for interviews—as well as for writing a superior resume.

7. **Follow up on all contacts.** Following up can make a big difference in the results you get in your search for a new job. Parts 4 and 5 have tips for sending thank-you notes.

No one should ever say that looking for a job is easy. But you can take steps to make the process a bit easier and shorter than it typically is. Getting your resume together is something that hangs many people up for entirely too long. The next two chapters help you solve that problem.

# CHAPTER 2

# Write a Simple Resume in About an Hour

You can write a basic resume in about an hour. It will not be a fancy one, and you may want to write a better one later, but I suggest you develop the simple one first. Even if you decide to create a more sophisticated resume later, doing a quick one now will allow you to use it in your job search within 24 hours.

The activities in this chapter also prepare you to take better advantage of the material in other chapters. So don't resist—get out your pen and get to work.

Keeping things simple has its advantages. This chapter does just that by presenting information, examples, and an Instant Resume Worksheet to help you write a basic chronological resume in about an hour. It also includes tips to improve your basic resume that are worth a little more time.

A chronological resume is easy to develop, which gives this format a big advantage over other styles. The chronological format works best for those who have had several years of experience in the same type of job they are seeking now. This is because a chronological resume clearly displays your recent work experience. If you want to change careers, have been out of the workforce recently, or do not have much paid work experience related to the job you want, a chronological resume might not be the best format for you. In these instances, you might want to use a skills resume, which is presented in chapter 3.

Most employers find a chronological resume perfectly acceptable, as long as it is neat and has no errors. You can use it early in your job search while you work on a more sophisticated resume. The important point is to get an acceptable resume together quickly so you won't be sitting at home worrying about your resume instead of being out job hunting.

# Two Chronological Resume Samples

Before starting your own chronological resume, you might find it helpful to see a couple of samples. Two sample resumes for the same person follow, and both use a chronological format. The first (figure 2.1) is a simple one, but it works well enough in this situation because Judith is looking for a job in her present career field, has a steady job history, and has related education and training. Note that she wants to move up in responsibility and emphasizes the skills and education that will help her do so.

One nice feature is that this job seeker put her recent business schooling in both the education and experience sections. Doing this filled a job gap and allows her to present recent training as equivalent to work experience. This resume also includes a "Strengths and Skills" section, where she presents some special qualifications and technical skills.

This same resume is then improved in the second example (figure 2.2). The improved resume adds a number of features, including a more thorough job objective, a "Special Skills and Abilities" section, and more accomplishments and skills. Notice, for example, the impact of the numbers she adds to this resume in statements such as "top 30% of my class" and "decreased department labor costs by more than $30,000 a year."

You should be able to write a resume like the one in figure 2.2 with an hour or two of additional work over the one in figure 2.1. Most employers will be impressed by the additional positive information it provides.

Besides being fairly quick to create, these two resumes have an added benefit in an Internet-oriented world. If you plan to submit your resume to an online database or via e-mail, this format requires only minor modification. Fancier resumes with graphics, bullets, borders, and other special formatting must be stripped of their more decorative elements to become an electronic resume.

**FIGURE 2.1: A SIMPLE CHRONOLOGICAL RESUME.**

# Judith J. Jones

115 South Hawthorne Avenue
Chicago, Illinois 66204
tel: (312) 653-9217
email: jj@earthlink.com

## JOB OBJECTIVE

A position in the office management, accounting, or administrative assistant area that enables me to grow professionally.

## EDUCATION AND TRAINING

Acme Business College, Lincoln, IL
Graduate of a one-year business program.

John Adams High School, South Bend, IN
Diploma, business education.

U.S. Army
Financial procedures, accounting functions.

Other: Continuing-education classes and workshops in business communication, spreadsheet and database applications, scheduling systems, and customer relations.

## EXPERIENCE

2006–present—Claims Processor, Blue Spear Insurance Co., Wilmette, IL. Process customer medical claims, develop management reports based on created spreadsheets and develop management reports based on those forms, exceed productivity goals.

2005–2006—Returned to school to upgrade business and computer skills. Completed courses in advanced accounting, spreadsheet and database programs, office management, human relations, and new office techniques.

2002–2005—E4, U.S. Army. Assigned to various stations as a specialist in finance operations. Promoted prior to honorable discharge.

2001–2002—Sandy's Boutique, Wilmette, IL. Responsible for counter sales, display design, cash register, and other tasks.

1999–2001—Held part-time and summer jobs throughout high school.

## STRENGTHS AND SKILLS

Reliable, hardworking, and good with people. General ledger, accounts payable, and accounts receivable. Proficient in Microsoft Word, WordPerfect, Excel, and Outlook.

## FIGURE 2.2: THE IMPROVED CHRONOLOGICAL RESUME.

# Judith J. Jones

115 South Hawthorne Avenue
Chicago, IL 66204

jj@earthlink.com
(312) 653-9217 (cell)

### JOB OBJECTIVE

A position requiring excellent business management expertise in an office environment. Position should require a variety of skills, including office management, word processing, and spreadsheet and database application use.

### EDUCATION AND TRAINING

Acme Business College, Lincoln, IL
Completed one-year program in **Professional Office Management.** Achieved GPA in top 30% of class. Courses included word processing, accounting theory and systems, advanced spreadsheet and database applications, graphics design, time management, and supervision.

John Adams High School, South Bend, IN
Graduated with emphasis on **business courses.** Earned excellent grades in all business topics and won top award for word-processing speed and accuracy.

Other: Continuing-education programs at own expense, including business communications, customer relations, computer applications, and sales techniques.

### EXPERIENCE

2006–present—**Claims Processor, Blue Spear Insurance Company,** Wilmette, IL. Process 50 complex medical insurance claims per day, almost 20% above department average. Created a spreadsheet report process that decreased department labor costs by more than $30,000 a year. Received two merit raises for performance.

2005–2006—**Returned to business school to gain advanced office skills.**

2002–2005—**Finance Specialist (E4), U.S. Army.** Systematically processed more than 200 invoices per day from commercial vendors. Trained and supervised eight employees. Devised internal system allowing 15% increase in invoices processed with a decrease in personnel. Managed department with a budget equivalent of more than $350,000 a year. Honorable discharge.

2001–2002—**Sales Associate promoted to Assistant Manager, Sandy's Boutique,** Wilmette, IL. Made direct sales and supervised four employees. Managed daily cash balances and deposits, made purchasing and inventory decisions, and handled all management functions during owner's absence. Sales increased 26% and profits doubled during tenure.

1999–2001—**Held various part-time and summer jobs through high school while maintaining GPA 3.0/4.0.** Earned enough to pay all personal expenses, including car insurance. Learned to deal with customers, meet deadlines, work hard, and handle multiple priorities.

### STRENGTHS AND SKILLS

Reliable, with strong work ethic. Excellent interpersonal, written, and oral communication and math skills. Accept supervision well, effectively supervise others, and work well as a team member. General ledger, accounts payable, and accounts receivable expertise. Proficient in Microsoft Word, Excel, PowerPoint, and Outlook; WordPerfect.

# The Major Sections of a Chronological Resume

Now that you have seen what both basic and improved chronological resumes look like, it's time to create your own chronological resume. An Instant Resume Worksheet follows this section. I encourage you to use it to complete each part of your basic chronological resume. You may find it helpful to complete each worksheet section after you read its related tips here.

## Heading

In the past you might have seen a resume that included the word "Resume" at the top, just in case the reader didn't know what it was. But these days, everyone will know what it is, so the heading is really not necessary.

## Name

This one seems obvious, but you want to avoid some things. For example, don't use a nickname; you need to present a professional image. Even if you have to modify your name a bit from the way you typically introduce yourself, it's important to sound professional by using your full name.

**QUICK NOTE**

Refer to the appropriate chapter in part 2 for substantial additional information on handling specific parts of a resume. You can also look at the many sample resumes in part 3 to see how others have handled various situations.

## Address

Don't abbreviate words such as "Street" or "Avenue." Do include your ZIP code. If you move during your job search, or expect that you might, ask a relative, friend, or neighbor in the new location whether you can temporarily use his or her address for your mail. Forwarded mail will be delayed and can cause you to lose an opportunity. Get an address at the new location so that you appear to be settled there.

**QUICK TIP**

If you're looking for a job in another location and don't know anyone there whose address you could use on your resume, look into the option of having a drop box that gives a real street address rather than a post office box. These are available for a small fee through local office-supply shops and national shipping chains such as The UPS Store and Mail Boxes, Etc.

## Phone Numbers and E-mail Address

An employer is more likely to phone or e-mail you than to contact you by mail, so giving an employer this contact information is essential.

Use a phone number that will be answered throughout your job search. Always include your area code. Because you often will be gone (at your current job or out looking for a new one), you must have an answering machine or voice-mail service.

**QUICK ALERT**

Keep in mind that an employer could call at any time. Make sure that anyone who will pick up the phone knows to answer professionally and take an accurate message, including a phone number. Practice with these people if you need to. Nothing is as maddening as a garbled message with the wrong number—or no message at all.

Call your answering machine or voice-mail. Listen to what the outgoing message says, and how. If it has some cute, boring, or less-than-professional message, change it to one you would like your next employer to hear. You can go back to your standard howling-wolves answer after you get your next job.

As you look at this book's sample resumes, notice that some provide more than one phone number or an explanation following the number. For example, "555-299-3643 (messages)" quickly communicates that the caller is likely to be asked to leave a message rather than reach you in person. Adding "555-264-3720 (cell)" gives employers another calling option.

If you have an e-mail address, definitely include it. If you don't have an e-mail account, give serious consideration to getting one. Many services, such as Hotmail.com and Yahoo.com, offer free e-mail. Even if you don't have Internet access at home, you can check your mail at a public library or on a friend's computer. Just be sure that if you do give out an e-mail address, you will check it regularly to see whether you've received any mail.

---

### Do It Now

*Now, take a moment to complete the identification section in the Instant Resume Worksheet on page 30.*

---

## Job Objective

Although you could put together a simple resume without a job objective, it is wise to include one. Doing so enables you to select resume content that directly supports your candidacy for the job you want. In a more advanced version of your resume, you might choose to omit the objective and include a Summary of Qualifications section instead. For now, the objective will help you focus your thinking and create a targeted resume.

Carefully write your job objective so that it does not exclude you from jobs you would consider. For example, if you use a job title like "administrative assistant," ask yourself whether doing so would exclude you from other jobs you would consider. Look at how Judith Jones presented her job objective in her basic resume (figure 2.1):

> A position in the office management, accounting, or administrative assistant area that enables me to grow professionally.

This resume keeps her options open more than saying "administrative assistant." And her improved resume's job objective says even more:

> A position requiring excellent business management expertise in an office environment. Position should require a variety of skills, including office management, word processing, and spreadsheet and database application use.

A good job objective allows you to be considered for more responsible jobs than you have held in the past, or to accept positions with different job titles that use similar skills.

I see many objectives that emphasize what the person wants but that do not provide information on what he or she offers the employer. For example, an objective that says "Interested in a position that allows me to be creative and that offers adequate pay and advancement opportunities" is not good. Who cares? This objective, a real one that someone wrote, displays a self-centered, "gimme" approach that will turn off most employers. Yours should emphasize what you can do, your skills, and how you can help a company meet its objectives.

Refer to the following examples of simple but useful job objectives. Most provide some information on the type of job the candidate seeks as well as on the skills he or she offers.

**QUICK TIP**

The best objectives avoid a narrow job title and position you to be considered for a range of appropriate jobs. They also focus on what you can do for the company—not what *they* can do for *you.*

The sample resumes throughout this book include job objectives that you can review to see how others have phrased them. Browse these objectives for ideas.

---

### Do It Now

*Jot down your own draft job objective and refine it until it sounds right to you. Then rewrite it on page 30 of the Instant Resume Worksheet.*

---

## SAMPLE JOB OBJECTIVES

Responsible general office position to utilize solid clerical and computer skills in a fast-paced, medium-sized organization.

Management position in the warehousing industry requiring supervisory, problem-solving, and organizational skills.

Computer programmer or systems analyst position. Prefer an accounting-oriented emphasis and a solution-oriented organization.

Medical assistant or coordinator in a physician's office, hospital, or other health services environment.

Responsible position that requires skills in public relations, writing, and reporting.

An aggressive and success-oriented professional, seeking a sales position offering both challenge and growth.

Desire position in office management requiring flexibility, strong organizational skills, and an ability to interact with people at all levels of the organization.

## Education and Training

Lead with your strengths. Recent graduates or those with good academic or training credentials but weak work experience should put their education and training toward the top because it represents a more important part of their experience. More experienced workers with work history related to their job objective can put their education and training toward the end.

You can drop the Education and Training section if it doesn't support your job objective or if you don't have the credentials typically expected of those seeking similar positions. This is particularly true if you have lots of work experience in your career area. Usually, however, you should emphasize the most recent or highest level of education or training that relates to the job.

**QUICK TIP**

Drop or downplay details that don't support your job objective. For example, if you have a degree but not in the preferred field, tell employers what you do have. Include details of relevant courses, good grades, related extracurricular activities, and accomplishments.

Depending on your situation, your education and training could be the most important part of your resume, so beef it up with details if you need to.

---

### Do It Now

*Look at the sample resumes in part 3 for ideas. Then, on a separate piece of paper, rough out your Education and Training section. Then edit it to its final form and write it on pages 30–31 of the Instant Resume Worksheet.*

---

## USE ACTION WORDS AND PHRASES

Use active rather than passive words and phrases throughout your resume. Here is a short list of active words to give you some ideas:

| | | |
|---|---|---|
| Achieved | Expanded | Organized |
| Administered | Implemented | Planned |
| Analyzed | Improved | Presented |
| Controlled | Increased | Promoted |
| Coordinated | productivity | Reduced |
| Created | (profits) | expenses |
| Designed | Initiated | Researched |
| Developed | Innovated | Scheduled |
| Diagnosed | Instructed | Solved |
| Directed | Modified | Supervised |
| Established policy | Negotiated | Trained |
| Established priorities | | |

## Work Experience

This resume section provides the details of your work history, starting with the most recent job. If you have significant work history, list each job along with quantified details of what you accomplished and special skills you used. Emphasize skills that directly relate to the job objective on your resume. Use numbers wherever possible.

Volunteer and military work experience are usually listed in separate sections after your paid civilian work history. You can, however, include volunteer work in the regular Work Experience section if you have limited paid work experience or if the volunteer work is highly relevant to your job objective. Similarly, you can include military experience in the Work Experience section if you consider your military experience to be a significant part of your career history.

## Previous/Current Job Titles

You can modify the titles you've had to more accurately reflect your responsibilities. For example, if your title was sales clerk but you frequently opened and closed the store and were often left in charge, you might use the more descriptive title of Night Sales Manager. Always check with your previous supervisors to make sure they approve of this and will back you up when a prospective employer checks your references.

**QUICK TIP**

If you were promoted, handle the promotion as a separate job under the same employer heading, listing the dates that you held each position to show how you progressed with the organization.

## Previous/Current Employers

Provide the organization's name and list the city, state, or province in which it was located. A street address or supervisor's name is not necessary—you can provide those details on a separate sheet of references if you are asked for them.

## Employment Dates

If you have large gaps in employment that are not easily explained, use full years instead of including the months in which you started and left. Doing so deemphasizes the gaps. Chapter 8 has additional information on handling this and other problems. If there was a significant period when you did not work, did you do anything that could explain it in a positive way? School? Travel? Raise a family? Self-employment? Even if you mowed lawns and painted houses for money while you were unemployed, that could count as self-employment. Employers will look on this more favorably than if you say you were unemployed.

## Duties and Accomplishments

In writing about your work experience, be sure to use action words and emphasize what you accomplished. Quantify what you did and provide evidence that you did it well. Take particular care to mention skills that directly relate to doing well in the job you want now.

If your previous jobs are not directly related to what you want to do now, emphasize skills you used in previous jobs that could be used in the new job. For example, someone who waits on tables has to deal with people and work quickly under pressure—skills needed in many other jobs such as accounting and managing.

### QUICK TIP

Look up the descriptions of jobs you have held in the past and jobs you want now in a book titled the *Occupational Outlook Handbook (OOH)*. This book, which is available in most libraries, tells you the skills needed to succeed in the new job. Emphasize these and similar skills in your resume. (See chapter 7 for more about the *OOH*.) You can also access the *OOH* online at www.bls.gov/oco.

---

### *Do It Now*

*Use separate sheets of paper to write rough drafts of what you will use in your resume. Edit it so that every word contributes something. When you're done, transfer your statements to pages 33–36 of the Instant Resume Worksheet.*

---

## *Professional Organizations*

This is an optional section where you can list your activities with job-related professional, humanitarian, or other groups. These activities may be worth mentioning, particularly if you were an officer or were active in some other way. Mention accomplishments or awards you earned during these affiliations. Many of the sample resumes in this book include statements about accomplishments to show you how to do this.

**QUICK TIP**

Emphasize accomplishments! Think about the things you achieved in jobs, school, the military, and other settings. Make sure that you emphasize these things in your resume, even if it seems like bragging.

---

### Do It Now

*Go to page 36 in the Instant Resume Worksheet and list your job-related efforts in professional organizations and other groups.*

---

## Recognition and Awards

If you have received any formal honors or awards that support your job objective, consider mentioning them. You can create a separate section for your awards if you have at least two to list, or you can put them in the Work Experience, Skills, Education, or Personal section.

## Personal Information

Years ago, resumes included personal details such as height, weight, marital status, hobbies, leisure activities, and other trivia. Please do not do this. Current laws do not allow an employer to base hiring decisions on certain points, so providing this information can cause some employers to toss your resume. For the same reason, do not include a photo of yourself.

**QUICK NOTE**

International resumes, often called CVs or *curriculum vitae,* do include personal information such as marital status. In America, however, including this information is taboo.

Although a Personal section is optional, I sometimes like to end a resume on a personal note. Some resumes provide a touch of humor or playfulness as well as selected positives from outside school and work. This section is also a good place to list significant community involvements, a willingness to relocate, or personal characteristics an employer might like. But keep it short.

***Do It Now***

*Turn to page 36 in the Instant Resume Worksheet and list any personal information that you feel is appropriate and relevant.*

## References

It is not necessary to include the names of your references on a resume. You can do better things with the precious space. It's also not necessary to state "references available on request" at the bottom of your resume, because that is obvious. If an employer wants your references, he or she knows to ask you for them.

Line up references in advance. Pick people who know your work as an employee, volunteer, or student. Make sure that they will express nice things about you by asking what they would say if asked. Push for negatives and don't feel hurt if you get some. Nobody is perfect, and it gives you a chance to delete references before they do you damage. Once you know who to include, type a list of references on a separate sheet. Include names, addresses, phone numbers, and details of why they are on your list. You can give this to employers who ask for references.

Be aware that some employers are not allowed to give references over the phone. I have refused to hire people who probably had good references but about whom I could not get information. If this is the case with a previous employer, ask the employer to write a letter of reference for you to photocopy as needed. This is a good idea in general, so you might want to ask employers for one even if they have no rules against phone references.

### QUICK TIP

One way to give employers positive information from past supervisors is to include a short quote from a performance evaluation or other correspondence directly on your resume. Part 3 shows examples of resumes that include supervisor quotes.

# The Final Draft

At this point you should have completed the Instant Resume Worksheet on pages 30–36. Carefully review dates, addresses, phone numbers, spelling, and other details. You can use the worksheet as a guide for preparing a better-than-average chronological resume.

Use the sample chronological resumes from this chapter as the basis for creating your resume. Additional examples of resumes appear in chapters 3, 4, 10, 11, and 12. Look them over for writing and formatting ideas. The sample resumes in chapter 3 tend to be simpler and easier to write and format than some of the more advanced samples found in chapters 10 through 12 and will provide better models for creating a resume quickly.

## QUICK TIP

Most word-processing programs have resume templates or "wizards" that will help make your resume look good.

Once you have completed the Instant Resume Worksheet, you have the information you need for a basic resume. If you have access to a computer, go ahead and put the information into the form of a resume.

If you do not have access to a computer, have someone else type and format your resume. But whether you do it yourself or have it done, carefully review it for typographical or other errors that may have slipped in. Then, when you are certain that everything is correct, have the final version prepared.

# Instant Resume Worksheet

## Identification

Name _____

Home address _____

_____ ZIP code _____

Phone number and description (if any) ( ) _____

_____

Alternate phone number and description ( ) _____

_____

E-mail address _____

## Your Job Objective

_____

_____

_____

_____

_____

_____

## Education and Training

**Highest Level/Most Recent Education or Training**

Institution name _____

City, state/province (optional)_____

Certificate or degree _____

Specific courses or programs that relate to your job objective _____

_____

_____

**Related awards, achievements, and extracurricular activities** _____

_____

_____

**Anything else that might support your job objective, such as good grades** _____

_____

_____

_____

_____

**College/Post High School**

**Institution name** _____

**City, state/province (optional)** _____

**Certificate or degree** _____

_____

**Specific courses or programs that relate to your job objective** _____

_____

_____

**Related awards, achievements, and extracurricular activities** _____

_____

_____

**Anything else that might support your job objective, such as good grades** _____

_____

_____

_____

_____

(continued)

(continued)

**High School**

Institution name _____

City, state/province (optional)_____

Certificate or degree _____

Specific courses or programs that relate to your job objective _____

_____

_____

Related awards, achievements, and extracurricular activities _____

_____

_____

Anything else that might support your job objective, such as good grades _____

_____

_____

_____

_____

**Armed Services Training and Other Training or Certification**

Institution name _____

Specific courses or programs that relate to your job objective _____

_____

_____

Related awards, achievements, and extracurricular activities _____

_____

_____

Anything else that might support your job objective, such as good grades _____

_____

_____

**Related Workshops, Seminars, Informal Learning, or Any Other Training**

_____

_____

_____

_____

_____

_____

## Experience

**Most Recent Position**

Dates: from _____ to _____

Organization name _____

City, state/province _____

Your job title(s) _____

Duties _____

_____

_____

Skills _____

_____

_____

Equipment or software you used _____

_____

_____

Promotions, accomplishments, and anything else positive _____

_____

_____

_(continued)_

(continued)

**Next Most Recent Position**

Dates: from _____ to _____

Organization name _____

City, state/province _____

Your job title(s) _____

Duties _____

_____

_____

Skills _____

_____

_____

Equipment or software you used _____

_____

_____

Promotions, accomplishments, and anything else positive _____

_____

_____

**Next Most Recent Position**

Dates: from _____ to _____

Organization name _____

City, state/province _____

Your job title(s) _____

Duties _____

_____

_____

Skills _____

_____

_____

Equipment or software you used _____

_____

_____

Promotions, accomplishments, and anything else positive _____

_____

_____

### Next Most Recent Position

Dates: from _____ to _____

Organization name _____

City, state/province _____

_____

Your job title(s) _____

_____

Duties _____

_____

_____

Skills _____

_____

_____

Equipment or software you used _____

_____

_____

Promotions, accomplishments, and anything else positive _____

_____

_____

*(continued)*

(continued)

**Any Other Work or Volunteer Experience**

_____

_____

_____

_____

## Professional Organizations

_____

_____

_____

_____

## Personal Information

_____

_____

_____

_____

# CHAPTER 3

# Write a Skills Resume in Just a Few Hours

Although it takes a bit longer to develop a skills resume than it does a chronological resume, there are a variety of reasons to write one. This chapter shows you why a skills resume may be good to consider and how to write one.

Be sure to read chapter 1 and do the activities in chapter 2 (particularly the Instant Resume Worksheet) before completing the skills resume described here.

This chapter shows you how to write a resume organized around the key skills you have that are needed in the job you want.

In its simplest form, a chronological resume is little more than a list of job titles and other details. If you want to change your career or increase your responsibility, the chronological style can often be ineffective. This chapter helps you highlight the skills you can use to transition to a new career or promotion.

Employers and recruiters usually look for candidates with a work history that fits the position they have to fill. If they want to hire a cost accountant, they look for someone who has done this work. If you are a recent graduate or have little experience in the career or at the level you now want, you will find that a simple chronological resume emphasizes your lack of related experience rather than your ability to do the job.

A skills resume avoids these problems by highlighting what you have done under specific skills headings rather than under past jobs. If you hitchhiked across the country for two years, a skills resume won't necessarily display this as an employment gap. Instead, under a heading called "Market Knowledge," you could say "Traveled extensively throughout the country and am familiar with most major market areas." That could be very useful experience for certain positions.

**QUICK ALERT**

Because a skills resume can hide your problems, some employers don't like it. But if a chronological resume would highlight a weakness, a skills resume may help get you an interview (with an employer who doesn't dislike skills resumes) instead of getting screened out. Who wins? You do.

Even if you don't have anything to hide, a skills resume emphasizes your key skills and experiences more clearly. And you can always include a chronological list of jobs at the end of the resume, thus making it a combination of the skills and chronological formats. So everyone should consider a skills resume.

## A Sample Skills Resume

Following is a basic skills resume (see figure 3.1). The example is for a recent high school graduate whose only paid work experience is in fast food. Read it and ask yourself: If you were an employer, would you consider interviewing Lisa? For most people, the answer is yes.

**QUICK NOTE**

This resume is a good example of how a skills resume can help someone who does not have the best credentials. It allows the job seeker to present school and extracurricular activities to good effect. It is a strong format choice because it lets her highlight strengths without emphasizing her limited work experience. It doesn't say where she worked or for how long, yet it gives her a shot at many jobs.

Although the sample resume is simple, it presents Lisa in a positive way. She is looking for an entry-level job in a nontechnical area, so many employers will be more interested in her skills than in her job-specific experience. What work experience she does have is presented as a plus. And notice how she listed her gymnastics experience next to "Hardworking."

**FIGURE 3.1: A SAMPLE SKILLS RESUME.**

### Lisa M. Rhodes
813 Lava Court • Denver, CO 81613
Home: (413) 643-2173 (leave message)
Cell: (413) 442-1659
lrhodes@netcom.net

### Objective
Sales-oriented position in a retail sales or distribution business.

### Skills and Abilities

| | |
|---|---|
| **Communications** | Good written and verbal presentation skills. Use proper grammar and have a good speaking voice. |
| **Interpersonal Skills** | Able to get along well with coworkers and accept supervision. Received positive evaluations from previous supervisors. |
| **Flexible** | Willing to try new things and am interested in improving efficiency on assigned tasks. |
| **Attention to Detail** | Concerned with quality. Produce work that is orderly and attractive. Ensure tasks are completed correctly and on time. |
| **Hardworking** | Throughout high school, worked long hours in strenuous activities while attending school full-time. Often managed as many as 65 hours a week in school and other structured activities while maintaining above-average grades. |
| **Customer Service** | Routinely handled as many as 500 customer contacts a day (10,000 per month) in a busy retail outlet. Averaged lower than a .001% complaint rate and was given the "Employee of the Month" award in second month of employment. Received two merit increases. |
| **Cash Sales** | Handled more than $2,000 a day ($40,000 a month) in cash sales. Balanced register and prepared daily sales summary and deposits. |
| **Reliable** | Excellent attendance record; trusted to deliver daily cash deposits totaling more than $40,000 a month. |

### Education
Franklin High School, 2005–2008. Classes included advanced English. Member of award-winning band. Excellent attendance record. Superior communication skills. Graduated in top 30% of class.

### Other
Active gymnastics competitor for four years. Learned discipline, teamwork, how to follow instructions, and how to work hard. Ambitious, outgoing, and reliable, and have solid work ethic.

If you have more work experience than shown in this example, look at the sample resumes at the end of this chapter and at those in part 3. There are examples of skills resumes for people with more education and experience.

**QUICK ALERT**

You'll get the best results from a skills resume by using it when you have a referral to an organization instead of using it to apply cold or to an ad. Because the skills resume usually doesn't list specifics of work history, many employers will toss it out in favor of your competitors' resumes that do. So, stick with using the skills resume primarily when you're networking for a job.

# Writing a Skills Resume

The skills resume format uses a number of sections similar to those in a chronological resume. This chapter discusses only those sections that are substantially different—the Job Objective and Skills sections. Refer to chapter 2 for information on sections that are common to both types of resumes. The samples at the end of this chapter give you ideas on skills resume language, organization, and layout, and how to handle special problems.

Don't be afraid to use a little creativity in writing your skills resume. You can break some rules if it will help you present yourself more authentically.

**QUICK TIP**

It is essential that your resume emphasize the skills you have that directly support your ability to do the job you want. You will benefit greatly from the skills identification activities in chapter 4. These include lists of skills that are of particular value to employers.

## *Job Objective*

Whereas a simple chronological resume doesn't require a career objective section, a skills resume does. Without a reasonably clear job objective, it is not possible to select and organize the key skills you have to support that job objective. It may be that the job objective you wrote for your chronological resume is good as is, but for a skills resume, your job objective statement should answer the following questions:

- **What sort of position, title, or area of specialization do you seek?** After reading the information on job objectives in chapter 2, you should know how to present the type of job you are seeking. Is your objective too narrow and specific? Is it so broad or vague as to be meaningless? If necessary, turn to chapter 6 to identify your job objective more clearly.

- **What level of responsibility interests you?** Job objectives often indicate a level of responsibility, particularly for supervisory or management roles. If in doubt, always try to keep open the possibility of getting a job with a higher level of responsibility (and, often, salary) than your previous or current one. Write your job objective to include this possibility.

- **What are your most important skills?** What are the two or three most important skills or personal characteristics needed to succeed on the job you've targeted? These are often mentioned in a job objective.

**QUICK TIP**

Review the sample job objectives in chapter 2 and look over the sample resumes at the end of this chapter and in part 3. Notice that some resumes use headings such as "Position Desired" or "Career Objective" to introduce the job objective section. Many people think that these headings sound more professional than "Job Objective." Choose the wording that works best for your situation.

## The Skills Section

This section can be called "Areas of Accomplishment," "Summary of Qualifications," "Areas of Expertise and Ability," or something else. Whatever you choose to call it, this section is what makes a skills resume. To construct it, you must carefully consider which skills you want to emphasize.

Your task is to feature the skills that are essential to success on the job you want and the skills that you have and want to use. You probably have a good idea of which skills meet both criteria, but you may find it helpful to review chapter 5 on developing your skills language.

### QUICK TIP

A good place to look for skills to feature is in the job posting or job description for the job you seek or jobs that are similar.

Note that some resumes in this book emphasize skills that are not specific to a particular job. For example, "well organized" is an important skill in many jobs. In your resume, you should provide specific examples of situations or accomplishments that show you possess such skills. You can do this by including examples from previous work or other experiences.

## Key Skills List

Following is a list of skills considered key for success on most jobs. It is based on research on the skills employers look for in employees. So, if you have to emphasize some skills over others, include these—assuming you have them, of course.

### Key Skills Needed for Success in Most Jobs

| Basic Skills | Key Transferable Skills |
|---|---|
| *Considered the Minimum to Keep a Job* | *That Transfer from Job to Job and Are Most Likely to Be Needed in Jobs with Higher Pay and Responsibility* |
| Basic academic skills | Instructing others |
| Accepting supervision | Managing money and budgets |
| Following instructions | Managing people |
| Getting along well with coworkers | Working with the public |
| Meeting deadlines | Working effectively as part of a team |
| Good attendance | Negotiating |

## Key Skills Needed for Success in Most Jobs

| Basic Skills | Key Transferable Skills |
|---|---|
| *Considered the Minimum to Keep a Job* | *That Transfer from Job to Job and Are Most Likely to Be Needed in Jobs with Higher Pay and Responsibility* |
| Punctuality | Organizing/managing projects |
| Good work ethic | Public speaking |
| Productivity | Communicating orally and in writing |
| Honesty | Organizational effectiveness and leadership |
| | Self-motivation and goal setting |
| | Creative thinking and problem solving |

In addition to the skills in the list, most jobs require skills that are specific to that particular job. For example, an accountant needs to know how to set up a general ledger, use accounting software, and develop income and expense reports. These job-specific skills can be quite important in qualifying for a job.

## QUICK TIP

If you want to identify more of your job-specific skills, chapter 5 will work you to distraction. You can probably write a fine skills resume without chapter 5 and the other material in part 2, but many will find the activities helpful.

## Identify Your Key Transferable Skills

Look over the preceding key skills list and write any skills you have and that are particularly important for the job you want. Add other skills you possess that you feel you must communicate to an employer to get the job you want. Write at least three, but no more than six, of these most important skills:

1. _____
2. _____
3. _____
4. _____
5. _____
6. _____

# Prove Your Key Skills with a Story

Now, write each skill you listed above on a separate sheet of paper. For each skill, write two detailed examples of when you used it. If possible, you should use work situations; but you can use other situations such as volunteer work, school activities, or other life experiences. Try to quantify the examples by giving numbers such as money saved, sales increased, or other measures to support those skills. Emphasize results you achieved and any accomplishments.

Here's an example of what one person wrote for a key skill:

EXAMPLE OF A KEY SKILL STORY

Key skill: Meeting deadlines

*I volunteered to help my social organization raise money. I found out about special government funds, but the proposal deadline was only 24 hours away. So I stayed up all night and submitted it on time. We were one of only three whose proposals were approved, and we were awarded more than $100,000 to fund a youth program for an entire year.*

## Edit Your Key Skills Proofs

If you carefully consider the skills needed in the preceding story, there are quite a few. Here are the most obvious ones:

- Hard work
- Meeting deadlines
- Willing to help others
- Good written communication skills
- Persuasiveness
- Problem solving

### QUICK TIP

You can use your proof stories to demonstrate in your resume and in an interview that you have the skills to do a particular job.

Review each proof sheet and select those proofs that are particularly valuable in supporting your job objective. You should have at least two proof stories for each skill area. Once you have selected your proofs, rewrite them using action words and short sentences. Write the skills you needed to do these things in the margins.

When you're done, convert these to bulleted accomplishment statements you can use in your resume. Rewrite your proof statements and delete anything that does not reinforce the key skills you want to support.

Following is a rewrite of the proof story I provided earlier. Do a similar editing job on each of your own proofs until they are clear, short, and powerful. You can then use these statements in your resume, modifying them as needed.

KEY SKILL REWRITE

Key skill: Meeting deadlines

*On 24-hour notice, submitted a complex proposal that successfully obtained more than $100,000 in funding.*

You could easily use this same proof story to support other skills listed earlier, such as hard work. So, as you write and revise your proof stories, consider which key skills they can best support. Use the proofs to support those key skills in your resume.

# Tips for Editing Your Draft Resume into Final Form

Before you make a final draft of your skills resume, look over the samples that follow for ideas on content and format. Several show interesting techniques that might be useful for your situation. For example, if you have a good work history, you can include a brief chronological listing of jobs. This jobs list could be before or after your skills section. If you have substantial work history, you could begin your skills resume with a summary of experience to provide the basis for details that follow.

When you have the content from the proof stories that you need for your skills resume, write your first draft. Rewrite and edit it until the resume communicates what you really want to say about yourself. Cut anything that does not support your objective. When you are done, ask someone to review it *very carefully* for typographical and other errors.

If you are having someone else prepare your resume, have someone in addition to yourself review the "final" copy for errors you might have overlooked. Only after you are certain that your resume contains no errors should you prepare the final version.

Your objective is to get a good job, not to keep working on your resume. So avoid the temptation to make a "perfect" resume and, instead, get this one done. Today. Then use it tomorrow. If all goes well, as I hope it does, you may never need a "better" resume.

## QUICK TIP

Searching for jobs on the Internet requires a special resume format. Chapter 4 describes electronic resumes and provides information on modifying your resume to this format.

# More Sample Skills Resumes (and JIST Cards)

Look over the sample resumes that follow to see how other job seekers have adapted the basic skills format to fit their situations. These examples are based on real resumes (although the names and other details are not real). I have included comments to help you understand details that might not be apparent.

The formats and designs of the resumes are intentionally basic and can be done with any word-processing software. Part 3 has many other skills resumes, including many with fancier graphics and designs. But remember that it is better to have a simple and error-free resume—and be out there using it—than to be at home working on a more elaborate one.

A JIST Card® precedes each skills resume. The JIST Card is a job search tool I developed many years ago. It is a mini-resume you can use in a variety of ways. You can attach JIST Cards to applications or resumes; give them to friends and other people in your network of contacts; enclose them in thank-you notes before or after an interview; and even put them on car windshields (really, this has been done, and with good results).

Employers like JIST Cards. The cards are short, are quick to read, and present essential information in a positive way. And the many, many people who have used them tend to have good stories about how well they work.

**QUICK TIP**

The more JIST Cards you have in circulation, the better they work. For more about JIST Cards, see chapter 13.

## A JIST Card and Resume for a Career Changer

Figure 3.3 is a resume of a career changer with substantial work experience in another occupation. After working for an alarm and security systems company and at a variety of other jobs, Darrel went back to school and learned computer programming. The skills format allows him to emphasize his past business experience to support his current job objective. His resume includes no chronological jobs listing and no education dates, so it is not obvious that he is a recent graduate with little formal work experience as a programmer.

Darrel does a good job of presenting previous work experience and includes numbers to support his skills and accomplishments. Even so, the relationship between his previous work and current objective could be improved. For example, collecting bad debts requires discipline, persistence, and attention to detail—the same skills required in programming. And, although he is good at sales, his resume does not relate the skills required for sales to his new job objective of programming.

Darrel's job objective could be improved. If Darrel were here to discuss it, I'd ask him if he wants to use his selling skills *and* his programming skills in a new job. If so, he could modify his job objective to include jobs such as selling technology or computer consulting services. Or, if he wants to be a programmer, I would suggest he emphasize other transferable skills that directly support his programming objective, such as his history of meeting deadlines. Still, this resume is effective in relating his past business experience to his ability to be a programmer in a business environment.

You will notice that a JIST Card is quite small. Darrel has to pack a lot of information in a very small space. This means that every word has to support his objective. Note, for example, that the first sentence does not mention he is a new graduate, but it indicates that he is very experienced. The next few sentences present his "credentials," followed by the last line, which lists several key transferable skills.

**FIGURE 3.2: DARREL'S JIST CARD.**

---

**Darrel Craig**                                          **(412) 437-6217**
                                          darrelITguy@comcast.net

**Position Desired:** Programmer/Systems Analyst

**Skills:** More than 10 years of combined education and work experience in business, data processing, and related fields. Proficient with Access, FoxPro, JADE, Oracle, and Microsoft SQL Server. Microsoft Certified Systems Engineer. Knowledge of various database and applications programs in networked PC and mainframe environments. Substantial business experience including accounting, management, sales, and public relations.

---

**FIGURE 3.3: DARREL'S RESUME.**

## Darrel Craig

**Career Objective**

A challenging position in programming or related areas that would best use expertise in the business environment. Position should have opportunities for a dedicated individual with leadership abilities.

**Programming Skills**

Experience with business program design including payroll, inventory, database management, sales, marketing, accounting, and loan amortization reports. Knowledgeable in program design, coding, implementation, debugging, and file maintenance. Familiar with distributed PC network systems (LAN and WAN) and working knowledge of DOS, UNIX, BASIC, FORTRAN, C, and LISP, plus Access, FoxPro, JADE, Oracle, and Microsoft SQL Server.

**Applications and Network Software**

Microsoft Certified Systems Engineer familiar with a variety of applications, including Lotus Notes, Novell NetWare, and Windows 2003 Server network systems, database and spreadsheet programs, and accounting and other software.

**Communication and Problem Solving**

Interpersonal communication strengths, public relations capabilities, innovative problem solving, and analytical talents.

**Sales**

A total of eight years of experience in sales and sales management. Sold security products to distributors and alarm dealers. Increased company's sales from $36,000 to more than $320,000 per month. Organized creative sales and marketing concepts. Trained sales personnel in prospecting techniques and service personnel in more efficient and consumer-friendly installation methods. Result: 90% of all new business was generated through referrals from existing customers.

**Management**

Managed security systems company for four years while increasing profits yearly. Supervised 20 personnel in all office, sales, accounting, inventory, and installation positions. Worked as assistant credit manager, responsible for more than $2 million per year in sales. Handled semi-annual inventory of five branch stores totaling millions of dollars.

**Accounting**

Balanced all books and prepared tax return forms for security systems company. Four years of experience in credit and collections. Collection rates were more than 98% each year; was able to collect a bad debt in excess of $250,000 deemed "uncollectible."

**Education**

School of Computer Technology, Pittsburgh, PA
Graduate of two-year Business Application Programming/TECH EXEC Program—3.97 GPA

Robert Morris College, Pittsburgh, PA
Associate degree in Accounting, minor in Management

**2306 Cincinnati St., Kingsford, PA 15171**
**(412) 437-6217**
**DarrelITguy@comcast.net**

## A Combination Skills/Chronological Resume (with JIST Card)

The resume in figure 3.5 combines elements of the chronological and skills formats. Thomas's resume breaks some rules, but for good reasons.

Thomas has kept his job objective quite broad and does not limit it to a particular industry or job title. Because he sees himself as a business manager, it does not matter to him in what kind of business or industry he works. He prefers a larger organization, as his job objective indicates. His education is near the top because he thinks it is one of his greatest strengths.

Thomas has worked with one employer for many years, but he presents each job there as a separate one. This allows him to provide more details about his accomplishments within each position and more clearly indicate that these were promotions to increasingly responsible jobs. His military experience, although not recent, is listed under a separate heading because he thinks it is important. Note how he presented his military experience using civilian language.

This resume could have been two pages, and doing so would allow him to provide additional details on his job at Hayfield Publishing and in other areas. The extra space could also be used for more white space and a less crowded look, although the resume works fine as is.

**FIGURE 3.4: THOMAS'S JIST CARD.**

**Thomas Marrin**

**Cell: (716) 223-4705; E-mail: tmarrin@techconnect.com**

**Objective:** Business-management position requiring skills in problem solving, planning, organizing, and cost management.

**Skills:** Bachelor's degree in Business Administration and more than 10 years of management experience in progressively responsible positions. Managed as many as 40 people and budgets in excess of $6 million/year. Consistent record of getting results. Excellent communication skills. Thorough knowledge of budgeting, cost savings, and computerized database and spreadsheet programs. Enjoy challenges, meet deadlines, and accept responsibility.

Willing to relocate.

Results-oriented, self-motivated, good problem-solving skills, energetic.

## FIGURE 3.5: THOMAS'S RESUME.

### THOMAS P. MARRIN
80 Harrison Ave. • Baldwin L.I., New York 11563
Cell: (716) 223-4705
tmarrin@techconnect.com

#### POSITION DESIRED

Mid- to upper-level management position with responsibilities including problem solving, planning, organizing, and budget management.

#### EDUCATION

University of Notre Dame, B.S. in Business Administration. Course emphasis on accounting, supervision, and marketing. Upper 25% of class. Additional advanced training: time management, organizational behavior, and cost control.

#### PROFESSIONAL EXPERIENCE

Wills Express Transit Co., Inc., Mineola, NY
*Promoted to Vice President, Corporate Equipment*—2006 to Present
Control purchase, maintenance, and disposal of 1,100 trailers and 65 company cars with more than $8 million operating and $26 million capital expense responsibilities.

- Schedule trailer purchases for six divisions.
- Operated 2.3% under planned maintenance budget in company's second best profit year while operating revenues declined 2.5%.
- Originated schedule to correlate drivers' preferences with available trailers, decreasing driver turnover 20%.
- Developed systematic Purchase and Disposal Plan for company-car fleet.
- Restructured company-car policy, saving 15% on per-car cost.

*Promoted to Assistant Vice President, Corporate Operations*—2002 to 2006
Coordinated activities of six sections of Corporate Operations with an operating budget of more than $10 million.

- Directed implementation of zero-base budgeting.
- Developed and prepared executive officer analyses detailing achievable cost-reduction measures. Resulted in cost reduction of more than $600,000 in first two years.
- Designed policy and procedure for special equipment-leasing program during peak seasons. Cut capital purchases by more than $1 million.

*Promoted to Manager of Communications*—2000 to 2002
Directed and managed $1.4 million communication network involving 650 phones, 75 WATS lines, 3 switchboards, and 15 employees.

- Installed computerized WATS Control System. Optimized utilization of WATS lines and pinpointed personal abuse. Achieved 100% system payback six months earlier than projected.
- Devised procedures that allowed simultaneous 20% increase in WATS calls and a $75,000/year savings.

Hayfield Publishing Company, Hempstead, NY
*Communications Administrator*—1998 to 2000
Managed daily operations of a large communications center. Reduced costs 12% and improved services.

#### MILITARY EXPERIENCE

U.S. Army—2nd Infantry Division, 1996 to 1998. First Lieutenant and platoon leader stationed in Korea and Ft. Knox, Kentucky. Supervised an annual budget equivalent of nearly $9 million and equipment valued at more than $60 million. Responsible for training, scheduling, supervision, mission planning, and activities of as many as 40 staff. Received several commendations.
Honorable discharge

## *Another Combination Resume and JIST Card*

Peter lost his factory job when the plant where he worked closed. He got a survival job as a truck driver and now wants to make truck driving his career because it pays well and he likes the work.

Notice how his resume (figure 3.7) emphasizes skills from previous jobs and other experiences that are essential for success as a truck driver. This resume uses a combination format—it includes elements from both skills and chronological resumes. The skills approach allows him to emphasize specific skills that support his job objective, and the chronological list of jobs allows him to display a stable work history.

The jobs he had years ago are clustered under one grouping because they are not as important as more recent experience. Also, doing so does not reveal that he is older. Yes, I realize employers are not supposed to discriminate based on age, but Peter doesn't want to take a chance because it's been known to happen.

For the same reason, Peter does not include dates for his military experience or high school graduation, nor does he separate them into categories such as Military Experience or Education. They just aren't as important in supporting his job objective as they might be for a younger person.

Unusual elements are comments about health and not smoking or drinking. These comments work for his objective. Peter figures that an employer will think that a healthy and sober truck driver is better than the alternative. Note how he presented his military experience as another job, with an emphasis on the truck driving and diesel experience.

Peter has another version of this resume that changed his job objective to include the supervision and management of trucking operations and added a few details to support this. When it made sense, he used the other version. If you are considering a promotion as one of your options, you can use this strategy, too.

**FIGURE 3.6: PETER'S JIST CARD.**

---

**Peter Neely**                    Messages: (237) 649-1234
                                        Cell: (237) 765-9876
                              E-mail: petethetrucker@yahoo.com

Position: Short- or Long-Distance Truck Driver

Background and Skills: More than 15 years of stable work history, including no traffic citations or accidents. Formal training in diesel mechanics and electrical systems. Familiar with most major destinations and have excellent map-reading and problem-solving abilities. Track record of getting things done and handling responsibility.

Excellent health, good work history, dependable.

---

# A Resume for a Recent High School Graduate

This resume (figure 3.9) uses a simple format with few words and lots of white space. It looks better than more crowded resumes. I would like to see more numbers used to indicate performance or accomplishments. For example, what was the result of the more efficient record-keeping system she developed? And why did she receive the employee-of-the-month awards?

As a recent high school graduate, Andrea does not have substantial experience in her field, having had only one full-time job since graduation. This resume's skills format allows her to present her strengths better than a chronological resume would. Because she has formal training in retail sales, she could have given more details about specific courses she took or other school-related activities that would support her objective. Even so, her resume does a good job of presenting her basic skills to an employer in an attractive format.

Andrea's JIST Card uses the same education and experience with more emphasis on the skills needed to make a transition to higher-paying marketing or sales jobs. She used it with a slightly refocused resume to apply for promotions.

**FIGURE 3.7: PETER'S RESUME.**

**Peter Neely**

203 Evergreen Rd.
Houston, TX 39127
Messages: (237) 649-1234      Cell: (237) 765-9876
E-mail: petethetrucker@yahoo.com

**POSITION DESIRED:** Short- or Long-Distance Truck Driver

| | |
|---|---|
| **Summary of Work Experience:** | More than 15 years of stable work history, including substantial experience with diesel engines, electrical systems, and driving all types of trucks and heavy equipment. |

**SKILLS**

| | |
|---|---|
| **Driving Record/ Licenses:** | Have current Commercial Driving License and Chauffeur's License and am qualified and able to drive anything that rolls. No traffic citations or accidents for more than 20 years. |
| **Vehicle Maintenance:** | Maintain correct maintenance schedules and avoid most breakdowns as a result. Substantial mechanical and electrical systems training and experience enable me to repair many breakdowns immediately and avoid towing. |
| **Record Keeping:** | Excellent attention to detail. Familiar with recording procedures and submit required records on a timely basis. |
| **Routing:** | Thorough knowledge of most major interstate routes, with good map-reading and route-planning skills. Get there on time and without incident. |
| **Other:** | Not afraid of hard work, flexible, get along well with others, meet deadlines, excellent attendance, responsible. |

**WORK EXPERIENCE**

| | |
|---|---|
| 2005–Present | CAPITAL TRUCK CENTER, Houston, TX<br>Pick up and deliver all types of commercial vehicles from across the United States. Entrusted with handling large sums of money and complex truck-purchasing transactions. |
| 2001–2005 | QUALITY PLATING CO., Houston, TX<br>Promoted from production to Quality Control. Developed numerous production improvements, resulting in substantial cost savings. |
| 1991–2001 | BLUE CROSS MANUFACTURING, Houston, TX<br>Received several increases in salary and responsibility before leaving for a more challenging position. |
| Prior to 1991 | Truck delivery of food products to destinations throughout the South. Also responsible for up to 12 drivers and equipment-maintenance personnel. |

**OTHER**

Four years of experience in the U.S. Air Force, driving and operating truck-mounted diesel power plants. Responsible for monitoring and maintenance on a rigid 24-hour schedule. Stationed in Alaska, California, Wyoming, and other states. Honorable discharge.

High school graduate plus training in diesel engines and electrical systems. Excellent health, love the outdoors, stable family life, nonsmoker, and nondrinker.

**FIGURE 3.8: ANDREA'S JIST CARD.**

---

**Andrea Atwood**             **Home: (303) 447-2111**
                              **andrea_a@aol.com**


**Position Desired:** A responsible position in retail sales or
marketing.

**Skills:** Two years of sales and marketing training including
promotional writing, advertising design, and business
processes. Computer skills in desktop publishing, graphics
design, word processing, and Web page design. Good written
and verbal communication skills. Experienced in dealing with
customers, direct sales, and problem solving. Punctual, honest,
reliable, and hardworking.

---

## A Combination Resume with Lots of White Space and Brief Copy (and No Dates)

Linda's resume (figure 3.11) is based on one included in David
Swanson's book, *The Resume Solution*. This resume shows the style
that David prefers: lots of white space, short sentences, and brief but
carefully edited narrative. Short. Like promotional copy. Like this.

This is another skills resume that breaks rules. It uses a skills format
but the skills are really ways to organize job-related tasks. Some skills
include references to specific employers. So this is really a combination resume.

**QUICK TIP**

The design for this resume is based on a resume template from a popular
word-processing program. Most programs offer several predetermined
resume design options that include various typefaces and other simple but
effective format and design elements. This makes it much easier to create a
resume more quickly.

**FIGURE 3.9: ANDREA'S RESUME.**

**ANDREA ATWOOD**
3231 East Harbor Road
Grand Rapids, Michigan 41103
Home: (303) 447-2111
andrea_a32@aol.com

**Objective:** A responsible position in retail sales or marketing.

**Areas of Accomplishment:**

*Customer Service*
- Communicate well with people of all ages.
- Able to interpret customer concerns to help them find the items they want.
- Received six Employee-of-the-Month awards in 3 years.

*Merchandise Display*
- Developed display skills via in-house training and experience.
- Received Outstanding Trainee Award for Christmas toy display.
- Dress mannequins, arrange table displays, and organize sale merchandise.

*Inventory Control*
- Maintained and marked stock during department manager's 6-week illness.
- Developed more efficient record-keeping procedures.

*Additional Skills*
- Operate cash register and computerized accounting systems.
- Willing to work evenings and weekends.
- Punctual, honest, reliable, and hardworking.

**Experience:**
Harper's Department Store
Grand Rapids, Michigan
2003 to present

**Education:**
Central High School
Grand Rapids, Michigan
3.6/4.0 grade-point average
Honors Graduate in Distributive Education

Two years of retail sales training in Distributive Education. Also courses in business writing, computerized accounting, and word processing.

Linda's resume is short but presents good information to support her job objective. I would like to see some numbers or other measures of results, although it is clear that Linda is good at what she does.

Did you notice that this resume includes no dates? You probably wouldn't notice until you had formed a positive impression. Well, it turns out that Linda did this on purpose, to hide the fact that much of her work was as a self-employed freelancer. Linda is also a bit older. She thought these things could work against her in getting a job, so she left off the dates.

**FIGURE 3.10: LINDA'S JIST CARD.**

---

**Linda Marsala-Winston / Voice Mail: (415) 555-1519 / lmw@netmail.net**

**Career Objective:** Copywriter or account executive in an advertising or public relations agency

**Skills:** More than seven years of experience in promoting various products and services. Advanced education and training in journalism, advertising, writing, design, psychology, and communications. Excellent written communication skills; several awards for writing excellence. Creative in solving problems and getting results.

Persuasive, innovative, meet deadlines.

---

**FIGURE 3.11: LINDA'S RESUME.**

## Linda Marsala-Winston

6673 East Ave.
Lakeland, CA 94544
**(415) 555-1519** (voice mail)
lmw@netmail.net

**Objective:** Copywriter or account executive in advertising or public relations agency

### Professional Experience

**Copywriter**

Developed copy for direct-mail catalogs featuring collectible items, real-estate developments, and agricultural machinery and equipment.

**Writer**

Wrote many articles for *Habitat* magazine. Specialized in architecture, contemporary lifestyles, and interior design.

**Sales Promotion**

Fullmer's Department Store, Detroit. Developed theme and copy for grand opening of new store in San Francisco Bay area.

**Fabric Designer**

Award-winning textile designer and importer of African and South American textiles.

**Other Writing and Promotion**

News bureau chief and feature writer for college newspaper; contributor to literary magazine. Script writer for fashion shows. Won creative writing fellowship to study in Mexico. Directed public relations for International Cotton Conference. Summer graduate fellow in public information, United Nations, New York City.

### Education

University of California, Berkeley
Bachelor of Arts Degree in English. Graduate study, 30 credits completed in Journalism.

California State University, Fresno
Master of Arts Degree in Guidance and Counseling.

### Professional Membership

San Francisco Women in Advertising

## *A Resume for a Candidate Without Recent Formal Experience*

Figure 3.13 is a resume based on one in a book by Richard Lathrop titled *Who's Hiring Who*. Although Richard calls it a "Qualifications Brief," this is a pure-form example of a skills resume.

This resume is unconventional in a variety of ways. It clearly takes advantage of the skills format by avoiding all mention of a chronology of past jobs. There are no references to specific employers, to employment dates, or even to job titles. (The reason for this is that Sara was a stay-at-home mom who gained relevant skills and experience from running the household.)

This is a clever example of how a well-done skills resume can present a person effectively in spite of a lack of formal paid work experience—or cover other problems. Students, career changers, and others can benefit in similar ways.

**FIGURE 3.12: SARA'S JIST CARD.**

---

**Sara Smith**                                            **(416) 486-3874**
                                              **sarasmith@gmail.com**


**Job Objective:** Program development, coordination, and administration

**Skills:** B.A. degree plus more than 15 years of experience in management, budgeting, and problem solving. Good financial management skills including cost control, purchasing, and disbursement. Able to organize and manage multiple tasks at one time and meet deadlines. Excellent communication skills.

Well organized, efficient; can delegate and accept responsibility.

---

## FIGURE 3.13: SARA'S RESUME.

**Sara Smith**
1516 Sierra Way • Piedmont, CA 97435 • (416) 486-3874
sarasmith@gmail.com

### OBJECTIVE

**Program Development, Coordination, and Administration**

…especially in a people-oriented organization where there is a need to ensure broad cooperative effort through the use of sound planning and strong administrative and persuasive skills to achieve common goals.

### MAJOR AREAS OF EXPERIENCE AND ABILITY

**Budgeting and Management for Sound Program Development**

With partner, established new association devoted to maximum personal development and self-realization for each of its members. Over a period of time, administered budget totaling more than $1,000,000. Jointly planned growth of group and related expenditures, investments, programs, and development of property holdings to realize current and long-term goals. As a result, holdings increased twenty-fold over the period, reserves invested increased 1200%, and all major goals for members have been achieved or exceeded.

**Purchasing to Ensure Smooth Flow of Needed Supplies and Services**

Made purchasing decisions to ensure maximum production from available funds. Determined ongoing inventory needs, selected suppliers, and maintained a strong continuing line of credit while minimizing financing costs. No significant project was ever adversely affected by lack of necessary supplies, equipment, or services on time.

**Personnel Development and Motivation**

Developed resources to ensure maximum progress in achieving potential for development among all members of our group. Frequently engaged in intensive personnel counseling to achieve this. Sparked new community progress to help accomplish such results. Although arrangements with my partner gave me no say in selecting new members (I took them as they came), the results produced by this effort are a source of strong and continuing satisfaction to me. (See "Some Specific Results.")

**Transportation Management**

Determined transportation needs of our group and, in consultation with members, ensured specific transportation equipment acquisitions over a broad range of types (including seagoing). Contracted for additional transportation when necessary. Ensured maximum utilization of limited motor pool to meet frequently conflicting requirements demanding arrival of the same vehicle at widely divergent points at the same moment. Negotiated resolution of such conflicts in the best interest of all concerned. In addition, arranged four major moves of all facilities, furnishings, and equipment to new locations.

**Other Functions Performed**

Duties periodically require my action in the following additional functional areas: crisis management; proposal preparation; political analysis; nutrition; recreation planning and administration; stock market operations; taxes; building and grounds maintenance; community organization; social affairs administration (including VIP entertaining); catering; landscaping (two awards for excellence); contract negotiations; teaching; and more.

**Some Specific Results**

Above experience gained in 10 years devoted to family development and household management in partnership with my husband, Harvey Smith, who is equally responsible for results produced. *Primary achievements:* Daughter Sue, 12, a leading candidate for the U.S. Junior Olympics team in gymnastics; a lovely home in Piedmont (social center for area teenagers). *Secondary achievements:* Vacation home at Newport, Oregon (on the beach); president of Piedmont High School PTA, two years; organized successful citizen protest to stop incursion of Oakland commercialism on Piedmont area.

### PERSONAL DATA AND OTHER FACTS

Bachelor of Arts (Business Administration), Cody College, Cody, California. Highly active in community affairs. Have learned that there is a spark of genius in almost everyone that, when nurtured, can flare into dramatic achievement.

# CHAPTER 4

## Develop an Electronic Resume in Less Than an Hour

More and more people are looking for jobs online and posting their resumes on the Web for employers to view. This technology requires you to have an electronic version of your resume so that you can make your credentials available to more employers online. Resumes on the Web are stored in electronic databases that are designed to save space and will be viewed by employers with many variations in computers and software. This means that most resumes are *not* stored as graphic images but, instead, as text files. Simple text files take up much less space than graphic files and can be read easily by any word processor or database program. Employers can also search text files for keywords, which are discussed later in this chapter.

Also, in the recent past, many employers took paper resumes they received and scanned them into electronic form. This enabled employers to put resume information into their own searchable databases. Although the popularity of this method is waning, some companies still use it. Scanning can introduce text errors and odd formatting due to the imperfect science of scanning technology. What this means is that your resume's carefully prepared format-and-design elements get stripped out, reducing your resume to a simple text format. So, you are better off making the modifications yourself if you know your resume will be scanned, if you will be submitting it to resume banks, or if you will be e-mailing it.

# Applying Directly on Employer Web Sites

In addition to searching resume banks or databases on the Internet, employers are asking applicants to put their personal information directly into their databases by typing it into boxes on the Web site. This saves them time and money. Larger employers get thousands of resumes, so it is impractical for them to store and retrieve paper resumes as jobs open up. Yet employers do want to retrieve resumes as positions become available and, for specialized positions, they want to consider applicants who submitted resumes weeks or even months in the past. To show you how this works, here are the instructions from one large employer's Web site on how to submit a resume.

## INSTRUCTIONS FROM A LARGE EMPLOYER ON HOW TO SUBMIT YOUR RESUME

*Registering is the first step. Registering gives you full access to the careers site tools:*

- **My Homepage:** *Your personalized home page, which provides quick and easy access to your most commonly used site tools.*

- **My Profile:** *Provides you with a central location for entering and updating personal information. My Profile allows you to enter the information just once—the information will automatically carry over to site tools, plus you can update this one-stop profile page at any time. My Profile information helps us to personalize your Careers home page. My Profile information also helps the staffing department match your skills to suitable career opportunities at the company.*

- **Resume:** *Use this tool to build and/or submit your resume to the company. Registered users can save a resume on the site for future access and submission to open jobs.*

- **Job Agent:** *Create up to five job search agents, which will automatically search for positions that match your specific search criteria and notify you of the results.*

- **Job Cart:** *Allows you to save job cart contents online for future visits, allowing you to reference or add to it at any time.*

*The Resume Builder is the most efficient way to submit your resume. This tool allows you to build and save your resume to submit for specific positions at a later date, modify your resume as needed, and provides the staffing department members the ability to match your skills and qualifications to available career opportunities almost immediately.*

*Alternatively, the Copy and Paste option allows you to submit an existing resume. When choosing this option it is highly recommended that you complete the entire form, in addition to pasting in your resume. This will give staffing department members the ability to review your skills and qualifications while your resume is processed.*

The methods for submitting a resume are pretty clear: No matter what your resume looks like now, this company wants just text and no fancy formatting (it does say that it will accept a mailed paper resume, but it's their least-preferred application option). This means that the best way to ensure that a resume is handled well electronically is to revise it into the most universally accepted electronic form, as the following example shows.

## A Sample Text-Only Resume, with All Graphics and Formatting Removed

Look at the sample resume in figure 4.1, adapted from one by Susan Britton Whitcomb in *Résumé Magic*. This resume has had all formatting and graphic elements removed for submission in electronic form.

It has the following features:

- No graphics
- No lines (it uses equal signs instead)
- No bold, italic, or other text variations
- Only one easy-to-scan font (which is Courier)
- No tab indentations
- No line or paragraph indents
- Keywords added

## FIGURE 4.1: A SCANNABLE RESUME.

```
AMY RICCIUTTI
Greenville, ME
(203) 433-3322
aricciut@compuserve.com

PROFESSIONAL EXPERIENCE
===========================================================================

ROCKWOOD INSURANCE, Augusta, ME
10/98-Present

Independent agency specializing in commercial coverage for
transportation and lumber industries.

Underwriting Manager ...

Recruited by partner/sales manager to manage underwriting in support of
aggressive expansion/business development campaign.  Liaison to five
agents and some 50 companies.  Underwrite $6 million in renewal coverage
and $200,000 in new business on a priority basis (commercial and
personal lines).  Collaborate with agents to protect loss ratios.
Aggressively process submissions to meet critical deadlines and offer
better premium to customers.

*** Contributions ***

+ Developed focus and structure for newly created position; established
underwriting and customer service infrastructure to support a projected
$500,000 increase in annual revenue.

+ Achieved new agency record for retaining renewal accounts.

+ Earned accolades from insurance companies for having "most complete
submissions."

+ Trained two Customer Representatives, equipping them with technical
knowledge to service complex accounts.

+ Designed and introduced Quote Worksheet and Agent Checklist to
standardize and streamline underwriting.

+ Diplomatically mitigated circumstances involving premium increases and
noncoverage of claims.


COAST INSURANCE SERVICES, Brunswick, ME
1995-1998

Senior Customer Service Representative ...

Accountable for policy maintenance, renewal retention, new business
submissions, claims, CSR training, and liaison work for independent
agency with $7 million in premiums.
```

*(continued)*

*(continued)*

```
*** Contributions ***

+ Assisted with AMS Novell network upgrade (resident expert for
software installation, troubleshooting).

+ Took on several new books of business during tenure without
need for additional support staff.


SUPPORTING SKILLS, INFORMATION
====================================================================

   *** Education *** INS 21 (Principles of Insurance).  INS 23
   (Commercial Principles of Insurance).  Personal Lines
   (Property and Auto).  Commercial Lines (Property).  E&O
   Coverage.  Employee Practices Liability.  Property & Casualty
   Agent (# 760923)

   *** Computer *** Windows 3.1. Windows 95 and 98.  MS Works.
   MS Office.  WordPerfect.  AMS Novell.  DOS and UNIX-based
   programs.  Redshaw.  OIS and FSC Rating Systems.  PS4 Proposal
   System.

   *** Affiliations *** National Association of Insurance Women.
   National Association of Female Executives.  Volunteer, Marine
   Mammal Center.
```

Yes, this resume looks boring, but it has the advantage of being universally accepted into company or Web resume databases, whether pasted into the Web site or e-mailed.

> **QUICK ALERT**
>
> It is important to provide a short, clear, and concise electronic resume. Some scanners and databases stop reading resumes after a certain number of lines, often after about one and a half pages, so be sure that your most important information appears early in the resume.

## Adapting Your Resume for Electronic Use

You can easily take your existing resume and reformat it for electronic submission. Here are some quick guidelines to do so:

1. Open your regular resume file and select the Save As command on your toolbar, usually located under the File menu. Select Text Only, Plain Text, or ASCII as the type.

2. Close the file and then reopen it to make sure you are working from the new text-only version. You'll see that most graphic elements such as lines, images, and bullet point symbols have now been eliminated. But if they haven't, go ahead and delete them. You may use equal signs in place of lines or borders and replace bullet points with plus symbols (+), asterisks (*), or hyphens (-).

3. Limit your margins to no more than 65 characters wide.

4. Use a plain, easy-to-scan font, such as Courier, Times New Roman, Arial, or Helvetica.

5. Eliminate bold, italics, and underlining if any remain after saving the file as text-only.

6. Introduce major sections with headings in all uppercase letters, rather than in bold, italics, or underlining.

7. Keep all text aligned to the left.

8. Rather than bullets, use a standard keyboard character, such as the asterisk.

9. Instead of using the Tab key or paragraph indents, use the space key to indent.

10. When you're done, click Save or OK. Then reopen the file to see how it looks. Make any additional format changes as needed (such as fixing indents or adding more line spaces).

Now test your electronic resume by e-mailing it to a friend or two. When you send it, paste the electronic resume into the body of the e-mail instead of sending it as an attachment. That way, they will be able to tell you how it looks when it shows up in their e-mail system and whether it is legible. After getting their feedback, make any adjustments necessary to fix it.

# The Importance of Keywords

Creating an electronic resume is more than just putting it into a plain format. This is because employers look for qualified applicants in a resume database by searching for keywords, which are various skills and attributes that they seek (for example, *bachelor's degree, Microsoft Word,* and *general ledger*). Your task is to add keywords to your electronic resume so that your chance of being selected for appropriate jobs is increased.

## *Keyword Technology*

The technology used by databases to search for your resume is very sophisticated. Software first extracts keywords and sorts them into major categories such as education, work history, personal traits, job skills, job titles, and others. The keywords from your resume are then sorted into the appropriate category. This allows an employer to search thousands of resumes to find the ones that meet very specific criteria.

**QUICK TIP**

See the sites recommended at the end of chapter 15 for more on how to use electronic resumes effectively.

For example, an employer could start with major criteria such as only those with a job objective in human resources, four or more years of experience in the field, and a four-year college degree in a related area. From this group the employer could then sort for those with specific skills such as interviewing, fringe benefit administration, grievance complaint handling, and EEOC policy compliance. The database would then search for those resumes that met these criteria, overlooking others that did not specifically state these things (and, often, thereby passing over good applicants who did not include the right words).

So if you plan on putting your resume on the Internet or submitting it to employers electronically, revise it to include as many key skill words as you can. Many resumes in part 3 include a keyword approach that will make them more likely to be selected from a resume database. Some consist almost entirely of keywords organized into groupings. This does not make for a very readable resume for humans, but can result in high "hit rates" for employers searching a database for someone with specific skills.

### QUICK ALERT

Avoid submitting a resume that contains lots of disjointed lists of keywords. The database might love you, but when a human gets ahold of your resume, it won't make much sense.

## Quick Tips for Selecting Keywords to Include in Your Resume

You probably already have many terms in your regular resume that can be used in a keyword section in your electronic resume. Leave them where they are, but repeat some of the most important ones in a "Key Skills" section near the top of your resume. In addition to using words you already have, here are some keyword tips for you to keep in mind:

- **Think like a prospective employer.** Think of the jobs you want, and then include the keywords you think an employer would use to find someone who can do what you can do. Emphasize technical terms, specific equipment or software names, certifications, and other specific terms an employer might use to fill the position. The job ads you read on the Internet or in newspapers are great ways to figure out what keywords employers are looking for.

- **Review job descriptions from major references.** Read the descriptions for the jobs you seek in major references like the *Occupational Outlook Handbook* or the *O\*NET Dictionary of Occupational Titles*. These and other references are described in chapter 7 and are available in both print and online formats. They will give you a variety of keywords you can use in your electronic resume.

- **Include all your important skill words.** When you complete the exercises in chapters 5 and 6, you will identify key skills that can help you develop keyword sections on your resume.

- **Look for examples of keywords in the sample resumes in part 3.**

Some of the sample resumes in part 3 contain keywords. These are noted in the handwritten comments on the resumes. The resumes in chapter 12 were specifically designed to be easily scanned, e-mailed, or posted to Web sites. Some provide a list of keywords in a separate section, in addition to the many keywords used throughout the resume. Look to them for inspiration on how to add more keywords to your own electronic resume.

**QUICK TIP**

Most people have two or more resumes—one that looks good to humans and another that e-mails and posts to Web sites well (but is still readable to humans). Having both, to be used in different situations, will give you a competitive edge.

# Using the Internet to Go Beyond the Resume

*By Kirsten Dixson, Brandego*

Now that you've seen how you can use the Internet to effectively distribute your resume, it's also important to understand that others will be using the Internet to find and research you.

More and more, you will be googled in your job search. A Harris Interactive poll showed that 23 percent of people search for the names of business associates or colleagues on the Internet before meeting them, and 75 percent of recruiters are googling candidates. There are classes popping up for HR professionals on googling candidates and peoples' Friendster profiles are even being reviewed in the recruiting process. It's clear that your online identity now has an impact on your career.

Have you googled yourself? Try typing your first and last name into Google, and then try it in quotes (like, "Mike Farr"). When you do, you could discover one of the following:

- You don't show up at all, making potential employers wonder how important you are.

- You have a common name, and it's hard to find anything relevant to you.

- There are negative results about you (arrests, firings, opinionated comments on non-professional blogs, or other unflattering information).

- Your personal blog or family Web site comes up high in the search results and it isn't something that you would want potential employers to find as a first impression.

- There are quite a few professionally relevant and positive results about you, but these snippets of information make it difficult to get a comprehensive picture.

- You have a Web site that comes up highly ranked in the search results and paints a clear picture of your professional self.

You can guess from these scenarios that everything that you post online or that is written about you becomes a part of your online identity. You'll want to consider the impact, positive or negative, that a comment on someone's blog or a review on epinions.com will have.

## Your Own Blog

One of the easiest and most economical ways to get an online presence that is well-designed and search-engine friendly is to create a professional *blog* (short for *Weblog*). With TypePad or Blogger, you don't have to know HTML to start posting articles about your area of expertise. Just make sure that your posts are professional and relevant to your target audience. Use this vehicle to demonstrate your knowledge, experience, and current grasp on happenings in your industry. On your blog, you can make your resume available for download (include text, Word, and PDF versions), link to other relevant sites, and include your career bio on the "about" page.

Figure 4.2 shows the blog of job seeker Nina Burokas. Nina uses a blog as part of her career strategy because it sets her apart from other job seekers, demonstrates her skills, and helps establish her personal "brand."

**FIGURE 4.2: A BLOG FOR CAREER MANAGEMENT.**

## Online Career Portfolios

To go beyond the blog and create a more comprehensive picture of who you are and what you have done, you can create an online career portfolio. A Web portfolio is the traditional paper portfolio concept reinvented for the online medium with links and multimedia content. Portfolios are more than Web-based resumes in that they *must* contain tangible evidence of your past performance, including work samples, testimonials, articles, video, photographs, charts, and so on.

Providing this depth of information earlier in the career search process weeds out jobs you're not qualified for and establishes virtual rapport with your interviewers. The portfolio concept also helps prove the facts on your resume because it shows and not just tells. Prospective employers and clients want to see that you have solved problems like theirs.

If you say that you have strong presentation skills, show a video clip! Articles, awards, graphs, audio references, white papers, case studies, press releases, and schedules of appearances are just some of the options you have to prove your expertise.

Figure 4.3 shows the Web portfolio of Cindy Eng, Vice President and Editorial Director for Scholastic At Home. Says Cindy, "I landed a great new job as a direct result of a networking contact finding my Brandego portfolio and seeing that my background was a perfect match for a position that his executive recruiter was trying to fill. My Web portfolio made it easy to distribute my resume and show examples of projects during my interviews. My new colleagues told me that they were reassured by my qualifications when they googled me after the announcement of my hire. I like that when I'm googled, my portfolio is the first thing that is found."

You can check out more Web portfolio examples at www.brandego.com/gallery.php.

**FIGURE 4.3: A WEB PORTFOLIO.**

## QUICK ALERT

Because most personal Web sites are not well executed, there has been some media backlash about using them for career marketing. Many Web-based career "portfolios" do look amateurish and are a risky mix of personal information (religion, politics, lifestyle, and so on), family photos, and career-related content. What this means for you is that you have a real opportunity to stand out by getting it right.

Maybe there will come a time where the Web career portfolio is as ubiquitous as the resume; but for now, there is a lot of opportunity to stand out from your competition and be extraordinary by having one. Of course, if the design and content of your portfolio is as unique as you are, that will further differentiate you. And, like any other Web site, there has to be a compelling reason to drive traffic to it. You must go way beyond the content that is in your resume.

The bottom line? You will be googled, and when the average job lasts only about 3.5 years, it certainly makes sense to constantly foster professional visibility both online and offline.

## QUICK ALERT

Don't get fired for blogging! What goes in a career-management blog? There are no rules, but common sense and good writing apply. There have been cases where people have been fired for blogging about proprietary corporate information or making unflattering remarks about their work environment. Ninety percent of your posts should be relevant to your professional target audience. Because blogs are expected to reveal your personality, you should occasionally write about your interests—but only the ones that you'd also include on a resume.

*Special thanks to **Kirsten Dixson** of Brandego (www.brandego.com) for lending her resume and cutting-edge technology expertise to the update of this section. Kirsten is a true pioneer in leveraging technology to help people increase their career success. She is a Founding Partner of Brandego, where she works with her clients to develop and manage their online identities with branded Web portfolios and blogs, and she is the cofounder of the Reach Branding Club, a virtual coaching environment for personal branding. She and partner William Arruda are the authors of* Career Distinction: Stand Out by Building Your Brand *(Wiley). Kirsten also serves as the Technology Master for the Career Masters Institute/Career Management Alliance.*

# Part 2

# A More Thorough Approach to Resume Writing and Career Planning

Each chapter in this part helps you build specific content for a powerful resume. While you are working on the activities needed to write a superior resume, you will also learn important things for your career and life planning. For example: What are you really good at? What sorts of things do you enjoy? What values do you need satisfied in your next job? What sort of job will you be looking for, specifically?

One big question you will have to answer in an interview is "Why should I hire you?" By completing the activities in this part, you will be able to better handle this essential interview question.

**Chapter 5: Develop a Powerful New Skills Language   77**

**Chapter 6: Document the Many Details of Your Work and Life Experience   87**

**Chapter 7: Identify Your Perfect Job and Industry   105**

**Chapter 8: Highlight Your Strengths and Overcome "Problems" on Your Resume   133**

**Chapter 9: Write a Better Resume Now   153**

# CHAPTER 5

# Develop a Powerful New Skills Language

This is an important chapter with some useful activities that are well worth your time. It provides a helpful list of skills to include on your resume. But this chapter is far more important than that. Knowing your skills is key to making good decisions about your future, interviewing effectively, and finding a job that matches what you do well.

Knowing what you do well is an essential part of writing a good resume. But it is also important to you in other ways. For example, unless you use skills you enjoy and are good at, it is unlikely you will be fully satisfied with your job.

Most people are not good at telling others what skills they have. When asked, few people can quickly say what they are good at, and fewer yet can quickly present the specific skills they have that are needed to succeed in the jobs they want. So knowing your skills and communicating them well will give you an advantage over other job seekers.

Surveys of employers have often shown that as many as 80 percent of the people they interview cannot adequately define the skills they have to support their ability to do the job. They may *have* the necessary skills, but they can't communicate them. It is problem number one in the interview process. So, this chapter is designed to help you fix that problem—on your resume and in an interview.

# Three Major Types of Skills

Analyzing the skills needed to perform even a simple task can become quite complicated. A useful way to organize skills is to divide them into three basic types:

- Adaptive skills

- Transferable skills

- Job-related skills

This is sometimes known as the Skills Triad. Figure 5.1 illustrates this system.

The system of dividing skills into three categories is not perfect because some overlap exists between the three skills categories. A skill such as being organized can be considered either adaptive (a personality trait) or transferable (a skill you can use on many different jobs). For our purposes, however, the Skills Triad is still a useful system for identifying skills that are important in the job search.

**FIGURE 5.1: THE SKILLS TRIAD.**

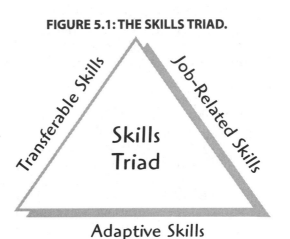

The following sections explain each skill type briefly. The rest of this chapter helps you identify your own key skills.

## *Adaptive Skills (Personality Traits)*

Adaptive skills are skills you use every day to survive and get along. They are called adaptive or self-management skills because they allow you to adapt or adjust to a variety of situations. Some of them also could be considered part of your basic personality. Examples of adaptive skills that employers value include getting to work on time, honesty, enthusiasm, and interacting well with others.

## Transferable Skills

These are general skills that can be useful in a variety of jobs. For example, writing clearly, good math skills, and the ability to organize and prioritize tasks are desirable skills in many jobs. These are called transferable skills because they can be transferred from one job—or even one career—to another. As a result, these are skills that you need to focus on when you're planning a career change. Your resume should emphasize them, and you should be able to give examples in interviews of how you have used these skills.

## Job-Related Skills

Job-related skills are the ones people typically first think of when asked, "Do you have any skills?" These skills are related to a particular job or type of job. An auto mechanic, for example, needs to know how to tune engines and repair brakes. An accountant needs to know how to create a general ledger, use computerized accounting programs, and perform other activities related to that job.

### KEEP UP YOUR COMPUTER SKILLS

If you don't have computer skills, you are at a great disadvantage in the job market because employers require computer literacy at all levels. If you have not kept up with computer skills related to your career area, consider taking some classes on the applications used most in the jobs you want. This might be word processing, spreadsheet, database, graphics, Web design, or some other type of program. Local adult education and community colleges often offer low-cost courses. You can also read computer magazines to familiarize yourself with the most current concepts, capabilities, and language.

# Identify Your Skills

Because it is so important to know your skills, this chapter includes checklists and other activities to help you identify the skills that are most important to highlight on your resume. Completing the activities will help you develop a skills language that can be very useful during interviews and throughout your job search—and your life.

Begin your skills identification process with the simple activity that follows.

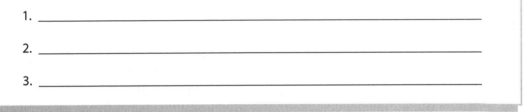

### Three Good Worker Traits

On the following lines, list three things about yourself that you think make you a good worker. Take your time. Think about what an employer might like about you or the way you work.

1. _____

2. _____

3. _____

The skills you wrote might be among the most important points an employer will want to know about you. Most (but not all) people write adaptive skills when asked this question. Whatever you wrote, these are key details to mention in interviews and to back up with examples of how you've demonstrated these skills. In fact, presenting these skills well—and the examples that provide evidence of them— often might allow a less experienced job seeker to get the job over someone with better credentials. It's simple, but this list may be the most critical element to remember from this whole book—but only if you learn how best to use the information.

## Identify Your Adaptive Skills

Following is a list of adaptive skills that are important to employers. The ones listed as "The Minimum" are those that most employers consider essential for a person to keep a job. Employers usually won't hire someone who has problems in these areas. The remaining adaptive skills are important to employers for a variety of reasons. Look over the list and put a check mark next to each adaptive skill that you have. Put a second check mark next to those skills that are particularly important to use or include in your next job.

# Adaptive Skills Checklist

### The Minimum

- ❏ Follow instructions
- ❏ Get along with supervisor
- ❏ Get along with coworkers
- ❏ Good attendance
- ❏ Hardworking, productive
- ❏ Honest
- ❏ Meet deadlines
- ❏ Punctual

### Other Adaptive Skills

- ❏ Able to coordinate
- ❏ Ambitious
- ❏ Apply new skills
- ❏ Assertive
- ❏ Capable
- ❏ Cheerful
- ❏ Competent
- ❏ Complete assignments
- ❏ Conscientious
- ❏ Creative
- ❏ Dependable
- ❏ Discreet

- ❏ Eager
- ❏ Efficient
- ❏ Energetic
- ❏ Enthusiastic
- ❏ Expressive
- ❏ Flexible
- ❏ Formal
- ❏ Friendly
- ❏ Good-natured
- ❏ Helpful
- ❏ Humble
- ❏ Imaginative
- ❏ Independent
- ❏ Industrious
- ❏ Informal
- ❏ Intelligent
- ❏ Intuitive
- ❏ Learn quickly
- ❏ Loyal
- ❏ Mature
- ❏ Methodical
- ❏ Modest
- ❏ Motivated

- ❏ Natural
- ❏ Open-minded
- ❏ Optimistic
- ❏ Original
- ❏ Patient
- ❏ Persistent
- ❏ Physically strong
- ❏ Reliable
- ❏ Resourceful
- ❏ Responsible
- ❏ Self-confident
- ❏ Sense of humor
- ❏ Sincere
- ❏ Solve problems
- ❏ Spontaneous
- ❏ Steady
- ❏ Tactful
- ❏ Take pride in work
- ❏ Tenacious
- ❏ Thrifty
- ❏ Trustworthy
- ❏ Versatile
- ❏ Well organized

*(continued)*

*(continued)*

**Add Any Other Adaptive Skills That You Think Are Important**

Include here any adaptive skills that you included in your "good worker traits" earlier, as well as any other skills that are important for your target job.

❑ _____   ❑ _____
❑ _____   ❑ _____
❑ _____   ❑ _____
❑ _____   ❑ _____
❑ _____   ❑ _____
❑ _____   ❑ _____
❑ _____   ❑ _____

## Your Top Three Adaptive Skills

Carefully review the skills checklist you just completed and select the three adaptive skills you feel are most important to tell an employer about or that you most want to use in your next job. The three skills you choose for this list are extremely important to include in your resume and to present to an employer in an interview.

1. _____

2. _____

3. _____

# Transferable Skills Checklist—Skills That Transfer to Many Jobs

Following is a list of transferable skills that are important in a wide variety of jobs. In the checklist that follows, the skills listed as "Key Transferable Skills" are those that are most important to many employers. These key skills are also those often required in jobs with more responsibility and higher wages, so it pays to emphasize these skills if you have them.

The remaining transferable skills are grouped into helpful categories. Check each skill you are strong in; then check twice the skills you want to use in your next job. When you are finished, you should have checked 10 to 20 skills at least once.

# Transferable Skills Checklist

## Key Transferable Skills

- ❏ Accept responsibility
- ❏ Control budgets
- ❏ Communicate in writing
- ❏ Increase sales or efficiency
- ❏ Instruct others
- ❏ Manage money or budgets
- ❏ Manage people
- ❏ Meet deadlines
- ❏ Meet the public
- ❏ Multitask
- ❏ Negotiate
- ❏ Organize/manage projects
- ❏ Plan
- ❏ Prioritize
- ❏ Solve problems
- ❏ Speak in public
- ❏ Supervise others

## Other Transferable Skills

### Dealing with Things

- ❏ Assemble or make things
- ❏ Build, observe, inspect things
- ❏ Construct or repair buildings
- ❏ Drive or operate vehicles
- ❏ Operate tools and machinery
- ❏ Repair things
- ❏ Use complex equipment
- ❏ Use my hands

### Dealing with Data

- ❏ Assemble or make things
- ❏ Analyze data or facts
- ❏ Audit records
- ❏ Budget
- ❏ Calculate, compute
- ❏ Classify data

- ❏ Compare, inspect, or record facts
- ❏ Count, observe, compile
- ❏ Detail-oriented
- ❏ Evaluate
- ❏ Investigate
- ❏ Keep financial records
- ❏ Locate answers or information
- ❏ Manage money
- ❏ Negotiate
- ❏ Research
- ❏ Synthesize
- ❏ Take inventory

### Working with People

- ❏ Administer
- ❏ Care for
- ❏ Confront others
- ❏ Counsel people
- ❏ Demonstrate

(continued)

*(continued)*

- ❏ Diplomatic
- ❏ Help others
- ❏ Interview others
- ❏ Insightful
- ❏ Kind
- ❏ Listen
- ❏ Negotiate
- ❏ Outgoing
- ❏ Patient
- ❏ Persuade
- ❏ Pleasant
- ❏ Sensitive
- ❏ Sociable
- ❏ Tactful
- ❏ Teach
- ❏ Tolerant
- ❏ Tough
- ❏ Trust
- ❏ Understand

## Using Words, Ideas

- ❏ Communicate in writing
- ❏ Articulate
- ❏ Communicate verbally

- ❏ Correspond with others
- ❏ Create new ideas
- ❏ Design
- ❏ Edit
- ❏ Inventive
- ❏ Logical
- ❏ Remember information
- ❏ Research
- ❏ Speak in public
- ❏ Write clearly

## Leadership

- ❏ Arrange social functions
- ❏ Competitive
- ❏ Decisive
- ❏ Delegate
- ❏ Direct others
- ❏ Explain things to others
- ❏ Get results
- ❏ Mediate problems
- ❏ Motivate people
- ❏ Negotiate agreements
- ❏ Plan
- ❏ Run meetings
- ❏ Self-controlled

- ❏ Self-motivated
- ❏ Solve problems
- ❏ Supervise others
- ❏ Take risks

## Creative, Artistic

- ❏ Artistic
- ❏ Dance, body movement
- ❏ Draw, sketch, render
- ❏ Expressive
- ❏ Music appreciation
- ❏ Perform, act
- ❏ Play instruments
- ❏ Present artistic ideas

## Add Any Other Transferable Skills That You Think Are Important

Include here any transferable skills that you included in your "good worker traits" earlier, as well as any other important transferable skills that aren't listed.

- ❏ _____
- ❏ _____
- ❏ _____
- ❏ _____

## Your Top Five Transferable Skills

List the five top transferable skills you want to use in your next job.

1. _____

2. _____

3. _____

4. _____

5. _____

**QUICK TIP**

If you are changing careers and want further help in discovering your transferable skills, you can take an assessment called the *Transferable Skills Scale (TSS)*. You can take and score this test on your own in about 25 minutes. In addition to identifying your skills, the TSS helps point out jobs that are a good match for your skills. Find out more about it from your career counselor or online at www.jist.com.

## *Identify Your Job-Related Skills*

Many jobs require skills that are specific to that occupation. An airline pilot obviously needs to know how to fly an airplane. Thankfully, good adaptive and transferable skills aren't enough to be considered for that job. You might have gained your job-related skills in a variety of ways, including education, training, work, hobbies, or other life experiences. Chapter 6 reviews your education, work, and other experiences and helps you use this as a basis for identifying your key job-related skills, which you can then present in your resume and interviews.

## THE TOP SKILLS EMPLOYERS WANT

Based on a variety of research studies, here are the skills employers consider most important in the people they hire. Note that all but computer literacy are adaptive or transferable skills because once a person has the minimum required job-related skills, these skills are the ones an employer looks for in making a hiring decision.

- *Analytical ability/critical thinking*
- *Computer literacy*
- *Decision-making*
- *Honesty/Integrity*
- *Interpersonal skills*
- *Leadership*
- *Motivation/Initiative/Enthusiasm*
- *Oral and written communication*
- *Organization/Coordination*
- *Problem-solving*
- *Results-orientation*
- *Self-confidence*
- *Strong work ethic*
- *Teamwork*
- *Time management*
- *Willingness to learn*

Source: Surveys by the U.S. Department of Labor and QuintCareers.com.

### QUICK TIP

If you need further help in deciding which jobs to pursue, the book *150 Best Jobs for Your Skills* (JIST Publishing) has extensive lists and descriptions to help you match your skills with good jobs.

# CHAPTER 6

# Document the Many Details of Your Work and Life Experience

All employers require you to provide information about what you have done in the past. Employers use applications, resumes, cover letters, e-mail interaction, phone contacts, and interviews to collect this information. If you can present yourself well in these ways, you are far more likely to be hired than if you do poorly. This chapter helps you collect the basic information needed to create a resume. It also encourages you to consider your accomplishments, identify additional skills, and develop specific examples of when and where you used those skills. These additions to the dry facts can make your resume a much more powerful tool for presenting yourself well.

I admit that this is a tedious chapter, with lots of worksheets to complete. For that reason, you would be forgiven for not wanting to do them all. But the details this chapter asks for will help you recollect specifics that later will help you develop a superior resume and, more importantly, better handle interviews. So filling out the worksheets in this chapter is worth your time.

## Quick Tips for Completing the Forms

Several forms in this chapter ask for information on your education, training, work and volunteer history, and other life experiences. Although you might have provided some of this information in part 1, the forms in this chapter are considerably more detailed. When filling out these forms, emphasize the key skills you identified in chapter 5. Those skills, as well as your accomplishments and results, are of particular interest to most employers.

Pay attention to experiences and accomplishments you really enjoyed; these often demonstrate skills that you should try to use in your next job. When possible, include numbers to describe your activities or their results. For example, "spoke to groups as large as 200 people" has more impact than "did presentations."

In some cases, you may want to write a first draft on a separate sheet before completing the forms. Use an erasable pen or pencil on the worksheets to allow for changes. In all sections, emphasize the skills and accomplishments that best support your ability to do the job you are seeking.

# The Worksheets

Following are three worksheets for organizing details of your work and life experience:

- Education and Training Worksheet (p. 88)
- Work and Volunteer History Worksheet (p. 92)
- Other Life Experiences Worksheet (p. 101)

## Education and Training Worksheet

### High School

This worksheet is an important source of resume information for recent high school graduates. For those with more experience, it can still be helpful to emphasize highlights from this time, particularly those that support your ability to do the job you want now.

Name of school(s) and years attended _____

_____

Subjects you did well in or that directly relate to the job you want _____

_____

_____

_____

_____

Extracurricular activities _____

_____

_____

_____

_____

Accomplishments/things you did well in or out of school _____

_____

_____

_____

Related hobbies or recreational activities _____

_____

_____

_____

## Post–High School Training (Other Than College)

List any training after or outside of high school that might relate to the job you want. Include military and on-the-job training, workshops, and informal training, such as from a hobby.

Training/dates/certificates _____

_____

_____

_____

_____

_____

_____

*(continued)*

(continued)

Specific things you can do as a result _____

_____

_____

_____

_____

_____

_____

Specific things you learned or can do that relate to the job you want _____

_____

_____

_____

_____

_____

_____

_____

_____

_____

## College

If you graduated from college or took college classes, this will interest an employer. If you are a new graduate, these experiences are especially important. Consider points that directly support your ability to do the job. For example, working your way through school proves that you are hardworking. If you took courses that specifically relate to your job, you can include details on these as well.

Name of school(s) and years attended _____

_____

Courses related to job objective_____

_____

_____

_____

_____

Extracurricular activities, including hobbies and leisure activities  _____

_____

_____

_____

_____

Accomplishments/things you did well in or out of school  _____

_____

_____

_____

Specific things you learned or can do related to the job you want _____

_____

_____

_____

_____

# Work and Volunteer History Worksheet

Virtually all resumes include information on work you have done in the past. Use this worksheet to list each major job you have held and information related to it. Begin with your most recent job.

Include military experience and unpaid work. Both are work and are particularly important if you don't have much paid civilian work experience. Create additional sheets to cover all of your significant jobs or unpaid experiences as needed. If you have been promoted, consider listing each position with that employer as a separate job.

Whenever possible, provide numbers to support what you did: number of people served over one or more years; number of transactions processed; percent sales increased; total inventory value you were responsible for; payroll of the staff you supervised; total budget you were responsible for; and other data. Think about any gauge you could use to measure your results on each job and, as much as possible, use numbers here, too.

This chapter includes four job worksheets, but if you need more, please feel free to photocopy extras.

## Job 1

Name of organization _____

Address _____

_____

Employed from_____ to _____

Job title(s) _____

Supervisor's name _____

Phone number (      ) _____

Machinery or equipment you used _____

_____

_____

_____

Computer skills developed or used, including software _____

_____

_____

_____

Data, information, or reports you created or used _____

_____

_____

People-oriented duties or responsibilities to coworkers, customers, others _____

_____

_____

_____

_____

_____

Services you provided or goods you produced_____

_____

_____

_____

_____

_____

Promotions or salary increases, if any_____

_____

_____

_____

_____

*(continued)*

(continued)

Details on anything you did to help the organization, such as increase productivity, simplify or reorganize job duties, decrease costs, increase profits, improve working conditions, reduce turnover, or other improvements. Quantify results when possible; for example, "Increased order processing by 50%, with no increase in staff costs.

_____

_____

_____

_____

_____

Specific things you learned or can do that relate to the job you want  _____

_____

_____

_____

_____

_____

What would your supervisor say about you?_____

_____

_____

_____

_____

## Job 2

Name of organization _____

Address  _____

_____

Employed from_____ to _____

Job title(s)  _____

Supervisor's name _____

Phone number (    ) _____

Machinery or equipment you used _____

_____

_____

_____

Computer skills developed or used, including software _____

_____

_____

_____

Data, information, or reports you created or used _____

_____

_____

_____

People-oriented duties or responsibilities to coworkers, customers, others _____

_____

_____

_____

_____

Services you provided or goods you produced_____

_____

_____

_____

_____

Promotions or salary increases, if any_____

_____

_____

(continued)

*(continued)*

Details on anything you did to help the organization, such as increase productivity, simplify or reorganize job duties, decrease costs, increase profits, improve working conditions, reduce turnover, or other improvements. Quantify results when possible; for example, "Increased order processing by 50%, with no increase in staff costs." _____

_____

_____

_____

_____

_____

Specific things you learned or can do that relate to the job you want _____

_____

_____

_____

_____

_____

What would your supervisor say about you? _____

_____

_____

_____

_____

_____

## Job 3

Name of organization _____

Address _____

_____

Employed from _____ to _____

Job title(s) _____

Supervisor's name _____

Phone number ( ) _____

Machinery or equipment you used _____

_____

_____

_____

Computer skills developed or used, including software _____

_____

_____

Data, information, or reports you created or used _____

_____

_____

_____

People-oriented duties or responsibilities to coworkers, customers, others _____

_____

_____

_____

_____

Services you provided or goods you produced _____

_____

_____

_____

_____

Promotions or salary increases, if any_____

_____

_____

*(continued)*

(continued)

Details on anything you did to help the organization, such as increase productivity, simplify or reorganize job duties, decrease costs, increase profits, improve working conditions, reduce turnover, or other improvements. Quantify results when possible; for example, "Increased order processing by 50%, with no increase in staff costs." _____

_____

_____

_____

_____

_____

Specific things you learned or can do that relate to the job you want  _____

_____

_____

_____

_____

_____

What would your supervisor say about you? _____

_____

_____

_____

_____

_____

## Job 4

Name of organization _____

Address  _____

_____

Employed from  _____ to _____

Job title(s)  _____

Supervisor's name _____

Phone number (    ) _____

Machinery or equipment you used _____

_____

_____

_____

Computer skills developed or used, including software _____

_____

_____

_____

Data, information, or reports you created or used _____

_____

_____

_____

People-oriented duties or responsibilities to coworkers, customers, others _____

_____

_____

_____

Services you provided or goods you produced_____

_____

_____

_____

_____

Promotions or salary increases, if any_____

_____

_____

(continued)

(continued)

Details on anything you did to help the organization, such as increase productivity, simplify or reorganize job duties, decrease costs, increase profits, improve working conditions, reduce turnover, or other improvements. Quantify results when possible; for example, "Increased order processing by 50%, with no increase in staff costs." _____

_____

_____

_____

_____

_____

Specific things you learned or can do that relate to the job you want _____

_____

_____

_____

_____

_____

What would your supervisor say about you? _____

_____

_____

_____

_____

_____

_____

# Other Life Experiences Worksheet

Use this worksheet to describe accomplishments or other significant information from hobbies, family responsibilities, family business employment, recreational activities, travel, and any other experiences in your life. Write any that are particularly meaningful to you, and name the key skills that were involved in these accomplishments. Make extra copies of this sheet as needed.

## Situation 1

_____

_____

_____

_____

Details and skills used _____

_____

_____

Specific things you learned or can do that relate to the job you want _____

_____

_____

_____

## Situation 2

_____

_____

_____

_____

Details and skills used _____

_____

_____

(continued)

*(continued)*

Specific things you learned or can do that relate to the job you want _____

_____

_____

_____

## Your Most Important Accomplishments and Skills to Tell an Employer

Here are three questions to help you consider which items from your history are most important to include in your resume and to mention in an interview. Emphasize these skills in your resume and in interviews!

1. What are the most important accomplishments and skills you can tell an employer regarding your education and training?

_____

_____

_____

_____

2. What are the most important accomplishments and skills you can present to an employer regarding your paid and unpaid work experiences?

_____

_____

_____

_____

3.  What are the most important accomplishments and skills you can present
    to an employer regarding your other life experiences?

    _____

    _____

    _____

    _____

# CHAPTER 7

# Identify Your Perfect Job and Industry

Regardless of whether you choose to include an actual Job Objective statement near the top of your resume, you should always have a clear job objective in mind. Even a general objective helps you to select details for your resume that best support what you want to do. If you have a very clear job objective, you could skip ahead to the next chapter; however, this chapter shows you how to explore career and job alternatives you might not have considered. So it's worth your time to read it.

This chapter helps you do the following:

- More clearly identify the range of jobs you can target in your job search.

- Obtain more information related to jobs that interest you.

- Write your resume's Job Objective statement and support it with skills and other details.

- Make good career decisions.

## Why Your Resume Needs a Job Objective

One of the worst things you can do with your resume is to try to make it work for "any" job. Although it is acceptable for you to consider a broad range of jobs, applicants who don't have a clear idea of what they want to do impress few employers. This means that all but the simplest resumes deserve to include a job objective.

Another mistake many people make on resumes is not emphasizing skills that support the job objective. So, if you are not clear about what sort of job you want, it's difficult to present the skills you have to do the job.

### QUICK TIP

As you may know, deciding on a job objective can be quite complicated. The U.S. Department of Labor defines more than 12,000 job titles, and it would be impractical to consider all alternatives. You probably have some idea of jobs that either interest you or that you are most likely to consider. If you have no idea about what you want to do, you need to figure it out (or make it appear as if you have) before you write your resume.

This chapter helps you learn more about the job options available to you—and how to use career information sources in constructing your resume. If you are not sure what sort of job you want or are considering additional education or training, plan to thoroughly explore your career options and consider this chapter as an introduction to a more thorough process.

## Consider Jobs Within Groups of Related Occupations

Most people overlook many job opportunities. They do this simply because they don't know about all the occupations that are suited to someone with their skills, interests, and experience. Most people go about their lives and their work with very little information about the universe of career and job possibilities. They may go to school and take courses that interest them, but later find jobs in a haphazard way. Their careers develop almost by accident. That's how it happened for me during my early years, and it was probably that way for you. Things simply happened.

But I think most of us can do better. I am not suggesting that career planning is a simple process; however, you can do a few simple things to make better decisions. And, in this chapter, I present a few points that I think can be particularly helpful.

The first step is to look at several ways that labor market experts have organized jobs and information about jobs. Fortunately, the more than 12,000 job titles are not in random order. Someone has spent a lot of time arranging them into groups of related jobs (known as "clusters"). Knowing these arrangements can help you identify possible job targets, prepare for interviews, consider long-term career plans, and write a better resume.

# The U.S. Department of Labor's *Occupational Outlook Handbook*

I consider the *Occupational Outlook Handbook (OOH)* one of the most helpful books on career information available. I urge you either to buy one or to access it online throughout your job search because it is so useful in a variety of ways.

The *OOH* provides descriptions for about 270 of America's most popular jobs, organized within clusters of related jobs. Although that may not sound like many jobs, about 87 percent of the workforce works in these jobs.

The *OOH* is updated every two years by the U.S. Department of Labor and provides the latest information on salaries, growth projections, related jobs, skills required, education or training needed, working conditions, and many other details. Each job is described in a readable, interesting format.

**QUICK TIP**

Appendix A includes a job description from the *Occupational Outlook Handbook*. Although that particular job might not interest you, reading the description helps you understand how useful the *OOH* job descriptions can be.

## Some Ways to Use the OOH

You can use the *OOH* in many ways. Here are some suggestions:

- **To identify the skills needed in the job you want.** Look up a job that interests you, and the *OOH* will tell you the transferable and job-related skills it requires. Assuming that you have these skills, you can then emphasize them on your resume and in interviews.

- **To find skills from previous jobs to support your present objective.** Look up *OOH* descriptions for jobs you have had in the past. A careful read will help you identify skills that can be transferred and used in the new job. Even "minor" jobs can be valuable in this way. For example, if you waited on tables while going to school, you would discover that this requires the ability to work under pressure, deal with customers, and work quickly. If you are now looking for a job as an accountant, you can see how transferable skills used in an apparently unrelated past job can support your ability to do another job. If you are changing careers or don't have much work experience related to the job you want, describing your transferable skills can be very important.

- **To identify related job targets.** Each major job described in the *OOH* lists other jobs that are closely related. The description also provides information on positions that the job might lead to through promotion or experience. And, because the jobs are listed within clusters of similar jobs, you can easily browse descriptions of related jobs you might have overlooked. All of this detail gives you options to consider in your job search as well as information to include in the Job Objective section of your resume.

- **To find out the typical salary range, trends, and other details.** Although you should never (well, almost never) list your salary requirements in a resume or cover letter, the *OOH* will help you know what pay range to expect and which trends are affecting the job. Note that local pay averages and other details can differ significantly from the national information provided in the *OOH*. You can get more localized salary information from sites such as Salary.com or HomeFair's Salary Calculator (www.homefair.com/Find_A_Place/Calculators/SalaryCalc/).

- **To get more specific information on this and related jobs.** If a job interests you, it is important to learn more about it. Each *OOH* job description provides helpful sources, including a cross-reference to the O*NET career information, related professional associations, Internet sites, and other sources.

## QUICK TIP

You can access the *OOH* information online at www.bls.gov/oco.

# *A Complete List of the 259 Jobs in the* Occupational Outlook Handbook

Following are the jobs in the current edition of the *OOH*, arranged in the same clusters used there. The clusters give you an idea of related jobs you might want to consider when writing your resume and conducting your job search.

Put a check mark by any job that interests you or that you have done in the past. Later, you can look up these jobs in the *OOH* and obtain additional information related to each.

## QUICK TIP

A very useful book titled the *Enhanced Occupational Outlook Handbook* includes the complete text of each job description in the current *OOH* plus brief descriptions for more than 1,100 O*NET jobs and more than 6,000 more specialized job descriptions from the *Dictionary of Occupational Titles*. This approach allows you to quickly identify the many specialized job titles in a simple-to-use format.

## List of Jobs in the *OOH* Within Clusters of Related Jobs

### Management and Business and Financial Operations Occupations

**Management Occupations**

Administrative services managers

Advertising, marketing, promotions, public relations, and sales managers

Computer and information systems managers

Construction managers

Education administrators

Engineering and natural sciences managers

Farmers, ranchers, and agricultural managers

Financial managers

Food service managers

Funeral directors

Human resources, training, and labor relations managers and specialists

*(continued)*

(continued)

Industrial production managers

Lodging managers

Medical and health services managers

Property, real estate, and community association managers

Purchasing managers, buyers, and purchasing agents

Top executives

**Business and Financial Operations Occupations**

Accountants and auditors

Appraisers and assessors of real estate

Budget analysts

Claims adjusters, appraisers, examiners, and investigators

Cost estimators

Financial analysts and personal financial advisors

Insurance underwriters

Loan officers

Management analysts

Tax examiners, collectors, and revenue agents

## Professional and Related Occupations

**Computer and Mathematical Occupations**

Actuaries

Computer programmers

Computer software engineers

Computer support specialists and systems administrators

Computer systems analysts

Mathematicians

Operations research analysts

Statisticians

**Architects, Surveyors, and Cartographers**

Architects, except landscape and naval

Landscape architects

Surveyors, cartographers, photogrammetrists, and surveying technicians

**Engineers**

**Drafters and Engineering Technicians**

Drafters

Engineering technicians

**Life Scientists**

Agricultural and food scientists

Biological scientists

Medical scientists

Conservation scientists and foresters

**Physical Scientists**

Atmospheric scientists

Chemists and materials scientists

Environmental scientists and hydrologists

Physicists and astronomers

**Social Scientists and Related Occupations**

Economists

Market and survey researchers

Psychologists

Urban and regional planners

Social scientists, other

**Science Technicians**

**Community and Social Services Occupations**

Counselors

Probation officers and correctional treatment specialists

Social and human service assistants

Social workers

**Legal Occupations**

Court reporters

Judges, magistrates, and other judicial workers

Lawyers

Paralegals and legal assistants

**Education, Training, Library, and Museum Occupations**

Archivists, curators, and museum technicians

Instructional coordinators

Librarians

Library technicians

Teacher assistants

Teachers—adult literacy and remedial education

Teachers—postsecondary

Teachers—preschool, kindergarten, elementary, middle, and secondary

Teachers—special education

**Art and Design Occupations**

Artists and related workers

Commercial and industrial designers

Fashion designers

Floral designers

Graphic designers

Interior designers

Designers

**Entertainers and Performers, Sports and Related Occupations**

Actors, producers, and directors

Athletes, coaches, umpires, and related workers

Dancers and choreographers

Musicians, singers, and related workers

**Media and Communications-Related Occupations**

Announcers

Broadcast and sound engineering technicians and radio operators

Interpreters and translators

News analysts, reporters, and correspondents

Photographers

Public relations specialists

Television, video, and motion picture camera operators and editors

Writers and editors

**Health Diagnosing and Treating Occupations**

Audiologists

Chiropractors

Dentists

Dietitians and nutritionists

Occupational therapists

Optometrists

Pharmacists

Physical therapists

Physician assistants

Physicians and surgeons

Podiatrists

Radiation therapists

Recreational therapists

Registered nurses

Respiratory therapists

Speech-language pathologists

Veterinarians

**Health Technologists and Technicians**

Athletic trainers

Cardiovascular technologists and technicians

Clinical laboratory technologists and technicians

Dental hygienists

Diagnostic medical sonographers

Emergency medical technicians and paramedics

Licensed practical and licensed vocational nurses

Medical records and health information technicians

(continued)

*(continued)*

Nuclear medicine technologists

Occupational health and safety specialists and technicians

Opticians, dispensing

Pharmacy technicians

Radiologic technologists and technicians

Surgical technologists

Veterinary technologists and technicians

## Service Occupations

### Healthcare Support Occupations

Dental assistants

Massage therapists

Medical assistants

Medical transcriptionists

Nursing, psychiatric, and home health aides

Occupational therapist assistants and aides

Pharmacy aides

Physical therapist assistants and aides

### Protective Service Occupations

Correctional officers

Fire fighting occupations

Police and detectives

Private detectives and investigators

Security guards and gaming surveillance officers

### Food Preparation and Serving-Related Occupations

Chefs, cooks, and food preparation workers

Food and beverage serving and related workers

### Building and Grounds Cleaning and Maintenance Occupations

Building cleaning workers

Grounds maintenance workers

Pest control workers

### Personal Care and Service Occupations

Animal care and service workers

Barbers, cosmetologists, and other personal appearance workers

Child care workers

Fitness workers

Flight attendants

Gaming services occupations

Personal and home care aides

Recreation workers

## Sales and Related Occupations

Advertising sales agents

Cashiers

Counter and rental clerks

Demonstrators, product promoters, and models

Insurance sales agents

Real estate brokers and sales agents

Retail salespersons

Sales engineers

Sales representatives, wholesale and manufacturing

Sales worker supervisors

Securities, commodities, and financial services sales agents

Travel agents

## Office and Administrative Support Occupations

### Financial Clerks

Bill and account collectors

Billing and posting clerks and machine operators

Bookkeeping, accounting, and auditing clerks

Gaming cage workers

Payroll and timekeeping clerks

Procurement clerks

Tellers

**Information and Record Clerks**

Brokerage clerks

Credit authorizers, checkers, and clerks

Customer service representatives

File clerks

Hotel, motel, and resort desk clerks

Human resources assistants, except payroll and timekeeping

Interviewers

Library assistants, clerical

Order clerks

Receptionists and information clerks

Reservation and transportation ticket agents and travel clerks

**Material Recording, Scheduling, Dispatching, and Distributing Occupations**

Cargo and freight agents

Couriers and messengers

Dispatchers

Meter readers, utilities

Postal Service workers

Production, planning, and expediting clerks

Shipping, receiving, and traffic clerks

Stock clerks and order fillers

Weighers, measurers, checkers, and samplers, recordkeeping

**Other Office and Administrative Support Occupations**

Communications equipment operators

Computer operators

Data entry and information processing workers

Desktop publishers

Office and administrative support worker supervisors and managers

Office clerks, general

Secretaries and administrative assistants

## Farming, Fishing, and Forestry Occupations

Agricultural workers

Fishers and fishing vessel operators

Forest, conservation, and logging workers

## Construction Trades and Related Workers

Boilermakers

Brickmasons, blockmasons, and stonemasons

Carpenters

Carpet, floor, and tile installers and finishers

Cement masons, concrete finishers, segmental pavers, and terrazzo workers

Construction and building inspectors

Construction equipment operators

Construction laborers

Drywall installers, ceiling tile installers, and tapers

Electricians

Elevator installers and repairers

Glaziers

Hazardous materials removal workers

Insulation workers

Painters and paperhangers

Pipelayers, plumbers, pipefitters, and steamfitters

*(continued)*

*(continued)*

Plasterers and stucco masons

Roofers

Sheet metal workers

Structural and reinforcing iron and metal workers

### Installation, Maintenance, and Repair Occupations

**Electrical and Electronic Equipment Mechanics, Installers, and Repairers**

Computer, automated teller, and office machine repairers

Electrical and electronics installers and repairers

Electronic home entertainment equipment installers and repairers

Radio and telecommunications equipment installers and repairers

**Vehicle and Mobile Equipment Mechanics, Installers, and Repairers**

Aircraft and avionics equipment mechanics and service technicians

Automotive body and related repairers

Automotive service technicians and mechanics

Diesel service technicians and mechanics

Heavy vehicle and mobile equipment service technicians and mechanics

Small engine mechanics

**Other Installation, Maintenance, and Repair Occupations**

Coin, vending, and amusement machine servicers and repairers

Heating, air-conditioning, and refrigeration mechanics and installers

Home appliance repairers

Industrial machinery mechanics and maintenance workers, except millwrights

Line installers and repairers

Maintenance and repair workers, general

Millwrights

Precision instrument and equipment repairers

### Production Occupations

**Assemblers and Fabricators**

**Food Processing Occupations**

**Metal Workers and Plastic Workers**

Computer-control programmers and operators

Machinists

Machine setters, operators and tenders—metal and plastic

Tool and die makers

Welding, soldering, and brazing workers

**Printing Occupations**

Bookbinders and bindery workers

Prepress technicians and workers

Printing machine operators

**Textile, Apparel, and Furnishings Occupations**

**Woodworkers**

**Plant and System Operators**

Power plant operators, distributors, and dispatchers

Stationary engineers and boiler operators

Water and liquid waste treatment plant and system operators

**Other Production Occupations**

Inspectors, testers, sorters, samplers, and weighers

Jewelers and precious stone and metal workers

Medical, dental, and ophthalmic laboratory technicians

Painting and coating workers, except construction and maintenance

Photographic process workers and processing machine operators

Semiconductor processors

**Transportation and Material Moving Occupations**

**Air Transportation Occupations**
Aircraft pilots and flight engineers

Air traffic controllers

**Motor Vehicle Operators**
Bus drivers
Taxi drivers and chauffeurs
Truck drivers and driver/sales workers
**Rail Transportation Occupations**
**Water Transportation Occupations**
**Material Moving Occupations**

**Job Opportunities in the Armed Forces**

**QUICK TIP**

If the information in the *OOH* is a bit too dry for your taste, you might prefer the new *EZ Occupational Outlook Handbook* from JIST. It describes the same aspects of the same jobs, but it does so in a more entertaining style.

# Other Important Sources of Occupational Information

There are a variety of useful career information sources and I present here the ones I consider most important.

## The Occupational Information Network (O*NET)

The U.S. Department of Labor maintains an up-to-date database of occupational information. Called the O*NET, it provides detailed information for almost 1,200 jobs. Although the *OOH* is more useful for most situations, the O*NET describes many more jobs (and more specialized jobs) and provides more details on each.

The O*NET database offers basic descriptions for each of its jobs, plus 450 additional data elements for each job. Keep in mind that the O*NET is a complex database and much of the detailed information it provides is not of much use for most job seekers—it is simply too much and too detailed if used in its database form.

Fortunately, career counselors have developed more helpful versions of the O*NET database. A book version published by JIST, *O*NET Dictionary of Occupational Titles,* was designed to provide the O*NET information of greatest value to most job seekers in an easy-to-use book format.

The job descriptions in this book are packed with information, including the following:

- **O*NET Number:** Allows you to cross-reference other systems using this number.

- **O*NET Occupational Title:** The job title most often used for this job.

- **Education/Training Required:** What it takes to prepare for the job.

- **Employed:** The total number of people who work in that job.

- **Annual Earnings:** The average annual earnings for people employed in the job.

- **Growth:** The projected percent of new jobs in the field each year.

- **Annual Job Openings:** The number of job openings per year projected for the job.

- **O*NET Occupational Description:** A brief but useful review of what a person working in that job would typically do.

- **GOE Interest Area and Work Group:** Cross-reference to related jobs.

- **Personality Type:** Tells you what personality type the job best fits into in the system used in Holland's Self-Directed Search or other interest inventories.

- **Work Values:** Lists any of the job's 21 work values with high scores in the O*NET database.

- **Skills:** Skills needed to perform the job.

- **Abilities:** Enduring attributes that influence a worker's job performance.

- **General Work Activities:** Lists the general types of work activities needed to perform the job described.

- **Physical Work Conditions:** Work setting, environmental conditions, job hazards, body positioning, and work attire.

- **Other Job Characteristics:** Includes several types of information such as error consequences, automation, and repetition.

- **Experience:** Lists the work or other experience the job requires.

- **Job Preparation:** Provides specific information on the training or education level the job requires.

- **Knowledges:** Knowledge required to perform the job successfully.

- **Instructional Programs:** A cross-reference to a system that provides information on the type of training and education typically required for entry into the occupation.

- **Related *SOC* Job:** Lists the related job title from the Standard Occupational Classification, a government job-classification system.

- **Related *OOH* Job:** Helps you find information on the same or similar job in the *OOH*.

- **Related *DOT* Jobs:** Cross references the job to an older classification system—the *Dictionary of Occupational Titles*.

The complete set of O*NET information is available on the Internet at http://online.onetcenter.org/. I recommend, however, that you use the book version because it was designed for career exploration and job seeking.

# *The* Guide for Occupational Exploration

After extensive research, the U. S. Department of Labor developed an easy-to-use system that organized all jobs by interest. For example, if you are interested in artistic activities, this system enables you to identify the many jobs related to this area. This interest-based system is presented in a book titled the *Guide for Occupational Exploration (GOE)* and is used in a variety of print and computer career information systems.

The current edition, called the *New Guide for Occupational Exploration*, organizes all jobs into 16 major interest areas. These areas are further divided into more specific groupings (called work groups) of related jobs. While the *GOE* system is easy to understand and use, it is powerful enough to allow thousands of job titles to be organized into its various work groups.

The *GOE* allows you to quickly identify groups of jobs that are most closely related to what you want to do. All along the way, from major interest areas to the more specific work groups, helpful information is provided related to each group of jobs. So, even if some jobs are not familiar to you, the *GOE* gives you enough information to help you understand the jobs within that group and what they require. In a quick and logical way, you can use the *GOE* to narrow down the thousands of job possibilities to the dozen or so that most closely match what you want to do and are good at.

## The *GOE*'s Major Interest Areas

The current edition of the *Guide for Occupational Exploration* is published by JIST and includes the following 16 major interest areas:

1. Agriculture and Natural Resources
2. Architecture and Construction

3. Arts and Communication

4. Business and Administration

5. Education and Training

6. Finance and Insurance

7. Government and Public Administration

8. Health Science

9. Hospitality, Tourism, and Recreation

10. Human Service

11. Information Technology

12. Law and Public Safety

13. Manufacturing

14. Retail and Wholesale Sales and Service

15. Scientific Research, Engineering, and Mathematics

16. Transportation, Distribution, and Logistics

## *GOE* Work Groups: A Quick Way to Find Related Jobs

Each of the *GOE*'s Interest Areas is broken down into more specific groups of related jobs. This is a very helpful approach because it allows you to quickly identify groups of jobs that are of most interest to you.

To show you how the *GOE* is organized, I've provided a sample listing of one *GOE* Interest Area here: "Arts, Entertainment, and Media." Under it, listed in bold text, are the various work groups for this Interest Area. In regular type following each work group name are the job titles from the O*NET that fit into each group. As you can see, this allows you to quickly find a work group that interests you and then review the job titles within that group. You can then use the *GOE* to read job descriptions for the jobs that interest you most or to get more details on the education, training, type of work, and other information for the jobs in that work group.

## SUBGROUPINGS WITHIN THE *GOE* ARTS, ENTERTAINMENT, AND MEDIA INTEREST AREA
GOE INTEREST AREA: 3. ARTS AND COMMUNICATION

### Work Group: Managerial Work

O*NET jobs: Agents and Business Managers of Artists, Performers, and Athletes; Art Directors; Producers; Program Directors; Public Relations Managers; Technical Directors/Managers

### Work Group: Writing and Editing

O*NET jobs: Copy Writers; Creative Writers; Editors; Poets and Lyricists; Technical Writers

### Work Group: News, Broadcasting, and Public Relations

O*NET jobs: Broadcast News Analysts; Caption Writers; Interpreters and Translators; Public Relations Specialists; Reporters and Correspondents

### Work Group: Studio Art

O*NET jobs: Cartoonists; Craft Artists; Painters and Illustrators; Potters; Sculptors; Sketch Artists

### Work Group: Design

O*NET jobs: Commercial and Industrial Designers; Exhibit Designers; Fashion Designers; Floral Designers; Graphic Designers; Interior Designers; Merchandise Displayers and Window Trimmers; Set Designers

### Work Group: Drama

O*NET jobs: Actors; Costume Attendants; Directors—Stage, Motion Pictures, Television, and Radio; Makeup Artists, Theatrical and Performance; Public Address System and Other Announcers; Radio and Television Announcers

### Work Group: Music

O*NET jobs: Composers; Music Arrangers and Orchestrators; Music Directors; Musicians, Instrumental; Singers; Talent Directors

### Work Group: Dance

O*NET jobs: Choreographers; Dancers

### Work Group: Media Technology

O*NET jobs: Audio and Video Equipment Technicians; Broadcast Technicians; Camera Operators, Television, Video, and Motion Picture; Film and Video Editors; Multi-Media Artists and Animators; Photographic Hand Developers; Photographic Reproduction Technicians; Photographic Retouchers and Restorers; Professional Photographers; Radio Operators; Sound Engineering Technicians

### Work Group: Communications Technology

O*NET jobs: Air Traffic Controllers; Airfield Operations Specialists; Central Office Operators; Directory Assistance Operators; Dispatchers, Except Police, Fire, and Ambulance; Police, Fire, and Ambulance Dispatchers

### Work Group: Musical Instrument Repair

O*NET jobs: Keyboard Instrument Repairers and Tuners; Percussion Instrument Repairers and Tuners; Reed or Wind Instrument Repairers and Tuners; Stringed Instrument Repairers and Tuners

The current edition of the *Guide for Occupational Exploration* includes descriptions for more than 900 jobs described in the O*NET, plus substantial additional information on the jobs in each Interest Area and work group. Among many other things, the *GOE* enables you to identify jobs by your work activities, work preferences, skills and knowledges, preparation, and education. You should be able to find the *GOE* in most libraries, and the GOE system is also used in various computerized career information systems you may have access to.

## Also Consider Industries in Your Job Search

Although much of this chapter is devoted to occupational choices, the industry you work in can be just as important. For example, an information technology professional with an interest in health and wellness might be happier working in an IT role at a hospital rather than in aircraft manufacturing or some other industry of lesser interest.

Look for an industry that interests you or that you know something about from your hobbies, family business, volunteer work, or other life experiences. Some industries also pay better than others for essentially the same work. Being clear about what industry you want to work in, and why, can give you a competitive edge over those who don't have a preference.

Following is a list of about 40 major industries from a book titled *Career Guide to Industries* by the U.S. Department of Labor. The book gives details on the nature of the industry, working conditions, employment opportunities, types of occupations it employs, training needed, earnings, outlook, and more for each industry.

## 40 Major Industries to Consider

**Agriculture, Mining, and Construction**

Agriculture, forestry, and fishing

Construction

Mining

Oil and gas extraction

**Manufacturing**

Aerospace product and parts manufacturing

Chemical manufacturing, except pharmaceutical and medicine manufacturing

Computer and electronic product manufacturing

Food manufacturing

Machinery manufacturing

Motor vehicle and parts manufacturing

Pharmaceutical and medicine manufacturing

Printing

Steel manufacturing

Textile, textile product, and apparel manufacturing

**Trade**

Automobile dealers

Clothing, accessory, and general merchandise stores

Grocery stores

Wholesale trade

**Transportation and utilities**

Air transportation

Truck transportation and warehousing

Utilities

**Information**

Broadcasting

Internet service providers, web search portals, and data-processing services

Motion picture and video industries

Publishing, except software

Software publishers

Telecommunications

**Financial Activities**

Banking

Insurance

Securities, commodities, and other investments

**Professional and Business Services**

Advertising and public relations services

Computer systems design and related services

Employment services

Management, scientific, and technical consulting services

Scientific research and development services

**Education and Health Services**

Child daycare services

Educational services

Health care

Social assistance, except child day care

**Leisure and Hospitality**

Arts, entertainment, and recreation

Food services and drinking places

Hotels and other accommodations

**Government**

Advocacy, grantmaking, and civic organizations

Federal government, excluding the Postal Service

State and local government, excluding education and hospitals

# Values, Preferences, and Other Factors to Consider in Defining Your Job Objective

Following is a brief review of points that others have found important in making career plans. Although this won't replace a thorough career planning process, you may find it helpful to consider a variety of issues that relate to deciding on a job objective, working on your resume, and making career plans.

## Eight Quick Questions to Help You Define Your Ideal Job

If you were to develop a profile of your ideal job, what would it include? As you probably realize, this includes more than picking out a job title. I have selected questions that you should consider in defining your ideal job. Of course, this involves a bit of reality (and I have included some of these elements), but dreams can never come true if you don't have them. So, I present the following very important but sometimes overlooked issues for you to consider in planning your job objective.

### What Skills Do You Have That You Want to Use in Your Next Job?

Review the skills lists you worked on in chapter 5. Think about the skills that you enjoy using and are particularly good at. Then list the five that you would most like to use in your next job.

*(continued)*

*(continued)*

1. _____

2. _____

3. _____

4. _____

5. _____

## What Type of Special Knowledge Do You Have That You Might Use in Your Next Job?

Perhaps you know how to fix radios, keep accounting records, or cook food. You don't need to have used these skills in a previous job to include them. Write down the things you have learned from schooling, training, hobbies, family experiences, and other sources. One or more of them could make you a very competitive applicant in the right setting. For example, an accountant who knows a lot about fashion would be a very special candidate if he or she just happened to be interviewing for a job with an organization that sells clothing. Can you see the possibilities?

1. _____

2. _____

3. _____

4. _____

5. _____

## What Types of People Do You Prefer to Work With?

It is unlikely you will be happy in a job if you're surrounded by people you don't like. One way to approach this is to think about characteristics of people that you would not want to work with. The opposite characteristics are those that you probably would enjoy. For example, if you don't like a boss or coworkers that are negative and constantly complaining, you can say that you prefer to work with people who are positive about their work and a boss who provides positive feedback. List the preferred characteristics of your supervisor and coworkers here.

1. _____

2. _____

3. _____

4. _____

5. _____

## What Type of Work Environment Do You Prefer?

Do you want to work inside, outside, in a quiet place, in a busy place, in a clean place, or a place with a nice view? For example, I like variety in what I do (since I am easily bored), so I want a work environment with lots of action and diversity—and a window. Once again, you can review what you have disliked about past work environments for clues on what you would most appreciate. Write those things that are most important to have on your next job.

1. _____

2. _____

3. _____

4. _____

5. _____

## Where Do You Want Your Next Job to Be Located— in What City or Region?

This could be as simple as finding a job that allows you to live where you are now (because you want to stay near your relatives, for example). Or, you might prefer to work in an area near certain necessities or conveniences, such as one close to a child-care center. If you were able to live or work anywhere, what would your ideal community be like? List its characteristics here.

1. _____

2. _____

3. _____

4. _____

5. _____

*(continued)*

*(continued)*

## How Much Money Do You Hope to Make in Your Next Job?

Many people will take less money if the job is great in other ways—or if they just need a job to survive. Think about the minimum you would take as well as what you would eventually like to earn. Realistically, your next job will probably be somewhere between your minimum and maximum amounts.

How much money do you hope to make in your next job? _____

What is the least you are willing to accept? _____

## How Much Responsibility Are You Willing to Accept?

In most organizations, those willing to accept more responsibility are often paid more there is typically a relationship between the two. Higher levels of responsibility often require you to supervise others or to make decisions that affect the organization. Some people are willing to accept this responsibility; and others, understandably, would prefer not to.

Decide how much responsibility you are willing to accept and write that here. _____

_____

_____

Also ask yourself whether you prefer to work by yourself, be part of a group, or be in charge. If so, at what level? Jot down where you see yourself, in terms of accepting responsibility for others, and in other ways within an organization. _____

_____

_____

## The Top Ten Values Employers Want

In completing some of these questions, it might help you to know the values that are most often cited in surveys of employers as being important in the people they hire:

1. Honesty/integrity/morality
2. Adaptability/flexibility
3. Dedication/hardworking/work ethic/tenacity
4. Dependability/reliability/responsibility

5.  Loyalty

6.  Positive attitude/motivation/energy/passion

7.  Professionalism

8.  Self-confidence

9.  Self-motivated/ability to work with little or no supervision

10. Willingness to learn

## What Things Are Important or Have Meaning to You?

What are your values? I once had a job where the sole reason for the organization's existence was to make money. Not that this is wrong—it's just that I wanted to be involved in something I could believe in. If money is the thing for you, fine. But some people prefer working to help others, clean up our environment, build things, make machines work, gain power or prestige, care for animals or plants, or many other possibilities. I believe that all work is worthwhile if it's done well, so the issue here is what is important to include in your next job, if you can. Write these values here.

1. _____

2. _____

3. _____

4. _____

5. _____

## Your Ideal Job

Use the eight preceding questions as a basis for defining your ideal job. Think about each question and select the points most important to you. You may want to include other issues not covered by the questions but that are particularly important to you.

You don't have to be practical here, nor do you need to write a job objective as it might appear on your resume. Just dream.

Now, write the five to ten most important elements you would like to include in your next job—your ideal job, if only you could find it.

(continued)

(continued)

1. _____

2. _____

3. _____

4. _____

5. _____

6. _____

7. _____

8. _____

9. _____

10. _____

# Write Your Resume's Job Objective

Now that you've worked to identify your ideal job, you have the ammunition you'll need to write your resume's job objective. For many, this can be more difficult than it might seem. It assumes, for example, that you have a good idea of the type of job or jobs you want.

You might need to spend more time researching career alternatives before settling on one you can use for your resume. If that's the case with you, consider putting together a resume around a broad job objective that makes the resume acceptable for a variety of jobs. Even if you're not sure that these are the ones you want long term, doing this allows you to conduct a job search while researching alternatives. In some cases, a job may present itself that is acceptable to you, even though it might be in a field you were not sure of. It happens.

It is also acceptable to create more than one resume, each with a different job objective. This approach allows you to write your resume's content to support each job objective in a specific way.

## QUICK TIP

If you still don't know what type of job you want, concentrate on what you want to do next. That might be working toward a long-term objective such as going back to school or starting your own business. In the meantime, you need to earn a living, so decide on a short-term job goal that you are qualified for and go after it. Make that short-term job goal the job objective for your resume.

---

### FOUR QUICK TIPS FOR WRITING A JOB OBJECTIVE

Although the job objective you write should meet your specific needs, here are some things to consider in writing it:

1. **Avoid job titles.** Job titles such as "administrative assistant" or "marketing analyst" can involve very different activities in different organizations. The same job can often have different job titles in different places, and using a title might limit you from consideration for such jobs as "office manager" or "marketing assistant."

   It's best to use broad categories of jobs rather than specific titles. You can then be considered for a wide variety of jobs related to your skills. For example, instead of "administrative assistant," you could say "responsible office management, support, and coordination position."

2. **Define a "bracket of responsibility" to include the possibility of upward mobility.** Although you may be willing to accept a variety of jobs related to your skills, you should include those that require higher levels of responsibility and pay. The preceding example keeps open the option to be considered for an office management position as well as clerical jobs.

   In effect, you should define a "bracket of responsibility" in your objective that includes the range of jobs you are willing to accept. This bracket should include the lower range of jobs that you would consider as well as those requiring higher levels of responsibility, up to and including those that you think you could handle. Even if you have not handled those higher levels of responsibility in the past, many employers might consider you if you have the skills to support the objective.

3. **Include your most important skills.** What are the most important skills needed for the job you want? Consider including one or more of these as required for the job you seek. The implication here is that if you are looking for a job that requires "organizational skills," then you

*(continued)*

*(continued)*

have those skills. Of course, your resume content should support those skills with specific examples.

4. **Include specifics if these are important to you.** If you have substantial experience in a particular industry (such as "computer-controlled machine tools") or have a narrow and specific objective that you really want (such as "art therapist with the handicapped"), it is fine to state this. But realize that by narrowing your alternatives, you will often not be considered for other jobs for which you might qualify. Still, if that's what you want, it just might be worth pursuing (although I would encourage you to have a second, more general resume just in case).

# The Job Objective Worksheet

Use this worksheet to create a draft of your resume's job objective. This worksheet includes questions and activities to help you decide what to include.

## What Sort of Position, Title, and Area of Specialization Do You Seek?

Write the type of job you want, as if you were explaining it to someone you know.

_____

_____

_____

_____

## Define Your "Bracket of Responsibility"

Describe the range of jobs that you would accept at a minimum as well as those you might be able to handle if given the chance. _____

_____

_____

_____

_____

## Name the Key Skills You Have That Are Important in This Job

Describe the two or three key skills that are particularly important for success in the job you seek. Select one or more of these that you are strong in and that you enjoy using. Write it (or them) here. _____

_____

_____

_____

_____

## Name Specific Areas of Expertise or
## Strong Interests That You Want to Use in Your Next Job

If you have substantial interest, experience, or training in a specific area and want to include it in your job objective, list that here. _____

_____

_____

_____

_____

## What Else Is Important to You?

Is there anything else you want to include in your job objective? This could include a value that is particularly important, such as "A position that allows me to help families" or "Employment in an aggressive and results-oriented organization"; a preference for the size or type of organization such as "A small to mid-size business"; or some other consideration.

_____

_____

_____

_____

_____

# Finalize Your Resume's Job Objective Statement

Look over the sample resumes in parts 1 and 3 to see how others have written their job objectives. Some don't include all the elements that are presented in the Job Objective Worksheet, and that's perfectly acceptable. Some are very brief, providing just a job title or category of jobs; others are quite long and detailed. Others don't include a Job Objective statement at all—it's just implied by the resume's content.

There are no rigid rules for writing your resume's Job Objective statement. You should include only information that is essential for an employer to know in considering you; this means that the objective should be brief. Each and every word should be important in some way.

Go ahead and write your job objective on the following lines just as you want it to appear on your resume. Edit it so that each word counts, and make certain that each word creates a positive impression.

_____

_____

_____

_____

_____

_____

_____

_____

_____

_____

_____

# CHAPTER 8

# Highlight Your Strengths and Overcome "Problems" on Your Resume

In a perfect world, we would be considered solely on the basis of our ability to do the job. But the reality is that employers are subjective, and their personal feelings about someone enter into the hiring decision.

This chapter presents common resume concerns voiced by job seekers over the years and gives you a positive way to present problems to employers. Employers are people, too, and most are more understanding than you might think.

## Never Highlight a Negative

A well-written resume often covers a job seeker's weaknesses or flaws. That is precisely the point. All of the resumes in this book are based on real ones written for and by real people. These resumes follow a primary resume-writing rule: *Never highlight a negative*. Because everyone has less-than-perfect credentials for a given job, all resumes hide one thing or another to some degree. In some cases, notes on the sample resumes point out how the writers have handled job-seeker problems. Use these as examples of how to handle similar problems in your resume.

Although I couldn't list every dilemma job seekers face, what follows will help you handle problems that many people deal with during their job search. If you have a different issue, this chapter will help you figure out what to do.

Note that these often are not just resume problems. They are also problems to resolve when completing applications or in interviews. Although the solutions in this chapter relate primarily to handling the problems on a resume, you should gain some insight on how to approach the same problems in other situations as well.

## Deal with "Problems" in an Interview, Not on Your Resume

A resume should present your strengths, so include only content an employer can interpret as positive. Try to think like an employer and exclude anything that *you* might interpret as a negative. Although you can't be dishonest, neither should you present negative information. In many cases, issues that concern or worry you may not be problems to employers at all.

If something does not support your job objective, you should eliminate it. No rule says you must include information in a resume that may not help you.

**QUICK TIP**

If you feel strongly that an employer needs to know something potentially negative about you, don't present it until you're in the interview. And even then, wait for the right opportunity to mention it and be sure to explain how you plan to overcome this negative.

## Some Problems Are Sensitive Subjects

Just mentioning that the issues covered here might be "problems" will upset some people. For example, some will object to any mention that people over 50 might experience discrimination in the labor market. Individuals over 50 know, however, that their age makes it harder to get a good job. Others will resent the implication that employers would consider such issues as race, religion, national origin, child-care arrangements, membership in the cigar-and-steak-lover's society, and other "politically sensitive" matters in evaluating people for employment.

So, with the certainty of offending someone, I have included information that is a bit sensitive for some. But I think that you, as a job seeker, need to accept reality and look for ways to overcome situations that some might consider to be problems. It can be done.

### QUICK NOTE

It's well known that some employers are unfair. Some consider factors in their hiring decisions that should not be factors. For example, many older people do have a harder time getting jobs than younger ones. Many employers are interested in whether a young woman has children (or is planning to in the near future). People are sometimes unfair, and employers are people.

I realize that some of these things are controversial and that you may not agree with some of my advice. But it is better that you consider these matters in advance and have a way to respond to them if they come up—or if you think one or more of them could be an issue to a given employer.

## General Guidelines for Handling "Problems"

Most employers are good people trying to do their jobs. They want to select people who will stay on the job, be reliable, and do well. That is usually why employers want to know as much as they can about you. Why, for example, are you new to this area? Do you plan on staying? If you are "overqualified," are you likely to be unhappy and leave after a short period of time?

### QUICK TIP

Employers want to determine whether they can depend on you and, to find out, they want to know more about you. You can either help them to know that, yes, you are reliable (and greatly increase your chances for a job offer, in spite of their technically inappropriate questions) or tell them to jump in the lake (which will likely not result in a job offer). But if someone asks really inappropriate (and maybe even illegal questions), take that as evidence of what it would be like to work for this employer.

Employers want to understand your true motivations. This can involve understanding issues such as how likely you are to stay in the area and other matters that are not work related.

Some of these points may arise when you're completing your resume, although they are often far more of an issue in an interview. In many cases, a cover letter provides additional details, but an interview is where you can best address most "problems." In that context, consider your situation in advance and be able to present to the employer that, in your case, the issue is simply not a problem at all, but an advantage.

In any case, an interview—and not a resume—is where you deal with problems. A resume is simply a preliminary piece of paper, and it should never, never present a problem of any kind. If yours does, you need to rework it until that problem is not evident.

In the interview, be truthful and present your problem as a potential advantage, should it come up. In that context, I hope that the following tips help you see that almost every problem has two sides. Here is my advice for handling a variety of problem situations on your resume.

## Gaps in Work History

Many people have gaps in their work history. If you have a well-understood reason for major gaps, such as going to school or having a child, you can simply state this on your resume. You could, in some situations, handle one of these gaps by putting the alternative activity on the resume, with dates, just as you would handle any other job.

**QUICK TIP**

Minor gaps, such as being out of work for several months, do not need an explanation. You can often simply exclude any mention of months on your resume. Instead, refer to the years you were employed such as "2005 to 2007."

## Being Out of Work

Some of the most accomplished people I know have been out of work at one time or another. One out of five people in the workforce experiences some unemployment each year, so you will be in good company. It's not a sin, and many people who are bosses have experienced it themselves, as have I. But the tradition is to try to hide this on the resume.

One technique is to put something like "(year you started) to present" on your resume when referring to your most recent job. This approach makes it look like you are still employed. Although this might be an acceptable approach in some cases, it may also require you to explain yourself early in an interview. This soft deception can start you off on a negative note and may not end up helping you at all. Another alternative is to write the actual month that you left your last job or to write some interim activity, such as being self-employed. Even if that means that you are working at a temporary agency, doing odd jobs, or helping a friend with his or her business, it's better than being deceitful.

**QUICK TIP**

A resume is the place for presenting positive information. If something might be interpreted as negative, do not include it. Use your judgment, and if you're in doubt, cut it out.

## Being Fired and Other Negatives in Your Work History

There is no reason for a resume to include details related to why you left previous jobs—unless, of course, they were positive reasons. For example, leaving to accept a more responsible job is to your credit, and your resume can say this. If you have been fired, analyze why. In most cases, it is for reasons that do not have to do with your performance. Most often, people are fired as a result of interpersonal conflicts. Personality clashes are quite common and do not necessarily mean you will have the same problem in a different situation. If your performance was the reason, you may have to explain why that would not be the case in a new job.

The resume itself should present what you did well in previous situations. Leave the discussion of problems for the interview, and take time in advance to practice what you will say about them if asked.

## Job History Unrelated to Your Current Job Objective

If your previous work experience was in jobs that don't relate to what you want to do next, your best bet is to use a skills resume. This resume format was presented in chapter 3, and you can see examples of it there and in part 3. In this situation, using a traditional chronological resume will display an apparent lack of preparation for the job you want.

The advantage of the skills resume in this situation is that it allows you to emphasize the transferable skills that you have developed and used in other settings. If you carefully select skills that are needed in the job you want next, you can draw from work and life experiences to demonstrate that you have the needed skills. And, of course, you would emphasize any education, training, and other experiences that directly prepared you for the job you now seek.

### QUICK TIP

Interview skills, including how to answer problem questions, are a topic of another book I wrote, *Next-Day Job Interview*. If you need more information on handling a problem that may come up in an interview, this book will help you handle most interview situations well.

## Changing Careers

This is a situation related to the preceding one and would also be handled through a skills resume. A change in careers does require some justification on your part, so that it makes sense to an employer.

For example, a teacher who wants to become a real-estate sales agent could point to his hobby of investing in and fixing up old houses. He could discuss his superior communications skills and his ability to get students to do what they are told in a classroom. And he could describe the many after-hours activities he has been involved in as a sign of a high energy level and a willingness to work the nights and weekends needed to sell real estate.

## *Recent Graduate*

If you have recently graduated, you probably are competing against people with similar levels of education but with more work experience. If you don't have a lot of work experience related to the job you want, you will need to emphasize your recent education or training. This might include specific mention of courses you took and other activities that most directly relate to the job you now seek.

**QUICK TIP**

Louise Kursmark, author of *Best Resumes for College Students and New Grads* (JIST), suggests that you look at a variety of school and life experiences for evidence of your abilities. For example, think about class/team projects, theses, research, clubs and organizations, summer jobs, volunteer activities, academic honors, travel, family background, and your own special skills and interests.

New graduates need to look at their school work as the equivalent of work. Indeed, school work is real work in that it requires self-discipline, completion of a variety of tasks, and other activities similar to those required in many jobs. You also may have learned a variety of things that are directly related to doing the job you want. A skills resume will allow you to present these experiences in the same way you might present work experiences in a chronological resume.

You should play up the fact, if you can, that you are familiar with the latest trends and techniques in your field and can apply these skills right away to the new job. And, because you are experienced in studying and learning new material, you will be better able to quickly learn the new job than someone who has been out of school for a while.

A skills resume also enables you to more effectively present transferable skills you used in other jobs (such as waiting tables) that don't seem to directly relate to the job you now want. These jobs can provide a wealth of adaptive and transferable skills that you can use, with some thought, to support your resume's job objective.

## *Too Little Experience*

Young people, including recent graduates, often have difficulty in getting the jobs they want because employers often prefer to hire someone with more experience. If this is your situation, you might want to emphasize your adaptive skills (see chapter 5) that tend to compensate for a lack of experience.

Once again, a skills resume allows you to present yourself in the best light. For example, emphasizing skills such as "hardworking" and "learn new things quickly" might impress an employer enough to consider you over more experienced workers. It happens more often than you might think.

**QUICK TIP**

Also consider expressing a willingness to accept difficult or less desirable conditions as one way to break into a field and gain experience. For example, "willing to work weekends and evenings" or "able to travel or relocate" may open up some possibilities.

Look for anything that might be acceptable as experience and emphasize it. This might include volunteer work, family responsibilities, education, training, military experience, or anything else you might present as legitimate activities that support your ability to do the work you believe you can do.

## *Overqualified*

It doesn't seem to make sense that you could have too much experience, but some employers might think so. They might fear you will not be satisfied with the available job and that, after awhile, you will leave for a better one. So what they really need is some assurance of why this would not be the case for you.

**QUICK NOTE**

If, in fact, you are looking for a job with higher pay than the one you are applying for—and if you communicate this in some way to an employer—it is quite likely that he or she will not offer you a job for fear that the company will soon lose you. And they may be right.

After a period of unemployment, most people become more willing to settle for less than they had hoped for. If you are willing to accept jobs where you may be defined as overqualified, consider not including some of your educational or work-related credentials on a version of your resume—although I do not necessarily recommend doing this. Be prepared to explain, in the interview, why you do want this particular job and how your wealth of experience is a positive and not a negative.

## Race, Religion, or National Origin

There is simply no need to make this an issue on your resume. The most important issue is whether you can do the job well. For this reason, I discourage people from including details that refer to these issues.

## Not Sure of Job Objective

As mentioned previously, including a job objective on your resume is highly desirable. If you really can't settle on a long-term job objective, consider a short-term one, and use that on your resume. You can also develop several resumes, each with its own job objective. This allows you to select information that will best support your various options.

## Recently Moved

Employers are often concerned that someone who has recently moved to an area may soon leave. If you are new to the area, consider explaining this on your resume (or, better yet, in your cover letter). A simple statement such as "Relocated to Cincinnati to be closer to my family" or any other reasonable explanation is often enough to present yourself as stable. Giving a reason eliminates the concern for most employers.

**QUICK TIP**

One way to differentiate your resume from the others and reassure employers that you are telling the truth is to have your resume certified. For $16 per credential, ResTrust (www.restrust.net) will verify your employment and education and stamp your resume as "certified." It saves the employer the expense of doing a background check on you and likely makes you a more attractive candidate.

## *No Degree or Less Education Than Typically Required*

If you have the experience and skills to do a job that is often filled by someone with more education, take special care in preparing the Education and Experience sections of your resume.

If you have substantial work experience, you can simply not include an Education section. Although this has the advantage of not presenting your lack of formal credentials in an obvious way, a better approach might be to present the education and training that you do have without indicating that you do not have a degree. For example, mention that you attended such-and-such college or program but don't mention that you did not complete it. Several sample resumes in part 3 take this approach (see pages 201, 202, and 219). It avoids you being screened out unnecessarily and gives you a chance at an interview you might not otherwise get.

### QUICK TIP

Note that I do not suggest you misrepresent yourself by overstating your qualifications or claiming a degree you do not have. That may result in your later being fired and is clearly not a good idea. But again, no law requires you to display your weaknesses. As I said earlier, the interview is where you can bring up any problems or explain any weaknesses.

## *Too Young*

Young people need to present their youth as an advantage rather than as a disadvantage. So consider just what aspects of your youth might be seen as advantages. For example, perhaps you are willing to work for less money, accept less desirable tasks, work longer or less convenient hours, or do other things that a more experienced worker might not. If so, say so.

Many employers prefer to hire workers with experience and demonstrated ability in jobs related to those they have available. Still, young people who present themselves effectively are often considered over those with better credentials.

# *Too Old*

Older workers need to present their wealth of experience and maturity as an advantage. If that sounds similar to the advice I offered for being "too young," you're right. In all cases, you need to look for ways to turn what someone might consider a negative into a positive. Older workers often have some things going for them that younger workers do not. On a resume, stress your years of experience as a plus, emphasize your loyalty to previous employers, and list accomplishments that occurred over time.

## QUICK NOTE

Labor experts project a huge shortage of available workers in the coming decade. As a result, companies are already seeing the importance of hiring and keeping older workers and persuading them to keep working after retirement age. So don't underestimate your value!

If you have more than 15 years or so of work experience, emphasize your more recent work experience. Once you have 10 or more years of work experience in a related field, you only need to write in your summary statement and cover letters "More than 10 years of experience in accounting," rather than a more specific number that could be used to indicate your age.

## QUICK TIP

If you are an older worker, select activities that best support your ability to do the job you are seeking and emphasize them on your resume. Unless it is clearly to your advantage, you don't need to provide many details on your work or other history from more than 20 years ago.

To avoid sounding "too old," consider not including graduation dates or any other date that can be used to indicate your age. You can cluster earlier jobs into one statement that covers them by saying something like "Various jobs requiring skills in engineering." In most cases, your more recent experiences are more important to an employer, anyway. Emphasize recent training, accomplishments, and responsibilities in your resume and include dates on these items as appropriate.

## *Family Status and Children*

There is absolutely no need for your resume to mention your marital status or whether you have children. The employer doesn't need to know these details of your life, and by law is not allowed to ask, so don't volunteer the information on your resume.

In certain jobs, however (such as daycare provider or children's book editor), having raised kids can be an advantage. But it's probably still best to leave this information off your resume and mention it in your cover letter instead.

## *Physical Limitations and Disabilities*

I assume that you will not seek a job that you can't or should not do. So that means you are looking for a job that you are capable of doing, right? And, that being the case, you don't have a disability related to doing this job at all.

For this reason, I see no need to mention any disability on your resume. Laws require employers to consider all applicants based on the requirements of the job and the ability of the applicant to do that job. This means that any disability you have is not supposed to be a limitation to being considered for a job that you are able to do.

Of course, employers are still able to use their judgment in selecting the best person for the job, and that means that people with disabilities have to compete for jobs along with everyone else. That is fair, so you will need to present to a prospective employer a convincing argument for why the employer should hire you over someone else. But on your resume, you should never mention a disability. Instead, focus on your *ability* to do the job.

**QUICK TIP**

For more advice on seeking, getting, and keeping jobs, see the federal government's site on employment for people with disabilities, DisabilityInfo.gov (www.disabilityinfo.gov).

## Negative References

Most employers will not contact your previous employers unless you are being considered seriously for the job. If you fear that a previous employer will not give you a positive reference, here are some things you can do:

- List someone other than your supervisor as a reference from that employer—someone who knew your work there and who will say nice things about you. Consider a coworker or someone from a different department that you worked closely with. You might also consider including outside contractors and vendors you worked with.

- Discuss the issue in advance with your previous employer and negotiate what this person will say. If what the former employer agrees to say is not good, at least you know this and can prepare potential employers.

- Get a written letter of reference. In many cases, employers will not give references over the phone—or negative references at all—for fear of being sued. Having a letter in advance allows you to give a copy to a prospective employer, and this may help the employer in making a decision.

**QUICK TIP**

If you're worried about what your references are saying about you, ask a friend to pose as a prospective employer and call your references. Or, if you're willing to pay a fee to check on them, hire a service such as Allison & Taylor, Inc. (www.myreferences.com) or use Yahoo.com's fee-based service of a confidential background check. If any negatives turn up, this gives you a chance to negotiate a more positive reference with a past employer, provide alternative references, or explain things in a positive way to a potential employer.

## Criminal Record

A resume should *never* include any negative information about you. So if you have ever been in trouble with the law, do not mention it in your resume. Labor laws prevent an employer from including such general questions on an application as "Have you ever been arrested?" and limit formal inquiries to "Have you ever been convicted of a felony?" because convictions for minor offenses are not supposed to be considered in a hiring decision.

In most cases, your criminal record would never be an issue on a resume because you would not mention it. In this country, we are technically innocent until proven guilty, thank goodness, and that is why employers are not allowed to consider an arrest record in a hiring decision. Being arrested and being guilty are two different things.

A felony conviction is a different matter. These crimes are more serious, and employment laws allow an employer to ask for and get this information—and to use it in making certain hiring decisions. For example, few employers would want to hire an accountant who had been convicted of stealing money from a previous employer.

If you have an arrest or conviction record that an employer has a legal right to inquire about, my advice is to avoid looking for jobs where your record would be a big negative. The accountant in the example should consider changing careers. I would advise people in this situation to avoid jobs where they could easily commit the same crime, since few employers would consider hiring them for that reason. Even if they did get such a job because they concealed their criminal history, they could be fired at any time for lying about it. Instead, I might suggest the above-mentioned accountant consider selling accounting software, starting his or her own business, or getting into a career completely unrelated to accounting.

### QUICK TIP

As always, your resume should reflect what you *can* do rather than what you can't. If you chose your career direction wisely and present a convincing argument that you can do the job well, many employers will, ultimately, overlook previous mistakes. So a criminal history really isn't an issue for a resume. Instead, it is a career planning, job search, and interview issue.

# Other Items to Include—or Not Include—on Your Resume

Here are some other items to include or not include on your resume.

## A Heading, Such as "Resume"

Few people would confuse a resume with something else, so using a header is not necessary. In some cases, this is done to make the resume appear more formal or, at times, just because the writer wanted it that way, but you really don't need to include one.

## A Way to Reach You by Phone or E-mail

Employers are most likely to try to reach you by phone or e-mail. For this reason, it is essential that you include a phone number and, if at all possible, an e-mail address.

Here are some essential things to consider for the phone number you include on your resume (e-mail is covered separately):

- **The telephone must always be answered.** In most cases, employers will call you during their regular business hours. If you are actively out looking for a job, you may be gone too often to reliably receive phone calls. The solution is to use an answering machine or voice-mail service. Although some people don't like leaving messages, most are used to it and are likely to leave a message asking you to return their call. This is far better than someone not being able to reach you.

**QUICK TIP**

It's acceptable (and sometimes preferable) to list your cell phone number on your resume. Just be sure to answer it professionally at all times if you don't recognize the incoming number. You might also consider letting the call go to voice mail if you are someplace where it would be difficult to conduct a professional conversation (around loud machinery, in a public place, or in front of your current boss).

- **The phone must be answered appropriately and reliably.** First impressions count, so make sure your phone is answered appropriately. If you are using your home phone, instruct anyone answering the phone during the day (when employers are most likely to call) to conduct themselves in a professional way. Make certain that anyone who answers the phone knows how to take reliable messages, including the name, organization, and phone number of the caller. And make certain your answering machine or voice-mail greeting is professional and clear. Keep in mind that an employer will hear this message, so be sure it presents you positively.

- **Your telephone number must include an area code.** Always include the correct area code for your phone number, even if you don't want to move to another area. Resumes have a way of getting circulated widely and in ways that you might not expect. In some cases, you may get a call from an employer who lives out of your area (at a corporate office, for example), but who has the authority to offer you a job where you are.

### QUICK TIP

Many cities now have multiple area codes, so don't assume that someone will know yours.

- **The phone number must remain the same throughout your job search.** Resumes can be filed for quite some time, which can result in an employer trying to reach you long after your resume was first put into circulation. So include a long-term phone number. If you are in the process of moving, you might consider using an answering machine, voice-mail service, cell phone, or pager until you no longer need it. You can even arrange for a local phone number to be used in a distant location by obtaining one of these services there. This will avoid creating the impression that you are not readily available.

In many situations, it is wise to include more than one phone number on your resume, and some resume examples in this book include two numbers. This allows you to use your home number (for example) as the primary place to reach you, as well as provide the employer an alternate number should the first one be unavailable, busy, or no longer in service. As you can see in the various sample resumes, you can simply indicate each phone number's type with words such as the following:

- Daytime
- Messages
- Cell or Mobile
- Fax
- Office
- Evenings
- Answering Service
- Pager
- Voice Mail
- Home

## YOUR RESUME SHOULD INCLUDE YOUR E-MAIL ADDRESS!

Many employers prefer to use e-mail instead of the phone because it takes less of their time. This is reason enough to include an e-mail address on your resume. In addition, people who don't include an e-mail address appear to be computer illiterate—not a good thing. Here are some tips on using your e-mail address to best effect:

- Handle your e-mail address just as you would your phone number, formatted in a similar way and placed near the top of your resume.

- If you don't want to use your personal e-mail address or if your regular address does not sound professional (like snakelady@hiss.com or whatever), set up a temporary address through a site like www.yahoo.com, www.msn.com, or www.hotmail.com.

- Check your e-mail daily throughout your job search and respond immediately to any employers who contact you that way.

- Remember that your e-mail response creates an impression, so make sure it's a positive one. Keep your e-mail responses short, professional, and friendly. And check them carefully to eliminate spelling and grammar errors.

## Alternative Addresses

In most cases, including your home address is enough. Just be sure to give your complete address and ZIP code. In rare situations, you might want to include either no address or an alternative one. For example, perhaps you don't consider your home address to be positive because it is in a "bad area," you live out of the area, or for some other reason. Before you exclude an address, consider asking someone reliable to accept your mail at his or her address and forward it to you.

If you are moving and know what the new address will be, you can list both the current and future locations. Add a statement like "After July 15" near the new address. This is not the best solution, but it can work.

## Personal Information

There is no need to include personal information on your resume such as height, weight, or marital status. The reason is that these things have little or nothing to do with your ability to do the job. In addition, labor laws introduced in the past prevent an employer from considering many of these things in their hiring decisions. As a result, most employers will throw away resumes that include this sort of information, to reduce their chances of being sued for using the information in their screening process.

There are exceptions, of course: Some resumes do effectively include personal details that reinforce their ability to do the job or reflect positively on their personality or style. For example, mentioning certain leisure interests, hobbies, or volunteer activities may reinforce your ability to do the job in some way. But these same things may also harm you, so be cautious in what you include. For example, your mention of involvement in a social or political organization, or of being a fan of a particular sport or team, may help you with some employers but harm you with others.

**QUICK TIP**

If personal information does not directly support your ability to do the job, it is best left out of your resume. A better place for some personal information might be your cover letter. But still, be careful what you share.

## Photographs

Unless you are applying for a position in modeling or the performing arts, never include your photograph with your resume. A photograph gives an indication of your age, gender, attractiveness, race, and other characteristics that an employer may later be accused of using in screening applicants. For this reason, many employers will not consider resumes that have photos attached.

**QUICK TIP**

A hot trend these days is a concept called video resumes. Candidates record two-minute videos of themselves talking about their credentials, post them online, and then send employers a link. Although this capitalizes on the popularity of Internet video and some employers like the idea of the convenience of it, others are concerned with discrimination issues. See www.interviewstream.com, www.workblast.com, and www.hirevue.com for more on video resumes and interviewing.

## References

Some resumes include a statement such as "References Available on Request" at the bottom. Older resume books typically advise you to do this, but it is no longer necessary. Employers know they can ask for references if they want to check them out.

In some cases, if you feel you have particularly good references, you may add a statement such as "Excellent References Available" to indicate that you have a good work history and nothing to hide. Some resumes incorporate this statement as narrative in another section rather than listed at the bottom.

**QUICK TIP**

An option is to include on your resume one to three positive quotes from previous employers attesting to what a good employee you are.

Although I don't suggest you list your references on your resume itself, I do suggest that you create a separate list of references. Having your references available in advance allows you to get them quickly to those employers who ask and conserves valuable space on your resume for use in documenting more important information. And don't forget to notify your references in advance that employers may be calling—and make sure they will have positive things to say about you.

# A Final Few Words on Handling Problems

Thankfully, a variety of laws and regulations require employers to consider applicants on their ability to do a job rather than such personal attributes as race, religion, age, disability, gender, or other unrelated criteria. Most employers are wise enough to avoid making decisions based on points that should not matter. They are often just like you are (you know: intelligent, good looking, humble, and so on). They will try to hire someone who convinces them that they can do the job well.

For this reason, it is *your* responsibility to present to your next employer a convincing argument as to why he or she should hire you over someone else. Even if your "problem" does not come up in the interview, it may be to your advantage to bring it up and deal with it. This is particularly true if you think an employer might wonder about this issue or that it might hurt you if you don't address it.

However you handle the interview, the ultimate question you have to answer is "Why should I hire you?" So provide a good answer, even if the question is not asked quite so obviously.

# CHAPTER 9

# Write a Better Resume Now

After completing chapters 5 through 8, you are ready to put together a "better" resume. By better, I mean one that is more carefully crafted than those you have already prepared, based on part 1.

This chapter helps you pull together what you have learned and create an effective resume. It also expands on the tips in part 1 on how to design, produce, and use your resume to best effect.

This chapter assumes that you have read and completed the activities in chapters 1, 2, 3, and 4. It also assumes that you finished a basic resume as outlined in those chapters and started using it right away while you worked on creating a "better" resume as time permitted.

If that information is not fresh in your mind, what follows won't make much sense because it is supplemental to the information presented in the first four chapters. And if you've worked through chapters 5 through 8, the results from that material will help you work through this chapter more easily. So now, here is additional information on writing an improved resume.

## If You Aren't Good at Writing a Resume, Get Some Help

I begin this chapter with some advice: If you aren't particularly good at writing and designing a resume, consider getting help. The following sections offer several sources of assistance.

## *Professional Resume Writers*

The fees that some resume writers charge are a bargain, whereas others charge entirely too much for what you get. Few regulations or requirements exist for setting up business as a resume writer, and the quality and pricing of services vary widely.

In reviewing a resume writer's capabilities, you need to have a good idea of the services you want and buy only those you need. For example, some resume writers have substantial experience and skills in career counseling and can help you clarify what you want to do. Helping you write your resume may be the end result of more expensive, time-consuming career counseling services that you may or may not need.

Most professional resume writers will ask you questions about your skills, experiences, and accomplishments so that they can use this information to improve your resume. This expertise benefits almost everyone. But, in some cases, the writer is essentially a keyboarder who takes the information you provide and puts it into a simple format without asking questions. This service does not have the same value and obviously should cost less.

**QUICK TIP**

Ask for prices and know exactly what is included before you commit to any resume-writing services. Many legitimate resume writers are happy to give you an upfront estimate.

Some resume writers provide additional services. These services include printing a number of resumes and matching envelopes, putting your resume on a computer disk (for future changes you can make), putting your resume into an electronic format for Internet posting, or posting your electronic resume on one or more Internet sites.

**QUICK TIP**

For a listing of more than 200 professional resume writers, along with their specialties, credentials, and samples, see the *Directory of Professional Resume Writers* (available at www.jist.com).

As mentioned earlier, writing a good resume helps you clarify what you want to do in your career. That process is not simple, and you might benefit greatly from the help of a true career-counseling professional who also happens to be a resume writer.

A variety of excellent resume writers contributed the sample resumes used in this book and you can find their contact information in Appendix B. Local resume writers are listed under "Resume Service" and similar headings in the Yellow Pages (although be sure to check that they have credentials). And many Internet career and job sites sell resume services or provide links to them.

## CHECK FOR PROFESSIONAL CREDENTIALS

There are six major associations of professional resume writers and each provides a Web site with links to professional writers:

- Association of Online Resume and Career Professionals (AORCP; www.aorcp.com)

- Career Directors International (CDI; www.careerdirectors.com)

- Career Management Alliance (The Alliance; www.careermanagementalliance.com)

- Career Professionals of Canada (www.careerprocanada.ca)

- National Résumé Writers' Association (NRWA; www.nrwa.com)

- Professional Association of Résumé Writers & Career Coaches (PARW/CC; www.parw.com)

Each of these associations has a code of ethics, so someone who belongs to these groups offers better assurance of legitimate services than someone who does not. Better yet is someone who has a designation such as Certified Professional Resume Writer (CPRW), Nationally Certified Resume Writer (NCRW), Master Resume Writer (MRW), Certified Expert Resume Writer (CERW), which they earned by passing resume-writing competency tests.

Members of these associations wrote many of the sample resumes in part 3. As you can see, those writers are very good at what they do and will be happy to help you with your resume if you contact them.

In any situation, ask for the credentials of the person who will provide the service, get a clear quote on services included in their prices, and see examples of the person's work before you agree to anything.

## Career or Job Search Counselors and Counseling Services

In your search for someone to help you with your resume, you may run into high-pressure efforts to sell you services. If so, buyer beware! Good, legitimate job search and career professionals are out there, and they are worth every bit of their fees. Many employers pay thousands of dollars for outplacement assistance to help those leaving find new jobs. But some career-counseling businesses prey on unsuspecting, vulnerable souls who are unemployed. Some "packages" can cost thousands of dollars and are not worth the price.

**QUICK TIP**

Two reputable organizations that can refer you to a career counselor or job search coach in private practice are Career Management Alliance (www.careermanagementalliance.com) and the International Association of Career Coaches (www.iaccweb.org).

I have said for years that many job seekers would gain more from reading a few good job search books than they might get from the less-than-legitimate businesses offering these services. But how do you tell the legitimate from the illegitimate? One clue is high-pressure sales and high fees. If this is the case, your best bet is to walk out quickly. Call the agency first and get some information on services offered and prices charged. If the agency requires that you come in to discuss this, assume that it is a high-pressure sales outfit and avoid it.

**QUICK TIP**

Low-cost services often are available from local colleges and One-Stop career centers (see www.servicelocator.org to locate one near you). These may consist of workshops and access to reading materials, assessment tests, and other services at a modest cost or even free. Consider these as an alternative to higher-priced services.

## Print and Photocopy Shops

Some of these businesses offer substantial services, including resume design, high-quality output, resume copying and printing, and a selection of good paper and matching envelopes. Their prices are often quite reasonable, although few are capable of providing significant help in writing your resume.

Look in the yellow pages under "Photocopying," "Copying & Duplicating," or "Printers" for local services. Read their ads and call a few; you may be surprised at what they offer.

# What Sort of Resume Will Work Best for You?

As you know, there are just a few basic resume types. But these types have many variations that could make sense for your situation. The basic resume types were covered in part 1, but here is a review, along with some additional information.

## The Simple Chronological Resume

Chapter 2 provides examples of a simple chronological resume. As you know, this resume arranges your history in reverse-chronological order, beginning with your most recent work experience. Education and training may come before or after your work history, depending on how long you've been out of school and how relevant your degree is to your target job.

Because a chronological resume organizes information by your work experience, it highlights previous job titles, locations, dates employed, and tasks. This is fine if you are looking for the same type of job you have held in the past or are looking to move up in a related field. However, it's less than ideal for some situations. For employers, the chronological resume presents a career progression and allows them to quickly screen out applicants whose backgrounds are not conventional or do not fit the preferred profile.

The chronological format is often not good for those who have limited work experience (such as recent graduates), who want to do something different, or who have less-than-ideal work histories such as job gaps.

## CONSIDER A MODIFIED CHRONOLOGICAL RESUME

While a basic, traditional chronological resume has limitations, you can add some information and modify its style in such a way that will help you. Here are some things you can do, depending on your situation:

- **Add a job objective.** Although a chronological resume might not include a job objective, yours certainly can. Although this has the disadvantage of limiting your resume to certain types of jobs, you should be focusing your job search in this way for other reasons. And including a job objective allows you to focus your resume content to best support that objective.

- **Emphasize skills and accomplishments.** Most chronological resumes simply provide a listing of tasks, duties, and responsibilities, but if you include a job objective, you should clearly emphasize skills, accomplishments, and results that support your job objective.

- **Expand your education and training section.** Let's say that you are a recent graduate who worked your way through school, earned decent grades (while working full time), and got involved in extracurricular activities. The standard listing of education would not do you justice, so consider expanding that section to include statements about your accomplishments while going to school.

- **Add new sections to highlight your strengths.** There is no reason you can't add one or more sections to your resume to highlight something you think will help you. For example, let's say you have excellent references from previous employers. You might add a statement to that effect and even include one or more positive quotes. Or maybe you got exceptional performance reviews, wrote some articles, edited a newsletter, traveled extensively, or did something else that might support your job objective. If so, nothing prevents you from creating a special section or heading to highlight these activities.

Some sample resumes in part 3 break the "rules" and include features that make sense for the individual. And that is one rule that really matters—that your resume communicates your strengths in an effective way.

## The Skills or Functional Resume

Chapter 3 presents the basics of writing a skills resume. This resume style arranges content under major skills rather than jobs previously held. A well-done skills resume emphasizes skills that are most important to succeed in the job stated in the job objective. Of course, you should possess these skills. These resumes are sometimes called functional resumes because they use a functional design that is based on the skills needed for the job sought.

**QUICK ALERT**

A skills resume is often used in situations where the writer wants to avoid displaying obvious weaknesses that would be highlighted on a chronological resume. For example, someone who has been a teacher but who now wants a career in sales could clearly benefit from a skills resume that deemphasizes a lack of sales experience and emphasizes skills learned in teaching that are also important in sales.

A skills resume can help hide a variety of other weaknesses as well, such as limited work experience, gaps in job history, or lack of educational credentials. This is one reason some employers don't like skills resumes: They make it harder for them to quickly screen out applicants. Personally, I like skills resumes. Assuming that you honestly present what you can do, a skills resume often gives you the best opportunity to present your strengths in their best light.

## The Combination Format

In a combination format, you might highlight your key skills related to your job objective and include a separate section that presents your work history in a conventional, chronological way. Some sample resumes in part 3 have successfully merged the skills resume and chronological resume formats—a good idea for many situations (see pages 226–227, 234–235, and 236). Consider using this approach if it can present you well.

## Creative Resumes

There is one other type of resume, and it defies easy description: These resumes use innovative formats and styles. Some use dramatic graphics, colors, and shapes. Graphic artists, for example, may use their resumes as examples of their work and include various graphic elements. An advertising or marketing person might use a writing style that approximates copy writing and a resume design that looks like a polished magazine ad.

I've seen all sorts of special resumes over the years; some are well done and create a good impression. Some do not. I haven't included many examples of these resumes in this book because they don't lend themselves to a book's format (black ink on white paper). How, for example, could I do justice to the resume I once saw that was written on a watermelon?

## QUICK TIP

I've seen many gimmicks, such as a dollar bill attached to a resume with a statement that this person would help the employer make lots of money. Some gimmicks work and you can try them, but I encourage you to stick to the basics: Write a resume that shows you deserve the interview.

So use your judgment. In some cases, creative resumes can make sense. Good design can certainly help, particularly in professions where good design skills are needed.

### PORTFOLIOS AND ENCLOSURES

Some occupations typically require a portfolio of your work or some other concrete example of what you have accomplished. Artists, copy-writers, advertising professionals, clothing designers, architects, radio and TV personalities, and many others know this and should take care to provide good examples of what they do. Examples can include writing samples, photographs of your work, articles you have written, sample audio or videotapes, artwork, a Web site you designed, and other samples of your work that support your job objective.

## Curriculum Vitae (CVs) and Other Special Formats

Attorneys, college professors, physicians, scientists, and people in various other occupations have their own rules or guidelines for preparing a "Professional Vitae" or some other special format. If you are looking for a job in one of these specialized areas, you should learn how to prepare a resume to those specifications. These specialized and occupation-specific resumes are not within the scope of this book and examples are not included, but many books and Web sites provide information on these special formats. For example, Purdue University's College of Liberal Arts has some helpful CV tips at www.cla.purdue.edu/careerservices/How%20to%20Write%20a%20Vita .htm.

### QUICK TIP

In Europe, the term *CV* refers to just a regular resume. People in all professions in Europe use CVs, not just those in academic and medical fields.

## Gather Information and Emphasize Accomplishments, Skills, and Results

Part 1 included activities and a worksheet designed to gather basic information for your resume. Chapters in part 2 provided more detailed information and activities to help you gather facts about yourself, identify key skills, and consider alternative ways to present what you want to include in your resume.

This chapter includes an expanded worksheet to help you gather the information that is most important to include in a resume. Some information is the same as that called for in the Instant Resume Worksheet in chapter 2; however, this new worksheet is considerably more thorough. If you complete it carefully, it will prepare you for the final step of writing a superior resume.

# Comprehensive Resume Worksheet

## Instructions

Use this worksheet to write a draft of the material you will include in your resume. Use a writing style similar to that of your resume, emphasizing skills and accomplishments. Keep your narrative as brief as possible and make every word count.

Use a pencil or erasable pen to allow for changes. You might find it helpful to use a separate sheet of paper for drafting the information in some worksheet sections that follow. When you have done that, go ahead and complete the worksheet in the book. The information you write on the worksheet should be pretty close to the information you will use to write your resume, so write it carefully. For some sections, you will probably need to refer back to the appropriate section of this book to find previously recorded information.

## Personal Identification

Name _____

Home address _____

_____

City, state or province, ZIP or postal code _____

_____

Primary phone number _____

Comment _____

Alternate/cell phone number _____

Comment _____

E-mail address _____

## Job Objective Statement

Write your job objective here, as you would like it to appear on your resume. Writing a good job objective is tricky business and requires a good sense of what you want to do as well as the skills you have to offer. You can refer to the work you did in chapter 7 and review sample resumes in part 3 before completing this. _____

_____

_____

_____

_____

## In Just a Few Words, Why Should Someone Hire You?

A good resume answers this question in some way. So, to clarify the essential reasons why someone should hire you over others, write a brief answer to the question in the following space. Then make sure that your resume gets this across in some way. _____

_____

_____

_____

_____

## Key Adaptive Skills to Emphasize in Your Resume

What key adaptive skills do you have that support your stated job objective? Review chapter 5 to identify your top adaptive skills and list those that best support your job objective in the following spaces. After each, write the accomplishments or experiences that best support those skills—your proof that you have these skills. Be brief and emphasize numbers and results when possible. Include some or all of these skills in your resume.

**Adaptive skill**_____

_____

Proof of this skill _____

_____

_____

_____

_____

**Adaptive skill** _____

_____

Proof of this skill _____

_____

_(continued)_

*(continued)*

_____

_____

_____

_____

**Adaptive skill** _____

_____

Proof of this skill _____

_____

_____

_____

_____

## Key Transferable Skills to Emphasize in Your Resume

Select your transferable skills that best support your stated job objective. Refer to chapter 5 as needed to help identify these skills and list them on the following lines, along with examples of when you used or demonstrated these skills. Use some or all of these in your resume.

**Transferable skill** _____

_____

Proof of this skill _____

_____

_____

_____

**Transferable skill** _____

_____

Proof of this skill _____

_____

_____

_____

_____

_____

**Transferable skill** _____

_____

Proof of this skill _____

_____

_____

_____

_____

**Transferable skill** _____

_____

Proof of this skill _____

_____

_____

_____

_____

**Transferable skill** _____

_____

Proof of this skill _____

_____

_____

_____

_____

_____

*(continued)*

(continued)

## What Are the Key Job-Related Skills Needed in the Job You Want?

Refer to chapter 7 to learn how to identify the key job-related skills needed in the job you want. If you have selected an appropriate job objective, you should have those very skills. Write the most important job-related skills (and more if you know them), along with examples to support these skills—and include them in your resume.

**Job-related skill** _____

_____

Proof of this skill _____

_____

_____

_____

_____

_____

**Job-related skill** _____

_____

Proof of this skill _____

_____

_____

_____

_____

_____

**Job-related skill** _____

_____

Proof of this skill _____

_____

_____

_____

_____

_____

**Job-related skill** _____

_____

Proof of this skill _____

_____

_____

_____

_____

_____

**Job-related skill** _____

_____

Proof of this skill _____

_____

_____

_____

_____

_____

_____

## What Specific Work or Other Experience Do You Have That Supports Your Doing This Job?

If you completed the worksheets in chapter 6, you have plenty of information to draw on in completing this section. If you are writing a chronological resume, organize the following information in order of the jobs you have held (most recent first). If you are writing a skills resume, organize the information within major skill areas.

There is space for both of these arrangements, and I suggest you complete both sections. In doing so, write the content as if you were writing it for use on your resume. You can, of course,

_(continued)_

*(continued)*

further edit what you write here into its final form, but try to approximate the writing style you will use in your resume. Use short sentences. Include action words. Emphasize key skills. Include numbers to support your skills; and emphasize accomplishments and results instead of simply listing your duties.

In previous jobs that don't relate well to what you want to do next, emphasize adaptive and transferable skills and accomplishments that relate to the job you want. Mention promotions, raises, or positive evaluations as appropriate. If you did more than your job title suggests, consider a more descriptive (but not misleading) title, such as "head waiter and assistant manager," if that is what you were, instead of "waiter." If you had a number of short-term jobs, consider combining them all under one heading such as "Various Jobs While Attending College."

You may need to complete several drafts of this information before it begins to "feel good," so use additional sheets of paper as needed.

## Experiences Organized by Chronology

**Most recent or present job title** _____

Dates (month/year) from _____ to _____

Organization name _____

City, state or province, ZIP or postal code _____

_____

Duties, skills, responsibilities, accomplishments _____

_____

_____

_____

_____

_____

**Next most recent job title** _____

Dates (month/year) from _____ to _____

Organization name _____

City, state or province, ZIP or postal code _____

_____

Duties, skills, responsibilities, accomplishments _____

_____

_____

_____

_____

_____

**Next most recent job title** _____

Dates (month/year) from _____ to _____

Organization name _____

City, state or province, ZIP or postal code _____

_____

Duties, skills, responsibilities, accomplishments _____

_____

_____

_____

_____

_____

**Next most recent job title** _____

Dates (month/year) from _____ to _____

Organization name _____

City, state or province, ZIP or postal code _____

_____

Duties, skills, responsibilities, accomplishments _____

_____

_____

_____

_____

_____

*(continued)*

(continued)

## Experience Organized by Skills

Look at the sample resumes in part 3 and you will see that some organize their experience under key skills needed for the job. These resumes often include statements regarding accomplishments and results as well as duties. They also often mention other skills that are related to or support the key skill as well as specific examples. These can be work-related experiences or can come from other life experiences.

Assume for now that your resume will organize your experience under key skills. Begin by listing the three to six skills you consider to be most important to succeed in the job you want.

There is space for up to six such skills in the worksheet. Once you have decided which ones to list, write examples of experiences and accomplishments that directly support these skills. Write this just as you want it to appear in your resume.

**Key skill 1** _____

Resume statement to support this skill _____

_____

_____

_____

_____

**Key skill 2** _____

Resume statement to support this skill _____

_____

_____

_____

_____

**Key skill 3** _____

Resume statement to support this skill _____

_____

_____

_____

_____

**Key skill 4** _____

Resume statement to support this skill _____

_____

_____

_____

_____

**Key skill 5** _____

Resume statement to support this skill _____

_____

_____

_____

_____

**Key skill 6** _____

Resume statement to support this skill _____

_____

_____

_____

_____

## What Education or Training Supports Your Job Objective?

Chapter 6 includes a worksheet that organizes your education and training in a thorough way. Go back and review that information before completing this section. In writing your Education and Training section, be sure to include any additional information that supports your qualifications for your job objective. New graduates should emphasize their education and training more than experienced workers and include more details in this section.

Use the space that follows to write what you want to include on your resume under the Education and Training heading.

**School or training institution attended** _____

Dates attended or graduated _____

*(continued)*

(continued)

Degree or certification obtained _____

_____

Anything else that should be mentioned _____

_____

_____

_____

_____

**School or training institution attended** _____

Dates attended or graduated _____

Degree or certification obtained _____

Anything else that should be mentioned _____

_____

_____

_____

_____

**School or training institution attended** _____

Dates attended or graduated _____

Degree or certification obtained _____

Anything else that should be mentioned _____

_____

_____

_____

_____

### Other Formal or Informal Training That Supports Your Job Objective

_____

_____

_____

### Other Resume Sections

If you want to include other sections on your resume, go ahead and write their headings and whatever you want to include. Examples might be "Summary of Experience," "Special Accomplishments," or others. See the headings of this kind among the sample resumes in part 3 for inspiration.

_____

_____

_____

_____

_____

_____

_____

_____

_____

# More Quick Resume-Writing Tips

Part 1 covered the basics of writing a resume. Here are some additional tips and information you might find helpful.

## As Much as Possible, Write Your Resume Yourself

I have come to realize that some people, even very smart people who are good writers, can't write or design a good resume. They just can't. And there is no good reason to force them to write one from start to finish. If you are one of these people, just decide that your skills are in other areas and don't go looking for a job as a resume writer.

Get someone else, preferably a professional resume writer, to do it for you.

But, even if you don't write your own resume, you should do as much as possible yourself. The reason is that, if you don't, your resume won't be truly yours. Your resume may present you well, but it won't be you. Not only may your resume misrepresent you to at least some extent, you also will not have learned what you need to learn by going through the process of writing your resume. You will not have struggled with your job objective statement in the same way and may not have as clear a sense of what you want to do as a result. You won't have the same understanding of the skills you have to support your job objective. As a result, you probably won't do as well in an interview.

### QUICK TIP

Although I encourage you to "borrow" ideas from this book's sample resumes, your resume must end up being yours. You have to be able to defend its content and prove every statement you've made.

Even if you end up hiring someone to help with your resume, you must provide this person with what to say and let him or her help you with how to say it. If you don't agree with something the writer does, ask the person to rework it until it works for you. However you do it, make sure that your resume is *your* resume and that it represents you accurately.

## Don't Lie or Exaggerate

Some job applicants misrepresent themselves. They lie about where they went to school or say that they have a degree that they don't have. They state previous salaries that are higher than they really were. They present themselves as having responsibilities and titles that are not close to the truth.

I do not recommend you do this. For one reason, it is simply not right, and that is reason enough. But there are also practical reasons for not doing so. The first is that you might get a job that you can't handle. If that were to happen, and you fail, it would serve you right. Another reason is that some employers check references and backgrounds more thoroughly than you might realize. Sometimes, this can occur years after you are employed and, if you're caught, you could lose your job, which would not be a pleasant experience. So, my advice is this: Honesty is the best policy. However, some things are better left unsaid, and a resume should present your strengths and not your weaknesses.

Being honest on your resume does not mean you can't present the facts in the most positive way. A resume is not a place to be humble. So work on *what* you say and how you say it, so that you present your experiences and skills as positively as possible.

## Use Short Sentences and Simple Words

Short sentences are easier to read. They communicate better than long ones. Simple words also communicate more clearly than long ones. So use short sentences and easy-to-understand words in your resume (like I've done in this paragraph).

Many people like to throw in words and phrases that are jargon. Some of this may be necessary, but too often I see language that is too specialized, which will turn off many employers. Good writing is easy to read and understand. It is harder to do but is worth the time.

## If It Doesn't Support Your Job Objective, You Should Probably Cut It Out

A resume is only one or two pages long, so you have to be careful in what you do and do not include. Review every word and ask yourself, "Does this support my ability to do the job in some clear way?" If that item does not support your job objective, it should go.

## Include Numbers

Many sample resumes in part 3 include some numbers (see pages 219, 239, and 257–258). Numbers can be used to refer to your word-processing speed, the number of transactions you processed per month, the percentage of increased sales, the dollar amount of costs you cut, or some other numerical measure of performance.

Numbers communicate in a special way, and you should include numbers to support key skills you have or that reflect your accomplishments or results.

## Emphasize Skills

It should be obvious by now that you should emphasize skills in your resume. Besides listing the key skills needed to support your job objective in a skills resume, you should include a variety of skill statements in all narrative sections of your resume. In each case, select skills you have that support your job objective.

## Highlight Accomplishments and Results

Anyone can go through the motions of doing a job, but employers want to know how *well* you have done things in the past. Did you accomplish anything out of the ordinary? What were the results you achieved? Chapter 5 includes many activities that will help you emphasize accomplishments and results from a variety of work and life situations.

## The Importance of Doing Drafts

It will probably take you several rewrites before you are satisfied with your resume's content. And it will take even more changes before you are finished.

**QUICK TIP**

Writing, modifying, editing, changing, adding to, and subtracting from content are important steps in writing a good resume. For this reason, I suggest that you write yours on a computer if you can, where you can make changes quickly.

Edit, edit, and edit again. Every word has to count in your resume, so keep editing until it's right. This might require you to make multiple passes and to change your resume many times. But, if you did as I suggested and have created a simple but acceptable resume, fretting over your "better" resume shouldn't delay your job search one bit. Right?

## Get Someone Else to Review Your Resume for Errors

After you have finished writing your resume, ask someone with good spelling and grammar skills to review it once again. It is simply amazing how errors creep into the most carefully edited resume.

# More Tips to Improve Your Resume's Design

Just as some people aren't good at resume writing, others are not good at design. Many resumes use simple designs, and this is acceptable for most situations. But you can do other things to improve your resume's appearance, and this section covers some basics.

**QUICK TIP**

When looking at the sample resumes in part 3, note how some have a better appearance than others. Some have rules and bullets; others do not. Some include lots of white space, while others are quite crowded. Compromises are made in most resumes, but some clearly look better than others. Note the resumes whose appearance you like and try to incorporate those design principles into your own resume.

## What to Do If You Don't Have the Best Computer Equipment or Design Experience

No problem. As I mentioned earlier, many people can help you with word processing and design. Just go out and have it done by a professional resume writer. At the beginning of this chapter, I provided referral services where you can find others to do your word processing and design work.

**QUICK TIP**

If you are not familiar with how to use a computer and its related software, now is not the time to learn. You can waste lots of time trying to use a computer to do simple tasks such as laying out a resume or printing a letter. If computers are new to you, let someone else create your resume on his or her computer system. Once you have your resume, you might have someone show you how to use the computer for tasks like correspondence. But avoid the fancy stuff.

## Increase Readability with Some Simple Design Principles

People who design advertising know what makes something easy or hard to read—and they work very hard to make things easy. Here are some things they have found to improve readability. You can apply these same principles in writing your resume.

- Short sentences and short words are better than long ones.
- Short paragraphs are easier to read than long ones.
- Narrow columns are easier to read than wide ones.
- Put important information on the top and to the left. People scan materials from left to right and top to bottom.
- Using plenty of white space increases the readability of the text that remains. And it looks better.
- Don't use too many (more than two) fonts on the same page.
- Use underlining, bold type, and bullets to emphasize and separate text—but use them sparingly.

## Avoid "Packing" Your Resume with Small Print

Sometimes it's hard to avoid including lots of detail, but doing so can make your resume appear crowded and hard to read. In many cases, crowded resumes can be shortened with good editing, which allows for considerably more white space.

## Use Two Pages at the Most

One page is often enough if you are disciplined in your editing, but two uncrowded pages are far better than one crowded one. Those with considerable experience or high levels of responsibility often require a two-page resume, but very, very few justify more than two.

**QUICK TIP**

If you end up with one-and-a-half pages of resume, add content or white space until it fills the whole two pages. It just looks better.

## Use Type Fonts Sparingly

Just because you have many fonts on your computer does not mean you have to use them all on your resume. Doing so creates a cluttered, hard-to-read look and is a sure sign of someone without design skills. Good resume design requires relatively few easy-to-read fonts in limited sizes. Look at the sample resumes in part 3—few use more than one or two fonts and most use bold and different font sizes sparingly.

## Consider Graphics

Part 3 includes some sample resumes that use graphic elements to make them more interesting (see pages 241 and 243). Although resumes with extensive graphic-design elements were not my focus for this book (this is a "quick" resume book), some resumes clearly benefit from this. Good graphic design is more important for those in creative jobs such as advertising, art, and desktop publishing.

## Edit Again for Appearance

Just as your resume's text requires editing, you should be prepared to review and make additional changes to its design. After you have written the content just as you want it, you will probably need to make additional editing and design changes so that everything looks right.

**QUICK TIP**

If someone else will help you with the design of your resume, show or e-mail this person copies of resumes you like as design examples. Be open to suggestions, but be willing to assert your taste regarding your resume's final appearance.

## Select Top-Quality Paper

Don't use cheap copy-machine paper. After all your work, you should use only top-quality paper. Most print shops are used to printing resumes and will have paper selections. The better-quality papers often contain a percentage of cotton or other fibers. I prefer an off-white or light cream color because it gives a professional, clean appearance. Pastel colors such as gray and light blue are also acceptable, but avoid bright colors such as pink, green, or red.

## Get Matching Stationery and Envelopes

Envelopes made of the same paper as your resume present a professional look. Select an envelope of the same paper type and color at the time you choose your resume paper. You should also get some blank sheets of this same paper for your cover letters and other job search correspondence. In some cases, you may also be able to obtain matching thank-you-note envelopes and paper.

## Good-Quality Photocopies and Laser-Printer Copies Are Fine

Most photocopy machines now create excellent images, and you can use them to reproduce your resume—as long as you use high-grade paper. Check out the copy quality first. Most laser printers also create good-quality images and can be used to make multiple resume copies.

**QUICK ALERT**

Use your judgment here and don't compromise. If the printing quality doesn't look better than good, find a different way to get it done.

## How Many Copies to Make

If you print your resume on your own printer, print enough to have extras on hand at all times. You just never know when you might need one. If you are photocopying your resume, make about 25 to 50 copies at any one time. You might want to make changes after you "field test" your resume, so don't make too many copies up front. If you are having the resume offset printed, the big cost is getting the job on the press; additional copies done at the same time are often quite inexpensive.

The best use of your resume is to get it into circulation early and often—so have enough so that you don't feel like you need to "save" them. Plan on giving multiple copies to friends, relatives, and acquaintances and sending out lots prior to and after interviews.

# Part 3

# A Stupendous Collection of Professionally Written and Designed Resumes

The resumes in this section were written by professional resume writers. As a result, they present a wonderful variety of writing and design styles and techniques. Each was written with great care and skill to present a real (but fictionalized) person in the best way possible.

There are many reasons to use different writing and design styles, and the resumes in this section show wide variety in all their elements. There are resumes for all sorts of people looking for all sorts of jobs. Some resumes include interesting graphic elements and others are quite plain. This variety will give you ideas for writing and creating your own resume. Feel free to experiment and use whatever style best suits you.

If you need help writing your resume—or with career planning or job search advice—I recommend you contact a writer whose work is included in this book (see appendix B for contact information).

**Chapter 10: Sample Chronological Resumes   183**

**Chapter 11: Sample Skills-Based and Combination Resumes   225**

**Chapter 12: Sample Electronic Resumes   267**

# CHAPTER 10

# Sample Chronological Resumes

The chronological resume is the most popular format among hiring managers because it makes it easy to see your employment history at a glance. Many people include a profile section at the beginning of the resume that highlights their skills; however, the focus in this type of resume is on employment experience.

The samples in this chapter are organized into clusters so that you can easily find ones that relate to your background or job objective. Categories covered in this chapter are the following:

- Business, management and executive, and finance (pages 185–189)
- Healthcare and medical (pages 190–195)
- Hospitality and culinary (pages 196–199)
- IT and engineering (pages 200–204)
- Students and new graduates with limited work experience (pages 205–208)
- Mechanical and skilled trades (pages 209–210)
- Media, information, and communications (pages 211–212)
- Sales (including retail) and marketing (pages 213–219)
- Education (pages 220–224)

One obvious way to use the samples is to turn to the section that seems most compatible with your career goals. Doing so enables you to see how others with similar experience or seeking similar jobs have handled their resumes. But I also encourage you to look at all the samples for formats, presentation styles, and content ideas to use in your resume. For example, some resumes have superior graphic design elements that may inspire you, even though your job objective is in a different area.

The comments written on the resumes point out features, provide information on the person behind the resume, or give other details. This unique approach gives insights into the strategies professional writers use.

*This senior executive needed a resume quickly to give to a recruiter who called unexpectedly, so the writer focused on key highlights and kept the resume to one page.*

# JOHN J. MONLEY

236 Kings Hwy. • Darien, CT 06820
203.655.2444 Res • 203.355.4323 Cell • jmonley@gmail.com

## FINANCIAL SERVICES EXECUTIVE

Senior Managing Director with more than 30 years of consistent success in the highly volatile fixed income markets. Excel in developing strategies and techniques to manage interest rate risk.

**Recognized as Top 3 in production nationwide every year for 26 years.**

**Earned 100% client retention rate over 26 years by providing savvy guidance and market expertise.**

**Effective Strategist** who blends technical acumen and market insight to develop effective hedging and investing strategies.

**Honest, ethical leader** with the highest level of integrity. Recognized for expert knowledge of regulatory rules and procedures.

## PROFESSIONAL EXPERIENCE

**MERRILL LYNCH ✦ NEW YORK, NY**                                    **1981–PRESENT**

<u>SENIOR MANAGING DIRECTOR, FIXED INCOME AND MUNICIPALS ✦ 1987–PRESENT</u>

Successively promoted to positions of increased responsibility based on consistently exceeding goals and expectations.

➤ *Started institutional practice* targeting middle market financial services firms. Assisted in developing client base through effective financial/portfolio analysis, tax swapping, trading, and investment strategies.

➤ Promoted to move to Chicago to run Institutional sales team (1987–2006). *Increased Chicago sales revenue 100% for each of first 2 years.*

➤ *Top 3 in production every year for 26 years.*

➤ *Earned #1 rank for performance in 23 of 26 years.*

➤ Became co-national sales manager in 1995 to improve performance of national sales force of 20. *Restructured organization and dramatically improved efficiencies* and client communications for fixed-income accounts.

➤ Recognized for introducing techniques in structured products and hedging instruments to improve returns and management of risk.

**LF ROTHCHILD ✦ NEW YORK, NY ✦ ASSOCIATE ✦ 1978–1980**

## EDUCATION

**BS, Banking & Finance**
Saint Johns University ✦ New York
Won numerous awards for Economics & Finance

*Submitted by Don Goodman*

# SHONYELL JOHNSON

*123 Palm Street    St. Petersburg, Florida 33710    (727) 555-1212    E-mail: creativeone@email.net*

## CAREER PROFILE

**RESULTS-ORIENTED BUSINESS MANAGEMENT PROFESSIONAL with 10+ years** of solid experience with small business ownership, education, and human services. Polished professional with a proven track record of success in strategic business planning, operations, relationship-partnering, sales, and vendor and community relations. Expertise in event planning, leadership development, mentoring, and case management. Former honors student who worked full-time while attending college full-time and maintaining volunteer activities in the community. Consistently exceed expectations on all job performance evaluations.

## PROFESSIONAL OBJECTIVE

Seeking to contribute to a company's growth and profitability as a Business Development Specialist.

## COMPUTER SKILLS

*Windows 2000 & XP    Microsoft Office 2003 (Access, Excel, PowerPoint, & Word)
Microsoft Outlook    Microsoft Outlook Express    Internet Research
Proprietary Educational and Human Services Software*

## EDUCATION

*Recently earned business degree is featured close to the top, even though she has more than 10 years of work experience.*

**B.S., BUSINESS MANAGEMENT, ECKERD COLLEGE PROGRAM FOR EXPERIENCED LEARNERS, ST. PETERSBURG, FLORIDA (2008)**
❖ G.P.A.: 3.6 / 4.0
❖ Worked full-time while attending college full-time.

### COURSE HIGHLIGHTS

*Accounting    Business Finance    Ethics in Management    Investment Finance
Management Leadership    Marketing    Microeconomics*

**A.A., ST. PETERSBURG COLLEGE, ST. PETERSBURG, FLORIDA**
❖ Worked full-time while attending college full-time.

## PROFESSIONAL EXPERIENCE

**CO-OWNER, EBONY GUESS, ST. PETERSBURG, FLORIDA, & ATLANTA, GEORGIA**
❖ Full profit & loss responsibility for a successful music sales business with revenue topping **$300,000** annually.
❖ As co-owner, started the business from its inception and successfully grew it into a profitable venture in under one year.
❖ Handle all strategic planning, marketing, financial, and accounting duties associated with the business.
❖ Maintain extensive records of all business transactions and plan for conservative future growth.
❖ Thoroughly learned all policies, procedures, licensing, permit, small business regulations, requirements, and standards for opening a business.
❖ Joined the Chamber of Commerce and the Midtown Economic Development Council.

*Submitted by Sharon McCormick*

*Prior experience in social services is relegated to page 2.*

**SHONYELL JOHNSON**                                                    Page Two

---

**STATE OF FLORIDA, DEPARTMENT OF HEATLH, HEALTHY FAMILIES PINELLAS / YWCA ST. PETERSBURG, FLORIDA**
*Family Support Worker (2003 to Present)*
- ❖ Work as part of a nationwide organization with **400+** offices across the country for a program considered to be the most successful child-abuse-prevention outfit in the United States.
- ❖ Work with several highly respected agencies including the *YWCA, Healthy Families Pinellas, the Department of Health,* and the *State of Florida.*
- ❖ Establish a trusting relationship with the parents of children considered at-risk for abuse and neglect to help them create healthier family environments.
- ❖ Create a *"Family Support Plan"* with specific goals, objectives, and activities in conjunction with the Program Supervisor.
- ❖ Assist in strengthening the parent/child relationship through improving parenting skills and meeting the basic needs of the family with the goal of community resource integration and self-sufficiency.
- ❖ Provide in-home visits with prenatal and postnatal parents every week and follow up with the family for up to five years.
- ❖ Enthusiastically teach parenting education to culturally diverse families with cutting-edge materials created by the national organization.
- ❖ Complete precise documentation per the program's requirements and utilize the computer for case planning.
- ❖ Thoroughly learned extensive community resource information and make referrals as needed.
- ❖ Consistently *"Exceed Expectations"* on annual job performance evaluations.

**PARENTS FOR CHILDREN PRESCHOOL, ST. PETERSBURG, FLORIDA**
*Assistant Director (2000 to 2003)*
- ❖ Performed human resources functions, including recruiting, hiring, coaching, supervising, disciplining, and terminating staff.
- ❖ Handled administrative office responsibilities for the preschool.
- ❖ Provided direct service to the children in classroom settings.
- ❖ Acted as a liaison for the children with professionals in the community as needed.
- ❖ Praised by parents for excellence in educational instruction with their children.
- ❖ Accepted more challenging position with the State of Florida.

**GREAT BEGINNINGS PRESCHOOL, ST. PETERSBURG, FLORIDA**
*Teacher (1995 to 1998)*
- ❖ Promoted a positive classroom setting for children by utilizing education and play activities.
- ❖ Prepared comprehensive lesson plans targeted toward different learning styles.
- ❖ Provided guidance, direction, understanding, and comfort to the children as needed.
- ❖ Accepted more responsible position at the Parents for Children Preschool.

## VOLUNTEER EXPERIENCE

**BROOKWOOD YOUNG WOMEN'S RESIDENCE, ST. PETERSBURG, FLORIDA**
*Volunteer (2007 to 2008)*
- ❖ Acted as a *Mentor* to up **50** troubled teenagers for a local young women's residential facility.
- ❖ Assisted with character-building and leadership-development activities for the teenagers.
- ❖ Praised by top management for communication and interpersonal skills with the residents.

**LAKEWOOD HIGH SCHOOL, ST. PETERSBURG, FLORIDA**
*Volunteer (2006 to 2007)*
- ❖ Acted as a *Mentor* to teenagers at a local high school with **1,000+** students.

*This manufacturing executive was in the same industry for his entire career. This resume helped him land a position at the senior VP level in another industry by focusing on his core competencies and outstanding achievements.*

## WILLIAM T. JOHNSON

35 Sunderland Drive
Shrewsbury, NJ 07702

E-mail: wtjohnson@compuserv.com

Home: (732) 530-5592
Mobile: (732) 530-6632

### PLANT / OPERATIONS / GENERAL MANAGEMENT EXECUTIVE

*Multi-site manufacturing plant/general management career building and leading high-growth, transition, and start-up operations in domestic and international environments with annual revenues of up to $680 million.*

**Expertise:** Organizational Development • Productivity & Cost Reduction Improvements • Supply Chain Management • Acquisitions & Divestitures • IPOs • Plant Rationalizations • Safety Performance • Customer Relations • Change Agent

### CORE COMPETENCIES

**Manufacturing Leadership**—Strong P&L track record with functional management experience in all disciplines of manufacturing operations • Developing and managing operating budgets • Spearheading restructuring and rationalization of plants and contracted distribution facilities • Initiating lean manufacturing processes, utilizing SMED principles • Establishing performance metrics and supply-chain management teams.

**Continuous Improvement & Training**—Designing and instituting leadership-enhancement training program for all key plant management • Instituting Total Quality System (TQS) process in domestic plants to promote the business culture of continuous improvement and leading the ISO 9001 certification process.

**New Product Development**—Initiating plant-based "New Product Development Think Tank" that developed 130 new products for marketing review, resulting in the successful launch of 5 new products in 2000.

**Engineering Management**—Oversight of corporate machine design and development teams • Developing 3-year operating plan • Directing the design, fabrication, and installation of several proprietary machines • Creating project cost tracking systems and introducing ROI accountability.

### PROFESSIONAL EXPERIENCE

**BEACON INDUSTRIES, INC., New York, NY (2000–Present)**
*Record of continuous promotions to executive-level position in manufacturing and operations management despite periods of transition/acquisition at a $680 million Fortune 500 international manufacturing company. Career highlights include*

**Vice President of Manufacturing (2003–Present)**

Senior Operating Executive responsible for the performance of 7 manufacturing/distribution facilities for a company that experienced rapid growth from 4 plants generating $350 million in annual revenues to 14 manufacturing facilities with revenues of $680 million. Charged with driving the organization to become a low-cost producer. Established performance indicators, operating goals, realignment initiatives, productivity improvements, and cost-reduction programs that consistently improved product output, product quality, and customer satisfaction.

*Accomplishments:*

- Selected to lead corporate team in developing and driving forward cost-reduction initiatives that will result in $21 million saved over the next 3 years through capital infusion, process automation, and additional rationalizations.

- Saved $13 million annually by reducing fixed spending 11% and variable overhead spending 18% through effective utilization of operating resources and cost-improvement initiatives.

- Cut Workers' Compensation costs 40% ($750,000 annually) by implementing effective health and safety plans, employee training, management accountability, and equipment safeguarding. Led company to achieve recognition as "Best in Industry" regarding OSHA frequency and Lost Workday Incident rates.

- Reduced waste generation 31%, saving $1 million in material usage by optimizing manufacturing processes as well as instituting controls and accountability.

- Enhanced customer service satisfaction 3% annually during past year (measured by order fill and on-time delivery percentage) through supply-chain management initiatives, inventory control, and flexible manufacturing practices.

- Trimmed manufacturing and shipping-related credits to customers from 1.04% to .5% of total sales in 2002, representing annual $1.8 million reduction.

- Decreased total inventories 43% from 1997 base through combination of supply-chain management, purchasing, master scheduling, and global utilization initiatives.

- Rationalized 3 manufacturing plants and 6 distribution facilities, saving $6 million over 3 years.

*Submitted by Louise Garver*

WILLIAM T. JOHNSON • Page 2

**General Manager, Northeast (2000–2003)**

Assumed full P&L responsibility of 2 manufacturing facilities and a $20 million annual operating budget. Directly supervised facility managers and indirectly 250 employees in a multi-line, multicultural manufacturing environment. Planned and realigned organizational structure and operations to position company for high growth as a result of acquiring a major account, 2 new product lines, and 800 additional SKUs.

*Accomplishments:*

- Reduced operating costs by $4.5 million through consolidation of 2 distribution locations without adverse impact on customer service.

- Accomplished the start-up of 2 new manufacturing operations, which encompassed a plant closing and the integration of acquired equipment into existing production lines for 2 new product lines without interruption to customer service; achieved 2 months ahead of target and $400,000 below budget.

- Increased operating performance by 15% while reducing labor costs by $540,000.

- Reduced frequency and severity of accidents by 50% in 3 years, contributing to a Workers' Compensation and cost avoidance reduction of $1 million.

- Decreased operating waste by 2% for an annual cost savings of $800,000 in 2 manufacturing facilities.

- Negotiated turnkey contracts for 2 distribution warehouses to meet expanded volume requirements.

- Maintained general management and administrative cost (GMA) at a flat rate as sales grew by 25% annually over 3 years.

**ROMELARD CORPORATION, Detroit, MI (1990–2000)**
**Division Manufacturing Director (1996–2000)**

Fast-track advancement in engineering, manufacturing, and operations management to division-level position. Retained by new corporate owners and promoted in 1997 based on consistent contributions to revenue growth, profit improvements, and cost reductions. Scope of responsibility encompassed P&L for 3 manufacturing facilities and a distribution center with 500 employees in production, quality, distribution, inventory control, and maintenance.

*Accomplishments:*

- Delivered strong and sustainable operating gains: increased customer fill rate by 18%; improved operating performance by 20%; reduced operating waste by 15%; and reduced inventory by $6 million.

- Justified, sourced, and directed the installation of $10 million of automated plant equipment.

- Implemented and managed a centralized master scheduling for all manufacturing facilities.

- Reduced annual Workers' Compensation costs by $600,000.

- Created Customer Satisfaction Initiative program to identify areas of concern and implemented recommendations, significantly improving customer satisfaction.

**Prior Positions with Romelard Corporation:** Manufacturing Manager (1990–1993); Plant Manager (1989–1990); Engineering Manager (1987–1989).

EDUCATION & PROFESSIONAL DEVELOPMENT

**Bachelor of Science** in Manufacturing Engineering
Syracuse University, Syracuse, NY

Continuing professional development programs in
Executive Management, Leadership, and Finance

# ERICA CLAYTON

2625 Trancas St. • Napa, California 94558 • (707) 257-1183 • eclayton@email.com

## DENTAL ASSISTANT
### Knowledgeable...Experienced...Professional

**PROFILE**

Graduate Dental Assistant with chairside, scheduling, reception, and telephone experience in general and endodontic practices. X-ray certified. Experienced in composite and amalgam fillings, oral surgery, root canals, impressions, molds, and crown preparation.

*Communicates candidate's enthusiasm.*

- Tactful, patient and courteous.
- Positive and enthusiastic.
- Professional telephone etiquette.
- Work well independently or as a team member.
- Punctual and responsible with a strong work ethic.

**EMPLOYMENT**

**William Mahoney, D.D.S.,** Napa, CA
*General Practice*                                                      11/07–present

*Highlights chairside experience.*

***Treatment & Case Coordinator, Chairside Assistant***
- Manage appointment schedules for three dentists to maximize available treatment time.
- Interface with doctors to implement course of treatment and with patients to arrange payment schedules and appointments.
- Coordinate with labs, suppliers, and office staff to ensure that all elements are in place to meet patients' treatment needs upon arrival for appointment, for example, x rays, impressions, prostheses, etc.
- Maintain supplies inventory to ensure consistent availability of all products.
- Provide patient education and encouragement.
- Assist dentists during treatment.
- Apply fluoride and sealant.

**Samuel Rutherford, D.D.S. & Dr. Roger Ingram, D.D.S.**
Napa, CA
*Endodontia*                                                          1/05–10/07

***Chairside Assistant & Front Office***
- Assisted in all aspects of treatment and in preparation for treatment, including sterilizing instruments, setting up trays, preparing injections, taking impressions, and pouring molds.
- Educated patients on dental hygiene and post-op care.
- Maintained inventory and ordered supplies.
- Assisted front office with reception, scheduling, filing, and telephones.

*Important formal training is listed here.*

**Part-time Positions (student)**                                     10/03–7/05

| | | |
|---|---|---|
| Hollywood Video | Glendale, CA | Assistant Manager & Trainer |
| Auntie Mary's Pretzel Palace | Northridge, CA | Shift Manager/Trainer |
| Runners, Inc. | Simi Valley, CA | Office Assistant |

**EDUCATION**       Certificate in Dental Assisting, ROP, Glendale, CA          6/05

**VOLUNTEER**      Girl Scouts of America, Glendale, CA (summers)          8/92–8/97
- Designed, coordinated, and implemented fun-filled week-long programs for younger scouts.

**COMPUTER SKILLS**    Basic knowledge of MS Word and Excel, Internet, and e-mail.

*Submitted by Gay Anne Himebaugh*

*This candidate successfully transitioned from janitor to medical assistant.*

## SHAWNTA NICOLE MARION

*789 Angel Lane   St. Petersburg, Florida 33733   (727) 555-1212   snm@yahoo.com*

### PROFESSIONAL OBJECTIVE

Seeking a position as a ***Medical Assistant*** for a Family or Geriatric medical practice that values compassion, dedication, integrity, and results.

### EDUCATION

**ST. PETERSBURG UNIVERSITY, ST. PETERSBURG, FLORIDA (2008)**
DIPLOMA—Medical Assisting
❖ **EXTERNSHIP, Palms Cardiology Practice, St. Petersburg, Florida** ——— *She was hired full-time before even starting her externship!*
❖ Successfully attended college and never missed a day of class or externship.

#### COURSE HIGHLIGHTS

*Anatomy & Physiology   Clinical Procedures   Medical Office Procedures
Practical Procedures   Health Care Automation*

**NORTH EAST HIGH SCHOOL, ST. PETERSBURG, FLORIDA (1998)**
DIPLOMA—General Studies
❖ Successfully attended high school and never missed a day of class.
❖ Worked **25** hours per week and sometimes up to **40** while attending high school full-time, by doing cleaning duties at Lakewood High School in St. Petersburg.
❖ Earned *As* and *Bs* while in high school.
❖ Volunteered with geriatric patients in the nursing department at *St. Anthony's Hospital* in St. Petersburg.
❖ Provided services to patients such as helping them by ensuring their comfort and well-being, checking on them daily, and bringing them beverages.
❖ Praised by management and patients for my communication, caring, compassion, and self-management skills.

### EMPLOYMENT EXPERIENCE

**PINELLAS COUNTY SCHOOL SYSTEM, LAKEWOOD HIGH SCHOOL, ST. PETERSBURG, FLORIDA**
*Plant Operator (1998 to Present)*
❖ Have never called in sick or missed one day of employment in TEN YEARS.
❖ Thoroughly cleaned 15 classrooms of 32 seats daily from 5:30pm until 10:30pm Monday through Friday.
❖ Used vacuum cleaners, mops, brooms, dust pans, and cleaning supplies to prepare the rooms for the next day's use.
❖ Utilized self-management skills to work independently every day.
❖ Consistently demonstrated personal pride, initiative, and drive to clean the classrooms to the best of my ability daily.
❖ Praised by two supervisors for my work ethic, dependability, and the quality control that I exhibit every day on the job.

#### COMPUTER SKILLS

*Points out her stellar work ethic.*   *Microsoft Office (Excel & Word)
Windows XP
Microsoft Outlook   Internet Research
Proprietary Medical Practice Management Software*

*Submitted by Sharon McCormick*

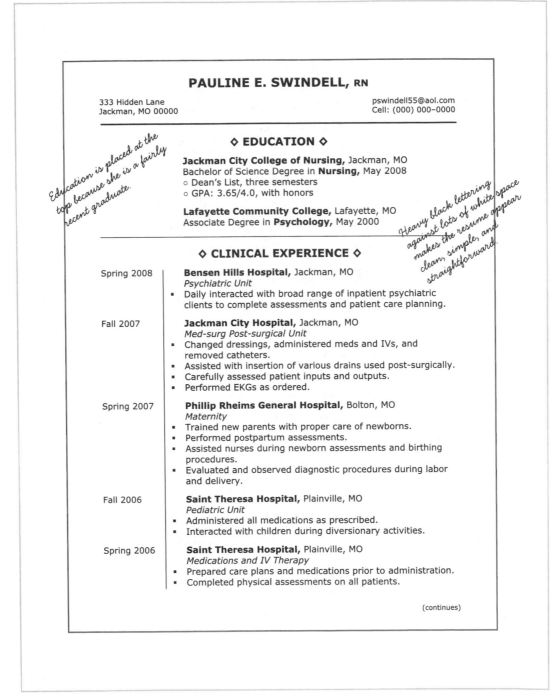

### PAULINE E. SWINDELL, RN

333 Hidden Lane
Jackman, MO 00000

pswindell55@aol.com
Cell: (000) 000–0000

*Education is placed at the top because she is a fairly recent graduate.*

## ◇ EDUCATION ◇

**Jackman City College of Nursing,** Jackman, MO
Bachelor of Science Degree in **Nursing,** May 2008
○ Dean's List, three semesters
○ GPA: 3.65/4.0, with honors

**Lafayette Community College,** Lafayette, MO
Associate Degree in **Psychology,** May 2000

*Heavy black lettering against lots of white space makes the resume appear clean, simple, and straightforward.*

## ◇ CLINICAL EXPERIENCE ◇

Spring 2008
**Bensen Hills Hospital,** Jackman, MO
*Psychiatric Unit*
- Daily interacted with broad range of inpatient psychiatric clients to complete assessments and patient care planning.

Fall 2007
**Jackman City Hospital,** Jackman, MO
*Med-surg Post-surgical Unit*
- Changed dressings, administered meds and IVs, and removed catheters.
- Assisted with insertion of various drains used post-surgically.
- Carefully assessed patient inputs and outputs.
- Performed EKGs as ordered.

Spring 2007
**Phillip Rheims General Hospital,** Bolton, MO
*Maternity*
- Trained new parents with proper care of newborns.
- Performed postpartum assessments.
- Assisted nurses during newborn assessments and birthing procedures.
- Evaluated and observed diagnostic procedures during labor and delivery.

Fall 2006
**Saint Theresa Hospital,** Plainville, MO
*Pediatric Unit*
- Administered all medications as prescribed.
- Interacted with children during diversionary activities.

Spring 2006
**Saint Theresa Hospital,** Plainville, MO
*Medications and IV Therapy*
- Prepared care plans and medications prior to administration.
- Completed physical assessments on all patients.

(continues)

*Submitted by Edward Turilli*

**Pauline E. Swindell**          Cell: (000) 000–0000          Page Two

| Fall 2005 | **James L. Betts Retirement Home,** Jackman, MO |
|---|---|

*PTs with ADLs*
- Intermingled with PTs during group meals.
- Administered medications to PTs as required.

## ◇ RELATED EMPLOYMENT ◇ ——
*Diamond motif helps candidate establish a unique brand identity.*

Jan 2006–
Present

**Jackman City Hospital,** Jackman, MO
*Mental Health Worker,* Part-time
- Assess and complete BIWA withdrawal assessment sheets.
- Interview PTs to wrap up daily process notes.
- Complete observation sheets with appropriate levels of observation for each patient.
- Always maintain safe milieu appropriate for patient safety.
- Provide crisis intervention as needed.
- Readily interact with peers and colleagues in a positive, professional, and therapeutic environment.

Aug 2004–
Jan 2006

**Lafayette Child and Family Services,** Lafayette, MO
*Residential Counselor,* Part-time
- Supervised residents' activities, recording daily personnel accountability.
- Administered prescription medication as prescribed.
- Daily interacted with peers to ensure safe and enjoyable environment.

## ◇ OTHER EMPLOMENT ◇

Summers
2002–2004

**Lafayette Summer Recreation Center,** Lafayette, MO
*Lifeguard, Swim & Safety Instructor*

## ◇ CERTIFICATIONS / SKILLS ◇

- Registered Nurse
- CPR, First Aid
- Lifeguard
- Health Care Provider
- American Red Cross
- Crisis Intervention

## ◇ VOLUNTEER ◇

- First Aid and Safety Member, U.S. Lifeguard Association
- Sylvan-Snyder Children's Care Center: Outpatient Services
- Jackman Youth Intervention Association

*Uses a two-column format to make headings easy to find.*

## MARK FRIEDMAN

23 Plainview Road • Plainview, New York 11590 • (516) 273-9981
markfriedman@optonline.net

| | |
|---|---|
| **PROFILE** | Physical Therapist who is able to work toward the restoration of function and the elimination of disability in individuals of all ages disabled by illness or an accident, or born with a handicap. Demonstrated skills working in hospitals and rehabilitation centers. Assist industry professionals in planning and directing patient care and preventative programs. Strongly motivated and dedicated to working with patients toward physical independence. |
| **EDUCATION** | Touro College • Bay Shore, NY<br>**Bachelor of Science in Health Sciences,** 9/08<br>**Master of Science in Physical Therapy,** 9/08<br><br>Long Island University at C.W. Post Campus • Brookville, NY<br>**Bachelor of Science in Physical Education Non-School,** 5/06<br>Concentration: Exercise Rehabilitation |
| **CLINICAL ROTATIONS 6/08 to 8/08 Level IV** | <u>STONY BROOK UNIVERSITY HOSPITAL</u> • Stony Brook, NY<br>**Acute Care**<br>~ Treated TKR, THR, CVA, and COPD diagnoses.<br>~ Provide D/C planning, evaluations, and exercise programs.<br>~ Associated with multiple disciplines in social work, nursing, and physician care.<br>~ Observed surgery: Hemiarthroplasty.<br>~ Participated in rounds and meetings.<br>~ Assisted Physical Therapists with patient care, exercise programs, and patient/family education.<br>~ Presented an in-service on Constraint Induced Movement Therapy. |
| **1/08 to 3/08 Level III** | <u>PLAINVIEW PHYSICAL THERAPY</u> • Plainview, NY<br>**Outpatient Orthopedic**<br>~ Evaluated, treated, and discharged patients with TKR, THR, ACL reconstruction, RC tear, shoulder impingement syndrome, sports/work-related injuries, LBP, and spinal orthopedic dysfunction; received experience in manual therapy.<br>~ Chronicled treatments in patients' charts; completed insurance forms.<br>~ Observed surgery: total knee replacement.<br>~ Presented an in-service on Total Knee Replacement. |

*Submitted by Donna Farrise*

# MARK FRIEDMAN
- Page Two -

| | |
|---|---|
| **4/07 to 6/07**<br>**Level II** | <u>ST. CATHERINE'S HOSPITAL</u> • Smithtown, NY<br>**Inpatient Geriatric Rehabilitation**<br>~ Reviewed charts, evaluated, treated, and discharged geriatric patients.<br>~ Primarily treated patients diagnosed with CVA, TKR, and THR.<br>~ Treated patients with balance problems and assisted with wound care.<br>~ Presented a case study on a patient with Parkinson's Disease and Chronic Obstructive Pulmonary Disease.<br>~ Presented an in-service on "The Effects of Tai Chi on Balance in the Elderly Populations." |
| **10/06 to 12/06**<br>**Level I** | <u>ST. MARY'S HOSPITAL</u> • Brooklyn, NY<br>**Outpatient Physical Therapy**<br>~ Evaluated, treated, and discharged adults/pediatrics from outpatient physical therapy.<br>~ Treated MS, CVA, BKA, AKA, patella tendonitis, bicep contractures, and Erb's Palsy diagnoses.<br>~ Observed wound care of amputated lower extremities. |
| **PROFESSIONAL EXPERIENCE**<br>**6/02 to 5/05** | <u>ALL CARE PHYSICAL THERAPY & REHABILITATION</u> • Freeport, NY<br>**Outpatient Rehabilitation Physical Therapy Aide**<br>~ Assisted with patient care, exercise programs, gym supervision, and application of heat, cold, electric stimulation, and ultrasound machines.<br>~ Educated patients and their families on treatment programs, care, symptoms, and potential complications.<br>~ *Designed a pool therapy packet for patients to be treated through aquatic therapy.* |

*Relevant experience before getting his degree is included later in the resume.*

| | |
|---|---|
| **CERTIFICATIONS** | Adult/Infant CPR & First Aid Certified, American Red Cross |
| **PROFESSIONAL MEMBERSHIPS** | American Physical Therapy Association (APTA)<br>Orthopedic Chapter & Sports Physical Therapy Section Member |
| **VOLUNTEER** | Empire State Games, Garden City, NY **(25 hours)**<br>Nassau County Medical Center, East Meadow, NY<br>- Outpatient Physical Therapy Department **(29 hours)** |

*Professional memberships show that the candidate is active in the PT field.*

*Candidate wants to transition from technical support to hospitality*

# MICHAEL R. BARKER
1411 Washington Street, Unit 3
Boston, MA 02118

(781) 264-4474                                    mikebarker@hotmail.com

*Resume high-lights transfer-able skills while deemphasizing specific techni-cal capabilities.*

## FOOD AND BEVERAGE SALES AND DISTRIBUTION

Creative professional with technical credentials and a degree in food and hospitality looking to transition back into the hospitality industry. Highly motivated and creative with excellent written and verbal communications capabilities and strong interpersonal relationship skills. An analytical thinker with problem-solving skills and the motivation to succeed. A team player able to perform with minimal direction.

*Education is placed near the beginning to highlight formal training in hospitality.*

## EDUCATION
**BA, Hospitality Management**—Johnson and Wales University, Providence, RI
**AS, Hotel/Restaurant Management**—Johnson and Wales University, Providence, RI
**Microsoft NT**—Sullivan and Cogliano, Waltham, MA
**Microsoft Windows**—Boston University, Boston, MA

## PROFESSIONAL EXPERIENCE
**Fidelity Investments,** Boston, MA                    2005–Present
**Software Support Analyst**
Responsible for providing PC and network support for 1,300 clients in the corporate office.

- Collaborated with engineers and software development to support the installation and integration of new enterprise applications.
- Acquired knowledge required to grow into a team leader.
- Coordinated teams to continually assess needs, identify resources, create schedules, monitor progress, and ensure resolution/fulfillment.
- Managed conversion teams to assist in migrating to new hardware and software systems.

**Fresenius Medical Care North America,** Lexington, MA          2002–2005
**Senior PC Support specialist**
Supplied PC and network support for more than 600 users in the corporate office—including troubleshooting hardware and software issues—and provided additional support for dialysis clinics and warehouses throughout the country.

- Managed software license compliance and ensured hardware standardization to maintain quality control.
- Researched, evaluated, and recommended new technology and managed technology agreements with vendors.
- Collaborated in needs assessments for new operating systems; supported these programs to ensure the technology met staff efficiency goals and lowered operating costs.
- Performed routine ongoing analysis to ensure that planned and actual expenditures met approved goals for performance.
- Conducted training sessions to ensure the proper use of company systems.

*Submitted by Judit Price*

**MICHAEL R. BARKER**                                                     Page 2

**CB Square Publications,** Middletown, NY                                2001–2004
**Field Representative**
Responsible for account support and developing prospects for a firm that serves the
strategic communications and information technology needs of school districts, not-for-
profits, and small to medium business.
- Communicated with customers to advise on and resolve product-related issues.
- Updated and maintained company managed websites.

**Harrison Conference Services**, Bank Conference Center, Waltham, MA    2000–2002
**Account Manager/Operations Director**
Responsible for the day-to-day operations of the facility. Managed a staff of 10 employees.
- Planned, coordinated, and delivered a range of conference activities.
- Contacted and qualified vendors, negotiated contracts, and provided oversight for all
  vendor service agreements.
- Recruited, hired, and trained the staff; processed payroll and benefit documentation
  and produced weekly and monthly status reports for management review.
- Instituted employee incentive programs and encouraged formal meetings to identify
  and implement areas of improvement.

**South Management Services,** Harvard Law School, Cambridge, MA         1998–2000
**Assistant Food and Beverage Director**
Assisted in directing the food service operation. Responsibilities included personnel, office
administration, marketing and sales, purchasing, security, and maintenance of the NCR
system. Managed a staff of 35.
- Recruited, hired, and trained new employees.
- Managed all funds and processed all reports; designed software to track and monitor
  inventories to reduce waste, yet maintain adequate supplies.
- Developed an ongoing set of promotions and innovative programs that increased
  sales. "Theme days"—with special menus, décor, and music—were very well
  received by the patrons. Expanded liquor sales by 10–15%.
- Established a planning process to ensure available staff for off-peak high-volume
  occasions.

**Sports Service, Fleet Center,** Boston, MA                             1997–1998
**Assistant Food and Beverage Director, Luxury Suites**
Supported all operational activities for the luxury suites. Managed a staff of 50.
- Directed all staffing schedules for the Bruins, Celtics, concerts, and other events.
- Organized all hot/cold food and beverage delivery schedules to ensure quality service.
- Managed all inventory, ordering, and receiving; monitored all beverages.
- Collaborated closely with the executive chef and the F&B director on cost control and
  food quality to ensure customer satisfaction.

*Good design, lots of white space, and few but well-chosen words make this an effective resume.*

# François J. Boudreau

88 Harbor Place
Rock Cove, ME 00000

(207) 555-5555
francois@foodie.com

**Objective:**    Assistant or Sous Chef

## Summary of Qualifications

- ✦ Associate's degree in Culinary Arts with training in American and international cuisines.
- ✦ Restaurant experience includes broiler, grill, sauté, fryer, expo, breakfast, and salads.
- ✦ Able to handle a multitude of tasks at once, meeting deadlines under pressure.
- ✦ Demonstrated ability to respond with speed and accuracy in a highly productive setting.
- ✦ Works cooperatively and harmoniously with coworkers and supervisors.
- ✦ Dedicated to quality in service and product.

## Experience

**Broiler/Prep Cook**    **Jacques Restaurant,** West Cove, Maine (9/2006–Present)
200-seat Four Diamond restaurant featuring an extensive menu of French and American cuisine

**Fry Cook**    **The Lobster Net,** Port Hancock, Maine (2004–2006)
Indoor and outdoor dining, specializing In fresh lobsters and seafood; takeout and banquet service.

**Fry/Prep Cook**    **The Weathervane,** Rocky Coast, Maine (2004)
Traditional New England seafood served in a casual setting.

## Education

Associate's Degree in Culinary Arts: Newbury College, Brookline, Massachusetts (2004)
Curriculum and Training included

- ✦ Soup, Stock, and Sauces
- ✦ Breads and Rolls
- ✦ Desserts
- ✦ Classical Bakeshop

- ✦ American Cuisine
- ✦ International Cuisine
- ✦ Garde Manger
- ✦ Sanitation and Dining Room

*Submitted by Becky J. Davis*

*Lists diverse responsibilities in a space-efficient format.*

### ROGER P. BARNES
196 East Goldwater Road
Tempe, Arizona 85858
(555) 555-5555
raj2008@comcast.net

**SUMMARY:** *Skilled Hospitality Manager with exceptional customer focus and organizational skills. Successful track record identifying niche markets, defining lounge/club concept, and implementing operating plan. Experienced in controlling costs, booking entertainment, and fostering repeat business with corporate clientele.*

## PROFESSIONAL EXPERIENCE

Jan. 2007–Present   **Manager, Time Square Lounge;** City, State.
*Accountable for day-to-day operations and overall management of nightclub grossing $50,000 monthly.*

- Book live music and DJs to play salsa, merengue, and hip-hop.
- Plan and implement advertising and promotion for musical acts.
- Control inventory and purchase all liquor.
- Negotiate purchase agreements with suppliers; control pour costs.
- Supervise 27 employees, including security staff.
- Account for daily receipts, prepare bank deposits, and administer payables.

**Major Accomplishments:**
*Increased gross revenues by more than 400%. Redefined club concept from Top 40 to salsa/hip-hop, successfully appealing to under-served niche market. Booked musical acts and designed promotional campaign to tout club's new focus.*

*An important section to show his results.*

Aug. 2005–Jan. 2007   **Bar Manager, Marriott Hotel;** City, State.
*Managed lounge seating 500 and grossing $60,000 monthly.*

- Hired, scheduled, and supervised bartenders and wait staff. Controlled inventory and pour costs.
- Booked corporate parties.
- Developed special promotions; implemented promotional campaigns.

**Major Accomplishments:**
*Increased bar gross revenues by up to 700%. Improved food revenues in lounge from virtually zero to $2,500 per week.*

July 2003–Aug. 2005   **Bartender, Mesa Mountain Ranch;** City, State.
*Serviced lounge seating 150, plus 15 wait staff serving adjacent pool area.*

- Developed rapport with customers and fostered cordial atmosphere.
- Up-sold patrons on food items, increasing overall revenue.
- Established corporate contacts that led to repeat business.
- Significantly reduced pour costs through negotiation with suppliers.

2000–2003   **Waiter/Bartender, High Falls Grill;** City, State.
*Served lunch and happy hour customers. Booked live entertainment and implemented promotions.*

1997–2000   **Room Service Supervisor/Waiter, Posh Resort;** City, State.
*Participated in the setup and launch of room service at this golf resort in suburban City, State.*

- Hired, trained, and supervised room service staff.
- Trained in bartending.

**EDUCATION**   A.A.S., Marketing; City Community College (2000); City, State.

*Submitted by Arnold Boldt*

# JAMES CARRO

408 Springmeadow • Holbrook, New York 11741 • (631) 567-9183
jcarro@aol.com

*Profile section summarizes the candidate's skills.*

## PROFILE

**Helpdesk/Desktop Support Specialist** able to provide theoretical and practical customer/user service and support to diagnose, troubleshoot, and repair hardware, software, and peripheral problems. Skilled in applying analytical and technical skills to produce practical solutions. Experienced in the installation of state-of-the-art hardware and software applications. Knowledge of equipment bases, digital switches, hubs, patch cables, routers, servers, administrator stations, network closet wiring, and installation procedures.

## TECHNICAL EDUCATION

### Install, Upgrade, Migrate & Configure

*Details of technical training*

**Hardware:** Pentium 4/D, Celeron
**Language:** HTML 4.01
**Operating Systems:** Windows XP/Server 2003
**Software:** MS Word/Office/Outlook/Access ▪ Lotus Notes ▪ Netscape Internet Explorer ▪ Norton Utilities
**Communications:** **Protocol**/SCSI/IDE/MFM/RLL/ESDI ▪ **Interface**/Modems/Network Cards/I/O Ports

## EDUCATION

Boston University, Boston, MA
**Windows Server 2003/HTML 4.01**
**Certification (in progress)**
PC Tech & Support Program, **A+ Certification, 2003**

*Certifications are included in the Education section.*

MEDICAL GROUP • Oakdale, NY — **2004 to Present**
**Independent Computer Support Contractor**
  Build computers from board level, install operating systems and software, and configure systems. Perform multiple installations of IE 6 and Fax Sr. from LAN.
  ~ *Researched components for value and reliability, resulting in substantial savings to customers.*

CERIDIAN PERFORMANCE PARTNERS • Boston, MA — **2001 to 2004**
**Fulfillment Coordinator**
  Performed as visibility liaison among company and human resource departments of subscribing Fortune 500 clients. Ensured timely and cost-efficient fulfillment of material for affiliate and client events. Worked with UPS Online System and Federal Express Powership updating and maintaining affiliate and client database. In conjunction with production department, defined and maintained online inventory system for offsite service facility.

LAURA ASHLEY GLOBAL DEVELOPMENT • Boston, MA — **1998 to 2001**
**Mail Services Supervisor**
  Distributed U.S. and interoffice mail, including payroll, to a staff of 300. Operated and upgraded Pitney Bowes mailing systems. Maintained database of 200 North American shops, U.K. headquarters, and European satellite offices.
  ~ *Contributed creatively to marketing department's nationwide window-display advertising.*
  ~ *Trained personnel in applications of UPS Online Shipping and Federal Express PowerShip.*

*Submitted by Donna Farrise*

*Profile highlights his computer training and goals orientation, along with other desirable transferable skills.*

*Mark's challenge was in not finishing college and having minimal work experience.*

### Mark W. Collington
1711 Crestview Road, Manhattan, KS 66506
785-532-5555 Home ▪ markcoll@popmail.com

---

**OBJECTIVE**

**Help Desk / Computer Support Technician** position

**PROFILE**

- ☑ Recent computer center graduate with proven organization abilities.
- ☑ Demonstrated track record of achieving goals in a team environment.
- ☑ Highly motivated and dependable—able to take responsibility for projects.
- ☑ Proven skills in problem solving, team leading, and customer relations.

**EDUCATION**

*Recent computer training (including coursework) is positioned for maximum exposure.*

**Tri-State Computer Learning Center,** Topeka, KS          2007–2008
Computer courses completed in
- ✓ Networking Essentials
- ✓ A+ Certification
- ✓ Intermediate Word 2003
- ✓ Beginning Word 2003
- ✓ Beginning Access 2003
- ✓ TCP/IP protocol
- ✓ Beginning Windows NT
- ✓ Administering Windows NT
- ✓ Windows NT Core Technologies
- ✓ Windows NT Support by Enterprise
- ✓ Beginning Business on the Internet
- ✓ Beginning FrontPage 2003

**University of Kansas,** Manhattan, KS          2005–2006
General first-year coursework in Bachelor's degree program.

**EMPLOYMENT**

**A Cut Above,** Topeka, KS          2007–2008
Receptionist/Cashier

- Successfully handled front desk and three incoming telephone lines for busy, upscale hair salon. Greeted and logged in steady stream of customers, coordinating appointments with hairdresser availability.

- Developed cooperative, team-oriented working relationships with owners and co-workers in this 8-station salon.

- Managed customer problems and complaints with tact and attention to prompt customer service.

- Experience gained in opening and closing procedures, cash register receipts, counter sales, light bookkeeping, and telephone follow-up.

**Plains Soccer Camp,** Manhattan, KS          2005, 2006 Summers
Trainer / Coach

- Assisted Women's Soccer Coach in 200-participant soccer camp. Worked with individuals as well as teams to improve their attitude and resulting soccer performance.

**ACTIVITIES & AWARDS**

**Kansas Cowboys** Soccer Semi-Pro Team—Center Half          2003–2007
- ✓ Team consistently ranked in top 10 semi-pro teams in the nation.

Manhattan High School Soccer Team          2002–2005
- ✓ Captain of team that won the state soccer title in 2003.
- ✓ Recognized as one of the top two midfielders in the state, 2005.

*Submitted by Susan Guarneri*

# William C. Hedges

555 Ridge Road, Princeton, NJ 08540
(609) 921-5555 Work • (609) 921-5566 Fax • billhedges@tgi.com

## QUALIFICATIONS

*Summary pinpoints career target and highlights technical skills.*

☑ **Database Programmer. Computer Programmer**—applications in C/C++ and Java
☑ Proactive team player with proven communications and organization talents.
☑ Computer skills: C/C++, STL (Standard Template Library), Java (JDK 1.2), Visual Basic 5, Oracle (SQL, SQL*Plus, PL/SQL), DataEase, Windows 2003, Windows XP, UNIX.

## PROFESSIONAL EXPERIENCE

*Experience includes class projects.*

### Technical Skills & Programming

- **Point-of-Sales, AR/AP System** for Technology Group, Inc.
  Created a normalized relational database (using DataEase) to provide complete invoicing, billing, and accounts receivable / accounts payable system for $1 million business with 300 active accounts and mailing list of 3,500. Currently running on Windows XP network.

- **Client-Server Sales Module in Java**—Class Project
  Using TCP/IP sockets, connected GUI front end to console application, allowing user to query server for price, availability, and credit status. Provided for simple update functionality.

- **C/C++**—Class Project
  Binary search tree. 2–3 search tree. Quick sort on linked list. String class. STL.

- **Sales Module in Visual Basic Connected to Access Database**—Class Project
  Created GUI front end to Access database (using Visual Basic) allowing input of customer information, part numbers, and quantities; and enabling users to place orders and print invoices and sales summaries.

- **Billing System in Oracle**—Class Project
  Generated users, tables, views, sequences and triggers using SQL, SQL*Plus, and PL/SQL to create Oracle database. Imported data and used Developer 2000 to create forms.

### Leadership & Organization Skills

- Spearheaded growth of mail-order business from $50,000 to $700,000 annually. Developed export customers in Europe, Africa, the Middle East, and Australia.

- Provide cross-functional expertise in overseeing daily operations, including technology, accounting, bookkeeping, taxes, purchasing, personnel, marketing, and customer relations.

## EDUCATION

Technology Institute of New Jersey, Somerset, NJ—2007 to 2008
Computer Science / Technology Coursework—19 credits, GPA 4.0
Data Structures and Algorithms, C++, Java, Visual Basic, Oracle/SQL, Networking

## EMPLOYMENT HISTORY

*Employment moved close to the end because it's not as relevant to his career goal.*

Owner / General Business Manager, Technology Group, Inc., Princeton, NJ—1994 to present
One of the largest beekeeping supply companies on the East Coast

## PROFESSIONAL ASSOCIATIONS

Computing Machinery Professionals Association—CMPA
New Jersey CMPA / TECE Joint Chapter
New Jersey Computer Users Group

*Submitted by Susan Guarneri*

## SHELLY DOE

2333 W. Addison, #A1
Oak Hill, IL 60689
Home: (773) 567-8910   Mobile: (312) 345-6789
shellydoe@hotmail.com

*Good, concise summary*

### SUMMARY

*Network and Senior Systems Engineer* with extensive and diverse experience in network LAN/WAN data communications equipment infrastructure engineering, as well as systems engineering. Experience includes installing, configuring, troubleshooting, and supporting routers, switches, hubs, servers, and network operating systems. Solid knowledge and experience working with both networks and systems.

*Tech skills are relevant enough to the objective to be placed early in the resume.*

### TECHNICAL SKILLS

| | |
|---|---|
| **Network Protocols:** | TCP/IP, IPX/SPX, FTP, TFTP, X.25, RIP, IGRP, HSRP, VTP, STP, PPP, ISDN |
| **Topologies:** | Ethernet and Token Ring |
| **Hardware:** | 3Com, HP, and Bay Hubs; Cisco Catalyst 2900XL and 5500 Series Switches and 2500, 3640, 1720 and 700 Series Routers |
| **Network Tools and System Management:** | Sniffer Protocol Analyzer, Cable Tracer, Openview, Compaq's Insight Manager Cisco IOS 11.3–12.2; MS Windows 2000, NT 4.0, and 3.51 Server, XP and 2000 Professional, 98, 95, 3.1, and 3.11; DOS 3.x–6.x; Novell NetWare 2.x–5.x |
| **Operating Systems:** | Cisco IOS 11.3–12.2; MS Windows 2000, NT 4.0, and 3.51 Server |
| **Applications:** | MS Internet Information Server 3.0 and 4.0; SQL Server 6.5; Exchange |
| **Business Applications:** | MS Office 2003, XP, and 97; Lotus SmartSuite and Freelance; Visio |

*Opening paragraph of each job entry gives overview of the role.*

### PROFESSIONAL EXPERIENCE

**PEBOTT SYSTEMS, Chicago, IL**                                                **2004 to Present**

*Senior Systems Engineer* with BTT Global Asset Management (2005 to Present)
Manage more than 100 Compaq servers with Microsoft BackOffice products in the Chicago and New York data centers. Design, purchase, and configure new HP/Compaq ProLiant platform servers, and Microsoft Windows 2000 Advanced Server and NT 4.0 Server products with IIS, MS SQL 6.5 and 2000, WINS, and DNS. Maintain, upgrade, and troubleshoot all related servers and products.

- Co-administer and support North American MS Exchange 5.5 servers.
- Co-design and implement global Windows 2000 production/test environment, including the migration of current production environment in Chicago and New York City to Win2K Active Directory. Co-design global DNS and WINS structures.
- Plan and implement physical server moves to brand new data center in downtown Chicago, including specification, implementation, and support of EMC Clarion SAN storage solution; implementation of NetIQ's AppManager and Security Manager server performance and security monitoring tools.

*Inet Engineer* with PBB Karson (2004 to 2005)
Managed Inet Engineering department computer lab, including management server hardware and software. Developed and implemented departmental intranet website focusing on the engineering of an automated document publishing and submission process, and the development of COM DLLs, MS Transaction Server packages, and VB6 IIS Applications to accommodate department informational needs.

- Engineered, troubleshot, and documented IIS solution; tested and administered Windows 2000 Developer's Pilot, including troubleshooting of Windows 2000 RC1/RC2 on 250 workstations and 6 servers.

*Systems Engineer* with PBB Brinson (2004 to 2004)
Managed Compaq hardware and Microsoft BackOffice products. Designed, purchased, configured, and installed Compaq ProLiant platform servers, and Microsoft Windows NT 4.0 Server and NT 4.0 Terminal Server products with IIS 4.0, MS SQL 6.5, and MS SQL 7.0, WINS, and DNS. Maintained, upgraded, and troubleshot all related servers and products.

Submitted by Hal Plantzer

(continued)

*(continued)*

Shelly Doe, Page 2

**MIDNIGHT COWGIRL MANAGEMENT COMPANY, Ft. Worth, TX**  2002 to 2003
*Senior Server and Network Administrator*
Administered National Windows NT 4.0/Exchange Server 5.5 for four boot manufacturing companies with more than 1,000 end users. Designed, implemented, and managed 47 Windows NT/BackOffice Servers, including 17 SAP R/3 systems with Oracle for NT 7.3.3 database. Sized and configured servers used in migration from IBM mainframe to SAP R/3 AFS business and SAP R/3 HR systems. Administered Windows NT network. Administered and maintained Microsoft Exchange 5.5 server, including Microsoft Outlook 97/98 electronic forms creation and distribution. Performed miscellaneous Microsoft Visual Basic programming. Managed WINS and DNS servers.
- Co-created and implemented desktop software standards.

**NFL OFFICE PRODUCTS INTERNATIONAL, Chicago, IL, and Arlington, TX**  2000 to 2002
*Client Network Specialist,* National Systems Division (2001 to 2002)
Administered National Windows NT 4.0/Exchange Server 4.0 with more than 2,300 users. Installed and configured new servers. Co-designed, implemented, and supported national MS Exchange servers and infrastructure. Maintained Corporate Internet Firewall network, as well as email connectivity problem identification and resolution. Performed troubleshooting for 40+ sites nationwide. Performed second- and third-line support for regional LAN administrators.
- Designed, implemented, and supported a national domain structure, including a migration plan and security design.
- Co-designed national desktop software and hardware standards.

*Bullets highlight key achievements.*

*LAN Administrator,* Great Lakes Region (2001)
Regional Windows NT 3.51/4.0 network administrator. Installed and configured all new servers (hardware and software) in 7 locations, as well as for connectivity across WAN utilizing TCP/IP. Designed and configured RAID systems. Coordinated WAN troubleshooting with provider. Designed and implemented regional domain structure and security. Maintained router and concentrator. Performed troubleshooting for connectivity problems both locally and between sites.

*Help Desk Analyst,* Chicago Division (2000)
Identified first-time problems and found solutions. Supported all internal and external customers, and provided all desktop-level support, including the installation of all new PCs and printers, as well as support for legacy terminal-based UNIX system. Also provided support for the Windows NT network administrator, including user creation and deletion, directory and share-level security control, printer creation, program installation, and all TCP/IP address assignments. Maintained router and concentrator, including installation of users and redirection from Sun terminal servers to PC network concentrators, and performed troubleshooting on connection problems both locally and between sites.

### CERTIFICATIONS

**Microsoft Certified Systems Engineer**

| | |
|---|---|
| Microsoft Windows NT Server 3.51 | Microsoft Systems Management Server 1.1 |
| Microsoft Windows NT Workstation 3.51 | Microsoft Exchange 5.5 |
| Microsoft Windows 95 | Microsoft Networking |

### EDUCATION

BFA, Art History, **Pennsyltucky State University,** Pennsyltucky, Ohio

*Clean, easy-to-read format—no frills; no fluff*

# TREVOR HANK WHITE

| 810 Lake Shore Drive, Evanston, IL 60612 | 713-555-1984 | trevorbusiness@xlt.com |

**FOCUS** Management Trainee—International Finance
Finance Degree with Spanish Minor and International Business Certificate

## QUALIFICATIONS

- Focused, disciplined, and competitive individual who is goal-driven and welcomes challenges.
- Outgoing, friendly, charismatic; strong relationship-building and interpersonal skills.
- Effective team leader and team member who strives for excellence in any endeavor.

## EDUCATION

**Northwestern University, Evanston, IL**                                          **May 2008**
**Bachelor of Business Administration**
- Major: Finance     Minor: Spanish     Certificate: International Business
- International Study Program: Madrid and Barcelona, Spring 2006
- Major GPA: 3.77/4.0  Cumulative: 3.84/4.0
- Presidential Scholar Award for Academic Excellence
- Valedictorian Scholar for Academic Excellence
- Student Scholarship for Academic Excellence
- World Class Scholarship for Academic Excellence

**Evanston Academy of Learning, Evanston, IL**                                     **2004**
- State of Illinois Scholar; National Merit Scholarship Finalist
- Academic All-State Scholar; Advanced Placement Scholar; Spanish Language Scholar
- Valedictorian Award—4.34/4.0 (Weighted Grades)
- Baseball Athletic & Academic Achievement Award
- Academic All-State Baseball Team Captain
- Varsity Baseball—Team Co-Captain & Captain; played baseball since age 8
- First Degree Black Belt—Tae Kwon Do Martial Arts
- Classical Pianist at local and state competitions

## CAMPUS ACTIVITIES

**Northwestern University:**
- Finance Committee Student Representative—Northwestern Alumni Foundation
- Sigma Alpha Beta—Active Member; Greek Week Coordinator; Committee Chair
- Greek Council Association—University Student Representative
- Dance Marathon—Personally raised more than $5,000 for Children's Hospital
- Northwestern Greek Council—Vice President of Operations

*Candidate has a well-rounded background and is well suited for various types of management trainee/entry-level positions.*

## EMPLOYMENT

Illinois High School Athletic Association, Springfield, IL, Summers 2005–Present
- Certified Baseball Umpire for high school baseball games in central Illinois.

Delta Gamma Alpha, Evanston, IL, 2006–2008
- House Hand in charge of preparing, serving, and meal clean-up for 120+ members.

Evanston Insulation Incorporated, Evanston, IL, Summers 2004–2007
- Laborer involved in tear-off, installation, and repair of commercial roofing systems.

*Resume language was chosen to strongly promote candidate's high scholarship, leadership, and related memberships to clearly emphasize his readiness to confidently pursue a successful career in law enforcement.*

# Alfred David Burton

<u>Current:</u>
100 Harold Point Avenue
Warren, WA 00000
(444) 222–6666

alfreddburton@aol.com

<u>Permanent:</u>
222 Jonathan Drive
Midtown, OR 00000
(000) 000-0000

## PERSONAL PROFILE

➢ Highly motivated to begin and achieve employment objectives in the criminal justice field.
➢ Proven experiences of working well under stressful conditions.
➢ Rule-oriented, fair, and disciplined in giving or carrying out orders.
➢ Dedicated, focused, and diligent in executing and maintaining the highest level of abilities to reach all planned objectives and goals.

## EDUCATION

**Stetson University,** Warren, WA
Bachelor of Arts degree in **Administration of Justice**                                   May 2008
**Horton-Davis College,** Lafayette, OR
Major in **Criminal Justice** (Transferred to Stetson University)                 2004–2005
**LaBelle Prep Academy,** Midtown, OR
College Preparatory Diploma                                                                        June 2003

### Honors / Scholarships:

► Stetson University, Dean's Scholarship, $6,000 per year
► Horton Davis Scholarship, one year, $8,000
► Horton Davis Grant, $1,000
► LaBelle Prep Academy College Scholarship, $1,500
► Grade-point Average: 3.8/4.0 (*magna cum laude*)
► Dean's List, Horton Davis College and Stetson University, three semesters
► Washington State Police Entrance Exam score: 90%
► National and Oregon State Honor Societies
► National Irish-American Honor Society

## RELATED WORK EXPERIENCE

**Department of Safety and Security,** Stetson University, Warren, WA
<u>Dispatcher</u>                                                                                              9/12/06–Present

▪ Dispatch vehicles to officers' campus beats and patrols.
▪ Capably relay emergency information to on-duty guards.
▪ Maintain day logs and incident reports.
▪ Keep professional radio contacts, serve as operator on emergency calls, and assist Warren Police with information on law violations.

*Quote from counselor adds weight to his candidacy.*

*"Alfred's integrity, sincerity, career focus, and personal achievements mark him for high success in life."*
—Brent Keenan, Guidance Counselor, LaBelle Prep Academy

*Submitted by Edward Turilli*

© JIST Publishing

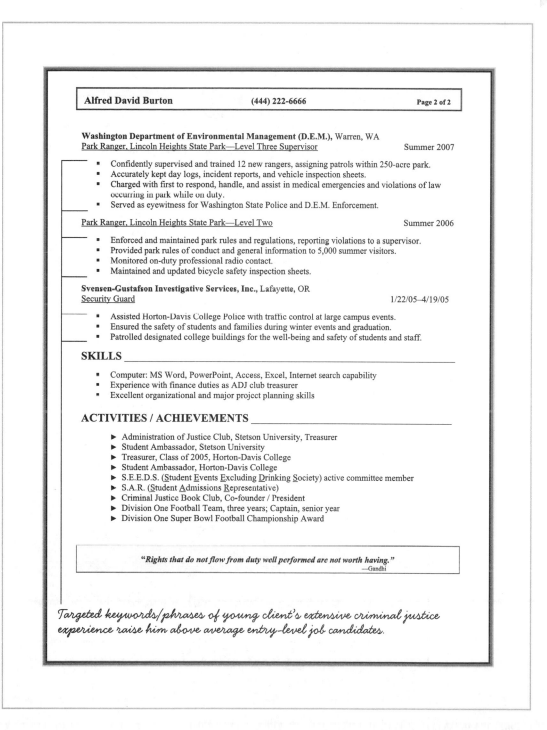

| Alfred David Burton | (444) 222-6666 | Page 2 of 2 |

**Washington Department of Environmental Management (D.E.M.),** Warren, WA
Park Ranger, Lincoln Heights State Park—Level Three Supervisor          Summer 2007

- Confidently supervised and trained 12 new rangers, assigning patrols within 250-acre park.
- Accurately kept day logs, incident reports, and vehicle inspection sheets.
- Charged with first to respond, handle, and assist in medical emergencies and violations of law occurring in park while on duty.
- Served as eyewitness for Washington State Police and D.E.M. Enforcement.

Park Ranger, Lincoln Heights State Park—Level Two          Summer 2006

- Enforced and maintained park rules and regulations, reporting violations to a supervisor.
- Provided park rules of conduct and general information to 5,000 summer visitors.
- Monitored on-duty professional radio contact.
- Maintained and updated bicycle safety inspection sheets.

**Svensen-Gustafson Investigative Services, Inc.,** Lafayette, OR
Security Guard          1/22/05–4/19/05

- Assisted Horton-Davis College Police with traffic control at large campus events.
- Ensured the safety of students and families during winter events and graduation.
- Patrolled designated college buildings for the well-being and safety of students and staff.

## SKILLS

- Computer: MS Word, PowerPoint, Access, Excel, Internet search capability
- Experience with finance duties as ADJ club treasurer
- Excellent organizational and major project planning skills

## ACTIVITIES / ACHIEVEMENTS

- Administration of Justice Club, Stetson University, Treasurer
- Student Ambassador, Stetson University
- Treasurer, Class of 2005, Horton-Davis College
- Student Ambassador, Horton-Davis College
- S.E.E.D.S. (Student Events Excluding Drinking Society) active committee member
- S.A.R. (Student Admissions Representative)
- Criminal Justice Book Club, Co-founder / President
- Division One Football Team, three years; Captain, senior year
- Division One Super Bowl Football Championship Award

*"Rights that do not flow from duty well performed are not worth having."*
—Gandhi

*Targeted keywords/phrases of young client's extensive criminal justice experience raise him above average entry-level job candidates.*

*This resume for a college student seeking an internship showcases the fact that she is committed to her career and has the work ethic to back it up.*

School
Alexandra Tamburro '08
19 Crossroads Drive
Conway, SC 29526

# Alexandra Tamburro

atamburro08@coastal.edu

Home
21 Sugarloaf Drive
Sugarloaf, NY 12906
Cell: 845.867.5309

### Objective: Internship Opportunities

*Eager to learn first-hand about government operations and gain insight into corporate culture and the international arena*

**PROFILE**

Energetic and career-minded individual with an academic record that reflects responsibility, leadership, and active involvement in the school community. Offering disciplined work habits, a high level of initiative, and a demonstrated ability to balance competing demands. Background also demonstrates a consistent effort to contribute to activities that require sound judgment, resourcefulness, and a significant amount of coordination.

**EDUCATION**

**Coastal Carolina University, Conway, SC** *(Anticipated Graduation)* **2009**
Candidate: B.S. in Political Science & Public Affairs *(Current GPA: 3.56)*
Minor: Spanish

**Extracurricular / Leadership Activities**
+ Student Activities (Music & Interactive Chair)
+ Student Activities Board Member
+ Model United Nations Club, Public Relations Chair
+ Spanish Club / JV Softball
+ Gold Key Society (candidate)
+ Big Events Volunteer Coordinator (2006/2007)
+ Big Events Executive Board: Communications Chair

**Academic and Leadership Involvement**
+ Judicial Board Representative (elected position)
+ Study Abroad (six weeks in Peru)
+ Presidential Scholarship Recipient
+ Prospective Student Overnight Host
+ Orientation Leader
+ Resident Assistant (named RA-of-the-Month, 9/07)
+ Relay for Life Entertainment Chair

**Frankfort High School, Poughkeepsie, NY** 2006
NYS Regents Diploma

**Academic Honors & Affiliations**
+ High Honor Roll / Honor Roll (2002–2006)
+ Dean's List (2006)
+ Spanish (three years)

**Extracurricular Activities**
+ Freshman Senior Day Leader
+ Art Club / Retreat Leader
+ JV Softball (3 years) / Captain (2005)

**ADDITIONAL EXPERIENCE**

**Coastal Carolina Ambassadors—Sophomore Coordinator** 2006 to Present
Represent the college at local high schools (Dutchess & Ulster County, NY) during college breaks. Deliver presentations to high school students, promoting academic offerings and discussing campus life. Responsible for contacting schools, coordinating visits, preparing summary reports, and meeting with head coordinator (senior-year representative). Position term continues through senior year and requires 10 hours of weekly work.

**Students in Free Enterprise,** *Coastal Carolina University* 2006 to Present
Team-oriented group that works on community-driven projects that promote free enterprise. Participate in regional and national SIFE competitions to present project results in front of numerous corporate executives. Current project (Edison Ethics) involves teaching high school students about business ethics.

**Model United Nations Security Council High School Conference,** *Conway, SC* Spring 2007
Served as a high-school advisor/coach for this professionally run program that provides a realistic simulation of the UN's practices and procedures as well as the issues that it addresses. Worked with students to help them prepare for the conference by providing an understanding of the workings of the UN as well as the various implications of its actions. Gained experience as a Secretary-General, Parliamentarian, and Secretariat.

**EMPLOYMENT**

**Herkimer Arts & Crafts,** *Herkimer, NY (Holidays & Summers)* 2004 to Present
**Coleman Staffing & Temp Service,** *Mohawk, NY* Summer 2007

**VOLUNTEER**

**Socastee Elementary School,** *Socastee, NY (Tutor/Arts & Crafts Leader)* 10/07 to 5/08
**After-School Program:** Worked with first, fourth, and fifth graders to help with homework and boost math and reading skills. Developed arts and crafts activities that were age-appropriate.

*Submitted by Kristin Coleman*

*Frank's experience, safety record, and strong qualifications should open up opportunities despite the fact that he is not affiliated with a trade union.*

# Frank Taglione

■ 203 Stonypoint Drive, Lewiston, ME 00000 ■
(555) 555-5555
frankietheplumber@email.com

### Pipefitter/Plumber skilled in mechanical and electrical installations

- Experience with pipes constructed of carbon steel, stainless steel, copper, alloys and galvanized metal, plastic-lined pipe, and prefabricated piping assemblies, as well as all related fittings and joining compounds.
- Five years of practice in different industrial settings, ranging from a water-treatment plant to a pharmaceutical testing lab.
- Own specialized hand tools to measure, cut, bend, and thread pipe to precise specifications.
- Excellent safety record for operation of forklift, hydraulic jack, arc welding equipment, and acetylene torch.
- Able to read piping assembly drawings and wiring schematics with understanding of system operations.
- Can identify such problems as pipe assemblies constructed of the wrong material or with incorrect dimensions.

## ■ Employment ■

2005–Present                                        HYDROPURE SYSTEMS, INC.
**Pipefitter/Plumber**                                          Lewiston, ME
- Fabricate, assemble, and install the interior and exterior piping of large water-treatment units.
  – Plan material layout.
  – Assemble prefabricated piping in accordance with engineering drawings.
  – Size and build threaded piping systems, including rigid electrical conduits to motor-operated valves.
  – Make and install steel pipe supports.
  – Hydro-test the finished units.
- Commended by management with regard to excellence in attitude, attendance, productivity, and the ability to learn new tasks.

*Many job-related skills are listed throughout, plus some very important adaptive skills.*

2000–2005                                 ADVANCED INDUSTRIAL MAINTENANCE
**Pipefitter/Plumber**                                         Portland, ME
- Assignments through this job shop have included running water lines for new installations in laboratories and manufacturing operations at AllCan Plastics, Wamesco, and Ultran corporations.
- Kept plumbing in good working order at these facilities.

1999–Present, Weekends                   GUIDO TAGLIONE, PLUMBING CONTRACTOR
**Plumber**                                                    Auburn, ME
- Assist with installation and service of residential plumbing fixtures, piping, boilers, and water heaters. Mainly called on to measure and cut pipe and to form either sweat-soldered or threaded connections.

## ■ Training ■

**Journeyman Pipefitter Certificate**—1999    STATE OF MAINE DEPARTMENT OF EDUCATION
- Completed four-year apprenticeship and course in the plumbing and pipefitting trades at Auburn Technical and Vocational High School.
- Currently enrolled in state-sponsored asbestos-removal training course.

*Submitted by Melanie Noonan*

*Packed with details, this resume's design and short statements keep it readable and effective.*

## Michelle Gibson

842 N. Main ■ Menasha, Wisconsin 54952 ■ (414) 784-8752 ■ beauty@yahoo.com

*Licensed Cosmetologist, State of Wisconsin*

**Summary of Attributes**

*These statements reinforce her strong business skills.*

- Enthusiastic professional with outstanding customer relation skills; upbeat, friendly, and genuinely care about providing good service.
- Strong sales techniques; consistently increase volume through additional product purchases.
- Carefully listen to clients to correctly address their needs/desires.
- Good business management aptitude; knowledgeable in all aspects of salon operation.
- Excellent technical skills evidenced through extremely loyal clientele and high referral rate.

**Experience**

The Ultimate Salon, Appleton, Wisconsin
**Independent Hairstylist/Makeup Artist**                     2004–Present
- Provide full range of services, including precision haircuts, permanent waving, color, and styling.
- Conduct one-on-one makeup consultations, providing hands-on instruction, individualized color selection, and written guidelines.
- Manage all aspects of business, including inventory control, bookkeeping, price determination, and marketing.

*Accomplishments:*
- Conceptualized and publish a quarterly client newsletter, which contributed to an increase in client base, as well as product sales.
- Specialize in creating unique images for bridal clients, incorporating various ornamentations into hairstyles.
- Researched and introduced a private-label makeup line.

A New You Salon, Menasha, Wisconsin
**Hairstylist/Makeup Artist**                     2001–2004
- Performed hairstylist duties, including cuts, styles, color, and permanent waves. Functioned as an apprentice, 2001–2004.
- Lead makeup artist for special occasions and one-on-one demonstrations.

*Accomplishments:*
- Achieved retail sales of 31% compared to national average of 15%.
- Orchestrated salon-wide Cut-A-Thon to benefit United Cerebral Palsy, including public relations, donation solicitation, and raffle organization. Tripled donations over previous year.
- Coordinated complimentary seminar to educate clients on new hair trends, products, and the benefits of various salon services.

**Education**

Northeast Wisconsin Technical College, Green Bay, Wisconsin          2001
Certificate of Completion; Cosmetology Training (included 400 hours of classroom instruction and 3,600 hours of on-the-floor supervised training)

**Industry Involvement**

Redken Symposium, Las Vegas, Nevada, January 2006
Redken Regional Seminar, Schaumburg, Illinois, 2004
- Assisted national and regional platform artists.
Acrial Hair Show, Stevens Point, Wisconsin, 2004
- Applied stage and runway makeup for models.

*Submitted by Kathy Keshemberg*

*An effective, space-efficient format*

## Karen A. Librarian
000 Any Street • Anywhere, Michigan 00000 • (000) 000-0000 • infoscience@gmail.com

*Strong opening*

### SUMMARY OF QUALIFICATIONS
More than 10 years of library and information science experience with 8 years at the supervisory level, maintaining a positive working environment. Possess excellent verbal and written communications skills and significant knowledge of reference materials. Conscientious and detail-oriented with ability to plan, organize, and direct library services and programs. Substantial computer experience, including Internet support.

### PROFESSIONAL EXPERIENCE

**Any Public Library**—Anywhere, Michigan                    *2005–Present*
***Assistant to the Director***
- ✓ Supervise, instruct, and schedule 11 staff members, including entire faculty in director's absence.
- ✓ Automation Project Manager for interlibrary loans, book status, and budgeting.
- ✓ Administer reference and reader advisory services to patrons; provide outreach services to senior center, and schedule various meetings.
- ✓ Lead adult book discussions, including book selections, and conduct library tours.
- ✓ Assisted in library expansion, design, and construction (2005–2006).

**Another Public Library**—Anywhere, Michigan                *2000–2005*
***Assistant to the Director*** (2002–2005)
- ✓ Supervised, instructed, and scheduled 9 staff members.
- ✓ Maintained microfiche and microfilm storage.
- ✓ Handled bookkeeping responsibilities and routine operations of the library.

***Children's and Young Adult Librarian*** (2000–2002)
- ✓ Selected books, periodicals, and nonprint material for collection development.
- ✓ Planned and implemented "Story Time" programs for preschool students, summer reading programs for grade school students, and "Computer Pix" for young adults.
- ✓ Updated reference and library materials to exhibit most current information.

**Another Branch Library**—Anywhere, California               *1999–2000*
***Reference Librarian (Temporary)***
- ✓ Examined ordered resources for collection development.
- ✓ Assisted coworkers and patrons in Internet usage.
- ✓ Handled book reservations and answered reference inquiries.

**Computer Experience**
- ✓ Microsoft Word, Excel, and PowerPoint
- ✓ Michigan Occupational Information Systems (MOIS)
- ✓ Data Research Associates (DRA), Intelligent Catalog-Bibliofile, TDD, Magnifiers, RLIN, CLSI, OCLC, GEAC, ERIC Data Base, and Info Track—Magazine Index.

### EDUCATION

**Texas Woman's University**—Denton, Texas
• Master of Library Science, 1999 • Bachelor of Library Science, 1997

*Submitted by Maria E. Hebda*

*A clean, disciplined format appropriate for a technical writer*

## Lizzy B. Wright

8888 Calla Lily Lane
Mountain View, CA 99999

lbwright@netcom.com
(650) 999-9999

**TECHNICAL WRITER—Highly Skilled, Technically Savvy, Energetic**

- Award-winning writer and editor of technical documentation (print and online) for Silicon Valley giant. Documents include manuals, guides, articles for trade journals, PR, proposals, course development, employee bulletins, and technical reports.

- Strong communication, training and interviewing skills. Translate "engineer-ese" into users' language with a clear and accurate writing style.

- Excellent cross-organizational skills and teamwork. Work closely with engineers, editors, other departments, and team members.

- History of learning applications with exceptional speed and handling multiple projects, from outline to finished product, within extremely tight schedules.

*Related training*

| | |
|---|---|
| **Systems:** | UNIX, Windows, Macintosh, VMS, Solaris, OpenWindows, All-in-One, Netware |
| **Applications:** | Framemaker, Framemaker+ SGML, Interleaf, MS Office, MS Project, PhotoShop, Illustrator, Lotus 1-2-3, Sun's workstation tools, Filemaker Pro |
| **Web Skills:** | HTML, graphics design and layout, information mapping, content development |

**MAJOR SILICON PLAYER, INC.,** Computerville, CA                     2004–Present

**Technical Writer II**

Promoted from Technical Writer I to Sustaining Project Lead, Illustration Project Lead, and Technical Writer II within a year. Produce documentation for online and print at all testing stages.

- Maintain document sets and all revisions for 4 mid-range servers and wrote section of Well-Known Hardware Platform Notes.

- Currently developing document set (hardware and software) for next generation of servers.

> Won *Touchstone Award* for Hardware Reference Category (one of three contributors) presented by Northern California Chapter of STC.

**Global Project Coordinator**

- Developed/maintained documentation and communications for 3 worldwide projects. Organized international team meetings and coordinated projects, including budget and metrics tracking.

- Designed award-winning intranet site. Served as webmaster and content developer for 50-page site containing Global Travel Policy (for 14 countries) and monthly Employee Newsletter.

- Designed user surveys, compiled information from hundreds of responses, and wrote 30–40-page recommendation reports used by Engineering in designing online tools.

**PREVIOUS EMPLOYMENT**

*Pertinent accomplishments from previous jobs moved here to avoid detracting from current accomplishments.*

- Edited journal articles, wrote news releases and speeches, and coordinated press relations for various contract positions, 1998–2004.

- Fully computerized busy six-doctor practice using Access database system, Medical Center of Northeast, 1997–1998.

- Developed information database used in health care reform initiatives, Regional Coalition for National Health Care, 1996.

**EDUCATION**

BA, Sociology (Vocal Performance), Oberlin College and Conservatory, Oberlin, OH

Pre-med Certificate Program, University of Massachusetts, Boston, MA

Information Architecture; Advanced Technical Communications, UC Berkeley Extension

C++ Programming, Foothill College, Los Altos, Hills, CA

*Languages:* Conversational Spanish, French, Italian

*Industry is not mentioned so that the candidate can apply to jobs in different industries.*

# John Belmont

E-mail: jbelmont@aol.com

978.555.8113

177 Washington Avenue • Boston, MA 95818

*Heading doubles as an adjective.*

## Sales Management

**Delivering consistent and sustainable revenue gains, profit growth, and market-share increases through strategic sales leadership of multi-site branch locations. Valued offered:**

- ✓ Driver of innovative programs that provide a competitive edge and establish company as a full-service market leader.
- ✓ Proactive, creative problem solver who develops solutions that save time, cut costs, and ensure consistent product quality.
- ✓ Empowering leader who recruits, develops, coaches, motivates, and inspires sales teams to top performance.
- ✓ Innovative in developing and implementing win-win solutions to maximize account expansion, retention, and satisfaction.

## Selected Career Achievements

RANFORD COMPANY • Boston, MA                                      1992 to 2008

**As Branch Manager, reinvigorated the sales organization, growing company revenues from $9MM to $45MM, expanding account base from 450 to 680, and increasing market share 15%.** Established new performance benchmark and trained sales team on implementing sales-building customer inventory rationalization programs.

*Focus is on results rather than respon- sibilities.*

- **Revitalized and restored profitability of 2 underperforming territories** by coaching and developing territory reps.
- **Penetrated 2 new markets** and secured a lucrative market niche in abrasive products. Staffed, opened, and managed the 2 branch locations with 22 employees in New Jersey—both sites produced $19.5 MM+ over 3 years.
- **Initiated and advanced the skills of the sales force to effectively promote and sell increasingly technical product lines** in response to changing market demands.

**Increased profit margins and dollar volume through product mix diversification and expansion.** Created product catalogs and marketing literature.

- **Ensured that the company maintained its competitive edge in the marketplace** by adding several cross-functional product lines.
- **Led highly profitable new product introduction with a 40% profit margin** that produced $100K annually in new business.

BERLIN COMPANY • Worcester, MA                                    1987 to 1992

**As Account Executive, rejuvenated sales performance of a stagnant territory. Turned around customer perception by cultivating exceptional relationships through solutions-based selling and delivering value-added service.** Recognized as a peak performer company-wide who consistently ranked #1 in sales and #1 in profits.

- **Positioned and established company as a full-service supplier** to drive sales revenues by translating customer needs to product solutions.
- **More than doubled territory sales from $700K to $1.6MM** during tenure and grew account base from 80 to 125 through new market penetration. **Landed and managed 3 of company's 6 largest accounts** and grew remaining 3.
- **Captured a lucrative account and drove annual sales from $100K in the first year to $400K in 3 years**—outperforming the competition without any price-cutting.
- **Mentored new and existing territory reps** on customer relationship management, solutions-selling strategies, advanced product knowledge, and customer programs.

## Education

B.S. in Business Management—Rhode Island University, Providence, RI

*Submitted by Louise Garver*

# Sam R. Wilson

3720 Broadview Terrace
Cedarville, OH 45314

s6496889@yahoo.com

(937) 641-0018 (Home)
(937) 649-6889 (Cell)

## SALES & MANAGEMENT

Food Industry

*Focus statement quickly summarizes the candidate's experience and tells how a company can benefit from hiring him.*

## FOCUS

Management professional with a distinguished 16-year career that will benefit gross margin improvement, comparable store sales, teamwork productivity, and effective merchandising.

## SALES & MANAGING EXPERIENCE

**Operations Manager**—*Pete's Meat Market,* Cedarville, OH          10/2007–03/2008

- Directed training, merchandising, and department sets.
- Category management of the entire market prior to opening.
- Directly responsible for $290K in sales the first 2 months of business.
- Weekly sales increases the first 10 weeks of 2008.
- Established and cultivated positive vendor relations.

**Store Manager**—*Stop 'n' Go Market,* Cedarville, OH          2001–2007

- Increased wine sales 150% from 2002–2007.
- Increased net profits by 3% per annum beginning in 2001.
- Sales growth of 15% from 2003–2007.

**Store Director**—*Jerry's Food Markets,* Cedarville, OH          2000–2001

- Reduced backroom inventory $100K in first quarter of 1998.
- Consistently exceeded company sales and gross profit objectives.
- Effectively supervised 8 department managers and over 100 employees.
- Reduced labor costs from 8.1% to 6.1% to add to bottom-line profits.

*Job titles are easy to read due to use of boldfacing, indents, and white space.*

**Meat Department Manager**—*Jerry's Food Markets,* Cedarville, OH          1992–1999

- Exceeded gross profit and labor objectives consistently.
- Highest-volume meat department with 10% sales increases annually.
- Acted as interim store manager in absence of market directors.

## EDUCATION

- **Spartan Foods Training Courses 1993–2001:** "Wings of the Future," "Sanitation," "Positive Discipline," "Effective Time Management," "Leadership," "Department Sales Growth," and "Merchandising"

- **Zig Zigler "See You At the Top" Motivational Seminar,** 1999—graduated first in class

*Submitted by Terry Ferrara*

## Mariah Masterson

9 Prospect Drive, Portland, ME 01069
mariahmast@yahoo.com / (417) 834-1429 (c) ● (417) 665-4345 (h)

### CAREER PROFILE

*Text is indented so that headings stand out to the reader.*

Highly motivated media sales professional seeking a challenging position where my skills and abilities will have maximum impact. Qualifications include

- Dedicated to superior customer service
- Proven track record of new business development
- High sales producer who consistently exceeds goals
- Resourceful problem solver with excellent organizational ability
- Outstanding communication, interpersonal, and self-management skills
- Strong team leader able to set high standards and motivate others to excel

### EXPERIENCE

**Account Executive,** Time Warner Cable, Portland, ME (2004–present)
Responsible for customizing campaigns for clients, selling airtime on 31 insertable cable networks, script writing, trafficking commercials as ordered, and keeping all billing at NET 30. Maintain and upsell current client base and manage aggressive new business development.

*Bullets are used sparingly to keep from diminishing their impact.*

*Accomplishments:*
- Named to "The President's Club" for outstanding sales for first year with the company.
- Generated a 65% increase of new business on client list over the past three years.
- Met and exceeded monthly and annual sales goals: Exceeded first annual budget by 24%.

**Account Executive,** New World Media, *The Daily Planet,* Portland, ME (2001–2004)
Responsible for selling advertising space in four regional alternative newsweeklies. Daily tasks included face-to-face client presentations, booking space and designing ads, gathering info from clients to meet space deadlines while maintaining the best collections in the office. Worked within clients' budgets to execute campaigns based on their needs cycle and balanced that with the policies of the company. Represented *The Daily Planet* at various business and social functions.

*Accomplishments:*    *"Accomplishments" subheadings allow the candidate to showcase*
- Managed a large client base and brought 55% new business to the paper. *special contributions*
- Exceeded sales goals by average of 21% during tenure.

**Account Executive,** WHCN, Madison, WI (1998–2001)
Responsible for bringing in new business as well as servicing and growing existing account base. Wrote commercial copy and produced spots; coordinated talent, effects, and input from clients. Kept collections current, routed traffic, and designed individual promotions and campaigns based on clients' needs and market research.

*Accomplishment:*
- Increased new business by 60% during tenure with the station.

### EDUCATION

University of Wisconsin, Madison, WI (1995)
Bachelor of Arts: Business Management

**REFERENCES:** Available upon request

*Submitted by Mary Hayward*

## Al Marchano
### entry-level commercial real estate professional

25 Crane Road
Center, Alabama 36000
☏ 334.555.5555 (home) − 334.555.6666 (cell)
✉almarch1111@hotmail.com

WHAT I CAN OFFER ACME PROPERTIES

- ❑ The drive and skill to build and **maintain a "pipeline" of potential deals.**
- ❑ The **personal contacts** among **key decision makers statewide,** including bankers, mayors, city council members, and elected officials.
- ❑ The **vision to see** and **close deals** others have **overlooked.**

RECENT AND RELEVANT WORK HISTORY WITH EXAMPLES OF PROBLEMS SOLVED

- ❑ **Majority Owner,** Standard Builders, LLC, Centerville, Alabama        Jul 06–Present

  *H&E serves the tri-county area building spec homes 1,800ft$^2$ and larger.*

  *The results of each story are placed first.*

  BUILDING RELATIONSHIPS WITH KEY PLAYERS IN COMMERCIAL REAL ESTATE

  Used my personal contact to persuade a banker to extend a major capital venture loan. Overcame a lack of a professional track record in building and partner's limited credit scores to prove we were a good financial risk. *Payoffs:* Loan **approved** in just two months.

- ❑ Major, Alabama Army National Guard, serving in a variety of assignments with increasing responsibility in Alabama and Saudi Arabia        Mar 91–Present

  FINDING AND SERVING CUSTOMERS OTHERS HAVE OVERLOOKED

  Turned around a product that customers didn't like—even though they were a "captive" market: a corporate newspaper. Recruited the right people to help me. Then went to where our readers lived to see what they wanted. Finally, overcame management's resistance to change to roll out an entirely new product. *Payoffs:* **Increased** circulation **by 100 percent.** We were pressed to keep up with customer demand—the strongest it had been in years.

  TURNING DIVERSE GROUPS INTO SOLID SUPPORTERS

  Went beyond changing the group I was asked to lead from dissatisfied strangers into a smoothly running team. Listened carefully, and then built their trust through demonstrated fairness every day. *Payoffs:* **Retention grew 15 percentage points. Met** my **goals** in this area for **30 consecutive months**—a rare feat.

  *Bold print guides the reader's eyes to payoffs they can use.*

- ❑ **District Director** and **Campaign Manager,** Office of Congressman Conrad Morton, Montgomery, Alabama        Mar 98–Dec 98 and Dec 03–Jan 04

  BUILDING COALITIONS AMONG PEOPLE WHO DRIVE COMMERCIAL REAL ESTATE

  Helped our candidate dominate the field by reaching out—personally—to mayors, city council members, and business leaders. Gave them clear and compelling proof

  *More indicators of performance* **Acme Properties** *can use …*

*Submitted by Don Orlando*

Al Marchano    **Entry-Level Commercial Real Estate Professional**    334.555.5555

that we were ready and able to meet their needs. ***Payoffs:*** Not only did we build solid support, we came across so powerfully that **not one competitor** from our party **entered the race.**

*Subheadings let readers jump to the stories most relevant to their needs.*

❑ **Executive Director**, Alabama Republican Party, Foley, Alabama    Aug 99–Dec 00
### PERSUADING BUSINESS LEADERS TO INVEST IN THEIR FUTURE

Found a better way to raise money that aligned our requirements with the business community's needs. Called on committees (you would call them sales forces) in every one of Alabama's 67 counties. Motivated each one to ask businesses to donate goods and services in a fund-raising auction. Drove nearly 4,000 miles in just nine days to make these "warm calls." ***Payoffs:* From plan to results**—from $100K in the red to $110K in the black—**in just five months.**

## EDUCATION AND PROFESSIONAL DEVELOPMENT

❑ BS, **Business Administration,** Troy University at Montgomery    93
*Granted two leadership scholarships under a competitive program that recognized top performers. Earned this degree while working up to 20 hours a week and carrying a full academic load at night.*

❑ AS, **Business Administration,** Alexander City Junior College, Alexander City, Alabama    88
*Granted a one-year scholarship. Held down a 20-hour-a-week job. Served as both Student Government Association Treasurer and Class President.*

❑ **"How to Generate Leads, Make Cold Calls, and Close Sales,"** Thomas Nelson, one week    06

## COMPUTER SKILLS

❑ An expert in Word and Adobe Photoshop; comfortable with advanced Internet search protocols; working knowledge of Excel

## LICENSES

❑ Alabama Real Estate License    Granted October 06

## COMMUNITY AFFILIATIONS

❑ Member and Treasurer, Sigma Chi, Montgomery Chapter    88–Present
❑ Former member of the Centerville Rotary Club    03
❑ Former member of Centerville Kiwanis    97

Page 2

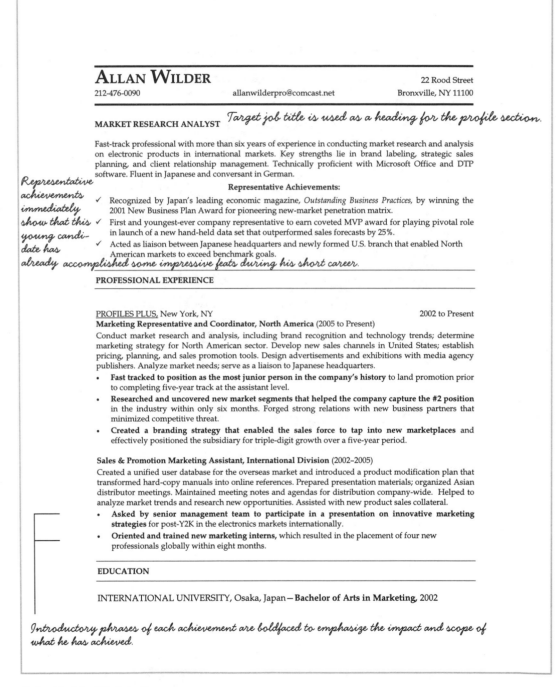

## ALLAN WILDER

212-476-0090  allanwilderpro@comcast.net

22 Rood Street
Bronxville, NY 11100

**MARKET RESEARCH ANALYST** *Target job title is used as a heading for the profile section.*

Fast-track professional with more than six years of experience in conducting market research and analysis on electronic products in international markets. Key strengths lie in brand labeling, strategic sales planning, and client relationship management. Technically proficient with Microsoft Office and DTP software. Fluent in Japanese and conversant in German.

### Representative Achievements:

*Representative achievements immediately show that this young candidate has already accomplished some impressive feats during his short career.*

✓ Recognized by Japan's leading economic magazine, *Outstanding Business Practices,* by winning the 2001 New Business Plan Award for pioneering new-market penetration matrix.

✓ First and youngest-ever company representative to earn coveted MVP award for playing pivotal role in launch of a new hand-held data set that outperformed sales forecasts by 25%.

✓ Acted as liaison between Japanese headquarters and newly formed U.S. branch that enabled North American markets to exceed benchmark goals.

### PROFESSIONAL EXPERIENCE

PROFILES PLUS, New York, NY                                             2002 to Present
**Marketing Representative and Coordinator, North America** (2005 to Present)
Conduct market research and analysis, including brand recognition and technology trends; determine marketing strategy for North American sector. Develop new sales channels in United States; establish pricing, planning, and sales promotion tools. Design advertisements and exhibitions with media agency publishers. Analyze market needs; serve as a liaison to Japanese headquarters.

- **Fast tracked to position as the most junior person in the company's history** to land promotion prior to completing five-year track at the assistant level.
- **Researched and uncovered new market segments that helped the company capture the #2 position** in the industry within only six months. Forged strong relations with new business partners that minimized competitive threat.
- **Created a branding strategy that enabled the sales force to tap into new marketplaces** and effectively positioned the subsidiary for triple-digit growth over a five-year period.

**Sales & Promotion Marketing Assistant, International Division** (2002–2005)
Created a unified user database for the overseas market and introduced a product modification plan that transformed hard-copy manuals into online references. Prepared presentation materials; organized Asian distributor meetings. Maintained meeting notes and agendas for distribution company-wide. Helped to analyze market trends and research new opportunities. Assisted with new product sales collateral.

- **Asked by senior management team to participate in a presentation on innovative marketing strategies** for post-Y2K in the electronics markets internationally.
- **Oriented and trained new marketing interns,** which resulted in the placement of four new professionals globally within eight months.

### EDUCATION

INTERNATIONAL UNIVERSITY, Osaka, Japan—**Bachelor of Arts in Marketing,** 2002

*Introductory phrases of each achievement are boldfaced to emphasize the impact and scope of what he has achieved.*

*Submitted by Jill Grindle*

## NOAH S. THOMAS

1029 Joshkate Avenue • Cincinnati, Ohio 45231
(513) 598-9100 • nst@printedpages.com

### Profile

Customer-focused manager with diversified experience in the retail/grocery/convenience store and restaurant industries, including stores that sell gasoline. Excellent analytical and problem-solving skills. Dependable and self-reliant; work equally well independently or as part of a team. Quick to learn procedures and assimilate new product knowledge. Core competencies: operations, ordering and inventory control, merchandising, employee scheduling and supervision, payroll, and record keeping. Excellent communication and interpersonal skills; proven ability to teach, lead, and motivate others.

### Experience

*Job duties are kept in paragraph form while accomplishments are bulleted for emphasis.*

SUPERSPEED USA, Cincinnati, OH                                                     11/05–Present
**General Manager**
Total P&L accountability for gas station/convenience store operation (open 24/7). Hired, trained, and supervised 15 employees.

▶ Reduced shrink 42% by implementing improved internal controls (inventory, receiving) and loss-prevention initiatives.

▶ Increased gross margin by more than 2% by focusing on fast-food area.

▶ Earned an award for highest increase in fountain beverage sales (out of 100+ stores in the district), 2 consecutive quarters.

FAST FOODS, INC., Cincinnati, OH                                                     9/01–10/05
**Unit Manager, Danny's Burgers**
Directed the activities of 20 Customer Service Representatives and 2–3 Assistant Managers in all aspects of restaurant operations.

▶ Turned around a failing store through a combination of retraining, encouraging teamwork, and controlling costs. Offset losses, producing $7,300 profit the first month and consistent profits ranging from $2,900 to $10,000+ each month thereafter.

▶ Improved drive-through speed an average of 32%.

▶ Developed computer programs and spreadsheets to schedule employees and track sales by product category and vendor.

▶ Recognized as Manager of the Month several times.

### Education

*Lack of a college degree is downplayed.*

CLAREMONT COMMUNITY COLLEGE, Pigeon Forge, TN                                        1998–2001
Completed classes in data processing, accounting, marketing, and management.

### Computer Skills

Proficient with MS Office (Word, Excel, Access), FoodSys, various Internet search engines, and e-mail programs.

**REFERENCES AND ADDITIONAL INFORMATION FURNISHED UPON REQUEST**

*Submitted by Michelle Mastruserio Reitz*

# ELIZABETH A. MOLINA

5 Thornton Avenue ♦ Rockville Centre, New York 11570 ♦ (516) 573-6288
emolina@msn.com

## PROFILE

Former educator with a record of fostering academic learning and enhancing students' critical thinking skills, *eager to return* to a **Social Studies Teacher** position. Utilize stimulating, artfully employed vocabulary to instruct students, and multisensory approach in presenting subject material. Versatile, solid experience with multiple intelligence school populations. Organized, accurate, and detail-oriented time-management skills. Partnered with community and business resources for the purpose of enhancing educational experience. Encourage strong inter-teacher cooperation and exchange of ideas. Maintain communication channels with parents.

*More recent credentials are high-lighted early in the resume.*

## CERTIFICATIONS

**New York State Certificate of Qualification in Secondary Education Social Studies (7–12th), 2002**
**New York State Extension Certificate (5–6th), 2002**
**Red Cross First Aid Certification for Coaching / CPR for Coaching, 2002**

*Older teaching experience comes before current job because candidate wants to return to teaching.*

## PROFESSIONAL TEACHING EXPERIENCE

NORTH SHORE CENTRAL SCHOOL DISTRICT • Sea Cliff, NY                1992
**Substitute Teacher / Social Studies, Grades Nine to Twelve • Assistant Varsity Track Coach**
• Devised and implemented well-received lesson plans in Social Studies.
• Taught document-based questions.
• Established learning environments that met the intellectual, social, and creative needs of all students.
• Encouraged an atmosphere of active student participation.
• Provided tutoring services for students needing extra help.
• Related to a wide range of students/administration crossing cultural lines.

OYSTER BAY–EAST NORWICH SCHOOL DISTRICT • Oyster Bay, NY             1991
**Substitute Teacher / Social Studies, High School • Assistant Football Coach**
• Created and implemented innovative teaching methodologies, strategies, and instructional techniques.
• Formulated well-received lesson plans from the Civil War to World War II utilizing New York State Curriculum.
• Selected textbooks, videos, and research materials.
• Developed cooperative learning activities; evaluated unit exams.
• Provided tutoring for students needing extra help.
• Attended various faculty meetings and subject team meetings.

*Submitted by Donna Farrise*

## ELIZABETH A. MOLINA
### - Page Two -

MANHASSET SCHOOL DISTRICT • Centereach, NY                    1981 to 1982
**Substitute Teacher / Social Studies, High School • Assistant Spring Track Coach / Head Winter Track Coach**
- Formulated unit plans and taught Social Studies and Government classes.
- Encouraged a learning atmosphere of active student participation.
- Challenged students to develop their own solutions to political problems.
- Provided group instruction and designed tests to evaluate student performance.
- Utilized group dynamics in assessing students.
- Supervised hall duties, study halls, and cafeteria duties.
- Attended multidisciplinary and faculty meetings, and parent-teacher conferences.

*Legal career is downplayed.* **PROFESSIONAL EXPERIENCE**

O'HALLERAN, FRENCH, & WINTERS • Holtsville, NY                    6/92 to Present
**Associate Attorney • 8/95 to Present**
   Independently arbitrate, negotiate, and litigate all aspects of criminal, civil, family, negligence, and contractual cases. Areas of concentration include, but are not limited to: preparing all papers necessary for litigation, settlement, and processing of appeals.
   - Perform client interviews; research information; draft affidavits, briefs, contracts, memoranda of law, and effect pleadings.
   - Conduct discoveries, plan case strategies, and try jury trials to verdict.
   - Analyze law sources; i.e., statutes, recorded judicial decisions, legal articles, treaties, constitutions, and legal codes.
   - Supervise paralegal and legal secretarial staff.

**Legal Assistant • 6/92 to 8/95**

### LICENSES

New York State Bar Association

### MEMBERSHIPS / ASSOCIATIONS

American Bar Association
Suffolk Bar Association
New York State Bar Association
Association of Trial Lawyers of America (ATLA)

### EDUCATION

New York University, New York, NY
**Juris Doctor, 1995**

St. John's University, Jamaica, NY
**Bachelor of Arts in Liberal Arts, 1992**

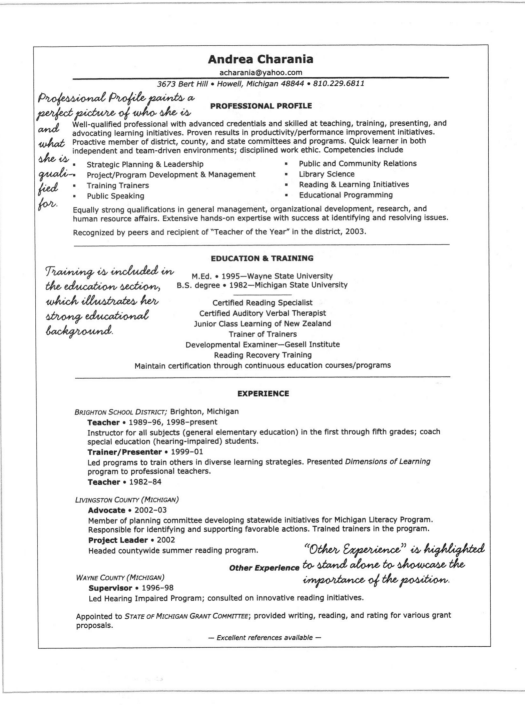

*Professional Profile paints a perfect picture of who she is and what she is qualified for.*

# Andrea Charania

acharania@yahoo.com

*3673 Bert Hill • Howell, Michigan 48844 • 810.229.6811*

## PROFESSIONAL PROFILE

Well-qualified professional with advanced credentials and skilled at teaching, training, presenting, and advocating learning initiatives. Proven results in productivity/performance improvement initiatives. Proactive member of district, county, and state committees and programs. Quick learner in both independent and team-driven environments; disciplined work ethic. Competencies include

- Strategic Planning & Leadership
- Project/Program Development & Management
- Training Trainers
- Public Speaking

- Public and Community Relations
- Library Science
- Reading & Learning Initiatives
- Educational Programming

Equally strong qualifications in general management, organizational development, research, and human resource affairs. Extensive hands-on expertise with success at identifying and resolving issues.

Recognized by peers and recipient of "Teacher of the Year" in the district, 2003.

## EDUCATION & TRAINING

*Training is included in the education section, which illustrates her strong educational background.*

M.Ed. • 1995—Wayne State University
B.S. degree • 1982—Michigan State University

Certified Reading Specialist
Certified Auditory Verbal Therapist
Junior Class Learning of New Zealand
Trainer of Trainers
Developmental Examiner—Gesell Institute
Reading Recovery Training
Maintain certification through continuous education courses/programs

## EXPERIENCE

*BRIGHTON SCHOOL DISTRICT;* Brighton, Michigan
**Teacher** • 1989–96, 1998–present
Instructor for all subjects (general elementary education) in the first through fifth grades; coach special education (hearing-impaired) students.
**Trainer/Presenter** • 1999–01
Led programs to train others in diverse learning strategies. Presented *Dimensions of Learning* program to professional teachers.
**Teacher** • 1982–84

*LIVINGSTON COUNTY (MICHIGAN)*
**Advocate** • 2002–03
Member of planning committee developing statewide initiatives for Michigan Literacy Program. Responsible for identifying and supporting favorable actions. Trained trainers in the program.
**Project Leader** • 2002
Headed countywide summer reading program.

*"Other Experience" is highlighted to stand alone to showcase the importance of the position.*

**Other Experience**

*WAYNE COUNTY (MICHIGAN)*
**Supervisor** • 1996–98
Led Hearing Impaired Program; consulted on innovative reading initiatives.

Appointed to *STATE OF MICHIGAN GRANT COMMITTEE*; provided writing, reading, and rating for various grant proposals.

— *Excellent references available* —

*Submitted by Lorie Lebert*

# Paula Redford

1112 W. 73rd St., New York, NY 10023
212-555-5555
predford@xyz.com

## SUMMARY

ESL/TOEFL Instructor with proven ability to teach adults of all levels of proficiency with varied educational and business backgrounds. Experience includes teaching conversational and written English. Knowledge of multiple cultures through travel and continuing contacts with people throughout Europe, Asia, South America, and Africa.

## EXPERIENCE

*Only the most recent and relevant jobs are included.*

**ESL Instructor**—New York Language Institute, New York, NY                1994–Present

- Teach ESL to private students and business executives; customize lessons according to occupation and level of English proficiency.
- Prepare students for the TOEFL exam.

**ESL Instructor**—Rutgers University                1994
Language Institute for English (L.I.F.E.) summer program at
The Juilliard School at Lincoln Center, New York, NY

- Taught specialized program for international musicians to improve English proficiency.

**ESL and TOEFL Instructor**—Pace University, New York, NY                1991–1993

- Taught ESL classes, from beginner to advanced levels, to American immigrants.

Previous experience includes positions as medical administrator at hospitals and for research programs, also tour guide and museum docent.

## EDUCATION

**B.A.,** *magna cum laude.* Columbia University, New York, NY          *Graduation date is omitted.*

**Graduate Studies:**
New York University, teaching methodology and applied linguistics
New School for Social Research, language learning and teaching

**License:**
New York State Teacher's License #1234

*Would you guess that this candidate is 81 years old? The word "retirement" is not in her vocabulary!*

*Submitted by Wendy Gelberg*

*This job seeker got two call-backs within one hour of faxing his resume to employers!*

# COLE A. THOMES

8 Thornton Way        Chicago, Illinois    60626    773-545-5555    cthomes@lsl.net

## PROFESSIONAL GOAL & PROFILE

*Lots of results*

### Financial Services—Training & Instruction

❖ Financial services experience of 20+ years in highly competitive markets. Areas of expertise:
- Training / Instructing
- Investment / Retirement Planning
- Disability Income Replacement
- Motivation of Sales Team / Agents
- Sales / Marketing
- Long-Term Care / Life Insurance / Annuities

❖ Valued by clients and colleagues for integrity, professionalism, and product knowledge.
❖ Effective in guiding others in investment vehicles, options, and choices to support desired goals.
❖ Readily earn the trust and confidence of others with "either / or" sales closing approach.
❖ Self-motivated and passionate in helping people feel good about where they invest their money.

## EXPERIENCE

**Major Market Investors, Inc.—Investment Strategist, Chicago, IL, 2006–Present**
❖ Recruited by principals of this property casualty and group benefits agency to expand market growth.
❖ Developed strong business relationships with existing clientele, specializing in retirement and pension plans, predominantly in the transportation industry.
❖ Trusted by clients for the ability to "manage money well in a down market."

**Investors Services, Inc.—Senior Investment Specialist, Chicago, IL, 1999–2006**
❖ Took agency from 49th place ranking (of 57) to rank of #3 within a two-year timeframe.
❖ Received numerous "Top Sales Achievement" awards for variable annuities and mutual funds.
❖ Trained, educated, and motivated agents and sales representatives.
❖ Accountable for compliance with NASD and Securities rules and regulations.

**Financials, Inc.—Securities Manager, Memphis, TN, 1993–1998**
❖ Established solid client and agent relationships based on confidence and consistency in helping others generate additional income. Served on the National Board of Financial Advisors for four-year term.
❖ Trained, educated, and motivated agents in sales / marketing of investment products.
❖ Named "Securities Manager of the Year" four consecutive years.
❖ Contributed to the #1 Agency ranking for Investment Sales four consecutive years.
❖ Recognized and appreciated by agents for exemplary performance in investment sales field.

**LBlythe Group, PC—Stockbroker Account Executive, Chicago, IL, 1991–1993**
❖ Built a strong client following through face-to-face contacts. Marketed and sold a complete line of financial products and services to individuals known from prior business endeavors.

**Thomes, Inc.—President, Chicago, IL, 1979–1991**
❖ Founder and developer of a highly successful record retail chain called Rock 4Ever. Promoted music venues throughout the country hosting big-name feature attractions. Recruited by PlayIt Studios, Detroit, for collaboration with artists / producers / engineers on musical direction of new songs.

## EDUCATION & INTERESTS

Vanderbilt University, Nashville, Tennessee, 1979
❖ **Bachelor of Business Administration** with Finance Emphasis—Music Minor
NASD Series 7 & 63; Health & Life Insurance Licenses; Certified Instructor in Power Sales Training
❖ Interests: stock market, baseball, golf, music, and family activities

*Submitted by Billie Ruth Sucher*

# CHAPTER 11

# Sample Skills-Based and Combination Resumes

Just as in chapter 10, the resumes in this chapter are organized around various job categories, but be sure to browse all the samples for ideas, not just the ones that relate to your targeted job.

- Business managers and executives (pages 226–228)
- Career changers (pages 229–231)
- Clerical and administrative (pages 232–235)
- Education and training (page 236)
- Entrepreneurs (page 237)
- Finance and accounting (pages 238–239)
- Healthcare, medical, and veterinary (pages 240–241)
- Hospitality (page 242)
- IT, engineering (pages 243–245)
- Mechanical and skilled trades, technology (pages 246–251)
- Media, arts, and communications (pages 252–255)
- Military-to-civilian transitions (pages 256–258)
- No degree/no college (pages 259–260)
- Sales (pages 261–262)
- Students and new graduates (pages 263–265)

*This combination resume highlights functional skills and achievements on page 1.*

# KATIE N. ANDERSON

1456 Apple Blossom Drive • Savannah, GA 31401
(912) 123-4567 • knanderson@abc.net

## OPERATIONS EXECTUTIVE

Highly motivated executive with more than 20 years of experience in contract administration, quality assurance, and new product development. Principal customer industries: procedure trays; boundary product; examination gloves; and federal, state, and local governments. Adept at analysis and business re-engineering, increasing bottom-line revenues and gross profits. Proven performer in recruitment and management encompassing personnel, contract negotiations, and customer relations. Areas of expertise include

> Operations & Materials Management
> Cost Controls & Reductions
> Market Share Strategies
> Major Client Management
> Competitive Maneuvering

> Purchasing Operations
> Sales & Marketing Management
> Vendor Management
> Organizational Development
> Staff Development

## OPERATIONS MANAGEMENT ACHIEVEMENTS

> Directed streamlining of multiple production sites to ultimately reduce shipping costs and increase gross profit margins 45%.

> Recruited to "clean house" and begin again. Re-engineered production planning, procurement, quality assurance, distribution, and sales administration departments. Increased overall productivity by 20%.

> Created product management system, which accelerated pricing, contract negotiations, and distribution agreements; increased profits by 27% through cost reductions and control.

> Negotiated multibillion-dollar group contract, which had been suspended for three years. Developed pricing strategy and fee payment program that overshot the competing bid by 15%, yet maintaining 20% gross profit.

> Generated $25M multiyear savings and accelerated productivity growth through development of private-brand products.

*Submitted by Tammy Chisholm*

*A brief summary of professional experience appears on page 2.*

Katie N. Anderson                                                    Page 2 of 2

## PROFESSIONAL EXPERIENCE

Xidus Medical, Inc.—Savannah, GA                              1999–2007
Ranked among the top medical manufacturers, offers broad spectrum of boundary and custom procedure tray products.
**Vice President, Operations**
Managed plant production and sales requirements while overseeing planning, scheduling, sales, quality control, and distribution. Direct 15 managers and 10 engineers with national P&L accountability.

Divad Custom Procedure Trays—Savannah, GA                    1978–1999
$1B leading national custom procedure tray manufacturer and distributor.
**Director, Sales Administration** (1995–1999)
Oversaw sales representative alignments, corporate account fee calculation/ distribution, and product catalog. Developed cost reduction and gross profit acceleration system for slow-moving product, increasing sales 54%.

**Manager, Marketing & Sales Services** (1978–1995)
Directed 50 sales and customer service representatives. Managed and trained sales representatives in custom procedure tray contents and sterilization methods. Developed and implemented bid and analysis processes to maximize profit and revenue growth.

---

## EDUCATION

**Master of Business Administration**
The Wharton School, University of Pennsylvania, Philadelphia, PA

**Bachelor of Science in Business**
Virginia Commonwealth University, Richmond, VA

---

## ORGANIZATIONS

**Executive Board,** United Way
**Vice Chairman,** Savannah Habitat for Humanity Chapter
**Board Member,** Hanover County Red Cross and Zoning Commission

*After many years as a production engineer, Stan wanted to switch to IT.*

**Stanley K. Larringer**
176 Woodhaven Drive, Eatontown, NJ 07724
(732) 927-5555 • StanLarringer@aol.com

**Web Applications Management**
**E-Commerce • B2B • Project Management**

## KEY QUALIFICATIONS

✓ **Technical Strengths:** Up-to-date, diverse training in e-Business Management coupled with years of experience in analytical, technical process engineering profession.

✓ **Project Coordination and Teamwork:** Highly productive in team environments as both team member and team leader. Efficient in handling multiple project priorities.

✓ **Communication:** Able to communicate technical information in an easily understandable way. Recognized for relationship building with team members and clients. An effective listener.

✓ **Personal Attributes:** Innovative problem solver. Committed to goal achievement. Dependable.

## EDUCATION

*His Education section shows that he has the technical training to segue into Web applications.*

☑ Cybersoft Internet Professional—CIP 1, Cybersoft, Inc., Woodbridge, NJ
**Certified e-Business Architect, e-Business for Managers**—December 2007
**Certified Cybersoft Communications 1000**—December 2005
Courses: Networking, Database, Web Development, Web Design, Multimedia, Internet Business

☑ Bachelor of Science, Industrial Engineering, Connecticut Institute of Technology

## TECHNICAL SKILLS

**e-Commerce:** e-Business and B2B Infrastructures and Consumer Payment Protocols
**Applications:** ERP, e-Procurement, Selling Chain Management, Customer Relationship Management
**Software Tools:** MS Word, MS Excel, MS Access, HTML, FrontPage 2000, JavaScript
**Operating Systems:** Windows NT, Windows 2000, Windows XP

## PROFESSIONAL EXPERIENCE

ENGINEERING SYSTEMS, INC., Astro Space Division, Eatontown, NJ          1990–2007
Manufacturing Engineer, Production Engineering Department

Provided assembly documentation and engineering floor support throughout all phases of production flow, including fabrication, assembly, and test operations, for manufacturer of diverse satellite products contracted by major government clients (USSA and U.S. Air Force).

### ACCOMPLISHMENTS

- Promoted to Team Leader for new equipment installation and upgrades. Performed research and analysis, and tested in production mode. Full authority to sign off fully tested equipment.

- Reduced cycle time by 30% through development of assembly and test tolling. Improved recycle characteristics and cut hazardous emissions into atmosphere by 40%.

- Collaborated with 60-person design engineering team to ensure that designs were producible in manufacturing environment. Provided cost-effective manufacturing recommendations.

- Trained 8 entry-level engineers in 4-month period to prepare efficient, labor-effective work plans for multi-line production floor in 80,000-square-foot facility.

*Accomplishments are given prime visibility in the Professional Experience section, showcasing the strengths mentioned in the Key Qualifications section.*

*Submitted by Susan Guarneri*

# Kristina R. Hill

1228 Cedar Ridge Avenue ♦ White Marsh, MD 21162
(301) 555-5019 – Home ♦ (240) 555-2735 – Cell ♦ krh@msn.com

**Job Target**

**Value Offered**

**Receptionist ♦ Customer Service ♦ Office Support**

- Personable and friendly; good conversationalist, with excellent face-to-face and telephone communication skills.
- Active listener who demonstrates an innate ability to ask the right questions at the right time.
- Task oriented with an ability to balance strong interpersonal skills with need for efficiency.
- Down-to-earth and practical; place high value on following procedures.
- Patient, persistent, and diplomatic while providing explanations.
- Extremely attentive to detail and producing high-quality work.
- Methodical about gathering information and data to present logical and systematic approaches to completing tasks.
- Artistic and creative; keen sense of style, balance, and use of color.
- Computer literate with self-taught skills in Windows, Internet, e-mail, basic word processing, and keyboarding.

*Mentions her ability to learn computer applications on her own*

**Employment History**

*Gained cross-functional office and customer service experience through various short-term positions while raising family and maintaining household (mid-1980s and 1990s.)*

*Explains the time she was out of the workforce to raise children*

- Supported business office operations for **Rich Lighting**. Managed incoming calls, assisted customers in selecting lighting fixtures, operated cash register, verified credit purchases, and tracked product inventory.
- Demonstrated and sold new and used cars for **Bowman Chevrolet**. Provided customers with information about vehicle features and benefits; completed extensive paperwork; set up and maintained account filing system; prospected for new business by phone and mail solicitation.
- Took over store management for Hagerstown branch of **Carpet Town**, including opening and closing responsibilities; customer service and sales; securing customer financing and calculating interest rates; office filing; and scheduling of installation projects.
- Answered phones, set up filing system, and helped organize office for a newly established restaurant/pub.
- Created and sold hand-drawn greeting cards. Designed and distributed monthly newsletter for Williamsport AmVets Post. Designed covers for high school graduation and baccalaureate pamphlets.

**Education**

Graduate, **Wye Mills High School,** Wye Mills, MD
Vocational Studies, **Commercial Art,** Career Studies Center, Wye Mills, MD

*Submitted by Norine Dagliano*

*Strong fonts and aggressive writing indicate the candidate's modern style and forward-thinking approach.*

# JULI STOLSON

824 BALSAM DRIVE, APEX, AZ 85365
(623) 972-0786    JSTOL@AOL.COM    CELL: (623) 506-4679

## PROFILE

*States what she can do and who she can do it for*

Available to handle internal human resource, accounting, and payroll duties for a small to mid-sized company. Analytical, outgoing, and organized employee who learns quickly, works well under pressure, and is attentive to detail.

Strong analytical and mathematical aptitude. Motto of "get it done, and get it done right," combined with high degree of accuracy and organizational talents. Outstanding communication skills used in answering questions/inquiries, doing research, and resolving issues. Demonstrate the spirit of helping others and "going the extra mile" when needed.

Excited by the challenge of learning new fields, procedures, and systems. Currently completing accounting degree.

*Three-column format draws reader's eye to her many talents.*

| | | |
|---|---|---|
| Customer Service | General Accounting | Quality Assurance |
| Human Resources | Bookkeeping | Bank Reconciliations |
| Payroll Processing | Taxes | Financial Statements |
| New Hires | Invoice / Client Billing | General Ledger |
| Terminated Employees | Spreadsheets | Word Processing |
| Writing | Government Agencies | Project Management |

## PROFESSIONAL EXPERIENCE

**SENIOR PAYROLL SPECIALIST**
**ADP CHECK PROCESSING**
Phoenix, AZ        (2004–Present)

Process client payrolls and resolve issues for this leading national provider of payroll, human resource, and benefits outsourcing solutions for small to medium-sized businesses. Manage more than 250 clients processing weekly, bi-weekly, semi-monthly, and monthly payrolls worth more than $6 million per month.

♦ Assist and advise clients with Human Resources issues, including paying terminated employees, new hire paperwork (W-4, A-4, I-9, etc.), name changes and name formatting for the Social Security Administration (SSA), and helping identify illegal workers through the SSA.

♦ Write letters to federal and state government agencies (IRS, Department of Revenue, etc.) responding to penalty notices or federal identification problems. Coworkers often reference past letters for helping write new letters.

*Submitted by Gail Frank*

# JULI STOLSON, PAGE 2

- Provide virtually error-free work; results are dramatically less than the company's minimum allowed number of free services to clients due to processing mistakes.
- Selected and trained to be backup "Taxpay Specialist" as an extra responsibility.
- Chosen as "Garnishment Specialist" due to high level of accuracy and understanding of wage garnishment procedures.
- Developed organizational spreadsheet that kept track of amended clients' complicated previous quarter tax returns. It was adopted as the office standard.
- Earned 15 commendations from regional manager for excellent service above 90% as reported by clients on survey cards.
- Expedited a request, reprinted data, and hand-delivered a client's lost quarterly tax return package.
- Secured a 35% corporate discount for a client who confided business and financial troubles. Evaluated services client was using and recommended cuts for unnecessary charges.
- Completed pre-hire math test with a perfect score, when more than 90% of applicants fail the test.
- Passed year-long intensive training program ranked in the Forbes Top 100 Training Programs.

## CUSTOMER CARE REPRESENTATIVE
## I-PAY CHECK SERVICES
SCOTTSDALE, AZ (2002–2004)
Provided customer service for this check warranty company that approved checks for merchants like Best Buy and Sears. Resolved customer issues for angry and upset customers who had just had checks declined at a merchant that used I-Pay.

- Answered over 90 customer calls per day and resolved issues within the allotted 3-minute period. Assisted clients with returned checks and helped ensure future check acceptance.
- Earned 5 "Special Recognition" certificates for exceeding department standards.
- Received several complimentary letters from appreciative customers.
- Helped other order-processing departments with their workload. Deciphered detailed spreadsheets and ran complicated computer programs for deadlines.
- Volunteered for overtime during busy season; often worked 12-hour+ shifts.

# EDUCATION & CERTIFICATIONS

**GLENDALE COMMUNITY COLLEGE,** Glendale, AZ, currently taking courses to complete accounting degree
**PASCO HIGH SCHOOL,** Dade City, AZ, high school degree, 2002

*Candidate is working toward her degree.*

- Graduated with honors.
- Awarded Merit scholarship, which covered 75% of college tuition.
- Won award for creative writing.

*This resume is a combination between chronological and functional formats.*

# ROBYN L. WRYGHT

3673 Bay View • Canton, Ohio 44705
234.229.6811

*The headline notes her job targets.*

## OFFICE MANAGER / ADMINISTRATIVE ASSISTANT

***Accounting — Payroll — Clerical Organization — AP/AR — Customer Service — Research & Writing***

Experienced Business Office Administrator, exceptionally loyal and organized. Dedicated professional with proven administrative credentials. Demonstrates strong interpersonal and communication skills.

*Professional Qualifications*

- Ability to *communicate* with all levels of management and colleagues.
- *Management expertise* in all areas of office administration.
- Experience in situations demanding extreme *confidentiality*.
- *Interacts professionally* with clients, salespeople, vendors, etc.
- *Executes* multiple tasks and *expedites* in an accurate, timely manner.
- Proficient in *prioritizing* projects and schedules with positive *decision-making skills*.
- Skilled at *organizing* and *coordinating* professional/personal calendars, and following up with appointments and schedules.
- *Computer skills* include Microsoft Word and Excel; Peachtree and other basic accounting applications; familiar with network environments and e-mail/Internet.

### PROFESSIONAL EXPERIENCE

*CHROMATECH;* Canton, Ohio
**Administrative Assistant** • 2004 to current
Provide all routine office assistance and functions in numerous cross-functional roles for international manufacturer of dies and pigments. Support sales team with correspondence needs, customer inquiries, and marketing materials.

- Function in all areas of accounting, accounts payable/accounts receivable, credit checking, and collections.
- Handle ordering of office supplies and purchasing of warehouse equipment as needed.
- Provide information and assistance to customers needing order/delivery and pricing help.
- Manage diverse special projects, presentations, and assignments.

*CHEMCENTRAL;* Columbus, Ohio
**Assistant Office Manager** • 1994 to 2004
Member of administrative team supporting one of the company's largest branches for national distributor of solvents and chemicals. Headed busy office with multiple cross-functional supervision and administration responsibilities.

- Oversaw accounting department clerks and activities to ensure accuracy and efficiency, including accounts payable and receivable, financial statements (monthly—yearly—taxes), payroll (attendance and hours for union—hourly—salary labor), journal entries, billing, and expenses.
- Assisted sales team and staff with research activities.
- Handled interoffice inquiries and internal conflicts to mutual resolution.
- Gave input on telephone systems and remodeling.
- Member of Quality Control Committee; investigated issues, gave advice, and resolved issues.
- Traveled to branch offices across the U.S. on special assignments.

*Education was omitted because of lack of college degree (if it's not noted, it's not a focal point).*

— *Excellent references available on request* —

*Submitted by Lorie Lebert*

# LISA J. CARTER

185 Spring Lane ◆ Plantsville, CT 06479-1018 ◆ 860-555-2222 ◆ lisajcarter@hotmail.com

*The top third of Lisa's resume provides critical information about the hard and soft skills she offers a prospective employer.*

## ADMINISTRATIVE PROFESSIONAL

### PROFILE

Detail-oriented, accurate, and observant. Well organized and proficient at multitasking. Excellent customer service aptitude. Outstanding interpersonal and communication skills. Quick learner who can rapidly retain information. Team player who easily establishes rapport and trust. Bilingual—English and Spanish. Computer skills include Microsoft Word, Excel, PowerPoint, and Outlook. Part-time student available for first and second shift.

### CORE SKILLS

- **Administrative Support**
- **Procedure Development**
- **Appointment Scheduling**
- **Correspondence**
- **Research & Analysis**
- **Event Coordination**
- **Customer Service**
- **Record Keeping**
- **Reception**

*Employment history is presented in an easy-to-follow format.*

### EMPLOYMENT HISTORY

CONNECTICUT SAVINGS BANK                    Hartford, CT                    9/04 to Present
**Administrative Assistant—Mortgage Department**

*Achievements in both positions are quantified and emphasized in boldface italics.*

- ❑ Process and prepare correspondence and documents for department director.
- ❑ Organize new client files. Maintain and update existing files and records.
- ❑ Respond to clients' in-person and phone inquires. Provide rate information.
- ❑ Conduct ongoing research on competitor products and services.
- ❑ Orchestrate administrative functions, including appointment scheduling, filing, and faxing.
- ❑ Arranged office promotional events, including Mortgage Education Night.
- ❑ *Researched and wrote 27-page office procedure manual adopted for use by 10 branches.*

THE COFFEE STAND                    Waterbury, CT                    5/92 to 9/04
**Shift Supervisor/Sales Associate**

- ❑ Oversaw activities, efforts, and training of 12 sales associates.
- ❑ Coordinated assignments and work schedules. Addressed and corrected shift problems.
- ❑ Assisted with processing customer orders, cleaning, and stocking.
- ❑ Balanced cash registers and processed bank deposits.
- ❑ *Received 2001 Employee of the Year Award in recognition of 55% sales increase.*

### EDUCATION

SOUTHERN CONNECTICUT STATE UNIVERSITY, New Haven, CT
*Completing Master of Science* (Part Time) ◆ Anticipated Date of Graduation—May 2010 (GPA 3.9/4.0)

UNIVERSITY OF CONNECTICUT, Storrs, CT
May 2006 ~ **B.A. in History** (GPA 3.2/4.0)

*Submitted by Ross Primack*

# NATALIE P. COLEMAN

20 Second Avenue ~ Hoboken, New Jersey 08873 ~ 201-963-8362 ~ npcoleman@hotmail.com

## SUMMARY OF QUALIFICATIONS

Motivated Customer Service Professional with several years of experience providing optimum levels of service to both internal and external customers. Resourceful and organized with excellent phone skills and a talent for resolving customer/client questions and complaints in a timely and courteous manner. Innovative, creative, intelligent, and disciplined with a proven record of turning disorganization and discontent into order and customer satisfaction. Developed an impressive record of advancement and achievement in diverse positions due to diligence, drive, strong work ethic, and creativity. Adept at quickly learning and applying new concepts, technologies, processes, and procedures. Highly skilled in dealing effectively with diverse clientele, including demanding clients with very discerning taste, business owners, city officials, and patrons of casual and fine-dining establishments. Technical proficiencies include MS Office, Photoshop, Illustrator, and Quark.

## CAREER HIGHLIGHTS

*The Career Highlights section takes information out of chronological order and places less emphasis on current position as a bartender.*

**PLANNING ASSOCIATES**

❖ Increased operational efficiency, communication, and employee morale by redesigning the entire work environment of one of the top ten Urban Planners in the country.

❖ Added value to the firm's end product and increased revenue by creating original watercolor portraits of employer's designs for presentation to clients.

❖ Ensured a seamless operation by recreating the firm's image library that was lost in a corporate relocation.

**BISTROT LEPIC**

❖ Promoted from Hostess to Manager of this top 10 fine-dining establishment within six months of employment.

❖ Saved over $13,000 in excess expenses as manager and increased clientele 50% after redesigning the interior to reflect a modern and aesthetically appealing atmosphere.

❖ Exceeded all expectations in this fast-paced, full-time position while balancing a full-time student course load.

**THE DESIGN STUDIO**

❖ Designed the Silver line of designer purses currently being sold in Saks Fifth Avenue, Bloomingdales, Neiman Marcus, and other high-end stores; designed the 12 purses in this line with an eye for detail and quality to suit the needs of discerning clientele.

**THE PRINTING PRESS**

❖ Promoted to Sales Representative as a result of ability to deal effectively with customers and provide suggestions to increase business.

❖ Worked with customers one-on-one to obtain their specifications and develop solutions that met their needs while remaining within their budget.

❖ Increased sales by translating marketing concepts into visually appealing materials; presented concepts via the use of various visual aids.

## EMPLOYMENT EXPERIENCE

*The Employment Experience section emphasizes her dealings with customers.*

**CHARLIE'S BAR AND GRILL,** New York, New York                                        2007–Present
**Bartender**

❖ Currently managing the bar of this popular eating establishment working both independently and in a team capacity to serve up to 200 patrons and ensure customer satisfaction.

**THE DESIGN STUDIO,** New York, New York                                        2007
**Purse Designer / Interior Decorator**

❖ Provided exceptional levels of customer service for customers of this high-end design studio.

❖ Designed home interiors according to customer specifications, providing appealing design options that suited their specific needs and budget while working in the Interior Design branch.

❖ Created contemporary purses with rich fabrics and colors to suit the needs and taste of discerning clientele.

**PLANNING ASSOCIATES,** Hoboken, New Jersey                                        2004–2006
**Corporate Consultant / Image Coordinator**

❖ Served as the front-line point of contact for new and existing customers of this top ten urban planner; fielded a high volume of calls and requests from city officials ensuring a smooth and efficient operation and maintaining the firm's professional image.

❖ Used Photoshop, Illustrator, Quark, and PowerPoint to edit images for client presentations.

*Submitted by Erika Harrigan*

# NATALIE P. COLEMAN

PAGE TWO

**BISTROT LEPIC,** New York, New York                                    2000–2002
**Manager**
- ❖ Recruited as Hostess and promoted to Manager within six months of employment as a result of providing exceptional customer service.
- ❖ Learned all aspects of the business to ensure that the needs of both the kitchen and the customers were met and to ensure a pleasurable dining experience for all patrons.
- ❖ Ensured a seamless operation by supervising and scheduling a staff of 30 waiters and effectively managing employee conflicts.

**THE PRINTING PRESS,** Jersey City, New Jersey                          1999–2000
**Sales Representative / Design Coordinator**
- ❖ Interacted heavily with customers over the phone to receive orders and resolve complaints for this full-service commercial printing company.
- ❖ Promoted to Sales Representative charged with working one-on-one with customers to obtain their specifications and develop solutions that met their needs while remaining within their budget.
- ❖ Used Photoshop and Illustrator to design flyers, brochures, and other visually appealing marketing documents for customers.

**FERRARI CONSTRUCTION INC.,** Elizabeth, New Jersey                     1997–2000
**Personal Assistant**
- ❖ Played an integral role in ensuring the success of this highly successful single-family home-building and masonry company by managing the billing, payroll, spreadsheets, and several other administrative details.

## EDUCATION

**PARSON'S SCHOOL OF DESIGN,** New York, New York, 2000–2003
Studied Painting, Art, Graphic Design, and Textiles
- ❖ Commissioned by the college to represent the Mixed Media department by designing a statue.
- ❖ Created a piece of Color Theory artwork that was purchased by Newark Airport.
- ❖ Designed a mural currently located in the lobby of the Hoboken City Council.

## COMMUNITY SERVICE ACTIVITIES

- ❖ Demonstrated leadership skills by donating more than 600 hours of community service.
- ❖ Served as Vice President of Walktoberfest and participated in beach sweeps, the Special Olympics, and tutoring mentally challenged individuals.

## Anna Maria Gomez

414 Acorn Court, Lawrenceville, NJ 08648
(609) 771-5555 ▪ annam@earthlink.net

### Spanish Teacher at the Middle or High School Level

*Resume leads off with her Education and Certification, most relevant to the new career she is pursuing.*

### EDUCATION & CERTIFICATION

New Jersey Teacher's Certification, Spanish K–12

BA, Spanish Language & Civilization / Teaching (cum laude), Rutgers University, New Brunswick, NJ
✓ Two semesters at University of Valencia, Spain. Summer study at University of Madrid.
MBA, International Business / Marketing, Columbia University, New York, NY

### PROFILE  *Profile showcases some of her unique qualifications and strengths.*

☑ Fluent Spanish. Basic conversational Portuguese and good reading ability. Familiar with French.
☑ Experienced Spanish teacher with demonstrated track record of obtaining outstanding results, utilizing highly effective interpersonal and communications skills.
☑ Detail-oriented, analytical professional with proven organizational and problem solving abilities.
☑ Computer literate: Windows 2003, MS Word, Excel, Outlook, Print Shop, and Internet Explorer.

### PROFESSIONAL EXPERIENCE  *Transferable skills most relevant to teaching are highlighted under Professional Experience.*

**TEACHING / COMMUNICATIONS**

▪ Designed Spanish-language curriculum and taught one 2½-hour class weekly for The Princeton Community School. Used text, multimedia, and visual aids to make classroom learning relevant to adults. Resulted in high re-registration rate for following semesters.

▪ Trained small groups of end users on computerized banking services for Mercantile Banking and Trust Company. Conducted product presentations and consultative interviews with clients and prospects. Created and implemented marketing plans for corporate clients in Latin America.

▪ Consulted with clients of International Research Corporation to determine specifications for customized market / opinion research projects. Wrote proposals and translated textbook chapters and questionnaires from Spanish to English. Developed marketing collaterals and account relationship management techniques to ensure top-notch company image and service.

**ORGANIZATION / PROJECT MANAGEMENT**

▪ Coordinated complex, multinational research projects for Research Analysis and International Research Corporation. Led and trained project teams and ensured timely completion of projects within budget.

▪ Coordinated translations from Spanish to English for scholarly magazine, obtaining and evaluating board member input on editorial content, all while meeting strict publication deadlines. Streamlined procedures for foreign-language advertisement and order fulfillment (Medical Learning Systems).

### EMPLOYMENT HISTORY

| | | |
|---|---|---|
| Director of International Marketing | International Research Corp., Somerset, NJ | 2002–2008 |
| Spanish I Teacher | Princeton Community School, Princeton, NJ | 2001–2006 |
| Field Administrator | Research Analysis Corp., Skillman, NJ | 2000–2001 |
| Coordinator—Latin American Services | Medical Learning Systems, Skillman, NJ | 1999–2000 |
| Senior Marketing & Sales Rep. | Mercantile Banking and Trust Co., New York | previously |

*Submitted by Lorie Lebert*

*Candidate's name and expertise stand out in this bold presentation.*

# DOLORES SMITH

2092 Recreation Drive • Powell, Ohio 43065
Home: 614-890-4499 • Cell: 614-276-4544
e-mail: dolores@worthingtonma.com

## COSMETIC ARTISTRY • COSMETIC SUPPLY SALES • PROFIT CENTER MANAGEMENT
### Leading-Edge Cosmetology Techniques/Methods • Esthetics • Spa Profit Protocols

**Customer-oriented cosmetology professional** with valuable blend of business ownership and management experience combined with noticeable talent in esthetic skin care leading to enhanced appearance and well-being of customers; utilizing 25-year history as licensed **Cosmetologist, Manager, and Instructor** to propel all facets of client care, organizational management, and strategic planning agendas. Extremely well organized, dedicated, and resourceful with ability to guide operations and associates to **technique improvements, maximized productivity, and bottom-line increases.**

## AREAS OF STRENGTH

• Relationship Building • Customer Service •
• Time Management • Creative/Strategic Selling •
• Follow-Up • Merchandising/Promotion •
• Relationship Management •
• Product Introduction • Inventory Management •
• Expense Control • Vendor Negotiations •
• Client Needs Analysis •

## EDUCATION

FINER ACADEMY OF COSMETOLOGY ... Finer, Ohio
• Cosmetology • Manager • Instructor •
Licenses

FINER ACADEMY OF HAIR DESIGN ... Finer, Ohio
Graduate in Hair Design

## SEMINARS & SPECIALIZED TRAINING

Continuing Education Units
(to meet requirements of 8 credits annually)

Certificate of Achievement for Advanced Basic
Esthetics and Spa Therapies, August 2006

Several seminars held by various cosmetics
associations

## ADDITIONAL BACKGROUND

**The Hair Artists** ... Dublin, Ohio
Manager of Licensed Cosmetologists
(1995–1998)

**Jean Bennett Salon** ... Worthington, Ohio
Licensed Cosmetologist
(1992–1995)

## PROFESSIONAL EXPERIENCE

STUDIO D@RENÉ.....DUBLIN, Ohio (May 1998 to October 2006)
*Full-service and independent customized hair, nails, and tanning boutique positioned in strip-mall (suburban locale) setting; operations staffed by 5 employees, contractors, and technicians.*

**Owner/General Manager**
**Directed total operation while simultaneously contributing as cosmetologist in one of four-station salon;** as single owner of small business, administered profit and loss, undertook all facets of decision-making, strategically guided salon operations and productivity, and assumed complete responsibility for revenue performance.

Management responsibilities included cosmetic and accessories sales, customer service, client management, accounting, finance, recruiting/hiring/training/scheduling, compliance, business/operations legal requisites, retail merchandising, advertising, inventory procurement/control, vendor relationships, contract negotiations, booth rental contracts, and leases to licensed cosmetologists and nail technicians.

→ **Successfully conceived and launched full scale of operations** and guided business to strong reputation for quality output of product and services; consistently met challenges of market conditions and business atmosphere to persevere throughout 8 years of ownership.

→ **Maintained operating costs at lowest possible point by reducing inventory and labor hours during seasonal periods;** also negotiated with vendors to secure better pricing for goods and services.

→ **Facilitated revenue increase by bringing in cosmetic line to enhance product offering to clients.**

→ **Recognized revenue opportunity** and spearheaded remodel of existing tanning space to provide for salon.

→ **Expanded market visibility by becoming member of Powell Chamber of Commerce.**

→ **Modified policies and procedures to ensure employee compliance with changing licensing regulations.**

→ **Worked in concert with American Cancer Society to provide styling services to cancer patients** with aims at improving appearance, outlook, confidence, and self-esteem.

*Two column-format enables her to pack lots of information on one page.*

Submitted by Jeremy Worthington

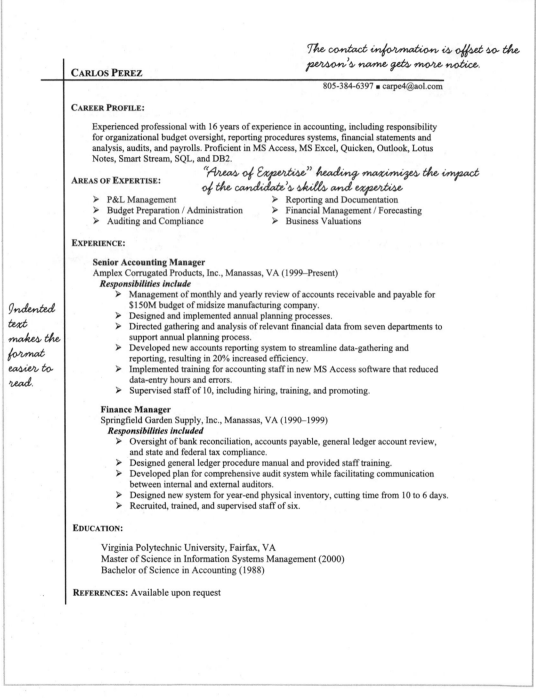

*The contact information is offset so the person's name gets more notice.*

## CARLOS PEREZ

805-384-6397 ∎ carpe4@aol.com

**CAREER PROFILE:**

Experienced professional with 16 years of experience in accounting, including responsibility for organizational budget oversight, reporting procedures systems, financial statements and analysis, audits, and payrolls. Proficient in MS Access, MS Excel, Quicken, Outlook, Lotus Notes, Smart Stream, SQL, and DB2.

**AREAS OF EXPERTISE:**

*"Areas of Expertise" heading maximizes the impact of the candidate's skills and expertise*

- ➢ P&L Management
- ➢ Budget Preparation / Administration
- ➢ Auditing and Compliance

- ➢ Reporting and Documentation
- ➢ Financial Management / Forecasting
- ➢ Business Valuations

**EXPERIENCE:**

**Senior Accounting Manager**
Amplex Corrugated Products, Inc., Manassas, VA (1999–Present)
*Responsibilities include*
- ➢ Management of monthly and yearly review of accounts receivable and payable for $150M budget of midsize manufacturing company.
- ➢ Designed and implemented annual planning processes.
- ➢ Directed gathering and analysis of relevant financial data from seven departments to support annual planning process.
- ➢ Developed new accounts reporting system to streamline data-gathering and reporting, resulting in 20% increased efficiency.
- ➢ Implemented training for accounting staff in new MS Access software that reduced data-entry hours and errors.
- ➢ Supervised staff of 10, including hiring, training, and promoting.

**Finance Manager**
Springfield Garden Supply, Inc., Manassas, VA (1990–1999)
*Responsibilities included*
- ➢ Oversight of bank reconciliation, accounts payable, general ledger account review, and state and federal tax compliance.
- ➢ Designed general ledger procedure manual and provided staff training.
- ➢ Developed plan for comprehensive audit system while facilitating communication between internal and external auditors.
- ➢ Designed new system for year-end physical inventory, cutting time from 10 to 6 days.
- ➢ Recruited, trained, and supervised staff of six.

**EDUCATION:**

Virginia Polytechnic University, Fairfax, VA
Master of Science in Information Systems Management (2000)
Bachelor of Science in Accounting (1988)

**REFERENCES:** Available upon request

*Indented text makes the format easier to read.*

*Submitted by Mary Hayward*

# Susan Danville

906 Riverview Road • San Ramon, CA 97786 • 974.588.9900
sdanville@cox.net

## Professional Summary

**Accounting/Finance Professional** with expertise in general accounting, financial analysis and reporting, financial systems, budget preparation, and cash management. Currently pursuing MBA in finance. *Current pursuit of MBA is emphasized.*

- Well versed in accounting principles, practices, and systems, as well as business operations.
- Team player who performs at high levels of productivity in fast-paced environments without missing a single deadline.
- Effective communicator and relationship builder with management, customers, staff, and financial institutions.
- Recognized for leadership and problem-solving strengths, as well as thoroughness and accuracy.

## Experience

THE LYDEN COMPANY, San Francisco, CA        1985–2008
   **Senior Accountant**        1993–2008
   **Accountant**        1989–1993
   **Accounting Technician**        1985–1989

Promoted through progressively responsible positions in accounting department in recognition of consistent performance results. Accomplishments: *Bulleted areas under experience focus on accomplishments.*

### *Accounting/Auditing*
- Managed accounts payable disbursements totaling more than $1.7 million annually, accounts receivable processing, and over $1 million in capital assets.
- Verified and maintained GL system. Developed and implemented accounting policies/procedures.
- Instituted internal control procedures, including suspense account reconciliations for premium collections, reducing write-offs by $75,000 annually.
- Coordinated audits with internal/external auditors and regulatory agencies. Compiled financial data for auditors. Prepared internal audit reports.

### *Financial Analysis & Reporting*
- Coordinated and prepared NAIC financial statements in accordance with SAP and premium tax return filings for more than $1.8 million in 48 states.
- Prepared financial statements in accordance with GAAP for the Board of Directors and shareholders and semiannual SEC filings for 6 portfolios totaling $1+ billion in net assets.
- Analyzed and prepared variance reports for all management levels throughout business unit.

### *Cash Management/Budgeting*
- Performed cash management functions to meet investment objectives and prepared timely corporate cash flow forecasts.
- Developed and implemented banking policies for accounting, premiums, commissions, and benefits.
- Coordinated $35 million budget-preparation process for all departments within business unit.

## Education

*To avoid repeating similar responsibilities, a skills-based format was used to group together the last three job titles with one recent employer.*

**M.B.A. candidate in Finance** • Anticipated May 2008
Stanford University • Berkeley, CA

**B.S., Accounting**
California State University • Sacramento, CA

Submitted by Louise Garver

*A simple functional format*

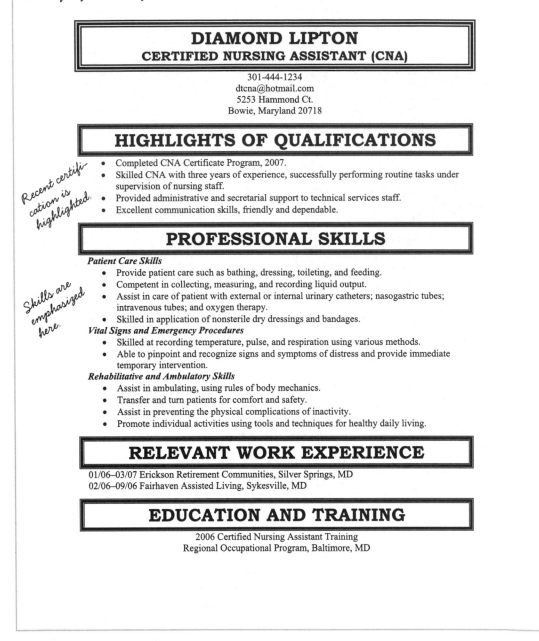

# DIAMOND LIPTON
## CERTIFIED NURSING ASSISTANT (CNA)

301-444-1234
dtcna@hotmail.com
5253 Hammond Ct.
Bowie, Maryland 20718

## HIGHLIGHTS OF QUALIFICATIONS

*Recent certification is highlighted.*

- Completed CNA Certificate Program, 2007.
- Skilled CNA with three years of experience, successfully performing routine tasks under supervision of nursing staff.
- Provided administrative and secretarial support to technical services staff.
- Excellent communication skills, friendly and dependable.

## PROFESSIONAL SKILLS

**Patient Care Skills**

*Skills are emphasized here.*

- Provide patient care such as bathing, dressing, toileting, and feeding.
- Competent in collecting, measuring, and recording liquid output.
- Assist in care of patient with external or internal urinary catheters; nasogastric tubes; intravenous tubes; and oxygen therapy.
- Skilled in application of nonsterile dry dressings and bandages.

**Vital Signs and Emergency Procedures**

- Skilled at recording temperature, pulse, and respiration using various methods.
- Able to pinpoint and recognize signs and symptoms of distress and provide immediate temporary intervention.

**Rehabilitative and Ambulatory Skills**

- Assist in ambulating, using rules of body mechanics.
- Transfer and turn patients for comfort and safety.
- Assist in preventing the physical complications of inactivity.
- Promote individual activities using tools and techniques for healthy daily living.

## RELEVANT WORK EXPERIENCE

01/06–03/07 Erickson Retirement Communities, Silver Springs, MD
02/06–09/06 Fairhaven Assisted Living, Sykesville, MD

## EDUCATION AND TRAINING

2006 Certified Nursing Assistant Training
Regional Occupational Program, Baltimore, MD

*Submitted by Brenda Thompson*

*This candidate landed a job from the very first resume she sent out!*

**PAULA MARTIN**
VETERINARY TECHNICIAN
pmartin@protypeltd.com

889 Westfield Street
Agawam, MA 06001
413.555.7644

*Profile reinforces the diverse clinical and soft skills she offers that relate to her objective.*

Compassionate and competent **Veterinary Technician** with 6+ years of experience assisting veterinarians in medical and surgical procedures, ranging from routine to emergency and critical care. Recognized as efficient, skilled in multitasking, and dedicated to providing prompt, courteous service. Effective communicator who enjoys working with people and animals and is able to educate owners on protecting their companion animals' health and well-being.

## PROFESSIONAL EXPERIENCE

**VETERINARY TECHNICIAN**
*Harrington Animal Clinic, Agawam, MA*                                      *2002 to Present*
   Assist 5 veterinarians in providing comprehensive veterinary care. Skilled in performing the following:

### *Medical & Surgical Procedures*
- Assist in all types of medical treatments (and with restraints), ranging from routine office examinations to critical care, emergency situations, euthanasia, and house calls.
- Set up all equipment and prep animals for surgery: shaving, intubating, inserting IV catheters, and administering intravenous/intramuscular drugs.
- Assist with surgeries, including spaying/neutering, exploratory, cystotomy, nasal scope, endoscopy, cruciate/luxating patella, abscess, declawing, and other procedures.
- Prepare and sterilize surgical packs in an autoclave; monitor anesthesia and patients' vital signs. Administer subcutaneous fluids. Perform complete dentistry.
- Accurately document anesthetic drugs used during surgery; handle post-surgical recovery: extubation, patient monitoring, and calling clients to provide follow-up/status reports.
- Prepare vaccines; refill/dispense medications; administer oral medications/vaccines under supervision and provide instructions to clients; assist with administration of chemotherapy.

### *Tests / Lab Work / Client Education*
- Conduct heartworm, Feline Leukemia, and FIV tests. Take glucose and blood (including jugular) samples. Read results of urinalysis and fecal samples.
- Perform and develop radiographs as required. Assist specialists in restraining animals during ultrasounds.
- Educate clients on diseases/preventive care, home care (post surgery, diabetic discharges, and administering subcutaneous fluids and medications), grooming, diet, geriatric care, declawing alternatives, and other aspects of animal health care.
- Groom and bathe animals, including fungal baths, lion clips, and reverse sedation according to veterinarian's instruction.

### *Front Office / Administration*
- Cross-trained to perform front office duties, including scheduling routine health exams and surgical appointments, invoicing/cashing out, providing estimates, and more. Greet clients and set up patients in exam rooms.
- Place orders for medications and various products per veterinarians' instructions. Sell products to clients.
- Utilize customized computer applications to process payments and enter patient records.
- Serve as resource to new technicians by answering questions on equipment, office, and other procedures.

## EDUCATION / TRAINING

**A.S., Veterinary Technician;** BRIARWOOD COLLEGE, Springfield, MA                           2002

**Additional Training:**
   Completed intensive on-the-job 3-month training under guidance of licensed veterinarians at Harrington Animal Clinic.

*Experience is organized within skill headings to reinforce the depth of her knowledge and capabilities to work with a wide range of animals.*

*Submitted by Louise Garver*

---

### HERNANDO R. DIAZ

11 River Street, Apt. #3C
Chicopee, MA 01020

e-mail: hernandochef@verizon.net

Cell: (413) 229-4511
Home: (413) 227-1894

*Career Focus immediately indicates to the employer the job level he aspires to.*

Career Focus: **CHEF de CUISINE**

#### PROFILE

*Profile provides highlights of his skills, experience, and achievements that build his candidacy for his job target.*

Food services professional with more than 9 years of progressive experience who enjoys experimenting with different flavors to create innovative dishes, with particular interest in Spanish, Italian, and Portuguese cuisines.

✓ Trained and worked for 2 years in positions of increasing responsibility at a restaurant rated as one of the "Top 50 Restaurants in the Pioneer Valley" by *The Valley Advocate*.

✓ Diligent and skilled at running a busy kitchen and staff while remaining calm under pressure at all times.

✓ Natural passion and flair for cooking; grew up helping to prepare ethnic family dishes blended with an ongoing interest in continuing to learn new culinary skills.

✓ Awarded a one-year scholarship to Holyoke Community College and won first place out of 14 high school teams with an authentic Spanish rice and braised beef dish in an *Entrees from Around the World Competition*.

#### PROFESSIONAL EXPERIENCE

**RIVERA RESTAURANT**, Springfield, MA                                2003–Present
**Sous Chef/Kitchen Manager**

Took on increased responsibilities to become an instrumental member in running a small, family-owned restaurant. Organize and overlook kitchen tasks that include developing prep lists, assigning duties to staff, and ensuring appropriate inventory levels. Participate in creation of seasonal menus and provide feedback on success of newly introduced dishes.

- Created a Spanish fish dish with caramelized onions, roasted tomatoes, garlic, and potatoes in a red-wine sauce that became a popular menu addition. Developed other signature entrée dishes with authentic flavors.
- Helped to prepare desserts such as tiramisu, rum bread pudding, dark chocolate cake, and a pear-almond tart that won over a following of loyal customers.

**NEVILLE BREAD COMPANY**, Agawam, MA                                2001–2003
**Assistant Kitchen Manager/Bread Baker**

Started out as an overnight baker, preparing breads and making pastries for wholesale and retail accounts. Ordered supplies and checked dry-goods stock. Later helped put together lunch menu with soups, salads, and sandwiches, and to-go suppers that included pasta dishes.

- Acted as resident expert on baking matters and taught others preparation methods.

**JORGE'S ON THE GREEN RESTAURANT**, Longmeadow, MA                                1999–2001
**Pantry Chef/Sauté Chef/Expediter**

Landed a position as the youngest member of the kitchen staff for a regionally acclaimed restaurant featured in *The Springfield Republican*, *Greater Western Mass Fine Dining*, and *The Valley Advocate*. Performed basic kitchen tasks and later helped with food preparation. Learned how to make pasta from scratch and many fine arts of gourmet Italian cooking.

- Advanced rapidly in food handling and cooking responsibilities for demonstrating enthusiasm and natural ability to master complex food-preparation techniques.

#### EDUCATION & TRAINING

*High school experience is mentioned because this shows a clear pattern of his interest in this field.*

Coursework toward an Associate degree in Culinary Arts, expected completion by 2009

Certificate in Bread Baking & Pastry, 2002

Gained basic cooking knowledge from part-time jobs as Banquet Chef and Pantry Chef while in high school

*Submitted by Jill Grindle*

*An interesting and relevant graphic draws attention to her technology, process, and equipment experience.*

## Sherry Gray

107 Pigeon Street ■ Oakville, Ontario ■ L5M 2R2
sgray789@hotmail.com

### Mechanical Engineer & Applied Sciences Student

### Technology

- ☑ CAD
- ☑ AutoCAD
- ☑ Maple
- ☑ MATLAB
- ☑ C++
- ☑ G-Code
- ☑ MS Excel

### Processes

- ☑ Design Requirements
- ☑ Design Drawings
- ☑ Design Documentation
- ☑ Database Development
- ☑ Quality Assurance

### Equipment

- ☑ Coordinates Measuring Machine (CMM)
- ☑ MasterCam
- ☑ Milling Machines
- ☑ Computer Aided Machining (CAM)

### Qualifications Summary

Energetic, highly motivated, and organized mechanical engineering student with experience in design and development. Well-rounded research and organizational skills along with outstanding communication skills. Personable, independent, and committed to producing top-quality work and results. Positive and upbeat attitude; well liked and respected by peers. Attentive to detail; excellent analytical and problem-solving skills; proven self-starter with strong communication and interpersonal skills. Eager to learn new skills and gain valuable working experience.

### Education & Training

University of Ontario, Toronto, Ontario—2005 to present
**Bachelor of Engineering and Applied Science**

Oakville District High School, Oakville, Ontario—2005
**Ontario Secondary School Diploma (O.S.S.D)**
- Graduated with Honours

**WHIMIS Safety Training—2007**

*Project and extracurricular experience sets this candidate apart from the competition.*

### Project Experience

- Led, motivated, and organized project team of 3 people in the conceptualization, design, and manufacturing of an electronic monorail system. Resulted in 4$^{th}$ place achievement in competition.

- Added value to students in the faculty and their learning experience through the revitalization of the Executive Committee and membership of the Mechanical Engineering Course Union. Promoted series of inspirational guest speakers that discussed "real-world" job opportunities and requirements for success; redesigned the website to be more informative and interactive; and facilitated meetings on a regular basis.

### Volunteer Experience

University of Ontario, Toronto, Ontario—2007
**Executive Member, Mechanical Engineering Course Union**

The Kinsmen Club of Oakville, Oakville, Ontario—2007
**Volunteer**

Hospital for Sick Children, Toronto, Ontario—2007
**Volunteer**

Canadian Cancer Society, Toronto, Ontario—2007
**Volunteer**

Submitted by Denyse Cowling

# ROBERT M. SCHULTZ

2511 Rangeline Drive, Dallas, Texas 75999 · 452-555-5555 · rmschultz@evansresumes.com

*Summary section starts off the resume with skills and areas of expertise.*

## SENIOR NETWORK MAINTENANCE / ADVISORY ENGINEER

**Customer-focused technical professional with continual recognition for technical proficiency, leadership, and performance exceeding expectations.** Characterized as a versatile networking Subject-Matter Expert with demonstrated mastery of broadband and data technologies, as well as ATM, frame relay, Cisco routing, Adtran/Alcatel equipment, and critical NOC engineering standards. *Additional expertise and success in*

- Inventory Management
- Staff Mentoring & Training
- Equipment Staging Approvals
- Project Coordination
- Technical Documentation
- Procedures Standardization
- Customer Requirements
- Shipping & Warehousing
- Equipment Troubleshooting

## TECHNICAL BACKGROUND

*Certifications and hardware/software are placed in the prime spot on page 1.*

| | |
|---|---|
| **Certifications:** | TP76300; Level 4 Installer; Cisco 8850/8250, Lucent CBX500, Alcatel/Newbridge 36170/36177/36060/7670, GX 550, and Cascade 9000 Frame Equipment |
| **Hardware:** | Adtran TA3000/HDX DSLAM; Alcatel 7300 HD, LP-UD DSLAM, 7470/7670 ATM Switches; Cisco MGX-8850 ATM Switches, 2600 Routers/1900 Switches; Spirent 3577A CopperMax ADSL Test Head; RT DSLAM DC Power Plants |
| **Software:** | Microsoft PowerPoint, Word, Excel; Remedy Ticket Systems |
| **Networking:** | TCP/IP; ATM; Frame Relay; DSL; ISDN; T-1 Circuits; Network Protocol Analyzers |

## PROFESSIONAL EXPERIENCE

**SUPERIOR TECHNICAL SOLUTIONS, INC. (MBC)**      1986–Present

### Senior Manager Maintenance Engineer, Richardson, TX, 2005–Present

Selected to fill elite technical advisory role, providing 24×7 network engineering services with oversight of 62 MBC central offices and 13-state area. Serve as Tier 2 support expert and first line of resolution for sophisticated network equipment preparation, testing, and installation. Collaborate with Tier 2 and 3 support groups, regional Subject-Matter Experts, Engineering, telephone companies, and Network Operation/Data Operation Center staff to deliver reliable network functionality. Oversee and monitor staging testing to ensure appropriate supplier performance and consistent service quality. Mentor and train maintenance engineers.

*Selected Accomplishments:*

- Supported 5,000 customers per switch, with responsibility for switches of up to 450G and $1.4M in value.
- Exceeded or met all Ready for Service dates, working closely with Implementation Engineering, Project Management, vendors, and installation teams.
- Authorized equipment readiness with final word on testing verifications, serving as expert resource instrumental in preserving installation integrity.
- Verified workaround solutions implementation and managed staff coordination to audit fulfillment of high-profile customer requirements.
- Tested Alcatel, Adtran, RPATS, AI/CODCN platforms, and fiber, DDP panel, and FOT panel equipment. Tuned and tested ATM, frame relay, LAN/WAN, Newbridge, TCP/IP, DSL, and Cisco equipment/protocols.

### Senior Maintenance Engineer, Richardson, TX, 2005–2007

Served as technical lead charged with 24×7 technical support, new service hardware and software deployment, and maintenance services for data and broadband technologies including ADSL, frame relay, ATM, and routing. Key functions included supporting field engineers in network system diagnostics, on-site technical assistance, and project management for enhancements and installations.

*Continued…*

*Submitted by Laura Smith-Proulx*

## ROBERT M. SCHULTZ                                        PAGE TWO

*Selected Accomplishments:*

- Ensured 100% system availability with timely problem resolution, network problem troubleshooting, and implementation of emergency procedures.
- Worked with regional Subject-Matter Experts to coordinate and implement all new products, FOAs, Engineering Complaints, Maintenance Engineering Flashes, and Product Change Notifications.
- Authored Maintenance Engineering Test & Acceptance procedures for Alcatel 7300 LP-UD DSLAM platform.
- Conducted technical reviews to identify and correct vulnerabilities and deviations from corporate standards.

### Maintenance Engineer / Manager Technical Support, Irving, TX, 2003–2005

Promoted to oversee ATM switch installations, as well as preparation for shipping readiness, in close collaboration with Cisco, Alcatel, and Lucent. Served as main regional point of contact. Staged switches according to engineering requests, with full testing to meet industry standards, and inventoried components while maintaining equipment database. Coordinated deliveries with site management, documenting movement and tracking warehouse inventory. Provided monthly hardware failure rate reporting.

*Selected Accomplishments:*

- Supported department as senior Subject-Matter Expert in Alcatel, Cisco, 7670 Multi-Shelf system, and all computer-related issues.
- Ensured timely replacement of defective equipment, initiating Return Material Authorizations with vendors.
- Supplied Tier 1 technical support to Dallas NOC Transport Technology Center, with TTC ISO 9000 team role critical to turn up, provisioning, maintenance, and upgrade process creation.
- Met 100% of project deadlines, working with diverse array of vendor equipment and keeping Methods of Procedures up-to-date.

### System Technician, McKinney, TX, 1986–2003

Installed all special circuits in product line, including OC48 rings, and installed vast array of technologies, including fiber. Detailed crew responsibilities, training and mentoring project technicians. Repaired and implemented DSL equipment on customer premises, and installed and corrected flaws in 911, ARM, OCS, and LAN equipment.

*Previous Experience:* **System Technician, MAJOR TELEPHONE COMPANY, Dallas, TX**

## EDUCATION & PROFESSIONAL DEVELOPMENT

*General Studies* ◆ RICHLAND COLLEGE, Richardson, TX

*A good strategy for presenting some college without a degree.*

*Professional Training:*

- Fiber Optics
- ATM Newbridge
- CCNA Boot Camp
- Disaster Recovery
- Hazard Recognition
- ISDN Installation & Maintenance
- Data Communications Technology
- SONET Overview
- Digital Synchronization
- Ethics in the Workplace
- Planning and Organizing
- Digital Circuit Technology
- Principles of Digital Transmission
- Network Data Link Lab and Protocols

## CIVIC AFFILIATIONS

*Certification Candidate and Member,* **Community Emergency Response Team (CERT)**

*Resume highlights skills and experiences that were specifically mentioned in the job posting.*

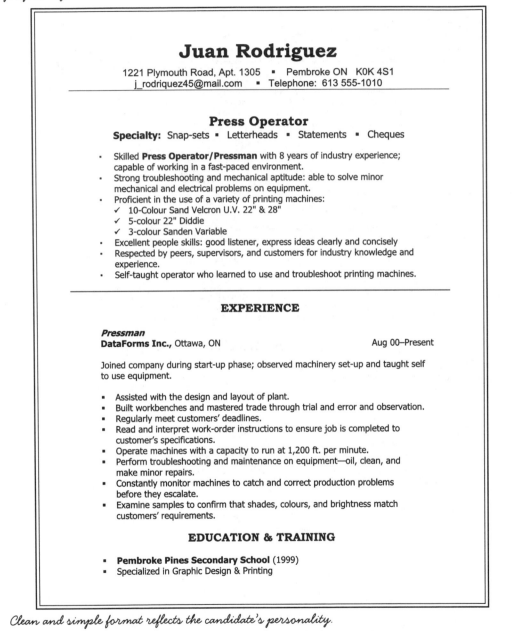

# Juan Rodriguez

1221 Plymouth Road, Apt. 1305  ▪  Pembroke ON  K0K 4S1
j_rodriquez45@mail.com  ▪  Telephone: 613 555-1010

## Press Operator

**Specialty:** Snap-sets ▪ Letterheads ▪ Statements ▪ Cheques

- Skilled **Press Operator/Pressman** with 8 years of industry experience; capable of working in a fast-paced environment.
- Strong troubleshooting and mechanical aptitude: able to solve minor mechanical and electrical problems on equipment.
- Proficient in the use of a variety of printing machines:
  - ✓ 10-Colour Sand Velcron U.V. 22" & 28"
  - ✓ 5-colour 22" Diddie
  - ✓ 3-colour Sanden Variable
- Excellent people skills: good listener, express ideas clearly and concisely
- Respected by peers, supervisors, and customers for industry knowledge and experience.
- Self-taught operator who learned to use and troubleshoot printing machines.

## EXPERIENCE

**_Pressman_**
**DataForms Inc.,** Ottawa, ON                          Aug 00–Present

Joined company during start-up phase; observed machinery set-up and taught self to use equipment.

- Assisted with the design and layout of plant.
- Built workbenches and mastered trade through trial and error and observation.
- Regularly meet customers' deadlines.
- Read and interpret work-order instructions to ensure job is completed to customer's specifications.
- Operate machines with a capacity to run at 1,200 ft. per minute.
- Perform troubleshooting and maintenance on equipment—oil, clean, and make minor repairs.
- Constantly monitor machines to catch and correct production problems before they escalate.
- Examine samples to confirm that shades, colours, and brightness match customers' requirements.

## EDUCATION & TRAINING

- **Pembroke Pines Secondary School** (1999)
- Specialized in Graphic Design & Printing

*Clean and simple format reflects the candidate's personality.*

*Submitted by Daisy Wright*

# Dan T. Harper

265 Charlotte Street, Asheville, NC 28801
(828) 254-7893 *Home,* (828) 230-1421 *Cell*

## Heavy Equipment Operator

*"I could pick an egg up off the ground and not break it."*

*Quote from the candidate himself speaks to his high skill level.*

**PROFILE**

DEPENDABLE, PATIENT HARD-WORKER with 32 years of experience in aggregate business operating **Drag Line** (9 years), **988 Loader** (7 years), **Hydraulic Shovel** (5 years), **Crane** (3 years), **Bulldozer** (3 years), **Trackhoe** (3 years), **Off-Road Truck** (2 years), and **Jaw Crusher** (1 year). Experience on computerized equipment.

**SUMMARY OF STRENGTHS**

*Summary shows exactly how he contributes to company profits.*

- At work 30 minutes early *always.*
- Willing to stay as long as it takes to get the job done.
- *Never* miss work.
- Willing to do whatever I'm asked.
- Machine-friendly—easy on equipment; keep it well maintained and clean. Often put on older equipment because I don't tear it up.
- Excellent record for safety of life and equipment.
- Friendly and even-tempered; get along very well with co-workers.
- Keep production as high as possible.
- Know the relationship to company bottom line.

**WORK HISTORY**

*Loyal and loved by his company, Dan has worked for the same company his entire career.*

BOONE GRAVEL—Asheville, NC                    1977–Present
*Portable plant, a subsidiary of RA Julius Industries, Mooreville, NC*

- Use crane to tear down rock crusher, conveyor belts, bends, loaders, and backhoes; transport plant to where it is needed and put it back up, as often as three times a year.
- Have worked on large and small projects all over North Carolina in all kinds of weather, including 7 degrees below zero.
- Projects include road and interstate highway construction (including pulling river stone out of rivers, crushing, and transporting to highway site), opening up new quarries (clearing land, removing overburden), and commercial construction.
- Train operators on trackhoe, loader, and off-road truck on safety and operation.

**EDUCATION**

**ADDITIONAL TRAINING**

City High School, Owensville, NC
High School Diploma, 1977

*Hundreds of hours of training:* North Carolina Safety courses (1-day annual refresher training).

*Submitted by Dayna Feist*

# KEN SANBORN

97 Moose Trail Path ▪ P.O. Box 1020 ▪ Soldotna, AK 99660
H: (907) 260-5987 ▪ C: (907) 631-2701 ▪ sanbornhunts@msn.com

**PROFILE** *Profile section clearly notes which jobs he is interested in.*

Industrious and dependable professional with 2 years of oil field experience seeking position as a Driver, Technician, Roustabout, or Expediter. Safety conscious with a QHSE passport. Accustomed to working long hours with demanding schedules in harsh climates, and under challenging physical and mental conditions. Solid employment references, strong work ethic, and levelheaded. **Qualifications include**

► Valid Class A CDL with HazMat, Tanker, Combo, and Air Brake endorsements and have a perfect driving record. Current N.S.T.C., Hazwoper and H2S.

► 100% drug free, on random drug testing with Worksafe through the U.S. Coast Guard.

► No safety incidents during 2 years on the slope; traveled by helicopter daily in one work hitch.

► Certified in first aid and CPR with valid endorsements.

► Hold a 100 Ton Masters License from the U.S. Coast Guard and can operate other heavy equipment, including bulldozers, loaders, and backhoes.

► Knowledgeable about welding and can quickly learn new technical/mechanical skills.

**HIGHLIGHTS OF WORK EXPERIENCE** *Highlights demonstrate his endurance, physical strength, and ability to work under extreme conditions in harsh climates.*

▪ Completed 12-week hitches on the slope as both a Straw Boss and Helper in the past 2 years.

▪ Run a halibut charter service during the summers, logging 12–16 hours a day, 7 days a week.

▪ Currently serve as a Bear Guard and Wildlife Specialist and as a Big Game Guide.

▪ Raised and worked on family cattle ranch, performing tasks requiring physical strength and stamina.

**EMPLOYMENT HISTORY**

| | |
|---|---|
| MOUNTAIN CAT ENTERPRISES, Helena, MN<br>**Bear Guard and Wildlife Specialist** | 2007 to Present |
| SCHLUTZ OILFIELD SERVICES, Fairbanks, AK<br>**Straw Boss** | 2007 |
| ENERGY SERVICES CONTRACTORS, Anchorage, AK<br>**Straw Boss and Helper** | 2006 |
| DEEP WATER FISHING, Seward, AK<br>**Charter Operator** | 2001 to Present |
| GREATER SOLDOTNA ALASKAN GUIDE SERVICES, Inc., Soldotna, AK<br>**Big Game Guide** | 1999 to Present |
| HALIBUT RUN CHARTERS, Juneau, AK<br>**Deckhand** | 2000 |
| BIG BLUE WATERS CHARTERS, Ninilchik, AK<br>**Deckhand** | 1999 |
| D-R-J RANCH, La Paz, CA<br>**Ranch Hand** | 1994 to 1999 |

*Because of his diverse work history, often with short-term jobs, a functional format worked best for this candidate.*

*Submitted by Jill Grindle*

*The Professional Profile captures some of her interpersonal/ transferable skills.*

# Susan R. Richards
6344 West View Road
Williamsport, MD 21795
(301) 555-5763

## Professional Profile

**Production** and **assembly worker** with more than 20 years of manufacturing and pharmaceutical laboratory experience. Work independently in assembling detailed circuit boards and sensors while remaining focused on quality and productivity. Experience working with chemicals to mix materials and reagents. Able to meet tight production deadlines by anticipating needs. Maintain good working relationships with co-workers and managers. Possess basic computer skills.

## Assembly Experience

*Breaks out two possible career paths (assembly and laboratory) into separate functional sections.*

**Senior Assembler, Mole Productions,** Martinsburg, WV                          1998–2008
- Built, tested, potted, and finished sensors for flow meters used by domestic and international waste and clean water treatment facilities.

**Mechanical Assembler, Smith Electronics,** Inwood, WV                          1975–1988
- Assembled printed circuit boards for communications equipment.

### Skills Set

- Used a variety of hand tools and equipment, including drills, sanders, Dremels, band saws, lathes, soldering guns, wiring cutting, and hot stamp machines.
- Mixed chemicals and poured molds for polyurethane and ceramic sensors, following written specifications.
- Followed blueprints and parts list to ensure correct assembly.
- Consistently adhered to procedures and guidelines established by ISO 9000 and Lean Manufacturing principles.

## Laboratory Experience

**Laboratory Technician, USDA,** Kearneysville, WV                          1997–1998
- Provided support and materials for research laboratories.

**Senior Laboratory Assistant, Hardin Labs,** Winchester, VA                          1994–1997
- Worked as a member of the support group assisting with manufacturing vaccine.

**Veterans Hospital,** Martinsburg, WV                          1989–1994
- Worked on a government contract supporting various research laboratories.

### Skill Sets

- Wrapped and sterilized glassware for laboratory use.
- Operated autoclaves, dryers, and washers.
- Mixed chemicals to make media and reagents.
- Cleaned and maintained work area to cGMP (current good manufacturing practices) and GLP (good laboratory practices) standards.

## Education

Currently pursuing GED, Washington County Board of Education, Maryland

*Submitted by Norine Dagliano*

*An example of a combination format resume.*

# DONALD JACOBS

## Confidential Security Clearance

1200 Peninsula Square
Cleveland, Ohio 44122

Home: (216) 333-1234
djacobs01@yahoo.com

A dedicated Electronics Technician with more than ten years of hands-on experience, with the ability to lead and motivate a diverse crew. Experienced in the utilization of creative problem-solving and solution techniques, while exuding decisive and confident decision-making abilities. Skilled in information systems management, with emphasis in program management, and internal control procedures.

*Skills are detailed up front.*

- *Computer Software*—Knowledgeable in MS Word and Excel. Understand C program language and able to perform some software program modifications.
- *Operator Mechanic*—Work closely with engineering personnel to assist in troubleshooting software and hardware using electronic schematics and technical procedures.
- *Quality Assurance*—Write quality reports for non-conformances and repairs conducted.
- *Test Planning*—Plan test environment using required equipment and documentation. Implement test plan with little or no supervision.
- *Troubleshoot and Repair*—Experience with troubleshooting mechanical, electrical, and electronic systems.

*Chronological work experience is listed later.*

# EXPERIENCE

**AVTRON MANUFACTURING., Independence, OH (2006–Present)**
**Field Service Engineer**
Primary responsibilities include writing service orders, distributing new technical bulletins to the site, training on maintenance practices and scanner operations, coordinating troubleshooting/maintenance with other vendor companies when needed, and assisting technical support group when special testing is being conducted.

**COX COMMUNICATIONS, Cleveland, OH (1998–2006)**
**Operator Mechanic**
Responsibilities include daily inspection of all mechanical, electrical, and electronic equipment; chemical analysis of all water systems; performed preventative maintenance and repairs on plant equipment; and wrote work orders for discrepancies.

**LINCOLN ELECTRIC, Cleveland, OH (1997–1998)**
**Mechanical Design Manufacturing Engineer**
Responsibilities included designing the in-house manufacturing equipment. Conceptualized equipment and tested the feasibility of the designs. Applied detailed analysis, design, fabrication, installation, debugging techniques, validation, and documentation. Used mechanical engineering theory and practice toward the design of all equipment.

*Submitted by Brenda Thompson*

# Donald Jacobs                                    Page –2–

UNITED STATES NAVY, Norfolk, VA (1994–1997)
**Nuclear Electronics Technician Second Class**
Completed more than 4,000 hours of reactor operating time and more than 7,000 hours of logged maintenance and troubleshooting of electronic and microprocessor-based equipment. Duties included repair and maintenance technician, departmental technical librarian, and repair section supervisor of the ship's calibration lab.

# EDUCATION

**Cleveland State University, Cleveland, OH (1997–2003)**
Major: Electrical Engineering
Credits: 64 college semester credits with an overall GPA of 3.68.

NAVY NUCLEAR POWER SCHOOL, Charleston, NC (1993–1994)
- Training consisted of a 24-week course in science and technology designed to provide theoretical background knowledge of nuclear power. It is presumed each officer has successfully completed at least one year of college-level physics and calculus, including integral calculus.

NAVY ELECTRONICS TECHNICIAN SCHOOL, Orlando, FL (1992–1993)
Certification: Electronics Technician
- A seven-month course concentrating on electricity and electronics, communications systems, digital logic, microprocessor-based equipment, and radar.
- Training consisted of the study of how to interpret schematic diagrams and use appropriate test equipment as well as hands-on experience on how to isolate and correct faults in both military and civilian electronic equipment.

*A two-column format allows for easy review of his qualifications.*

*The profile positions him for the director level in terms of management, leadership, and administration.*

# PETER BARISHNOVIC

678 MOUNTAIN VIEW ROAD
SEATTLE, WASHINGTON 98101
206.555.5877
PETERB@PROTYPELTD.COM

## EXPERTISE

Demonstrated proficiency in the development of unique circus-arts techniques as well as educational program design, development, and management.

## TECHNICAL SKILLS

International circus arts performer adept in juggling, balancing, hat manipulation, acrobatics, aerial acrobatics, trapeze, wire walking, teeterboard, rolling globe, unicycle, clowning, and magic.

## EDUCATION

School for Ballet and Circus Arts, Volgograd, Russia

Completed degree program in Classical Ballet, specializing in Acrobatic Skills

## AFFILIATIONS

Actors' Guild of Variety Artists

## DUAL CITIZENSHIP

United States
Russian

## LANGUAGE FLUENCY

English
Russian
French
Spanish

## INTERNATIONAL CIRCUS ARTS DIRECTOR

**CREATOR, INSTRUCTOR, AND DIRECTOR OF CIRCUS-ARTS PROGRAMS IN EDUCATIONAL INSTITUTIONS AND CORPORATE ENVIRONMENTS WORLDWIDE.**

➤ Innovator of teaching methodology to maximize students' potential, strengths, and self-confidence.

➤ Talented trainer and coach who has developed students of all ages.

➤ Award-winning member of the Volzisky Troupe performing worldwide with the Brothers Benson Circus.

➤ Invited as guest instructor and consultant at the renowned International Clown College to train future performers.

*The Accomplishments section reinforces the depth of his competencies.*

## ACCOMPLISHMENTS

• Initiated and expanded circus-arts education program at Washington University that doubled revenues in just 2 years.

• Designed workshops, trained staff, and coordinated circus-arts program for major corporations throughout the world.

• Instructed and developed numerous students who achieved success as celebrated performers in international circus programs.

• Created and performed peerless juggling acts, including "Unsupported Ladder" and Musical Drum Juggling, with internationally acclaimed Volzhskiy Troupe.

• Directed development of the successful Big Top circus program, an annual event for the past 15 years.

• Multiple award winner for "Best Performing Act" in the European World Circus Competition and Cirque Atarré.

## PROFESSIONAL EXPERIENCE

WASHINGTON UNIVERSITY • Seattle, Washington • 1991 to present
**Assistant Director of Circus-Arts Program**

Design and implement circus-arts instructional programs at the university. Recruit, supervise, and train instructors, building department from a staff of 3 to 10. Plan and manage program's operating budget. Coordinate instruction schedule and related activities; maintain and purchase equipment. Initiated design and implementation of effective safety standards for program.

SCHOOL FOR BALLET AND CIRCUS ARTS • Volgograd, Russia • 1982 to 1991
**Circus Instructor**

Created and instructed circus-arts program for students ranging from 7 to 18 years old. Developed and advanced the careers of numerous students who subsequently performed internationally.

**CONSULTING EXPERIENCE:** As consultant, provide expertise in the design and presentation of circus-arts workshops. Develop in-house trainers in creating circus productions to develop individual skills and promote teamwork (1991 to present).

**PRIOR PERFORMING EXPERIENCE:** International circus arts performer with the Volzhskiy Troupe, specializing in unique acrobatic/juggling acts.

*Submitted by Louise Garver*

© JIST Publishing

## KAREN B. EVERSLEY

9145 Ellicott Court, Manassas, VA 20111
Residence: 703-487-8541 ◊ Cellular: 703-458-7478 ◊ E-mail: keversley@yahoo.com

### SENIOR EDITOR / WRITER

#### QUALIFICATIONS PROFILE

☐ **Internal & External Communications:** Ten-plus years of experience creating compelling articles, marketing materials, promotional documents, and trade publications; recent experience in Web content / online editing.

☐ **Publications:** Prolific author with wide cross-section of articles and feature stories published in magazines, Web sites, and industry journals.

☐ **Web Portfolio:** Visually appealing, interactive presentation of written work, including cutting-edge stories, news features and special projects at *www.kareneversley.net*.       *Draws attention to a Web portfolio the*

☐ **Team Player:** Adept at building effective working relationships with content programmers, photo editors,      *candidate*
   promotion managers, and publishing staff.                                                              *created.*

☐ **Technical Skills:** Mac, PC, Word, WordPerfect, QuarkXPress, Photoshop, Illustrator, Dreamweaver, Flash, Adobe Photoshop for Newspapers, and Avid Xpress Pro.

*Education is listed early because*
*she has a new Master's*            #### EDUCATION & CERTIFICATIONS
*degree relevant*   **MA in Interactive Journalism**—American University, Washington, DC (2008)
*to her job target.*   **BA in Public Communication**—State University of New York College at Buffalo, NY (1996)
                         Federal Communications Commission (FCC) License (1991)

*Hands-on experience and academic training in*

| | | | |
|---|---|---|---|
| • Advanced Editing | • Article/Feature Writing | • Public Speaking | • Print Media |
| • Marketing Materials | • Digital Storytelling | • Multimedia Reporting | • Newsletter Creation |
| • Press Releases | • Brochures | • In-depth Journalism | • Web Studio |
| • Layout & Design | • Web Content Creation | • Proofreading | • Online Publications |
| • Headline Writing | • Online Editing | • Promotional Copy | • Newspapers/Magazines |

#### PROFESSIONAL EXPERIENCE

**Editor,** America Online, Dulles, VA (2007 to present)

▪ Serve as copy editor for high-traffic interactive company Web site with approximately 20 million paid subscribers and hits from 35 million visitors daily.

▪ Revise and edit "raw" script content into concise, audience-appropriate copy for major topics and events, including health, entertainment, commerce, and movies.

▪ Attend production and bimonthly network meetings to discuss upcoming promotions and special events; contribute unique story ideas to boost Web site readership.

▪ Support production managers to ensure smooth transition in Web content display and monitor deadlines.

**Editor,** American Newspaper Association, Vienna, VA (2005 to 2007)

▪ Translated broad information from wide variety of sources, including field experts and phone/e-mail questionnaires into engaging feature articles for bimonthly trade publication, *Newspaper Marketing*, reaching 5,000+ readers.

▪ Compiled and reviewed submissions from freelancers, colleagues, and other contributors to create editorial calendar; facilitated blue line, page count, and final print production.

▪ Played key role in the upgrade and redesign of magazine from layout, color selections, and font size; worked closely with senior vice president and creative services department.

*Submitted by Abby Locke*                                          *(continued)*

*(continued)*

*Positions on page 2 out-
line only the writing
parts of these jobs.*

KAREN B. EVERSLEY                                                    PAGE TWO

### PROFESSIONAL EXPERIENCE, continued

**Marketing Coordinator,** A+ Marketing Solutions, Fairfax, VA (2003 to 2005)

- Authored profile stories, "how-to," and trend feature pieces for international industry publications, *les nouvelles, esthetiques,* and *DERMASCOPE.*
- Developed full range of marketing and publicity documents—media pitch letters, press releases, brochures, banners, and direct mail; wrote copy for special events.

**Communications/Events Director,** Harpers Golf & Country Club, Sterling, VA (2001 to 2003)

- Managed corporate communications for community of more than 1,500 residents and club members.
- Launched monthly newsletter, *The Harpers Horn,* and grew publication from 4-page pamphlet to large size, 24-page color publication; enhanced publication with graphics and encouraged advertisements from local businesses.
- Contributed and wrote main articles; edited entire publication and oversaw entire print production process.

**Public Affairs Assistant,** Northern Virginia Association of Realtors, Fairfax, VA (1999 to 2000)

- Researched current industry events and issues, conducted interviews, and wrote relevant articles for monthly trade publication, *Realtor Keys,* which served more than 13,000 regional Realtors.

**Corporate Communications Assistant,** Fannie Mae, Washington, DC (1996 to 1999)

### AFFILIATIONS & MEMBERSHIPS

The Online News Association
American Writers Association

Additional portfolio of writing samples available upon request.

# KAREN B. EVERSLEY

9145 Ellicott Court, Manassas, VA 20111
Residence: 703-487-8541 ◊ Cellular: 703-458-7478 ◊ E-mail: keversley@yahoo.com

—Resume Addendum—

## ONLINE ARTICLES / PRINT PUBLICATIONS

*The resume addendum serves as a central place for listing her writing accomplishments and helps to dispel any perception that she is an underexperienced editor.*

### THE AMERICAN OBSERVER:

- House Bill, FBI Target Gang Violence
- Dentists Close Your Eyes
- Penny Pinching Turns Pastime

### YOGA PARADISE:

- The Heavenly Stretch

### NEWSPAPER MARKETING:

- Using Mobile Technology to Reach Young Readers, an International Perspective
- Are You Missing Out? The Rapidly Growing Hispanic Community
- Transformation of Advertising, Knowing and Understanding Your Competitor's Future
- Halt Declining Readership
- Audio and Video Streaming, Advanced Features Sure to Attract New Readers and Advertisers (cover story)

### DERMASCOPE:

- Beat the Summer Slump
- Haircare 101

### LES NOUVELLES ESTHETIQUES:

- A Little Advice, One Owner's Business Plan

### CELEBRITY CUTS:

- Ellie.Ellie Salon, Star Treatment

### M WOMAN:

- Wife Rights

### THE NVAR UPDATE:

- Photo spread with captions
- How to Profit from International Real Estate (cover story)
- How to Become a Real Estate Mentor (sidebar)

*Candidate was leaving the navy and wanted to apply his skills in maintenance, materials, and operations management in the private sector.*

## DAVID A. JONES

85 Ellington Street • Groton, CT 06098 • (203) 437-6779 • daj39@aol.com

### MAINTENANCE / MATERIALS / OPERATIONS MANAGEMENT
#### Transportation ~ Shipping Industry

*"David is an exceptional planner, organizer and innovative problem solver who has succeeded where others have failed ... he has exceptional operations expertise, strong leadership skills, and sound judgment."*

—Bertrand Fisher
Commanding Officer

**Management Professional offering 15 years of experience in electronics equipment maintenance, materials, operations, and security.**

- Promoted through increasingly responsible technical and supervisory positions based on expertise, demonstrated initiative, and contributions to operational efficiency.
- Effective trainer who develops and leads staff to peak performance.
- Expert in navigation and ship-handling operations and systems.
- Recipient of 15 achievement, commendation, and distinguished service awards throughout naval career.

### RELEVANT EXPERIENCE & ACCOMPLISHMENTS

**Maintenance & Materials Management**
- Improved operations through aggressive materials improvement and equipment refurbishment programs that were subsequently instituted throughout the organization.
- Supervised electronics technicians in maintenance/repair of various communications, radar, and other electronics systems, ensuring peak efficiency and reliability.
- Led implementation of efficient purchasing and JIT inventory management system.
- Oversaw hazardous cargo certification requirements, equipment maintenance, and safety deadlines.

**Operations Management**
- Managed the daily planning, coordination, and supervision of 45 staff members, effectively ensuring stringent compliance with vessel safety standards.
- Developed and executed detailed operational review plans for command administrative inspection, resulting in timely problem identification and corrective actions.
- Recognized for instrumental role in achieving "excellent" ratings in all areas during plant inspections.

**Staff Training & Management**
- Trained more than 500 military and civilian personnel in maintenance procedures, navigation, firefighting, damage control, security, and other areas.
- Turned around an underperforming division to rank #1 in productivity by improving the training curriculum.

### CAREER HISTORY

United States Navy • 1991 to Present
Patrol Boat Captain • 1989 to 1990; Legal & Administrative Officer • 1990 to 1991
Assistant Operations & Electronics Material Officer • 1988 to 1990

### EDUCATION

B.E., Electrical Engineering, Connecticut College • New London, CT
Additional Training: Electronics Material Management Training Program
Boat Group Management Training Program, Military Justice Legal Training Program

*His actual job titles are listed under Career History to deemphasize them while translating his relevant experience and accomplishments into three skill sections to help the reader understand his background.*

*Submitted by Louise Garver*

*This retiring army colonel had completed a successful command tour in Iraq and now was assigned to a staff leadership position in anticipation of his retirement.*

### ARTHUR ANDERSON, JR.
2 Custer Avenue
Fort Riley, KS 66442
Home: 785-706-3100
e-mail: arthuranderson1@yahoo.com

#### OBJECTIVE

A management position in operations or logistics in the retail industry.

#### SUMMARY OF QUALIFICATIONS

Twenty-four years of experience in leadership, command, and senior staff positions in medium and large complex organizations. Versatile, dynamic leader and high achiever who communicated positively and effectively with people at all levels of an organization. Demonstrated record of success in creating highly effective teams, logistics management, strategic planning, increasing efficiency, and establishing strong organizational systems.

- **Logistics Distribution**
- **Leadership**
- **Strategic Planning**
- **Organizational Management**
- **Team Building**
- **Training**

#### ORGANIZATIONAL MANAGEMENT

Supervised all aspects of a large, complex organization of 6,000 personnel. Efficiently executed an annual budget of $42M. Implemented aggressive management controls and cost-reduction initiatives that resulted in the savings of an average of $1M per quarter. Maintained and operated facilities, complex equipment, and vehicles with a total value in excess of $500M. Planned, prepared, and executed organizational oversight for task forces and peace support rotations. Used an active and positive After Action Report process to ensure task forces knew what happened, why it happened, and how they could fix problems.

*Writer chose to emphasize his skills in a functional format.*

#### TRAINING

Created an integrated team training approach to teach, coach, and mentor leaders of medium-sized organizations in all aspects of leadership and training. Prepared them to deploy to contingency locations to assist units as they complete preparations for war or peace. Created an environment where soldiers could focus on training to learn and gain confidence in their war-fighting skills while ensuring soldier and family readiness.

#### LEADERSHIP

Led and commanded small, medium, and large organizations of up to 6,000 personnel. Commanded a large multiservice organizational team of 6,000 personnel in Iraq and a medium organization of 1,000 in Bosnia. Coordinated the efforts and activities of army units, international humanitarian organizations, and nongovernmental agencies. Cited by General Officers for "always leading my soldiers from the front and never asking them to do anything I would not do myself" and "moving my command without regard for personal danger to ensure it was at the decisive point of the battle, at the right time."

*Submitted by James Walker*

(continued)

*(continued)*

**ARTHUR ANDERSON, JR.**

### LOGISTICS DISTRIBUTION AND MANAGEMENT

Created and maintained a complex logistics distribution network with thousands of lines of supply both in the United States and Iraq. Aggressive leadership and planning ensured on-time delivery and minimal lag time. Implemented highly effective systematic maintenance procedures and user responsibilities in the supply warehouse, resulting in increased readiness rates and better asset visibility.

### STRATEGIC PLANNING

Helped develop and execute the Fort Riley strategic training and logistics plans. Negotiated with numerous Iraqi, U.S. governmental officials, and other foreign nationals in planning and implementing a regional strategy for reconstruction. Responsible for administering $23.5 million in Iraqi reconstruction money. Effectively managed combat and civil affairs operations to support local governance initiatives as well as training for emerging Iraqi Security Forces.

### TEAM BUILDING

Planned, funded, and constructed a series of bases in Iraq exceeding $20M. Teamed with the Corps of Engineers, international contractors, and organizational units to complete the projects efficiently and effectively. Fostered a sense of cooperation and trust with rotational units that fed on my infectious enthusiasm and passion for learning how to lead, fight, and win. Created a command climate that was professional, healthy, stimulating, and extremely supportive for young officers and junior leaders.

### EMPLOYMENT HISTORY

- Director for Operations and Logistics, U.S. Army, Fort Riley, KS, November 2006–Present
- Commander, U.S. Army, Iraq and Fort Riley, KS, June 2005–October 2006
- Commander, U.S. Army, Fort Carson, CO, June 2004–May 2005
- Training Director, U.S. Army, Heidelberg, Germany, June 2002–June 2003
- Commander, U.S. Army, Bosnia and Fort Bragg, NC, May 2000–May 2002

### EDUCATION

- Graduate, Military Strategic Studies, 1 year, U.S. Army War College, Carlisle, PA
- Master of Science, Strategy, U.S. Army War College, Carlisle Barracks, PA
- Master of Arts, History, Temple University, Philadelphia, PA
- Bachelor of Science, Engineering, United States Military Academy, West Point, NY

# MARC SCHMIDT

8709 Bay Vista, Venice, Florida 34668
727-815-1307

MSchmidt@hotmail.com
Cell 727-243-5800

## PROFILE

**General Manager/CEO** with more than 25 years of extensive experience in the automotive and recreational vehicle field. Confident, aggressive, and responsible leader who motivates others and is results-oriented.

Consistent track record of improving bottom line and profitability through hands-on management of employees, marketing, service, parts, and inventory for new and used wholesale and retail vehicle sales. Independent turnaround specialist who can do it all. Laser focus on financial statements and profit-and-loss results.

Seeking business owner who needs a GM/GSM/CEO to take full responsibility for success. Must have the authority to bring about changes needed to improve the service and delivery process, and be able to hold employees accountable.

## PROFESSIONAL EXPERIENCE

### SALES MANAGER
LEISURE DAYS RV                    2005–2008    Orlando, Florida

**Challenge:** Succeed at selling recreational vehicles despite no prior knowledge of the business and add industry knowledge of this booming industry to portfolio of skills.

**Results:**
- Year 1: Selected as "Rookie of the Year"; achieved 100% of goal.
- Year 2: Achieved "Top 20" status within company.
- Year 3: "Top 10"; ranked #2 YTD 2006 of 158 salespeople.
- Currently travel with the American Coach travel team and as a member of the Leisure Days exclusive Crown Club team.
- Ranked as the #2 Fleetwood and the #2 American Coach salesperson.

### GENERAL MANAGER/PARTNER
VEHICLE MAX DEPOT                  2001–2005    Orlando, Florida

**Challenge:** Build startup used-car dealership with partner as an interim business venture.

**Results:**
- Built business from scratch to profitable level.
- Negotiated licensing and location contracts, bought vehicles, and started up business.
- Managed budget, purchasing, sales, inventory, service, and parts.
- Hired, trained, and managed employees.

*Summary is written in a direct style and indicates that he prefers autonomy in his work.*

*Resume uses a dramatic format of "Challenge" and "Results" because Marc is a problem-solver and has numbers and results to back him up.*

*(continued)*

## MARC SCHMIDT, PAGE 2

### CEO/DEALER/GENERAL MANAGER
SCHMIDT CHEVROLET                          1996–2001    Bentley, Georgia

*Challenge:* Increase dealership sales and profitability. Eventually secured financing and bought out dealership in 1998.

*Results:*
- Took dealership from $20K/month loss to $77K/month profit within 1 year.
- Hired, trained, and managed 40 employees.
- Handled all day-to-day operations, including service, parts, sales, inventory, accounting, body shop, and both new and used vehicle departments.
- Wrote, produced, and appeared in all TV advertising and managed all marketing efforts.
- Sold dealership in 2001 after significant area economic depression: 3 major manufacturing facilities closed and several natural disasters devastated the agricultural industry.

### GENERAL MANAGER
ROGER COPELAND HYUNDAI                      1994–1996    Houston, Texas

*Challenge:* Offered partnership and percentage of future profits to turn around this dealership that was losing money.

*Results:*
- Turned business around within 6 months. Changed from a loss of $125K/month to profitable venture.
- Hired, trained, and managed 45 employees.
- Created, wrote, and directed TV advertising and ran all marketing efforts.
- Ran all business operations, including inventory, P/L, hiring and firing, and factory communications.

### GENERAL SALES MANAGER / SALES MANAGER / SALES REPRESENTATIVE
RAYMOND AMC/JEEP                            1991–1994    Stuart, Florida

*Challenge:* Hired to help this struggling dealership that needed sales and service turned around.

*Results:*
- Increased sales from 8 sales a month to 33 sales per month.
- Hired, trained, and managed 8 employees.
- Promoted to Sales Manager and then to General Sales Manager. The owner functioned as General Manager, so there was no more upward mobility.

### AVIONICS ELECTRICIAN AND PLANE CAPTAIN
UNITED STATES MARINE CORPS

Maintained aircraft and worked with pilots training for air-to-ground control for Marine and Navy personnel.

*There are enough results that the employer will probably not notice that the "Education" section is omitted.*

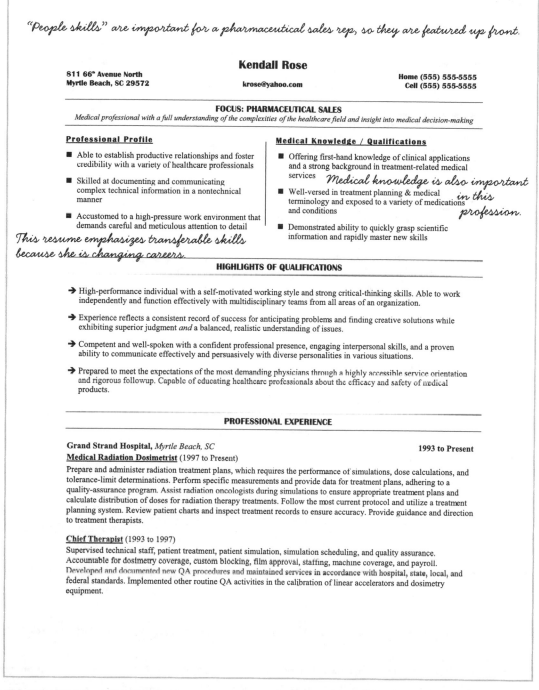

*"People skills" are important for a pharmaceutical sales rep, so they are featured up front.*

## Kendall Rose

811 66ᵃ Avenue North
Myrtle Beach, SC 29572

krose@yahoo.com

Home (555) 555-5555
Cell (555) 555-5555

### FOCUS: PHARMACEUTICAL SALES

*Medical professional with a full understanding of the complexities of the healthcare field and insight into medical decision-making*

### Professional Profile

- Able to establish productive relationships and foster credibility with a variety of healthcare professionals

- Skilled at documenting and communicating complex technical information in a nontechnical manner

- Accustomed to a high-pressure work environment that demands careful and meticulous attention to detail

### Medical Knowledge / Qualifications

- Offering first-hand knowledge of clinical applications and a strong background in treatment-related medical services

- Well-versed in treatment planning & medical terminology and exposed to a variety of medications and conditions

- Demonstrated ability to quickly grasp scientific information and rapidly master new skills

*Medical knowledge is also important in this profession.*

*This resume emphasizes transferable skills because she is changing careers.*

### HIGHLIGHTS OF QUALIFICATIONS

→ High-performance individual with a self-motivated working style and strong critical-thinking skills. Able to work independently and function effectively with multidisciplinary teams from all areas of an organization.

→ Experience reflects a consistent record of success for anticipating problems and finding creative solutions while exhibiting superior judgment *and* a balanced, realistic understanding of issues.

→ Competent and well-spoken with a confident professional presence, engaging interpersonal skills, and a proven ability to communicate effectively and persuasively with diverse personalities in various situations.

→ Prepared to meet the expectations of the most demanding physicians through a highly accessible service orientation and rigorous followup. Capable of educating healthcare professionals about the efficacy and safety of medical products.

### PROFESSIONAL EXPERIENCE

**Grand Strand Hospital,** *Myrtle Beach, SC*                                    **1993 to Present**
**Medical Radiation Dosimetrist** (1997 to Present)
Prepare and administer radiation treatment plans, which requires the performance of simulations, dose calculations, and tolerance-limit determinations. Perform specific measurements and provide data for treatment plans, adhering to a quality-assurance program. Assist radiation oncologists during simulations to ensure appropriate treatment plans and calculate distribution of doses for radiation therapy treatments. Follow the most current protocol and utilize a treatment planning system. Review patient charts and inspect treatment records to ensure accuracy. Provide guidance and direction to treatment therapists.

**Chief Therapist** (1993 to 1997)
Supervised technical staff, patient treatment, patient simulation, simulation scheduling, and quality assurance. Accountable for dosimetry coverage, custom blocking, film approval, staffing, machine coverage, and payroll. Developed and documented new QA procedures and maintained services in accordance with hospital, state, local, and federal standards. Implemented other routine QA activities in the calibration of linear accelerators and dosimetry equipment.

*Submitted by Kristin Coleman*

Kendall Rose                                                                Page Two

### PROFESSIONAL EXPERIENCE continued...

**Mohawk Valley Community Hospital,** *Utica, NY*                          1990 to 1993
<u>Chief Therapist / Department Supervisor</u>

Responsible for the daily operation of the Radiation Oncology area, which included the overall supervision of clerical and technological staff. Maintained departmental policies and procedures, objectives, safety, environmental, and infection-control standards. Established and maintained the quality-assurance program. Served on the Radiation Safety committee and as coordinator of oncology nursing programs and continuing-education programs.

**St. Agnes Hospital,** *White Plains, NY*                                 1984 to 1986
<u>Staff Radiation Therapist</u>

Delivered prescribed and planned course of radiation therapy to patients, obtained patient history, answered questions, and explained procedure. Interfaced extensively with physician and radiation oncologist. Reinforced recommendations given to patient by the physicians regarding reaction to treatment, care of the radiated area, and local side effects.

**Westchester Medical Center,** *Valhalla, NY*                            1983 to 1984
<u>Staff Radiation Therapist</u>

Provided skilled technical performance for delivery of radiotherapeutic treatments, as prescribed by the radiation oncologist. Accountable for patient treatments, simulation, filming, and student orientation/supervision. Acquired dosimetry experience.

### EDUCATION / CREDENTIALS

**University of South Carolina,** *Columbia, SC*        <u>Certification</u>
<u>Associate Degree in Radiologic Technology</u>          AIDS

<u>Licensures</u>
Registered Radiation Therapist, American Registry of Radiologic Technologists
Certified Radiologic Technologist—Radiotherapy

### PROFESSIONAL DEVELOPMENT

<u>Clinical Equipment</u>                                  <u>Clinical Treatment Planning Systmes</u>
➤ Various Simulators                                      ➤ Eclipse
➤ Varian Treatment Machines                               ➤ Theraplan
➤ Siemens Treatment Machines                              ➤ Render Plan

<u>Professional Affiliation</u>
➤ American Society of Radiologic Technologists (ASRT)

*Table of keywords based on her volunteer work, research position, and previous teaching experience highlights words that closely relate to social work and counseling.*

## SHARON PARKER

2807 Sky Park Manor
Houston, TX 77082
sharonparker@aol.com
Cellular: 713-758-4587

**CAREER OBJECTIVE: COUNSELOR — Advocacy • Family Services • Children & Youth • Women**

Client-focused young professional with degree in Psychology, demonstrated leadership capabilities, and strong interpersonal communication skills qualified for entry-level position in individual, group, or family counseling. Displays high degree of professionalism and empathy when dealing with victims and general public; able to create positive and trusting environments. Sensitive to diverse cultural, ethnic, and social backgrounds.

*Hands-on professional experience combined with academic training in the following areas:*

- Referral Servicing
- Program Coordination
- Hotline Services
- Goal Planning
- Youth Development
- Public Speaking
- Data Collection
- Group Counseling
- Community Resources
- Crisis Intervention
- Research & Analysis
- Self-help/Empowerment
- Client Needs Assessment
- Advocacy & Linkage
- Client Coaching/Motivation
- Womens' Group Work

## EDUCATION

Bachelor in Psychology with minor in Human Development & Family Studies
University of Houston, Houston, TX, 2008

**Key Coursework**: Introduction to Psychology, Social Psychology, Sociology, Abnormal Psychology, Personality Disorders, & Physiological Psychology

## PROFESSIONAL EXPERIENCE / VOLUNTEER WORK / ACADEMIC INTERNSHIPS

*Volunteer,* Houston Area Women's Center (HAWC), Houston, TX (2008)
- Aid female residents and call-in clients with crisis-intervention services. Conduct client needs assessment and provide one-on-one phone counseling on issues of domestic violence and sexual assault.
- Present callers and clients with service information and public education, and make referrals to community resources and service providers.
- Extend additional support and assistance to other departments, including Childcare Advocate and Group Counseling.

*Research Assistant,* University of Houston, Houston, TX (2008)
- Part of research team collecting data and categorizing information for in-depth study of couples and their relationships. Study is sponsored by the American Psychological Association (APA) and will be available for national review.

*Sales Lead Assistant,* Worktree.com, LLC, Houston, TX (2003 to 2007)
- Provided daily database management, sales assistance, and client relations support for fast-paced recruitment agency serving more than 13,000 members.

*Teacher's Aide* (Internship), Human Development Laboratory School, Houston, TX (Summer 2005)
- Helped lead teacher with daily activities, instructional materials, curriculum development, and general classroom activities for 15 to 20 elementary students. Attended skill-development and Parent Advisory Board meetings.

*Administrative Assistant,* AG Edwards, Houston, TX (2002 to 2003)
- Coordinated seminars, lecturers, and informational events for existing and potential clients. Scheduled meeting and client appointments for investment strategy/portfolio evaluation sessions with prospective clients.

*Held additional positions in retail sales and office administration to finance college education.*

## MEMBERSHIPS / AFFLIATIONS

Artistic & Marketing Director—Urban Students Association
Treasurer, Fellow Mentors, Inc.

*Creates assumptions about her personal strengths, such as focused, committed, hardworking, and driven.*

*Her leadership roles in student-based organizations show her well-rounded college experience and ability to take initiative.*

*Submitted by Abby Locke*

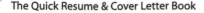

# Angela L. Ferris

| *Permanent Address:* | | *Current Address:* |
|---|---|---|
| After May 2008 | | Until May 2008 |
| 4190 E. Timberwood Drive | | 123 Main Street #3100 |
| Grand Rapids, MI 49500 | ferris@cedarville.com | Cedarville, OH 45314 |

## CURRENT FOCUS

*This college student is looking for an internship related to both her major and her minor.*

**INTERNSHIP:** Four months of volunteer experience, serving people in need in an underdeveloped or developing country, preferably India. Have had a three-year calling to work with the poor and AIDS victims showing Christ's love by being His hands and feet. Eager to learn and serve in micro-financing.

## SUMMARY OF ATTRIBUTES

- Passionate about serving the poor and AIDS victims in an underdeveloped country
- Able to achieve results independently and as a cooperative team member
- Caring
- Excellent time-management abilities
- Self-motivated & goal-driven to reach high achievement
- Good written, verbal, and interpersonal communications

## EDUCATION

CEDARVILLE UNIVERSITY, Cedarville, Ohio
International Studies Major; Bible minor, Fall 2007 to present

GATEWAY COMMUNITY COLLEGE, New Haven, Connecticut
International Studies Major, Fall 2006 to May 2007

NORTHWESTERN MICHIGAN COLLEGE, Grand Rapids, Michigan
English classes, Fall 2005 to May 2006

GRAND RAPIDS CENTRAL HIGH SCHOOL, Grand Rapids, Michigan
Honor graduate, National Honor Society, Graduated May 2006

## EMPLOYMENT HISTORY

- Piano Teacher, *FOOTE SCHOOL*, 9/06–4/07, New Haven, CT
- Cook & Cashier, *CEDARVILLE UNIVERSITY*, 9/07–5/08, Cedarville, OH
- Customer Service, *AMON ORCHARDS*, 5/07–8/07, Grand Rapids, MI
- Server, *BOB EVANS*, 3/05–9/05, Grand Rapids, MI

## ACTIVITIES      *College activities related to her internship target are included.*

- Trained with YOUTH WITH A MISSION (YWAM)—Axiom, a nonprofit Christian missions organization, for a year, including five weeks in South Africa, working with AIDS patients and orphans. This was an important time, giving and setting a vocational foundation for the future: loving Christ by helping those who cannot help themselves.
- CEDARVILLE UNIVERSITY—Involved in Women of Vision/World Vision, Photography Club, Campus Congress, Intercollegiate Council, traveling, reading, writing, film, guitar, discussions on poverty and development

EXCELLENT REFERENCES AVAILABLE

*Submitted by Terri Ferrara*

*This resume for a graduating high school student demonstrates his strong skills and previous work experience.*

# JOHN U. HIGHSCHOOL

**(410)-666-7777**
**juhschool@hotmail.com**

333 Third Street
Baltimore, MD 21075

**Retail Sales Clerk / Stockroom Helper**

## SUMMARY OF SKILLS

- Cashier experience
- Proficient in using computerized cash registers
- Accurate and careful in counting money
- Recorded daily cash activities
- Reliable, punctual, and steady worker

- Good customer service skills
- Honest and trustworthy
- Good attitude around customers, friendly and helpful
- Patient with ability to mediate stressful situations
- Courteous and confident

## PROFESSIONAL HISTORY

McDonald's Restaurant, Baltimore, MD
2006–Present Cashier/Cleaner
- Greet customers and assist in order taking and menu translations.
- Provide excellent service in a high-quality, clean, friendly, and fun atmosphere.
- Prepare food and provide quality guest service.
- Recognized as Employee of the Month 2006, 2007.

Lifeguard, Baltimore, MD
Summer 2005
- Instructed children on rules and regulations of aquatic facility.
- Monitored pool area for violations and potential hazardous situations.
- Assisted in maintaining pool and recreation areas.
- Instructed summer swimming classes.

Child Care, Baltimore, MD
Summer 2004
- Provided child care for several families after school, on weekends, and during school vacations.

## EDUCATION/VOLUNTEER

- Skyline High School, Baltimore, MD, Graduation pending June 2008, GPA 3.0
- Big Brothers / Big Sisters
- Maryland Literacy Program

*Submitted by Drenda Thompson*

# CHAPTER 12

## Sample Electronic Resumes

The sample resumes in this chapter are formatted especially for use on the Internet—for pasting into Web forms or e-mails. Formatting is very simple and uses easy-to-read fonts. Page length is not much of a concern for electronic resumes, so it's common for them to be as long as three or more pages.

- Accounting (pages 268–269)

- Education (pages 270–271)

- Executive (pages 272–274)

- Human Resources (pages 275–277)

- Information Technology (page 278)

- Manufacturing (pages 279–281)

- Public Administration (pages 282–284)

- Sales (pages 285–287)

*Skills format maximizes contributions made to one employer over 16-year tenure.*

GREGORY LAWRENCE, C.P.A.
445 Sunset Lane, Vernon, New York 60194
555-555-5555 - greglawrence@msn.com

============================================================

CORPORATE ACCOUNTING * PUBLIC ACCOUNTING * TAXATION

Certified Public Accountant with a master's degree in accounting and taxation
and business management experience. Versed in the different types of
corporations, consolidations and tax advantages. Proven analytical and financial
management skills. Critical thinker and creative problem solver with excellent
planning and organizational strengths. Technical skills: MS Office, JD Edwards,
and Peachtree Accounting. Key Skills:

General Accounting … Cost Accounting … Financial/Business Analysis … Asset and
Liability Management Cost/Benefit Analysis … Financial Modeling … Auditing …
Risk Assessment … Working Capital

*Equals signs double as a separator line.*

============================================================

CAPABILITIES - ACCOUNTING/FINANCE

Education and training provided a solid foundation in

* Setting up balance sheets, income statements, and cash-flow statements in
compliance with GAAP.
* Analyzing financial performance of business operations; tracking and analyzing
costs; creating and implementing cost-control systems to achieve corporate
objectives.
* Developing and administering budgets; familiar with capital budgeting process.
* Determining valuation of business assets, stocks and bonds prices,
depreciation schedules, and pro forma statements. Creating capital asset pricing
models and financial models.
* Calculating P/E ratios, DCF, EPS, discounted cash flow, and beta for equity
security analysis.
* Devising portfolio asset allocation strategies and conducting risk
assessments; developing business plans.
* Developing financial management and investment strategies for both individuals
and companies.


============================================================

EDUCATION

SIMMONS COLLEGE, NEW YORK, NEW YORK
M.S. in Accounting and Taxation, 2005
B.S. in Business Administration with concentration in Finance, 1980

Relevant Courses: Advanced Accounting, Intermediate Accounting, Managerial
Accounting, Governmental Accounting, Auditing, Finance, Business Law, Cost
Accounting, Tax Accounting

Certified Public Accountant - State of New York, 2003

*Submitted by Louise Garver*

```
============================================================
BUSINESS MANAGEMENT EXPERIENCE

Value Stores, Inc., New York, New York (1992 to present)

Store Manager (1995 to present) / Assistant Manager (1992 to 1995)

Promoted to manage the financial and day-to-day operations of $3 million
business, including P&L management, sales, merchandising, customer relations,
inventory, security, human resources, and training. Scope of responsibilities
encompasses auditing financial records, processing payroll, managing cash,
balancing drawers, entering inventory on computer system, adjusting inventory
retail values, and managing bank deposits and bank reconciliations.
Accomplishments:

* Significantly improved store's financial performance, bringing it from 10%
under budget to 3% above budget within the first month as manager by
   - Assessing and realigning employee skills with appropriate tasks/functions.
   - Improving inventory levels and product mix on sales floor.
   - Reducing turnover, hiring and training quality candidates, and implementing
a succession plan.
* Boosted profits by 20% over prior year, sales by 4% annually, and budgeted
profit forecasts by 6% per year.
* Winner of 3 Paragon Awards out of 15 managers in the district for achieving
excellence in customer service and exceeding profitability/sales targets. Tapped
as mentor, developing and training 25 new store managers.
```

Nancy A. Monroe
670 E. Higgins Road
Naperville, IL 60563
555.555.5555
namonroe2008@hotmail.com

>->->->->->->->->->->->->->->->->->->->->->->->->->->->

VALUE OFFERED AS DIRECTOR OF EDUCATION DELIVERY

*Value statement—what you can do for the company—replaces a self-serving objective.*

Demonstrated track record of improving and directing global education services programs that maximize instructor realization, curriculum quality, revenue growth, and profitability at technology organizations.

* Provide the vision, innovation, and leadership to improve internal processes in Education Services with a talent for identifying and resolving operational challenges to enhance revenues/profits.
* Effective in assessing and driving instructor skill-set development and budget and resource management, as well as partnering with internal departments to meet education needs for a diverse customer base.
* Experienced in the design and delivery of curriculum programs that support and achieve business objectives.
* Repeatedly built and empowered cohesive teams that achieved high standards of quality and productivity in competitive markets.

M.B.A. and B.S. in Education, Springfield College, Springfield, MA

>->->->->->->->->->->->->->->->->->->->->->->->->->->

PROFESSIONAL EXPERIENCE

SIMTECH CORPORATION, CHICAGO, IL     1999 to present

*Good spacing makes this resume easy for a person to read.*

Promoted through series of high-profile management positions in global Education Services and Customer Support: Global Support Programs Manager (2006 to 2008), Best Practices Manager (2003 to 2006), and Education Services Manager (1999 to 2003).

As Education Services Manager, repositioned, upgraded, and transformed Education Services department from an underperforming training function to a profit-generating global organization. P&L management accountability for 12 global Customer Education Centers, team of 17 instructors, curriculum design, facilities management/leasing negotiations, and budget growth to $4MM.

Achievements

* Introduced and educated team on concepts of adult learning theory to better serve students. Turned around team morale from a low of 2 to an average high of 4 as indicated by survey results.
* Determined core product offering, set revenue mix and gross profit margin, and developed knowledge transfer process in collaboration with Product Management and Customer Support departments.
* Established a consistent learning environment for all students globally that eliminated revenue delays and led unit's revenue growth from $4MM to $10MM in billable customer education during 12-month tenure.

*Submitted by Louise Garver*

* Implemented ASP model for online registration and payment. Produced $600K in additional revenue in first 3 months; achieved double annual quota in first 6 months; doubled revenues in 6 months.
* Succeeded in creating additional revenue stream with multimillion-dollar potential where previous team failed after acquiring $250K of software that could not be implemented.
* Created multi-level certification programs with validation protocol for customers, partners, and employees using ASP model for less than $50K. The certification program revenue potential is millions of dollars annually.
* Took charge of and delivered new education class for applications product line in just 3 months despite failure of consulting team to produce program after 9 months of effort.
* Enhanced company's ability to launch new product lines by designing and ensuring curriculum availability on all product lines by the rollout date. Created incremental education product updates for existing customers.

WORLDWIDE SOLUTIONS, NEW YORK, NY          1993 to 1999

As Operations Manager of Education Services, provided strategic planning and leadership effectiveness that drove Education Services revenue growth by 150% ($5MM to $7MM). Directed 12 instructors globally. Supervised curriculum development with team in Germany.

Achievements

* Managed the training channel, created certification program, conducted Partner Certification programs, and ensured accreditation of internal resources and third-party delivery resources (partners and subcontractors).
* Automated Education Services function and enrollment process using Access database, turning around employee morale and reducing customer calls from 500 a week down to just 25, while improving customer satisfaction.

David R. Cross
145 Commonwealth Avenue
Boston, MA 55555
davidrcross@gmail.com
O: (555) 555-5555

PROFESSIONAL SUMMARY
========================

SENIOR EXECUTIVE: PROFESSIONAL SERVICES

*Asterisks serve as bullets.*

* Document / Content Management Software
* Service Sales, Management, and Delivery
* Global Operations Start-up and Growth
* Consultant Training and Development

Differentiated by:

VISIONARY LEADERSHIP OF TOP-FLIGHT PROFESSIONAL SERVICES ORGANIZATIONS

Resulting in:

MULTIMILLION-DOLLAR, LONG-TERM ENGAGEMENTS WITH INDUSTRY GIANTS

Goal-focused, value-driven management executive. Consistently tapped to
open new markets and grow sales, profit margins, and market share.
Increase efficiencies through expert design of standardized
methodologies/processes. Deep cross-industry background in
document/content management software markets. On-time/budget management of
$1+ million implementation projects.

MANAGEMENT HIGHLIGHTS   *Headings and important text set off in all caps rather*
========================   *than boldface.*

VICE PRESIDENT & GENERAL MANAGER - NORTH AMERICA
Rightform Software - $12 million global developer of document management
software, Boston, MA (2005 to 2007)

Challenged with growing North American operations through direct
sales/services management and business partner development. Formed
organizational infrastructure and processes. Led all aspects of operations,
including P&L control, budgeting, and staffing.

* Grew revenues from $327,000 in 2005 to $2.7 million in 2007 with a 38%
profit margin.

* Strategized a North American marketing campaign that generated business
partnerships and major sales contracts.

Key Clients: Prominent healthcare, insurance, and financial services firms.

SENIOR PRACTICE DIRECTOR - GLOBAL DELIVERY SERVICES, SOUTHEAST REGION
T-10 Technologies - $400 million leader in business process software
solutions, Tampa, FL (2004)

Top management authority for the Northeast Consulting Group: sales,
delivery services, project development, and leadership of 12 direct/30+

*Submitted by Jean Cummings*

indirect reports in 3 locations. Refocused operations on a balanced mix of cost containment and profit growth.

* Captured $4 million in revenues and $6.4 million in bookings in the first year.

* Achieved a 50% increase in total revenues while maintaining 50+% profit margins throughout a period of downsizing.

* Reached 125% of revenue and booking goals by developing a partnership arrangement with license sales staff.

* Led turnaround of the product sales team by mentoring on business processes and developing individual action plans.

Key Clients: Leading companies in the travel, food, package delivery, technology, and banking industries.

VICE PRESIDENT - PROFESSIONAL SERVICES GROUP
ContentSystems Technologies - Document management software vendor, Tampa, FL (2001 to 2003)

Recruited to launch a U.S. presence and expand global operations for this UK-based software firm. Controlled $11 million operating budget and $21 million in revenues with a 52% profit margin. Managed 200+ direct and dotted-line reports. Participated in major sales initiatives in excess of $1 million for ECM/CRM solutions targeting financial services and insurance Fortune 100 clients.

* Transformed the group into a world-class organization through standardized processes and best-practices methodology.

* Piloted operations and strategy for build-out of Web Services and Integration Services startup business units that generated in excess of $1 million in revenue during the first year.

* Grew group revenues from $6 million to $21 million in under 2 years; surpassed sales goals 7 out of 9 quarters.

* Designed an implementation partners program composed of Big 5 and major ISVs to aid in closing and implementing mega-deal projects. Increased total revenue 35%.

* Core member of the leadership team credited with transforming the company into an ECM/CRM vendor, guiding entry into new markets, and positioning for a successful buyout.

* Increased staffing levels from 30 direct reports in a single location to 130 in 7 locations in less than a year.

Key Clients: Big brand companies in insurance and financial services.

SENIOR PRACTICE DIRECTOR - PROFESSIONAL SERVICES, EUROPEAN / US OPERATIONS
Premier Technology - $1 billion IT management software firm, New York, NY (1999 to 2001)

(continued)

*(continued)*

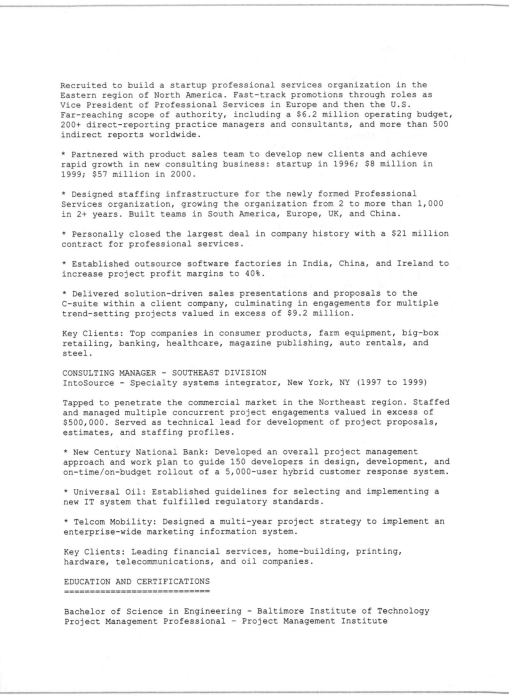

Recruited to build a startup professional services organization in the
Eastern region of North America. Fast-track promotions through roles as
Vice President of Professional Services in Europe and then the U.S.
Far-reaching scope of authority, including a $6.2 million operating budget,
200+ direct-reporting practice managers and consultants, and more than 500
indirect reports worldwide.

* Partnered with product sales team to develop new clients and achieve
rapid growth in new consulting business: startup in 1996; $8 million in
1999; $57 million in 2000.

* Designed staffing infrastructure for the newly formed Professional
Services organization, growing the organization from 2 to more than 1,000
in 2+ years. Built teams in South America, Europe, UK, and China.

* Personally closed the largest deal in company history with a $21 million
contract for professional services.

* Established outsource software factories in India, China, and Ireland to
increase project profit margins to 40%.

* Delivered solution-driven sales presentations and proposals to the
C-suite within a client company, culminating in engagements for multiple
trend-setting projects valued in excess of $9.2 million.

Key Clients: Top companies in consumer products, farm equipment, big-box
retailing, banking, healthcare, magazine publishing, auto rentals, and
steel.

CONSULTING MANAGER - SOUTHEAST DIVISION
IntoSource - Specialty systems integrator, New York, NY (1997 to 1999)

Tapped to penetrate the commercial market in the Northeast region. Staffed
and managed multiple concurrent project engagements valued in excess of
$500,000. Served as technical lead for development of project proposals,
estimates, and staffing profiles.

* New Century National Bank: Developed an overall project management
approach and work plan to guide 150 developers in design, development, and
on-time/on-budget rollout of a 5,000-user hybrid customer response system.

* Universal Oil: Established guidelines for selecting and implementing a
new IT system that fulfilled regulatory standards.

* Telcom Mobility: Designed a multi-year project strategy to implement an
enterprise-wide marketing information system.

Key Clients: Leading financial services, home-building, printing,
hardware, telecommunications, and oil companies.

EDUCATION AND CERTIFICATIONS
==============================

Bachelor of Science in Engineering - Baltimore Institute of Technology
Project Management Professional - Project Management Institute

```
SUSAN B. ALMANN
355 Birch Drive
Tarrytown, NY 90557
(555) 555-5555
Almann@aol.com


~~~~~~~~~~~~~~~~~~~~~~~~~~~~~~~~~~~~~~~~~~~~~~~~~~
CAREER PROFILE

Strategic Human Resources Executive and proactive business partner to senior
operating management to guide in the development of performance-driven,
customer-driven, and market-driven organizations. Demonstrated effectiveness in
providing vision and counsel in steering organizations through accelerated
growth as well as in turning around underperforming businesses. Diverse
background includes multinational organizations in the medical equipment and
manufacturing industries.


-------------------------------------------
Expertise in all generalist HR initiatives.
-------------------------------------------
Recruitment & Employment Management … Leadership Training & Development …
Benefits & Compensation Design … Reorganization & Culture Change … Merger &
Acquisition Integration … Union & Non-Union Employee Relations … Succession
Planning … Expatriate Programs … Long-Range Business Planning … HR Policies &
Procedures.


~~~~~~~~~~~~~~~~~~~~~~~~~~~~~~~~~~~~~~~~~~~~~~~~~~
PROFESSIONAL EXPERIENCE

MARCON MANUFACTURING COMPANY, Peekskill, NY

Vice President, Human Resources (1997-Present)

Challenge:
 Recruited to create HR infrastructure to support business growth at a $30
million global manufacturing company with underachieving sales, exceedingly high
turnover, and lack of cohesive management processes among business entities in
the U.S. and Asia.


Actions:
 Partnered with the president and board of directors to reorganize company,
reduce overhead expenses, rebuild sales, and institute solid management
infrastructure.


Results:

* Established HR with staff of 5, including development of policies and
procedures; renegotiated cost-effective benefit programs that saved company $1.5
million annually.
* Reorganized operations and facilitated seamless integration of 150 employees
from 2 new acquisitions within parent company.
* Reduced sales force turnover to nearly nonexistent, upgraded quality of
candidates hired by implementing interview-skills training and management-
development programs. Results led to improved sales performance.
```

*"CAR" format highlights achievements in a behavioral orientation.*

*Submitted by Louise Garver*

*(continued)*

*(continued)*

* Recruited all management personnel; developed HR policies, procedures, and plans; and fostered team culture at newly built Malaysian plant with 125 employees.
* Initiated business reorganization plan, resulting in consolidation of New York and Virginia operations and $6.5 million in cost reductions.

BINGHAMTON COMPANY, New York, NY
Director, Human Resources & Administration (1993-1996)

Challenge:
 Lead HR and Administration function supporting 1,600 employees at $500 million manufacturer of medical equipment. Support company's turnaround efforts, business-unit consolidations, and transition to consumer products focus.

Actions:
 Established cross-functional teams from each site and provided training in team building to coordinate product development efforts, implement new manufacturing processes, and speed products to market. Identified cost-reduction opportunities; instrumental in reorganization initiatives that included closing union plant in Texas and building new plant in North Carolina. Managed HR staff of 12.

Results:

* Instituted worldwide cross-functional team culture that provided the foundation for successful new product launches and recapture of company's leading edge despite intense competition.
* Led flawless integration of 2 operations into single, cohesive European business unit, resulting in profitable business turnaround.
* Restructured and positioned HR organization in the German business unit as customer-focused partner to support European sales and marketing units.
* Initiated major benefit cost reductions of $3 million in year one and $1 million annually while gaining employee acceptance through concerted education and communications efforts.

ARCADIA CORPORATION, New York, NY

Manager, Human Resources (1991-1994)
Assistant Manager, Human Resources (1990-1991)

Challenge:
 HR support to corporate office and field units of an $800 million organization with 150 global operations employing 4,500 people.

Actions:
 Promoted from Assistant Director of HR to lead staff of 10 in all HR and labor-relations functions. Established separate international recruitment function and designed staffing plan to accommodate rapid business growth. Negotiated cost-effective benefits contracts for union and non-union employees.

```
Results:

* Oversaw successful UAW, Teamsters, and labor contract negotiations.
* Established and staffed HR function for major contract award with U.S.
government agency.
* Introduced incentive plans for field unit managers and an expatriate program
that attracted both internal and external candidates for international
assignments in the Middle East.
* Managed HR issues associated with 2 business acquisitions while accomplishing
a smooth transition and retention of all key personnel.
* Restructured HR function with no service disruption to the business while
saving $500,000 annually.

~~~~~~~~~~~~~~~~~~~~~~~~~~~~~~~~~~~~~~~~~~~~~~~~~~~~~
EDUCATION

M.B.A., Cornell University, New York, NY
B.A., Business Administration, Amherst College, Amherst, MA

~~~~~~~~~~~~~~~~~~~~~~~~~~~~~~~~~~~~~~~~~~~~~~~~~~~~~
AFFILIATIONS

Society for Human Resource Management
Human Resource Council
```

*Brief format works for a candidate with limited experience.*

**BRANDON L. ANDERSON**
1234 Beach Road
Savannah, GA 31401
Home: (123) 456-7891
Cell (123) 456-7891
**blanderson@email.com**

**IT SYSTEMS ANALYST**

Highly motivated and dedicated professional seeking to utilize hands-on and educational experience providing innovative IT solutions. Expertise encompasses requirements gathering, systems analysis, application design, programming, testing, implementation, and project management. Talent for identifying and retaining emerging technologies to establish secure performance-driven systems. Active communicator with exceptional technical communication skills conveying end-user data management and training.

**CORE COMPETENCIES & KEYWORD SUMMARY**

*Keyword summary used to make resume show up in employers' database searches.*

Project Management, Test Development & Execution, IT Solutions Development, User Training & Support, Problem Resolution & Troubleshooting, System Design & Conversion, IT Storage Solutions, Backup & Recovery Strategies, Client Relationship Management

**TECHNICAL PROFICIENCES**

Platforms: Windows NT/XP/2000, Oracle 9.2, UNIX
Tools: C++; Java; JavaScript; HTML; Perl; MS SQL Server, Exchange, Visio, Word, Excel, PowerPoint, Outlook, and Internet Explorer; Acrobat Reader
Hardware: IBM, Dell, Toshiba, HP, Printers, Scanners, Cisco Routers, Switches, Dell PowerEdge Series Servers, Compaq/HP ProLiant ML Series Servers

**PROFESSIONAL EXPERIENCE**

Sunset Communications, Inc., Savannah, GA  2006 – Present
Systems Analyst
Manage all aspects of system design, programming, development, and implementation including performance test management and quality assurance. Identify and review business requirements, creating detailed system design specifications that include process flow and data mapping. Ensure disaster recovery backup preparedness. Support and educate end users, providing superior customer service.
Key Achievements:
* Designed and implemented new $2M hardware infrastructure, improving system performance and reducing down time 25%.

**EDUCATION**

Master of Science in Information Systems Technology, University of Houston, Houston, TX
Bachelor of Science in Information Technology, University of Georgia, Atlanta, GA

*Submitted by Tammy Chisholm*

Joseph M. Jackman
71824 Haines Rd.
Seattle, WA 82487
845-994-2274 (h)
845-995-3967 (c)
jmjack@hotmail.com

PRODUCTION  -  SAFETY  -  MANUFACTURING
Global Manufacturing / Precision Materials
Forward-thinking, performance-driven Production Management/Safety-Health Manager
with more than 20 years in production management, quality control, safety
programs, and staff retention. Expert in promoting quality, cost, and
performance improvement across production and safety issues to improve internal
processes and enhance bottom-line performance. Direct and coordinate human
resource functions and quality control activities among departments. Natural
communicator and proactive leader with the ability to motivate staff and create
synergy among teams. Highlights include
*Process Redesign & Performance Optimization
*Safety & Environmental Programs
*Behavioral-Based Plant Safety
*Vendor Management & Outsourcing
*Quality Control & Solutions Management
*Team Training & Development

*Lack of white space not crucial when resume is put into an online database, but would be somewhat difficult for a person to read.*

ACHIEVEMENTS IN DEPTH:   SAFETY PROGRAMS  -  MANUFACTURING  -  HR MGMT

Safety Leadership, Quality Control
**Safety Programs & Initiatives, Safety Committee**
-Conducted job-related accident investigations, monitored accident trends, and
recommended corrective actions to reduce workers' compensation costs.
-Took on and managed an entire machine guarding program at the Seattle,
Washington, facility, safeguarding all production equipment to OSHA standards
within a 2-year time period and a budget of $1 million. Supervised one employee
who built and designed guards. Collaborated with production personnel to create
guards that were practical enough for production equipment, yet offered the
maximum protection to workers.
-Led Safety Committee meetings; conducted safety audits and safety tours to
ensure compliance with plant, corporate, and OSHA safety requirements.
-Served as Radiation Safety Officer; properly stored materials and trained
employees in the proper handling of low-level radioactive materials. Found
alternatives for disposals that cut company costs and benefited the environment
by recycling the materials. Reported findings to Washington State and to the NRC
(Nuclear Regulatory Commission).
-Created and implemented a "behavioral-based safety program" to run in
conjunction with the existing safety programs.
-Maintained all records and reports required by government agencies; established
and implemented a Safety Management System (SMS) for ISO18001.
-Coordinated and implemented Hazardous Energy Control Program and Machine
Guarding Program.
-Evaluated workstations, mitigated employee repetitive trauma disorders, and
trained workers in ergonomics.
-Managed all workers' compensation injuries at each facility; attended workers'
comp hearings and cultivated relationships with key attorneys.
-Teamed with P.I.s to investigate fraudulent claims. Remained in touch with
employees on leave to keep lines of communication open.
-Implemented the Hazard Communication Program and Emergency Contingency Plan.

Submitted by Erin Kennedy

(continued)

*(continued)*

Joseph M. Jackman, Page 2 of 3

Continued…

-Developed and implemented programs for plant safety training programs and Personal Protective Equipment.
-"Safety Recognition" from Corporate Safety Office for Outstanding Achievement, 2003.
-"Safety Acknowledgement" from National Safety Council of Washington for improvements to incident rate, 1997, 1998.
"Safety Award" from National Safety Council of Washington for significant improvements, 1991.

Material Inventory, Plant & Environmental Safety
**Inventory Control, Plant Safety, Safety Audits**
-Governed all phases of raw materials, tooling supplies, and outside vendors; schedule and govern inventory-control functions.
-Administered all environmental issues, including ISO 14001 management system.
-Revamped the "product on time" delivery from 65% to 85% within the first year at AP Inc.
-Led plant hazardous waste, air, and water regulations and the Hazardous Materials Spill Team.
-Ran Phase II Environmental Site Assessments, including subsurface soil sampling and groundwater evaluation from bedrock aquifer.

Human Resources Management
**Employee Selection, Training & Development, Staffing & Retention**
-"Neighbor of Choice Team Leader"; serve as organizational representative to the community.
-Promoted and encouraged positive and productive employee relations through an "open-door" policy, effective complaint resolution, and equitable/consistent policy application.
-Trained all staff-level management to support diversity in the workplace; ensured selection, training, development, and performance management of employees (hourly/salaried).
-Created new operating policies and procedures for management.

CAREER CHRONOLOGY

*Chronological listing of work history follows extensive skills section.*

Aerospace Precision, Copenhagen, WA    2005 to Present
Materials & Safety Manager
Hired to manage all direct/indirect staff for this aeronautical manufacturing company. Serve as liaison for manufacturing, engineering, sales, and production schedules with customer requirements and streamline the facility and resources.

Bright Lights, Inc., Seattle, WA    1976 to 2004
Human Resources Manager (1999 to 2004)
Promoted to HR Manager to organize, direct, and evaluate all human resources activities for two facilities with more than 200 employees. Advised management on all state and federal employment regulations. Made recommendations to management about HR initiatives and how they related to business objectives and goals. Maintained HR policies and procedures for employees, including staffing and retention, labor relations, and wages/salaries. Conducted local wage surveys.

Joseph M. Jackman, Page 3 of 3

Continued…

Safety and Environmental Specialist (1990 to 1999)
Coordinated and led all aspects of plant safety and environmental issues for all
employees. Conducted job-related accident investigations, monitored accident
trends, and recommended corrective actions to reduce workers' compensation
costs. Developed and managed safety and environmental programs for multiple
facilities.

EARLY BRIGHT LIGHTS CAREER (1976 to 1990)    *Short summary of older (and less relevant) experience*

Began Bright Lights career during college and took on increasingly responsible
roles due to consistent successes. Gained valuable experience in safety and
environmental management, corporate compliance, and employee relations. Known as
the "go-to" person to get things done.

EDUCATION & TRAINING

BS, Industrial Technology, Western University, Brownstown, WA—1987
AS, Electro Mechanical Technology, Eagle Eye Community College, Afton, WA—1983

Examples of Training:
-Advanced Hazardous Waste/Hazardous Materials RCRA
-Powered Industrial Truck Trainer
-24/8 Hour Emergency Response Activities
-ISO 9000 Quality Systems Auditing
-Behavior Management for Safety
-Managing Hazardous Waste in Washington
-Understanding & Implementing ISO 9001:2000
-Environmental Regulations
-Certified Trainer for ZengerMiller/AchieveGlobal
-Global 8 D Problem Solving
-Basic Accident Prevention & OSHA Compliance
-Safe Lift Truck Operations
-Asbestos Abatement for Supervisors & Contractors
-Occupational Ergonomics

*Extensive on-the-job training*

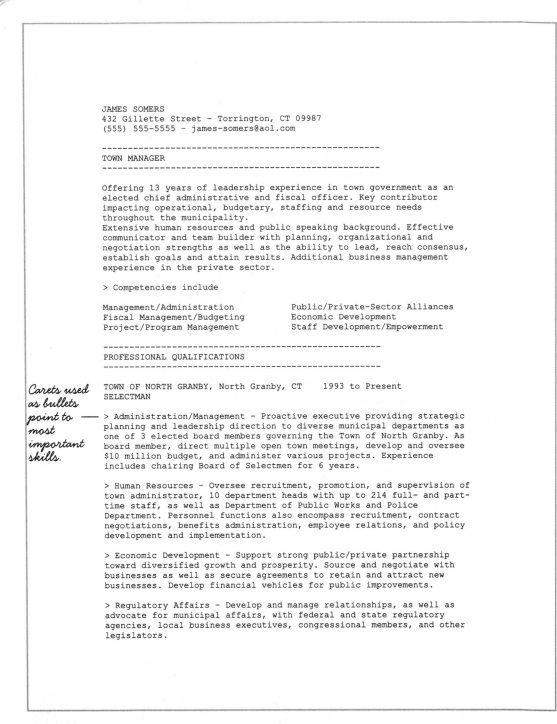

JAMES SOMERS
432 Gillette Street - Torrington, CT 09987
(555) 555-5555 - james-somers@aol.com

```
------------------------------------------------------
TOWN MANAGER
------------------------------------------------------
```

Offering 13 years of leadership experience in town government as an
elected chief administrative and fiscal officer. Key contributor
impacting operational, budgetary, staffing and resource needs
throughout the municipality.
Extensive human resources and public speaking background. Effective
communicator and team builder with planning, organizational and
negotiation strengths as well as the ability to lead, reach consensus,
establish goals and attain results. Additional business management
experience in the private sector.

> Competencies include

Management/Administration          Public/Private-Sector Alliances
Fiscal Management/Budgeting        Economic Development
Project/Program Management         Staff Development/Empowerment

```
------------------------------------------------------
PROFESSIONAL QUALIFICATIONS
------------------------------------------------------
```

*Carets used as bullets point to most important skills.*

TOWN OF NORTH GRANBY, North Granby, CT    1993 to Present
SELECTMAN

> Administration/Management - Proactive executive providing strategic
planning and leadership direction to diverse municipal departments as
one of 3 elected board members governing the Town of North Granby. As
board member, direct multiple open town meetings, develop and oversee
$10 million budget, and administer various projects. Experience
includes chairing Board of Selectmen for 6 years.

> Human Resources - Oversee recruitment, promotion, and supervision of
town administrator, 10 department heads with up to 214 full- and part-
time staff, as well as Department of Public Works and Police
Department. Personnel functions also encompass recruitment, contract
negotiations, benefits administration, employee relations, and policy
development and implementation.

> Economic Development - Support strong public/private partnership
toward diversified growth and prosperity. Source and negotiate with
businesses as well as secure agreements to retain and attract new
businesses. Develop financial vehicles for public improvements.

> Regulatory Affairs - Develop and manage relationships, as well as
advocate for municipal affairs, with federal and state regulatory
agencies, local business executives, congressional members, and other
legislators.

*Submitted by Louise Garver*

> Public/Community Relations - Instrumental in the enhancement of Town's image and building consensus with all boards. Active participant in numerous annual community events; act as spokesperson to the media.

Achievements

* Turned around employee morale and productivity, instituted training and employee recognition programs, and fostered interdepartmental cooperation, creating a positive work environment while restoring accountability and confidence in the administration. Town of North Granby is recognized by the state municipal association for having the "most responsive and best managed administration statewide."

* Orchestrated multiple town revitalization projects, following failed attempts by prior boards:
- $2.9 million renovations to Town Hall and $5 million public safety complex.
- $1.3 million public library project with state library grant offsets of $200,000.
- $15 million sewer project with more than $5 million secured in federal grant funding.

* Effectively negotiated with company CEOs to relocate their businesses back to North Granby. Results led to construction of new plants for 4 companies employing 2,550 people combined and an agreement to expand employee base.

* Instrumental in attracting and retaining businesses in the community by personally negotiating Tax Incentive Financing Agreements.

* Spearheaded search for new providers and negotiated improved employee benefits program while avoiding any rate increase.

---

BUSINESS MANAGEMENT EXPERIENCE

---

*Summary of experience not directly related to job target*

| | |
|---|---|
| MONROE & COMPANY, New York, NY | 1980 to present |
| Regional Manager | 2002 to present |
| District Manager | 1990 to 2002 |
| Account Manager | 1988 to 1990 |

Promoted to manage $23 million region that extends from the Northeast to Florida at a multibillion-dollar food processing manufacturer. Lead and motivate the direct sales team of 35 plus 5 broker organizations. Develop and execute sales and marketing programs. Manage $2.5 million annual marketing/advertising budget.

Achievements

* Created sales and marketing initiatives that turned around the region's ranking from #6 to #1 out of 8 regions nationwide. Consistently exceeded annual sales plan despite a declining industry.
* Led the region's successful transition from a direct sales force to a productive food-broker network; efforts charted an entirely new

*(continued)*

*(continued)*

```
          direction in the company and the new business model was adopted in all
          regions.
          * Drove expansion of existing account base while capturing 5 key
          accounts that generated $10.5 million in annual business volume for the
          district.
          * Elected to the Leadership Club in 1997, 1996, 1995, and 1994 for
          consistently ranking among the top 10% of account managers in overall
          sales performance throughout company.
          * Renegotiated marketing programs with major customers that increased
          sales and profits while achieving acceptable dollar spends.

          --------------------------------------------------
          EDUCATION / PROFESSIONAL DEVELOPMENT
          --------------------------------------------------

          BENTLEY COLLEGE, Bentley, VT
          M.B.A., Finance, 1999
          B.S., Business Administration, 1995

          Additional: Several seminars on municipal administration sponsored by
          Connecticut Municipal Association and Selectmen's Association

          --------------------------------------------------
          COMMUNITY AFFILIATIONS / LEADERSHIP
          --------------------------------------------------

          Selectmen's Association
          Vice President, North Granby Rotary Club
          Chairman, Conservation Commission
```

*Community affiliations are important for this job objective.*

```
DUDLEY DORIGHT
7000 Lexington East, #26A
New York, NY 10028
doright@nj.rr.com
212.856.8781


SENIOR SALES EXECUTIVE
~ Over 15 years of success managing Sales and Reseller / Channel Relations ~

Hard-charging Sales Executive with more than 10 years of successful sales
leadership in startup and territory expansion situations for some of the biggest
names in consumer products: Samsung, Philips, and Maytag. Consistently earned
top ranks in sales performance in every position by bringing revenues, profits,
and market share to new heights.

        * DESIGNED AND EXECUTED SAMSUNG SALES STRATEGY TO GROW SALES FROM
                $61M TO OVER $1B IN 4 YEARS.

        * REVITALIZED LOST ACCOUNT FOR PHILIPS AND DELIVERED
                $105M IN SALES IN 2 YEARS.

        * CONSISTENTLY RANKED AS TOP TERRITORY MANAGER.


GIFTED SALES STRATEGIST AND TACTICIAN who excels in driving revenues through
innovative and focused merchandising and sales force/channel development
programs. Noted for pioneering program to share personal sales best practices
with resellers that was subsequently adopted by all regions nationwide.

PRODUCT EVANGELIST AND SALES LEADER practiced in driving market enthusiasm
through public speeches to press, analysts, and industry trade groups.
Accomplished in turning mediocre performers into high-performance sales teams
and managing and motivating sales-channel teams.


CORE COMPETENCIES
-----------------
* Strategic Market Planning
* Business Development
* Territory Management
* Customer Acquisition & Penetration
* National Accounts
* Channel Sales Strategies
* Sales Force Development
* Merchandising & Promotions
* Sales Best Practices


PROFESSIONAL EXPERIENCE
========================

NATIONAL SALES MANAGER, HOME APPLIANCE - AUG 2006 - SEP 2008
SAMSUNG CONSUMER ELECTRONICS * RIDGEFIELD PARK, NJ
A global leader in semiconductor, telecommunication, digital media, and digital
convergence technologies with more than 90 offices in 48 countries.
```

*Core competencies are highlighted in a bulleted list before formal experience.*

*Submitted by Don Goodman*

(continued)

*(continued)*

Aggressively recruited to revitalize launch of the Home Appliance Division for Samsung Electronics in the United States. Challenged to jumpstart flailing efforts and build all new sales distribution channel across 4 segments: Mass Merchant, Home Improvement, Club, and large Regional accounts. Worked with product and marketing teams to create product differentiation and gain competitive advantage. Served as Product Champion, evangelizing products to press, analysts, and industry trade groups. Oversaw staff of 5.

*Emphasis on accomplishments shows the candidate gets results.*

NOTABLE ACCOMPLISHMENTS:
> Developed sales roadmap, which provides for +$2B in annual sales by 2011 compared to $61M in 2007. Analyzed existing sales-channel relationships and developed all new sales strategy focused on market leaders who could drive sales and market presence.
> Noted for driving 237% increased sales level in 2008.
> Targeted Lowes, second largest retailer of home appliances in the United States, and personally led sales charge. Credited with closing 5-year Alliance Partnership (1 of 2 appliance manufacturers with this designation) valued at $75M in first year and $1B in annual sales by 2011. Noted for leading all pricing negotiations and obtaining highly favorable margins. Developed national training program to educate 1,100 Lowes locations and more than 6,000 Lowes sales associates on products and sales best practices.
> Exited relationships with Sam's Club and Menards and closed stronger, more profitable agreement with Costco, valued at $30M in second year.
> Listened attentively to customers and conceived launch plan to introduce revolutionary product in January 2009, bringing entire new category into market with projected sales of $150M in first year.


NATIONAL ACCOUNT DIRECTOR - JUL 2003 - JUL 2006
PHILIPS CONSUMER ELECTRONICS * ATLANTA, GA
One of the world's top 3 consumer electronics companies, with a range of products based on world-leading digital technologies.
Recruited by CEO to reestablish relations with recently lost Sears account. Challenged to rebuild severely tarnished relationships. Oversaw staff of 4.

NOTABLE ACCOMPLISHMENTS:
> Led entirely new strategy designed to establish Philips as a value-added partner as opposed to a traditional supplier. Delivered detailed business plan identifying market opportunities and positioning Philips to deliver higher-margin business. Complemented strategy with comprehensive field operations plan, including product and sales training.
> Closed agreement that delivered $53.1M in sales for 2005 and $105M in 2006.
> Reinvented how sales team interacted with Sears by introducing team-selling concept. Increased SKUs by 340% and standard margins by 32% in 2006 by collaboratively shifting sales focus to high-margin items.
> Designed and executed a 12-month merchandising and sales training program at the last 3 feet to create sell-through. Created special promotions (e.g. free home theater giveaway with the purchase of a big-screen TV) that resulted in SKU expansion and $40M in increased category sales.
> Received prestigious President's Award for dramatically exceeding goals and targets.


REGIONAL SALES MANAGER - JUL 1994 - JUL 2003
MAYTAG APPLIANCES * WASHINGTON, D.C.
One of America's most trusted appliance manufacturers.
Recruited to oversee 12 sales professionals and expand 3-state territory.

```
        NOTABLE ACCOMPLISHMENTS:

> Grew Washington, D.C., territory into third largest domestic market (up from
sixth) with 36% sales increase to $19M.
> Delivered 112% of region's revenues goal, producing $64M in annual sales.
Noted for increasing sales to National Accounts by 8.7%
> Ranked as 1 of country's Top 5 Regional Managers.
> Recognized as only 1 of 20 Regional Managers to develop and clearly
communicate sales strategy and plan with defined performance metrics.
> Pioneered program to share sales best practices with retail sales forces
(audiences up to 200) from such retailers as Best Buy, Circuit City, and Sears.
Successful program was subsequently adopted nationwide.
> Credited for designing and executing new cooperative advertising newspaper
insert program with Washington Post that increased exposure, reduced marketing
costs, and caused Direct-Maytag retail store in DC to become second largest in
U.S. Huge success resulted in being asked to execute program for entire East
Coast.
> Asked to develop and deliver national presentation, "The Pillars of Success,"
which demonstrated effective personal sales and marketing techniques. Personally
delivered methodology at national sales meetings and was featured in corporate
videotape.


EDUCATION
=========

BACHELOR OF SCIENCE, BUSINESS ADMINISTRATION * 1993
University of Nebraska * Lincoln, Nebraska
```

# Part 4

# Quick Cover Letters, Thank-You Notes, JIST Cards, and Other Job Search Correspondence

You will probably send out a variety of correspondence in addition to your resume. For example, the majority of employers expect candidates to send a cover letter along with their resume. But there are several other useful written communications that many job seekers overlook.

Thank-you notes, for example, can make a big difference if you use them well. JIST Cards, an innovative mini-resume format, are another powerful job search tool. These and other related forms of written communication to employers and your network are the focus of the two chapters in this section.

**Chapter 13: The Quick Cover Letter and How to Use It   291**

**Chapter 14: Thank-You Notes and JIST Cards   315**

# CHAPTER 13

# The Quick Cover Letter and How to Use It

You shouldn't send a resume to someone without explaining why. Whether you're mailing, faxing, or e-mailing your resume, it's important to provide a letter along with it—a cover letter (or cover message, in the case of e-mailing). Even when you post your resume to a job bank or employer Web site, the site often has a place where you can upload or paste a cover letter. Depending on the circumstances, the letter would explain your situation and ask the recipient for some specific action, consideration, or response.

Entire books discuss the art of writing cover letters. Some authors go into great detail on how to construct "powerful" cover letters. Some suggest that a cover letter can replace a resume by providing information specifically targeted to the person receiving it. Although these ideas have merit, the objective here is to give you a simple, quick review of cover letter basics that will meet most needs.

**QUICK TIP**

Although most people think of a resume as one in printed form and a cover letter as a traditional letter on paper, increasingly these documents are sent as e-mail or an attachment.

# Only Two Groups of People Will Receive Your Cover Letters

If you think about it, you will send a resume and cover letter to only two groups of people:

- People you know
- People you don't know

Although this sounds overly simple, it's true. And this observation makes it easier to understand how to structure your letters to each group. Before you look at some useful and effective cover letter samples for both groups, let's first review some basics regarding writing cover letters in general.

**QUICK TIP**

Although many situations require writing a formal letter, a simple note will do in many instances (for example, when you know the person you are writing to). Chapter 14 gives additional information on writing informal notes.

# Seven Quick Tips for Writing a Superior Cover Letter in 15 Minutes

No matter who you're writing to, virtually every good cover letter should follow these guidelines.

## 1. Write to Someone in Particular

Never send a cover letter "To whom it may concern" or use some other impersonal opening. We all get enough junk mail, and if you don't send your letter to someone by name, it will be treated like junk mail. Make an effort to find out who the hiring manager is—call the company and ask, or do some research on their Web site. In the case of a "blind ad," however, where you don't even know what company you're applying to, you'll have to use a generic salutation.

## 2. Make Absolutely No Errors

One way to offend people quickly is to misspell their names or use incorrect titles. If you have any question, call and verify the correct spelling of the name and other details before you send the letter. Also, review your letters carefully to be sure they contain no typographical, grammatical, or factual errors.

## 3. Personalize Your Content

Don't use a form letter. Those computer-generated letters that automatically insert a name (merge mailings) never fool anyone, and cover letters done in this way can be a turnoff. Although some resume and cover letter books recommend that you send out lots of these "broadcast letters" to people you don't know, you will most likely find that doing so wastes time and money. Small, targeted mailings or e-mailings to a carefully selected group of prospective employers can be effective if you tailor your cover letter to each recipient.

**QUICK ALERT**

Check and double-check the address and salutation on your cover letter to make sure you don't accidentally put one person's name on it and then send it to another. Also, if you mention the company's name in the letter, be sure it's the same company you're sending the letter to. Employers report that they see mistakes like these often, and it's a huge strike against the candidate.

## 4. Present a Good Appearance

Your contacts with prospective employers should always be professional, so buy good-quality stationery and matching envelopes for times when you'll be mailing or hand-delivering a letter and resume. Use papers and envelopes that match or complement your resume paper. The best colors are white, ivory, and light beige. The standard 8½ × 11 paper size is typically used, but you can also use the smaller Monarch-size paper with matching envelopes.

Use a standard letter format that complements your resume type and format. Most word-processing software provides templates or "wizards" to automate your letter's format and design. I used such templates to create the formats for the sample letters in this chapter. And don't forget the envelope! It should be typed and printed carefully, without abbreviations or errors.

### 5. Provide a Friendly Opening

Begin your letter with a reminder of any prior contacts and the reason for your correspondence now. The examples later in this chapter give some ideas on how to handle this.

### 6. Target Your Skills and Experiences

To do this well, you must know something about the organization or person with whom you are dealing. Present any relevant background you have that may be of particular interest to the employer.

### 7. Close with an Action Statement

Don't close your letter without clearly identifying what you will do next. Don't leave it up to the employer to contact you; that doesn't guarantee a response. Close on a positive note and let the employer know that you desire further contact.

**QUICK NOTE**

Using a few simple techniques, it is possible to meet all sorts of people. Why waste time and money sending your resume or cover letter to strangers when it's relatively easy to make direct contact? Chapter 15 provides details on how to make contact with people you don't know.

## Writing Cover Letters to People You Know

It's always best if you know the person to whom you are writing. Written correspondence is less effective than personal contact, so the ideal circumstance is to send a resume and cover letter after having spoken with the person directly.

For example, it's far more effective to first call someone who has advertised a job than to simply send a letter and resume. You can come to know people through the Yellow Pages, personal referrals, and other ways. You might not have known them yesterday, but you can get to know them today.

So let's assume you have made some sort of personal contact before sending your resume. Within this assumption are hundreds of variations, but I will review the most common situations and let you adapt them to your own circumstances.

## The Four Types of Cover Letters to People You Know

When sending cover letters to people you know, you will be in one of four basic situations described here. Each situation requires a different approach. This chapter includes sample cover letters for each situation.

- **An interview is scheduled and a specific job opening may interest you.** In this case, you have already arranged an interview for a job opening that interests you. Your cover letter should provide details of your experience that relate to the specific job.

- **An interview is scheduled but no specific job is available.** Chapter 15 explains in more detail why this situation is such a good one for you to set up. In essence, this is a letter you will send for an exploratory interview with an employer who does not have a specific opening for you now but who might in the future. This is fertile ground for finding job leads where no one else may be looking.

- **You've already had an interview.** Many people overlook the importance of sending a letter after an interview. This is a time to say that you want the job (if you do) and to add any details on why you think you can do the job well.

- **No interview is scheduled yet.** There are situations where you just can't arrange an interview before you send a resume and cover letter. For example, you might be trying to see a person whose name was given to you by a friend, but that person is on vacation. In these cases, sending a good cover letter and resume makes later contacts more effective.

The four types of cover letters illustrate an approach that you can use to get interviews, which is the real task in finding a job.

## Sample Cover Letters to People You Know

The following are sample cover letters for the four situations. Look at the samples for each type of cover letter and see how, in most cases, they assume that personal contact was made before the resume was sent. Note that they use different formats and styles to show you the range of styles that are appropriate. Each addresses a different situation, and each incorporates all of the cover letter writing guidelines from the preceding section.

These samples should give you ideas on writing your own cover letters. Once you get the hang of it, you should be able to write a simple cover letter in about 15 minutes. Just keep in mind that the best cover letter is one that follows your having set up an interview. Anything else is just second best.

## FIGURE 13.1: SAMPLE COVER LETTER, PRE-INTERVIEW, FOR A SPECIFIC JOB OPENING.

**Comments:** This writer called first and arranged an interview, which is the best approach. Note how this new graduate included a specific example of how he saved money for a business by changing its procedures. Although it is not clear from the letter, his experience with lots of people was gained by working as a waiter. Note also how he included skills such as "hard worker" and "deadline pressure."

Richard Swanson
113 South Meridian
Greenwich, Connecticut 11721

March 10, 20XX

Mr. William Hines
New England Power and Light Company
604 Waterway Boulevard
Darien, Connecticut 11716

Dear Mr. Hines:

I am following up on the brief chat we had today by phone. After getting the details on the position you have open, I am certain that it is the kind of job I have been looking for. A copy of my resume is enclosed, providing more details of my background. I hope you have a chance to review it before we meet next week.

My special interest has long been in the large-volume order-processing systems that your organization has developed so well. While in school, I researched the flow of order-processing work for a large corporation as part of a class assignment. With some simple and inexpensive procedural changes I recommended, check-processing time was reduced by an average of three days. For the number of checks and dollars involved, this one change resulted in an estimated increase in interest revenues of more than $35,000 per year.

Although I have recently graduated from business school, I have considerable experience for a person of my age. I have worked in a variety of jobs dealing with large numbers of people and deadline pressures. My studies have also been far more "hands-on" and practical than those of most schools, so I have a good working knowledge of current business systems and procedures. This includes a good understanding of various computer spreadsheet and database programs, the use of automation, and experience with cutting costs and increasing profits. I am also a hard worker and realize I will need to apply myself to get established in my career.

I am most interested in the position you have available and am excited about the potential it offers. I look forward to seeing you next week. If you need to reach me before then, you can call me at (973) 299-3643 or e-mail me at rswanson@msn.net.

Sincerely,

Richard Swanson

**FIGURE 13.2: SAMPLE COVER LETTER, PRE-INTERVIEW, NO SPECIFIC JOB OPENING.**

**Comments:** This letter indicates that the writer first called and set up an interview as the result of someone else's tip. The writer explains why she is moving to the city and asks for help in making contacts there. Although no job opening exists here, she is wise in assuming that there might be one in the future. Even if this is not the case, she asks the employer to think of others who might have a position for someone with her skills. Assuming that the interview goes well and the employer gives her names of others to call, she can then follow up with them.

---

ANNE MARIE ROAD

February 20, 20XX
Ms. Francine Cook
Park-Halsey Corporation
5413 Armstrong Drive
Minneapolis, Minnesota 56317

Dear Ms. Cook:

When Steve Marks suggested I call you, I had no idea you would be so helpful. I've already followed up with several of the suggestions you made and am now looking forward to meeting with you next Tuesday. The resume I've enclosed is to give you a better sense of my qualifications. Perhaps it will help you think of other organizations that may be interested in my background.

The resume does not say why I've moved to Minneapolis and you may find that of interest. My spouse and I visited the city several years ago and thought it was a good place to live. He has obtained a very good position here and, based on that, we decided it was time to commit ourselves to a move.

As you can see from my work experience, I tend to stay on and move up in jobs, so I now want to research the job opportunities here more carefully before making a commitment. Your help in this task is greatly appreciated.

Feel free to contact me at (834) 264-3720 if you have any questions; otherwise, I look forward to meeting with you next Tuesday.

Sincerely,

Anne Marie Road

616 KINGS WAY ROAD
MINNEAPOLIS, MINNESOTA 54312
(834) 264-3720

---

## FIGURE 13.3: SAMPLE COVER LETTER, AFTER AN INTERVIEW.

**Comments:** This letter shows how you might follow up after an informational interview and make a pitch for solving a problem—even when no job formally exists. In this example, the writer suggests that she can use her skills to solve a specific problem she uncovered during her conversation with the employer. Although it never occurs to many job seekers to set up an interview where there appears to be no job opening, jobs are created as a result of such interviews.

---

**Sandra A. Zaremba**          115 South Hawthorn Drive
Dunwoody, Georgia 21599

April 10, 20XX

Ms. Christine Massey
Import Distributors, Inc.
417 East Main Street
Atlanta, Georgia 21649

Dear Ms. Massey:

I know you have a busy schedule so I was pleasantly surprised when you arranged a time for me to see you. Although you don't have a position open now, your organization is just the sort of place I would like to work. As we discussed, I like to be busy with a variety of duties, and the active pace I saw at your company is what I seek.

Your ideas on increasing business are creative. I've thought about the customer service problem and would like to discuss a possible solution. It would involve the use of a simple system of color-coded files that would prioritize correspondence to give older requests priority status. The handling of complaints could also be speeded up through the use of simple form letters similar to those you mentioned. I have some thoughts on how this might be done, too, and I will work out a draft of procedures and sample letters if you are interested. It can be done on the computers your staff already uses and would not require any additional cost to implement.

Whether or not you have a position for me in the future, I appreciate the time you have given me. An extra copy of my resume is enclosed for your files—or to pass on to someone else.

Let me know if you want to discuss the ideas I presented earlier in this letter. I can be reached at any time on my cell phone at (942) 267-1103. I will call you next week, as you suggested, to keep you informed of my progress.

Sincerely,


Sandra A. Zaremba

---

### FIGURE 13.4: SAMPLE COVER LETTER, NO INTERVIEW IS SCHEDULED.

**Comments:** This letter explains why the person is looking for a job as well as presents additional information that would not normally be included in a resume. Note that the writer got the employer's name from the membership list of a professional organization, one excellent source of job leads. Also note that the writer stated that he would call again to arrange an appointment. Although this letter might turn off some employers, many others would be impressed with his assertiveness and willing to see him. The card mentioned in this letter is a JIST Card and can be found in chapter 14.

8661 Bay Drive
Tempe, Arizona 27317
827-994-2765 (cell)

# Justin Moore

January 5, 20XX

Ms. Doris Michaelmann
Michaelmann Clothing
8661 Parkway Boulevard
Phoenix, Arizona 27312

Dear Ms. Michaelmann:

As you may know, I phoned you several times over the past week while you were in meetings. I hope that you received the messages. Since I did not want to delay contacting you, I decided to write. I got your name from the American Retail Clothing Association membership list. I am a member of this group and wanted to contact local members to ask their help in locating a suitable position. I realize that you probably don't have an available position for someone with my skills, but I ask you to do two things on my behalf.

First, I ask that you consider seeing me at your convenience within the next few weeks. Although you may not have a position available for me, you may be able to assist me in other ways. And, of course, I would appreciate any consideration for future openings. Second, you may know of others who have job openings now or might possibly have them in the future. Would you be able to refer me to someone else?

Although I realize that this is an unusual request and that you are quite busy, I do plan to stay in the retail clothing business in this area for some time and would appreciate any assistance you can give me in my search for a new job.

My resume is attached for your information along with a card that summarizes my background. As you probably know, Allied Tailoring has closed and I stayed on to shut things down in an orderly way. Despite their regrettable business failure, I was one of those responsible for Allied's enormous sales increases over the past decade and have substantial experience to bring to any growing retail clothing concern, such as I hear yours is.

I will contact you next week and arrange a time that is good for us both. Please feel free to contact me at any time regarding this matter.

Sincerely,


Justin Moore

# Writing Cover Letters to People You Don't Know

If it's not practical or possible to directly contact a prospective employer by phone or some other method, it's acceptable to send a resume and cover letter. This approach makes sense in some situations, such as if you are moving to a new location or responding to a blind ad that lists only a post office box number.

Although I don't recommend sending out "To Whom It May Concern" letters by the basketful, sending an unsolicited resume can make sense in some situations. There are ways to modify this "shotgun" approach to be more effective. For example, try to find something you have in common with the person you are contacting. By mentioning this link, your letter then becomes a very personal request for assistance. Look at the two letters that follow for ideas.

**QUICK TIP**

Microsoft Word includes several professional-looking letter templates and "Wizards." Using one of these speeds up the process of formatting your letter and ensures that it looks nice. Just be sure to use the same fonts on your letter as you do on your resume.

## FIGURE 13.5: RESPONSE TO A WANT AD.

**Comments:** This letter does a good job of outlining the candidate's credentials as relevant to the advertised position. The bullet points give the reader a quick overview of his qualifications. Then it provides more detail in case the reader wants to know more before turning to the resume.

---

### GORDON STRAW

straw@netzero.net

3731 Honeysuckle Hill     Bellingham, Washington 98225-2006     (360) 731-5704

---

September 30, 20XX

Illusion Software, Inc.
Seattle, Washington

**Reference ID:**   **2051-3**
                 **Project Manager**

Throughout my Project Management career, I have provided the strategic and tactical leadership to accelerate revenue and earnings gains for high-growth, technology-based corporations. Highlights include the following:

- More than 15 years of top-flight project management experience with leading high-technology corporations.
- Extensive project management and business development in the U.S. and Europe.
- Strong technical qualifications and experience with mainframe, mid- to high-range technologies, global information networks, numerous operating systems, and virtually all leading software packages.
- Created the RUMBA Developer and Web-to-Host Editions.

I am direct and decisive in my leadership style, yet flexible in responding to constantly changing markets, economies, and competitors. I set and drive clear priorities and can work autonomously as well as part of a team. I built and led U.S. and multinational teams responsible for product development, marketing, sales, technical support, internal MIS, human resources, and administration. I possess outstanding qualifications in all facets of the project lifecycle development from initial feasibility analysis and conceptual design through documentation, implementation, user training, and enhancement; my projects have always been completed on time (even while meeting tight deadlines) and within budget.

With a unique blend of MIS and general management experience, I have positioned each technology organization as a key partner to the operating management team, responding to their specific needs and recommending proactive systems solutions. Most recently, I transitioned my experience into nonprofits, providing them with competitive technologies to drive performance improvement.

Currently, I am exploring new professional challenges and opportunities. The enclosed resume shows that I meet most of your requirements for this position; therefore, I would welcome a personal interview to explore your needs for a strong and decisive project manager.

Thank you for your consideration.

Sincerely,


Gordon Straw

Enclosure

---

*Submitted by Myriam-Rose Kohn.*

## FIGURE 13.6: UNSOLICITED RESUME SENT TO OBTAIN AN INTERVIEW.

**Comments:** This is an example of a person conducting a long-distance job search using names obtained from a professional association, which is a good strategy. This letter also explains why he is leaving his old job and includes positive information regarding his references and skills that would not normally be found in a resume. John asks for an interview even though there might not be any jobs open now. He also asks for names of others to contact.

July 10, 20XX

Mr. Paul Resley
Operations Manager
Rollem Trucking Co.
I-70 Freeway Drive
Kansas City, Missouri 78401

Mr. Resley:

I obtained your name from the membership directory of the Affiliated Trucking Association. I have been a member for more than 10 years and I am very active in the Southeast Region. The reason I am writing is to ask for your help. The firm I had been employed with has been bought by a larger corporation. The operations here have been disbanded, leaving me unemployed.

Although I like where I live, I know that finding a position at the level of responsibility I seek may require a move. As a center of the transportation business, your city is one I have targeted for special attention. A copy of my resume is enclosed for your use. I'd like you to review it and consider where a person with my background would get a good reception in Kansas City. Perhaps you could think of a specific person for me to contact?

I have specialized in fast-growing organizations or ones that have experienced rapid change. My particular strength is in bringing things under control, and then increasing profits. Although my resume does not state this, I have excellent references from my former employer and would have stayed if a similar position existed at its new location.

As a member of the association, I hoped that you would provide some special attention to my request for assistance. I plan on coming to Kansas City on a job-hunting trip within the next six weeks. Prior to my trip I will call you for advice on who I might contact for interviews. Even if they have no jobs open for me now, perhaps they will know of someone else who does.

My enclosed resume lists my phone number and other contact information should you want to reach me before I call you. Thanks in advance for your help.

Sincerely,

John B. Goode
Treasurer, Southeast Region
Affiliated Trucking Association

*John B. Goode*
*312 Smokie Way        Nashville, Tennessee 31201*

# Additional Sample Cover Letters

Following are some additional cover letters that address a variety of situations. Although the formats are not fancy, they are acceptable and quick.

**FIGURE 13.7: NO INTERVIEW IS SCHEDULED.**

947 Cherry Street
Middleville, Ohio 01234

October 22, 20XX

Mr. Alfred E. Newman, President
Alnew Consolidated Stores, Inc.
1 Newman Place
New City, OK 03000

Dear Mr. Newman:

I am interested in the position of national sales director, which you recently advertised in the *Retail Sales and Marketing* newsletter.

I am very familiar with your company's innovative marketing techniques as well as your enlightened policy in promoting and selling environmentally sound merchandise nationwide. I have been active for some time now in environmental protection projects, both as a representative of my current employer and on my own. I recently successfully introduced a new line of kitchen products that exceeds federal standards, is environmentally safe, and is selling well.

The enclosed resume outlines my experience and skills in both sales and marketing in the retail field. I would like to meet with you to discuss how my skills would benefit Alnew Consolidated Stores. I will contact you soon to request an interview for current or future positions and may be reached at (513) 987-6543.

Thank you for your time and consideration.

Sincerely,


Robin Redding

**FIGURE 13.8: PRE-INTERVIEW, NO SPECIFIC JOB OPENING.**

# Linda M. Fletcher

3321 Haverford Road
Baldwin, North Carolina
12294

E-mail: lfletcher@yahoo.com
Phone: 400-541-0877
Fax: 400-541-0988

March 15, 20XX

Mr. Howard Duty
WXLC TV
10212 North Oxford Avenue
Halstead, South Carolina 12456

Dear Mr. Duty:

Thank you for agreeing to meet with me at 3 p.m. on March 23 to talk about job opportunities for broadcast technicians. Although I understand that you have no openings right now, I'm enclosing my resume to give you some information about my training and background.

You will see that I have worked on both up-to-date and as well as older equipment. Working part time for a small station, I've learned to monitor, adjust, and repair a variety of equipment including both the newer automated and computerized items as well as the older ones. Keeping a mix of older and newer equipment working smoothly has required me to learn many things and has been an invaluable experience. At Halstead Junior College, I have become the person to call if the new, state-of-the-art audio and video equipment does not perform as it should.

I look forward to graduating and devoting all my time and energy to my career. I greatly appreciate your help, particularly your invitation to spend more time observing field operations during your live election coverage.

Sincerely,


Linda M. Fletcher

P.S. I found your Web site and was ***very*** impressed that you did most of the work on it. You may be interested to know that I have created a Web site for our college TV station. If you have time, you can find it at www.halstead.edu/WNCSTV—I'd like your feedback!

Enclosure: resume

**FIGURE 13.9: NO INTERVIEW IS SCHEDULED.**

**JANE MAEYERS**
123 Alexandria Drive
Alexandria, Louisiana 71409
(318) 443-0101

October 23, 20XX

Attention: Ms. Brenda Barnes
Coordinator of Student Activities
Screening Committee
Coldgate University
Campus Box 7
Emporia, Kansas 66801

RE:  Position as Coordinator of Student Activities
     Organization & Special Events, or related
     position

Dear Screening Committee:

I have planned, developed, supervised, taught, and successfully completed numerous tasks assigned to me in my 10 years of experience as a recreation specialist. Now I'm ready to apply the same expertise and principles of hard work to starting a productive and challenging career as Coordinator of Student Activities Organization and Special Events, or related position, with your organization. Because this position matches my interests, qualifications, work, and education experience, I can be a productive and valuable director from day one.

The resume enclosed also outlines all the details of my career. background as a recreation specialist. With these credentials and my belief in quality and hard work, I will make a significant contribution to Coldgate University.

I am looking forward to working with your organization and would appreciate the opportunity to discuss employment opportunities with you soon.

Please inform by letter or call (318) 443-0101 to arrange a time when we can meet at your convenience. I can also be contacted via e-mail at jmaey@alexu.edu. Thank you for your time and consideration.

Sincerely,


Jane Maeyers

**FIGURE 13.10: NO INTERVIEW IS SCHEDULED.**

# ROBERT P. BARNES, CBCP
*Certified Business Continuity Professional*

1434 Madison Boulevard
Orlando, FL 38917
Residence: 954-555-1212
Mobile: 954-555-1212
robertpbarnes@earthlink.net

April 8, 20XX

Samuel Ryan, CIO
Global Financial Services, Inc.
495 Central Avenue
Orlando, FL 38917

Dear Mr. Ryan:

Development of a comprehensive, state-of-the-industry business-continuity program is critical to a company's ability to achieve its core mission. Employee safety, shareholder value, corporate reputation, revenues and profits, data integrity, and IT systems—these are some of the corporate interests that an effective business continuity program is designed to protect. My expertise is the ability to deliver, within a complex multinational organization, innovative business-continuity plans that are integrated with overall corporate strategy and aligned with corporate goals.

In my work as Business Recovery Manager at Morgan Summers Financial Services, I established just such a program. My groundbreaking thinking and writing promotes business-continuity planning as a strategic, business-driven process in which IT plays a supporting role. My contributions helped ensure that the company would mitigate risk, survive potential disruptions, and recover in a timely manner. Achievements included the following:

— Developed and executed business-continuity plans for an organization with $176 billion in assets under management, 40 business units, 800 employees, and 19 different IT systems running 200 applications.

— Promoted my visionary concept of the role of business-continuity planning throughout the organization and achieved buy-in for plan initiatives from 40 business units (including 6 IT business units) and 2 disaster-recovery vendors.

— Implemented a multifaceted employee-awareness program to help ensure that employees knew how to implement plans in the event of a business disruption.

I came up through the ranks as an IT professional and earned both my M.B.A. degree and my Bachelor's degree in Business Computer Information Systems. As an experienced BCP manager who is a Certified Business Continuity Professional, I am well credentialed for assuming a leadership position in business-continuity planning.

Please contact me if you are interested in my demonstrated ability to help a company mitigate risk and protect critical assets. I look forward to an opportunity to speak with you in person about your business requirements and will call you next week to set a mutually convenient time. Thank you.

Sincerely,

Robert P. Barnes

Enclosure

*Submitted by Jean Cummings.*

**FIGURE 13.11: PRE-INTERVIEW, FOR A SPECIFIC JOB OPENING.**

1768 South Carrollton Street
Nashville, Tennessee 96050
May 26, 20XX

Ms. Karen Miller
Office Manager
Lendon, Lendon, and Sears
Suite 101, Landmark Building
Summit, New Jersey 11736

Dear Ms. Miller:

Enclosed is a copy of my resume that describes my work experience as a legal assistant. I hope this information will be helpful as background for our interview next Monday at 4 p.m.

I appreciate your taking time to describe your requirements so fully. This sounds like a position in which I could make a significant contribution to your company. And my training in accounting—along with experience using a variety of computer programs—matches your needs.

Lendon, Lendon, and Sears is a highly respected name in New Jersey. I am excited about this opportunity and I look forward to meeting with you.

Sincerely,

Richard Wittenberg

## FIGURE 13.12: NO INTERVIEW IS SCHEDULED.

### Allan P. Raymond, CPA

29 Brookside Drive, Mystic, CT 06433
860.239.7671 • allanraymond@verizon.net

March 15, 20XX

Carol P. Graves, CPA
President, Graves & Andrews
254 Court Street
New London, CT 06320

Dear Carol:

I enjoyed our conversation at the recent CPA Society meeting and, as you suggested, I am forwarding my resume with this letter of interest in joining your firm.

You and I agreed that your clients deserve the best: the best accountants, the best strategies, and the greatest dedication to customer service. I am confident I can bring "the best" in both attitude and execution to your firm.

With more than ten years of accounting experience—the last five as a CPA and owner of an accounting firm specializing in tax—I have strong and well-proven professional skills. I thrive on the challenges and intricacies of tax accounting and stay up-to-date with tax code changes through both in-person and online training programs.

What satisfies me most in my professional life is the opportunity to help clients better manage, control, and benefit from their money. One of the keys to the good advice I give my clients is my deep understanding of the consequences of investment decisions on their tax situation. I have worked with businesses of all sizes from one person to complex multimillion-dollar organizations in diverse industries and have contributed strategies and planning recommendations as well as tax-related accounting services.

Having just concluded the sale of my business, I am eager for new professional challenges. I would like to explore my value as a tax accountant with your firm, and in pursuit of that objective I will call you next week to schedule a meeting. Thank you.

Best regards,

Allan P. Raymond

enclosure: resume

*Submitted by Louise Kursmark.*

**FIGURE 13.13: NO INTERVIEW IS SCHEDULED.**

4550 Parrier Street
Espinosa, California 94478

December 12, 20XX

Mr. Craig Schmidt
District Manager
Desert Chicken Shops
Post Office Box 6230
Los Angeles, California 98865

Dear Mr. Schmidt:

My resume (enclosed) outlines my four years of successful experience as a fast-food manager with a nationwide network of restaurants. I graduated from a Restaurant Management curriculum at Harman University with a 3.75 GPA in 2007.

I have been impressed with the rapid growth and exceptional quality of product and service for which Desert Chicken has become well known. This is the kind of organization I hope to work for now.

My experience includes positions as cook, night manager, assistant manager, and manager for my current employer.

I will call your office in a few days to see if we might schedule a convenient time to meet and discuss some areas of mutual interest.

Thanks very much for your consideration.

Sincerely,


Douglas Parker


Enclosure

© JIST Publishing

**FIGURE 13.14: NO INTERVIEW IS SCHEDULED.**

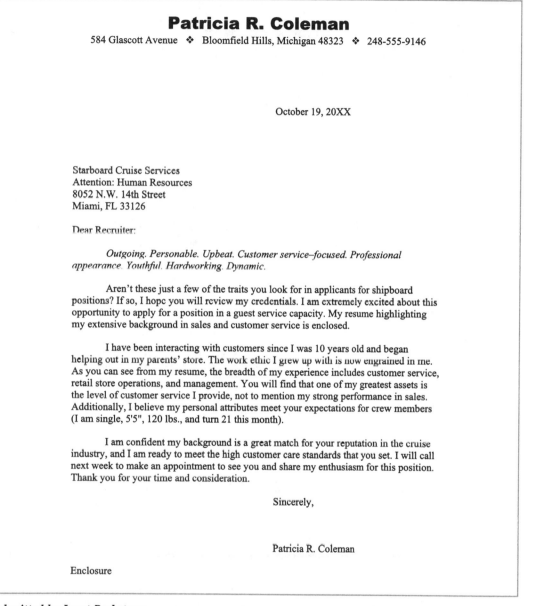

# Patricia R. Coleman

584 Glascott Avenue ❖ Bloomfield Hills, Michigan 48323 ❖ 248-555-9146

October 19, 20XX

Starboard Cruise Services
Attention: Human Resources
8052 N.W. 14th Street
Miami, FL 33126

Dear Recruiter:

*Outgoing. Personable. Upbeat. Customer service–focused. Professional appearance. Youthful. Hardworking. Dynamic.*

Aren't these just a few of the traits you look for in applicants for shipboard positions? If so, I hope you will review my credentials. I am extremely excited about this opportunity to apply for a position in a guest service capacity. My resume highlighting my extensive background in sales and customer service is enclosed.

I have been interacting with customers since I was 10 years old and began helping out in my parents' store. The work ethic I grew up with is now engrained in me. As you can see from my resume, the breadth of my experience includes customer service, retail store operations, and management. You will find that one of my greatest assets is the level of customer service I provide, not to mention my strong performance in sales. Additionally, I believe my personal attributes meet your expectations for crew members (I am single, 5'5", 120 lbs., and turn 21 this month).

I am confident my background is a great match for your reputation in the cruise industry, and I am ready to meet the high customer care standards that you set. I will call next week to make an appointment to see you and share my enthusiasm for this position. Thank you for your time and consideration.

Sincerely,

Patricia R. Coleman

Enclosure

*Submitted by Janet Beckstrom.*

## FIGURE 13.15: NO INTERVIEW IS SCHEDULED.

### JASON R. GOODSON

1843 Lake Johanna Blvd.      Roseville, MN 55112      651-555-6633

August 31, 20XX

Mr. Robert McCarthy, Director of Personnel
Roseville Area Schools
1251 W. County Road B2
Roseville, MN 55113

Dear Mr. McCarthy:

Thank you for this opportunity to formally express my interest in the Athletic Director position. I appreciated Bill Murphy's suggestion that I apply, especially because Bill is familiar with my abilities through our collaboration on Roseville's football coaching staff last fall. I understand you have my resume on file.

My qualifications for this position closely match those listed in your posting:

| *Desired Qualifications* | *My Qualifications* |
|---|---|
| ☐ M.A. in Education or School Administration | ☑ M.A. in Secondary Administration from U-M. |
| ☐ Minimum 5 years of teaching experience | ☑ Almost 10 years as classroom teacher. |
| ☐ Outstanding leadership and personal qualifications | ☑ Spearheaded drive for state-of-the-art health and fitness facility and monitored its construction. Developed and presented motivational program on interpersonal skills to high school students, families, and educators. |
| ☐ Successful coaching experience at varsity level | ☑ 9 years as varsity football coach. Led team to state semifinals. Received Tri-State Athletic League Coaches award as second-year coach. |
| ☐ Excellence in organizational skills and problem-solving strategies | ☑ Effectively balance roles as teacher, coach, and parent. Evaluated and implemented strategies to turn around poor-performing team to reach its first 7-consecutive-win season in 27 years. |
| ☐ Mental/physical ability and stamina | ☑ Actively participate in personal health and fitness plan to ensure peak performance. |

Throughout my career as an educator and coach, I have recognized the importance of my position as a role model and motivator for students. But I also relate well to parents and humbly state that I have an excellent reputation among game officials and coaching peers within Ramsey County.

I welcome the chance to speak with the selection committee about this position so that I can elaborate on my enthusiasm and commitment to Roseville Area Schools. I will call next week to set up an interview. Thank you again for this opportunity.

Sincerely,

Jason R. Goodson

*Submitted by Janet Beckstrom.*

## FIGURE 13.16: RESPONSE TO AN AD.

# JILL LaFLEUR
2101 Sweet Meadow Drive, Tampa, Florida 33624
813-687-6415 ♦ jlafleur@aol.com

## RE: PHARMACEUTICAL SALES REPRESENTATIVE POSITION

July 1, 20XX

careers@pharmaceuticalrecruit.com
ATTN: Pharmaceutical Recruiters
4020 Green Mount Crossing Drive
Suite 330
Fairview Heights, IL 62269

Dear Hiring Professional:

In response to your search for an entry-level pharmaceutical sales representative, I am ready to start my career!

I have several years of experience in health care and am used to working with doctors and nurses in a busy, hectic hospital setting. I recently earned my bachelor's degree in Biology and am looking to combine my academic knowledge and love of learning with my interest in health care and my goal of becoming an outstanding pharmaceutical sales rep.

Here is how I meet/exceed your needs listed in the job posting:

♦ *Diverse, dynamic professional:* I've held a variety of jobs in and out of the health care field, coupled with a degree in Psychology.

♦ *Verifiable record of achievement:* My 5-year employment at St. Joseph's Women's Hospital and my excellent and respected standing as an employee show my ability to stick with a job, be reliable, and be goal oriented.

♦ *Level-headed, competitive, assertive, self-motivated, one who works well independently, computer literate, and possesses a high energy level:* People who have worked with me will state I am all these things. In fact, my positions as a Patient Care Technician and Certified Nursing Assistant have demanded these exact qualities.

♦ *Call on physicians, hospitals, pharmacies, and other caregivers:* I currently work in a fast-paced medical-care setting, where relationships have to be built and maintained. I use my relationship-building and persuasive skills daily with medical professionals and patients.

♦ *Able to comply with legal and regulatory requirements governing the sale and promotion of the company's pharmaceutical products:* Working in a hospital requires knowledge of and compliance with many different legal and bureaucratic policies and procedures. I am used to navigating myriad important requirements.

My resume provides further details of my accomplishments. I look forward to discussing a new career opportunity with you. If I don't hear from you, I will contact you next week to arrange a meeting to discuss your company's needs in greater detail.

Sincerely,

Jill LaFleur

Enclosure

*Submitted by Gail Frank.*

**FIGURE 13.17: CAREER CHANGER.**

## LISA ANN CRAMMER

3550 Sunglow Drive ▪ Oroville, CA 96221 ▪ 533-226-5896

March 23, 20XX

Wendy Templeton, Human Resources Director
Northern California Regional Hospital
2801 Evergreen Way
Oroville, CA 96221

Dear Ms. Templeton:

After recently completing billing, coding, and medical terminology courses through the Meditec Support Services Training Program, I am currently exploring medical coding, billing, and records opportunities where I can utilize my strengths in program development, organization, and researching. After reviewing your company website, I have decided to contact you about possible job openings within your organization.

Two things really stood out and impressed me about your company. The first is your dedication to fostering positive relationships with both your patients and employees. Coming from a background in special education, I have always believed this to be the most essential goal for creating an environment where individuals can flourish and reach their fullest potential. The second thing that impressed me was your mission to provide personal and attentive care to every patient and his or her family. It is important for me to work for a company where patients' personal needs and well-being take top priority.

As you will see from my enclosed resume, I have completed my medical coding and billing training in the top tenth percentile of all students who have ever gone through the Meditec program. I am very detail oriented with strong research and analytical skills. As a resource specialist I utilized these skills on a daily basis. Through the detailed analysis of student work and test scores, I was able to create personalized learning experiences for learning-disabled students, which allowed them to learn important skills by maximizing their own unique learning capabilities.

These strengths will also be important for me to utilize in the medical support services area. As a medical support services employee, I will be committed to paying thorough attention to the details of my job, as I fully understand the importance of carefully examining all data when dealing with personal and confidential medical records and insurance forms. The ability to analyze data and extract the most specific and important information from coding references and other materials can greatly affect reimbursement payments and can have a significant influence upon compliance issues as well.

Should you have a need for someone with my qualifications and experience, please contact me at 533-226-5896. I look forward to hearing from you and will follow up next week by phone. Thank you for your time.

Sincerely,


Lisa Ann Crammer

Enclosure

*Submitted by Carla Barnett.*

# CHAPTER 14

# Thank-You Letters and JIST Cards

**M**uch of the information in this chapter is often overlooked in resume books. That's too bad because thank-you letters are a very effective job search tool. So are JIST Cards. Other related correspondence can also play an important part in a quick, successful job search.

This chapter gives the basic "whys" and "hows" of writing effective follow-up correspondence and handy JIST Cards for presenting your key credentials quickly.

## The Importance of Thank-You Letters

While resumes and cover letters get the attention, thank-you letters often get results. Sending thank-you letters makes both good manners and good job search sense. When used properly, thank-you letters can help you create a positive impression with employers. So here are the basics of writing and using thank-you letters.

## Three Times When You Should Definitely Send Thank-You Letters—and Why

Thank-you letters have a more intimate and friendly social tradition than other formal business correspondence. That's one reason they work so well—people respond to those who show good manners and say thank you. Here are some situations when you should use them, along with some sample letters.

## 1. Before an Interview

In some situations, you can send a less formal note before an interview, usually by e-mail (unless the interview is scheduled for a fairly distant future date). For example, you can simply thank someone for being willing to see you. Depending on the situation, enclosing a resume could be a bit inappropriate. Remember, this is supposed to be sincere thanks for help and not an assertive business situation. This also serves as a way to confirm the date and time of the scheduled interview and as a reminder to the recipient that you will be showing up at that time. Figure 14.1 shows a sample thank-you letter sent before an interview.

**FIGURE 14.1: SAMPLE THANK-YOU LETTER SENT BEFORE AN INTERVIEW.**

*April 5, 20XX*

*Ms. Kijek,*

*Thanks so much for your willingness to see me next Wednesday at 9 a.m.*

*I know that I am one of many who are interested in working with your organization, but I'm confident that you'll find my qualifications are a good fit for the role. I've enclosed a JIST Card that presents the basics of my skills for this job and will bring my resume to the interview.*

*I appreciate the opportunity to meet you and learn more about the position. Please call me if you have any questions at all.*

*Sincerely,*

*Bruce Vernon*

## QUICK TIP

Enclose a JIST Card with your thank-you letter when sending your letter through the mail. You can find JIST Card samples later in this chapter and in chapter 3. JIST Cards provide key information an employer can use to contact you. They also list key skills and other credentials that will help you make a good impression. And the employer might forward the card to someone who might have a job opening for you.

## 2. After an Interview

One of the best times to send a thank-you letter is right after an in
view. Here are several reasons why:

- Doing so makes a positive impression. The employer will assume
  you have good follow-up skills—as well as good manners.

- It creates yet another opportunity for you to remain in the
  employer's consciousness at an important time.

- It gives you a chance to get in the last word. You get to include a
  reminder of why you're the best candidate for the job and can
  even address any concerns that might have come up during the
  interview.

- If they have buried, passed along, or otherwise lost your resume
  and previous correspondence, a thank-you letter and correspon-
  ding JIST Card provide one more chance for employers to find
  your number and call you.

For these reasons, I suggest you send a thank-you letter right after the
interview and certainly within 24 hours. Figure 14.2 is an example of
such a letter.

**FIGURE 14.2: SAMPLE THANK-YOU LETTER SENT AFTER AN INTERVIEW.**

---

*August 11, 20XX*

*Dear Mr. O'Beel,*

*Thank you for the opportunity to interview for the position available in your production
department. I want you to know that this is the sort of job I have been looking for and I am
enthusiastic about the possibility of working for you.*

*Now that we have spoken, I know that I have both the experience and skills to fit nicely into
your organization and to be productive quickly. The process improvements I implemented at
Logistics, Inc., increased their productivity 34%, and I'm confident that I could do the same for
you.*

*Thanks again for the interview; I enjoyed the visit.*

*Sara Smith*

*(505) 665-0090*

---

**QUICK TIP**

Send a thank-you letter by e-mail or mail as soon as possible after an interview or meeting. This is when you are freshest in the mind of the person who receives it and are most likely to make a good impression.

## 3. Whenever Anyone Helps You in Your Job Search

Send a thank-you letter to anyone who helps you during your job search. This includes those who give you referrals, people who provide advice, or simply those who are supportive during your search. I suggest you routinely enclose one or more JIST Cards in these letters because recipients can give them to others who may be in a better position to help you. Figure 14.3 is a sample thank-you letter sent to someone who helped in a job search.

**FIGURE 14.3: SAMPLE THANK-YOU LETTER TO SOMEONE WHO HELPED IN A JOB SEARCH.**

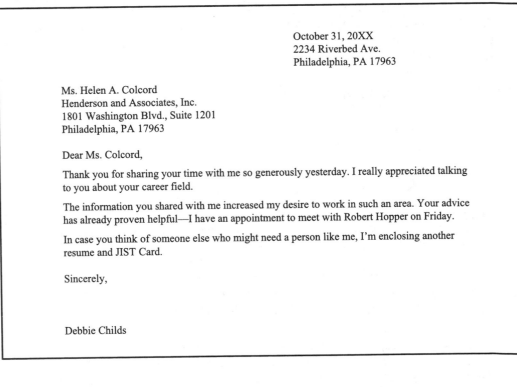

October 31, 20XX
2234 Riverbed Ave.
Philadelphia, PA 17963

Ms. Helen A. Colcord
Henderson and Associates, Inc.
1801 Washington Blvd., Suite 1201
Philadelphia, PA 17963

Dear Ms. Colcord,

Thank you for sharing your time with me so generously yesterday. I really appreciated talking to you about your career field.

The information you shared with me increased my desire to work in such an area. Your advice has already proven helpful—I have an appointment to meet with Robert Hopper on Friday.

In case you think of someone else who might need a person like me, I'm enclosing another resume and JIST Card.

Sincerely,

Debbie Childs

# *Eight Quick Tips for Writing Thank-You Letters*

Here are some brief tips to help you write thank-you letters that get results.

## 1. Decide Whether E-mail or Snail Mail Makes More Sense

Consider the timing involved and the formality of the person and organization you're sending it to. If you need to get a letter out quickly because it has to arrive before an interview that's coming up soon, or if it's a thank-you letter after an interview and you know the employer will be making a decision soon, e-mail is your best bet. Use regular mail if there's no rush and if you sense that the other person would appreciate the formality of a business letter printed on nice paper and received in the mail.

## 2. Use Quality Paper and Envelopes

For mailed thank-you letters, use good-quality paper with matching envelopes. It's best to use the same paper that your resume is printed on. Off-white and beige are the best colors.

## 3. Don't Handwrite It

Traditionally, thank-you letters were handwritten, but these days more are written on a computer and printed on resume paper. If you're sending a very quick note to someone you already know well, a handwritten note is acceptable. In all other cases, a formal, word-processed letter is better.

## 4. Use a Formal Salutation

Unless you know the person you are thanking, don't use a first name unless you've already met the person you're writing and he or she has asked you to use first names, or if you're writing to someone in a young, hip environment. Instead, use "Dear Ms. Smith" or "Ms. Smith," rather than the less formal "Dear Pam." Include the date.

## 5. Keep the Letter Short and Friendly

Keep your letter short and friendly. Remember, the letter is a thank you for what someone else did, not a hard-sell pitch for what you want. Make sure, however, that in a thank-you letter sent after an interview that you give a reminder of your skills or other qualifications that are relevant to the job. This lets the thank-you letter serve as an expression of appreciation as well as a chance to get the last word on why you should be hired. The more savvy members of your competition will be doing this, so you should too.

Also, make sure your thank-you letter doesn't sound like a form letter. Put some time and effort into it to tailor it to the recipient and the situation. Include specific details from any previous contacts you have had with the person.

As appropriate, be specific about when you will next contact the person. If you plan to meet soon, send a letter saying that you look forward to the meeting and say thank you for the appointment. And make sure that you include something to remind the employer of who you are and how to reach you. Your name alone may not be enough to be remembered.

## 6. Sign It

Sign your first and last name. Avoid initials and make your signature legible (unless you're being hired for your creative talents, in which case a wacky-looking, illegible signature could be a plus!).

### QUICK TIP

Always send a letter or e-mail after an interview, even if things didn't go well. It can't hurt.

## 7. Send It Right Away

Write and send your letter or e-mail no later than 24 hours after you make your contact. Ideally, you should write it immediately after the contact, while the details are fresh in your mind.

## 8. Enclose a JIST Card

Depending on the situation, a JIST Card is often the ideal enclosure with a printed thank-you letter. It's small, soft sell, and provides your contact information, in case the employer wants to reach you. It's both a reminder of you, should any jobs open up, and a tool to pass along to someone else (see the next section for details on writing JIST Cards).

## *More Sample Thank-You Letters*

Following are a few more samples of thank-you letters. They cover a variety of situations and will give you ideas on how to structure your own correspondence. Notice that they all contain very specific information and typically mention that the writer will follow up in the future—a key element of a successful job search campaign.

Also note that several of these candidates are following up on interviews where no specific job opening exists yet. As I've mentioned elsewhere in this book, getting interviews before a job opening exists is a very smart thing to do.

**FIGURE 14.4: SAMPLE THANK-YOU LETTER TO SOMEONE WHO HAS BEEN HELPFUL.**

## Allan P. Raymond, CPA

29 Brookside Drive, Mystic, CT 06433
860.239.7671 • allanraymond@verizon.net

March 30, 20XX

Ellen Farmer
President, Sound Financial
112 Front Street
New London, CT 06321

Dear Ms. Farmer:

Thank you for taking the time to meet with me. Your ideas were excellent, and I have already reached out to both of the contacts you suggested. Like you, both Mr. Avenida and Mr. Stroman felt that my background makes me a great fit for a small- to medium-sized CPA firm that needs an experienced professional. I am vigorously pursuing all leads and hope that you will keep me in mind as you interact with various business leaders in the New London area.

To that end, I have enclosed a few JIST Cards that are a convenient way for you to pass along my credentials.

As a small way of returning the favor, I have given your name and business cards to two people I know who are in financial transition (Mary McCormick is getting a divorce, and Chris Taylor recently came into a small inheritance) and suggested they give you a call. From what you told me, your services would be a great fit for their special circumstances.

If I can be of further help to you, please let me know. And as you suggested, I will follow up with you from time to time to keep you informed of my progress. Thanks so much!

Best regards,


Allan P. Raymond

enclosures

**FIGURE 14.5: SAMPLE THANK-YOU LETTER WHERE NO OPENING CURRENTLY EXISTS.**

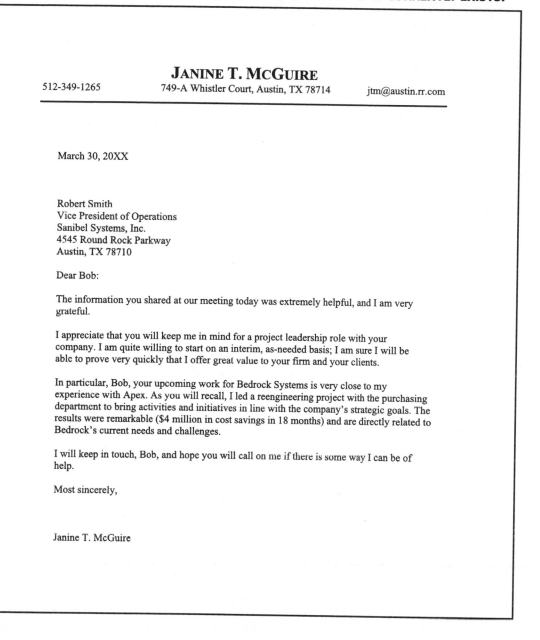

**JANINE T. MCGUIRE**

512-349-1265      749-A Whistler Court, Austin, TX 78714      jtm@austin.rr.com

March 30, 20XX

Robert Smith
Vice President of Operations
Sanibel Systems, Inc.
4545 Round Rock Parkway
Austin, TX 78710

Dear Bob:

The information you shared at our meeting today was extremely helpful, and I am very grateful.

I appreciate that you will keep me in mind for a project leadership role with your company. I am quite willing to start on an interim, as-needed basis; I am sure I will be able to prove very quickly that I offer great value to your firm and your clients.

In particular, Bob, your upcoming work for Bedrock Systems is very close to my experience with Apex. As you will recall, I led a reengineering project with the purchasing department to bring activities and initiatives in line with the company's strategic goals. The results were remarkable ($4 million in cost savings in 18 months) and are directly related to Bedrock's current needs and challenges.

I will keep in touch, Bob, and hope you will call on me if there is some way I can be of help.

Most sincerely,

Janine T. McGuire

**FIGURE 14.6: SAMPLE THANK-YOU LETTER REINFORCING THE CANDIDATE'S "FIT" FOR THE JOB.**

---

March 30, 20XX

Dear Samantha,

I know how busy you are, and I am extremely grateful that you were willing to share some time with me on Monday.

I realize that you do not have an opening for me at this time, but I am very interested in joining the Armanda team. From my research, backed up by what you told me on Monday, it is a great fit for not only my skills and expertise, but my preferred work style as well. There is nothing that motivates me more than a tough challenge and a tight deadline!

As you suggested, I will touch base with you in about a month to see whether things have changed.

In the meantime, if there is any way that I can be of help to you, please let me know.

Sincerely,


Ryder Wilson

---

## FIGURE 14.7: SAMPLE THANK-YOU LETTER ASKING FOR THE JOB.

# Kathy Miller

2943 Hillside Street, Unit 2-B ▪ Oakland, California 94624 ▪ 510-245-7450 ▪ kathymiller@verizon.net

March 30, 20XX

Steve Rostakoff
Western Regional Manager
NuTraders Network
9090 Mile High Drive
Denver, CO 80209

Dear Steve:

NuTraders has an exciting future, and I would like to help the Institutional Services division skyrocket to a market-dominant position in the West.

NuTraders' new offerings put the company in a short-term position of market advantage. To seize this advantage requires a "hit the ground running" sales approach. As we discussed, my experience with Schwab closely parallels your new Western Sales Manager position. I know the market... I know the key players... I know the industry and the products... and I have the experience and track record to deliver both immediate revenue results and sustainable long-term growth.

With the right person at the helm, the first-year goal of $100 million in sales is easily reachable. I believe I am that person. I hope you agree.

As you requested, I am attaching a list of professional references, and I will follow up with you on April 6 to see whether you have any additional questions. Thank you for sharing so much time and information with me this week; I am inspired by your enthusiasm and eager to play a part in building a strong Western Region for NuTraders.

Sincerely,


Kathy Miller

enclosure

# JIST Cards®—A Mini-Resume and a Powerful Job Search Tool

JIST Cards are a job search tool that gets results. I developed JIST Cards many years ago, almost by accident, as a tool to help job seekers. I was surprised by the positive employer reaction they received back then, so paid attention and developed them further. Over the years, I have seen them in every imaginable format, and forms of JIST Cards are now being used on the Internet, in personal video interviews, and in other electronic media.

In case you were wondering, the word "JIST" is an acronym originally created for a self-directed job search program I developed years ago. It stands for "Job Information & Seeking Training." The word JIST was later trademarked and has been used for many years now in various forms (including JIST Publishing) to identify self-directed job search, career, and other materials.

## Think of a JIST Card as a Very Small Resume

A JIST Card is carefully constructed to contain all the essential information most employers want to know in a very short format. It typically uses a 3-×-5–inch card format, but has been designed into many other sizes and formats, such as a folded business card, or as part of an e-mail.

Your JIST Cards can be as simple as handwritten or created with graphics and on special papers or electronic formats. You should create a JIST Card in addition to a resume because a JIST Card is used in a different way.

## JIST Cards Get Results

What matters is what JIST Cards accomplish—they get results. In surveys of employers, more than 90 percent of JIST Cards form a positive impression of the writer within 30 seconds. More amazing is that about 80 percent of employers say they would be willing to interview the person behind the JIST Card, even if they did not have a job opening now. I know of no other job search technique that has this effect. And to have this effect in about 30 seconds is simply amazing.

## *How You Can Use JIST Cards*

You can use a JIST Card in many ways, including these:

- Attach one to your resume or application.

- Enclose one in a thank-you letter.

- Give them to your friends, relatives, and other contacts—so that they can give them to other people.

- Send them to everyone who graduated from your school or who is a member of your professional association.

- Put them on car windshields.

- Post them on the supermarket bulletin board.

- Send them in electronic form as an e-mail.

I'm not kidding about finding JIST Cards on windshields or bulletin boards. I've seen them used in these ways and hear about more ways people are using them all the time.

## *JIST Card Paper and Format Tips*

JIST Cards are most often used in paper formats. Many office-supply stores have perforated light card stock sheets that you can run through your computer printer. You can then tear them apart into 3-×-5–inch cards. Many word-processing programs have templates that allow you to format a 3-×-5–inch card size. You can also use regular size paper, print several cards on a sheet, and cut it to the size you need. Print shops can also photocopy or print them in the size you need. Get a few hundred at a time. They are cheap, and the objective is to get lots of them in circulation.

**QUICK TIP**

You can include your JIST Card information in a signature line at the bottom of outgoing e-mail messages. Use it on every e-mail you send, because the more people who see it, the better your chances of finding a job opportunity.

## Sample JIST Cards

The following sample JIST Cards use a plain format, but you can make them as fancy as you want. So be creative. Look over the examples to see how they are constructed. Some are for entry-level jobs and some are for more advanced ones. The content of the samples, and of your own JIST Card, can be adapted for use as e-mail attachments, as part of an online or other portfolio, and other formats. So be creative and adapt the idea to best fit your own situation.

### QUICK TIP

JIST Cards are harder to write than they look, so carefully review the examples and use the content of your resume as a starting point for content. Once you have your own JIST Card, put hundreds of them in circulation. JIST Cards work, but only if they get to the people in your network.

**FIGURE 14.8: A SAMPLE JIST CARD FOR AN OFFICE WORKER.**

Sandy Nolan

Position: General Office/Clerical

Message: (512) 232-9213

More than two years of work experience plus one year of training in office practices. Type 55 wpm, trained in word processing, post general ledger, have good interpersonal skills, and get along with most people. Can meet deadlines and handle pressure well.

Willing to work any hours.

Organized, honest, reliable, and hardworking.

## FIGURE 14.9: SAMPLE JIST CARD FOR A SYSTEMS ANALYST.

Joyce Hua

Home: (214) 173-1659
Message: (214) 274-1436
E-mail: jhua@yahoo.com

Position: Programming/Systems Analyst

More than 10 years of combined education and experience in data processing and related fields. Competent programming in Visual Basic, C, C++, FORTRAN, and Java, and database management. Extensive PC network applications experience. Have supervised a staff as large as seven on special projects and have a record of meeting deadlines. Operations background in management, sales, and accounting.

Desire career-oriented position, will relocate.

Dedicated, self-starter, creative problem solver.

## FIGURE 14.10: SAMPLE JIST CARD FOR A CHEMIST.

Paul Thomas

Home: (301) 681-3922
Cell: (301) 927-9856
pthomas@chem.com

Position:    Research Chemist, Research Management
             in a small-to-medium-sized company

Ph.D. in biochemistry plus more than 15 years of work experience. Developed and patented various processes with current commercial applications worth many millions of dollars. Experienced with all phases of lab work with an emphasis on chromatography, isolation, and purification of organic and biochemical compounds. Specialize in practical pharmaceutical and agricultural applications of chemical research. Have teaching, supervision, and project management experience.

Married more than 15 years, stable work history, results and task oriented, ambitious, and willing to relocate.

**FIGURE 14.11: SAMPLE JIST CARD FOR AN ELECTRONICS INSTALLER.**

Richard Straightarrow

Home: (602) 253-9678
Message: (602) 257-6643
E-mail: RSS@email.com

**Objective:** Electronics installation, maintenance, and sales

Four years of work experience plus a two-year A.S. degree in Electronics Engineering Technology. Managed a $360,000/year business while going to school full time, with grades in the top 25%. Familiar with all major electronic diagnostic and repair equipment. Hands-on experience with medical, consumer, communication, and industrial electronics equipment and applications. Good problem-solving and communication skills. Customer service oriented.

Willing to do what it takes to get the job done.

Self motivated, dependable, learn quickly.

**FIGURE 14.12: SAMPLE JIST CARD FOR A WAREHOUSE MANAGER.**

**Juanita Rodriguez**

Message: (639) 361-1754
E-mail: jrodriguez@email.com

Position: Warehouse Management

Six years of experience plus two years of formal business coursework. Have supervised a staff as large as 16 people and warehousing operations covering over two acres and valued at more than $14,000,000. Automated inventory operations resulting in a 30% increase in turnover and estimated annual savings more than $250,000. Working knowledge of accounting, computer systems, time and motion studies, and advanced inventory management systems.

Will work any hours.

Responsible, hardworking, and can solve problems.

## FIGURE 14.13: SAMPLE JIST CARD FOR A HOTEL MANAGER.

**Deborah Levy**  Home: (213) 432-8064
Cell: (212) 876-9487
E-mail: debbielevy@yahoo.com

**Position:** Hotel Management Professional

Four years of experience in sales, catering, and accounting in a 300-room hotel. Associate degree in Hotel Management plus one year with the Boileau Culinary Institute. Doubled revenues from meetings and conferences. Increased dining room and bar revenues by 44%. Have been commended for improving staff productivity and courtesy. I approach my work with industry, imagination, and creative problem-solving skills.

Enthusiastic, well-organized, and detail-oriented.

## FIGURE 14.14: SAMPLE JIST CARD FOR A MANAGER.

**Jonathan Miller**  Cell: (614) 788-2434
E-mail: jonm@pike.org

Objective: Management

More than 7 years of management experience plus a B.S. degree in business. Managed budgets as large as $10 million. Experienced in cost control and reduction, cutting more than 20% of overhead while business increased more than 30%. Good organizer and problem solver. Excellent communication skills.

Prefer responsible position in a medium-to-large business

Cope well with deadline pressure, seek challenge, flexible.

# Other Job Search Correspondence

Besides thank-you letters and JIST Cards, you can send a variety of other items to people during your job search. Following are brief comments about some of these methods of communication.

## Follow-Up Letters After an Interview

After an interview, you might want to send follow-up correspondence to solve a problem the employer mentioned or to present a proposal. The preceding section showed examples of letters and letters that were sent following an interview. You can easily adapt the content for use in follow-up e-mails.

In some instances, a longer or more detailed letter is appropriate. The objective is to provide additional information or to present a proposal. The sample letter from Sandra A. Zaremba in chapter 13 is an example of a follow-up letter that suggests a specific proposal.

In some cases, you could submit a much more comprehensive proposal that would essentially justify the employer creating a job for you. If a job opening is available, you can submit an outline of what you would do if hired. In writing such a proposal, it is essential that you be specific in telling an employer what you would do and what results these actions would bring. For example, if you propose to increase sales, how would you do it and how much might sales increase?

## Enclosures and E-mail Attachments

In some cases, you may want to include items along with the correspondence, such as a writing sample. This can be appropriate, but don't send too much material unless the employer requests it. Never send originals unless you are willing to lose them. Assume, in all cases, that what you send will not be returned to you.

## Self-Sticking Notes

You have surely used those little notes that stick to papers, walls, and other things. There's a size usually called "flags" that are smaller and narrower than most of the square stick-on notes you probably use. Some even have an arrow design on them. These can be useful when calling attention to specific points on attachments or to provide additional details.

**QUICK TIP**

Use one or two self-sticking notes at the most. Avoid making your correspondence look like a patchwork quilt. The fewer notes you attach, the more impact they will have.

## List of References

Once employers begin to get serious, they might want to contact your references as part of their final screening process. To make this easier for them, I suggest that you prepare a list of people to contact. This list should include the complete name, title, organization, address, phone number, and e-mail address for each reference. You should include information about how each person knows you. For example, indicate that Ms. Rivera was your immediate supervisor for two years.

Be sure to inform those on your list that they might be contacted and asked to provide references. Take the time to prepare them for the call by sending information on the types of jobs you now seek, a current resume, a JIST Card, and other details.

**QUICK TIP**

If you have any question whether a person will provide you with a positive reference, discuss this in advance so that you know what the individual is likely to say about you. If it is not positive, drop this person from your list.

## Letters of Reference

Many organizations fear lawsuits as the result of giving out negative information regarding an ex-employee. For this reason, it can often be difficult for an employer to get any meaningful information about you over the phone. I recommend that you request previous employers and other references to write a letter or e-mail of reference that you can submit to others when asked.

If the letters are positive, the advantages are clear. Even if the letter is negative, at least you now know that there is a problem with this reference. Depending on the situation, you might contact this previous employer and negotiate what he or she will say when called.

## Unsolicited Letters Requesting an Interview or Other Assistance

Once more, I want to discourage you from sending out unsolicited letters or e-mail as a primary job search technique. Even though many resume books recommend sending out lots of unsolicited resumes, the evidence is overwhelming that this method does not work for most people. Doing the same thing on the Internet often results in the same outcome. The rare exception is if your skills are very much in demand.

Sending a letter or e-mail to people with whom you share a common bond, such as alumni or members of a professional group, can be reasonably effective. This is particularly so if you are looking for a job in another city or region and you send a letter or e-mail asking someone to help you by providing names of contacts. Several of the sample cover letters in chapter 13 provide examples of this very technique. It can work, particularly if you follow up by phone and e-mail.

# Part 5

# How to Find a Job Fast

This could be the most important section in this book. It consists of two chapters focused on finding a good job quickly. It gives you all the tools you will need to conduct a quick and effective job search. Remember that a resume alone can't get you a job. That's why I'm providing this extra information—so that your job search will be as short as possible and that you will find the right job for you.

**Chapter 15: Get a Good Job in Less Time   337**

**Chapter 16: Quick Tips for Using the Internet in Your Job Search   365**

# CHAPTER 15

# Get a Good Job in Less Time

This chapter provides you with an overview of career planning and job seeking skills. It illustrates quick but helpful techniques that you can use to shorten the time it takes to get a job.

Hopefully you have jumped to this chapter after finishing one of the basic resumes in part 1. With resume in hand, you can set out to accomplish your real objective: getting a job.

## Career Planning and Job Search Advice

Although a resume is a tool to help you get a job, few resume books provide good advice on job seeking. In fact, most resume books give bad advice. For example, they often tell you to send out lots of resumes and get them into the stacks on employers' desks. Then, if your resume (or cover letter) is good enough, employers will pick it out of the pile and ask you in for an interview.

This advice is old fashioned and downright harmful. It puts you at the mercy of some employer whose mindset is to screen people out. It encourages you to be passive and wait for employers to call you. And, worst of all, it assumes that the job search is limited to talking to employers who have job openings now and excludes all those who do not—but who might soon.

## QUICK NOTE

If you are planning your career or need to know more about finding a job, I strongly encourage you to learn more. You can find more details in longer job search books such as *The Very Quick Job Search* (by Mike Farr), *Job Search Magic* (by Susan Britton Whitcomb), and *The Ultimate Job Search* (by Richard Beatty).

So I think the traditional advice on resumes and job seeking is not good. You can use techniques that are far more effective than the traditional ones. The best job search techniques are based on common sense. They encourage you to be clear about what you want and then to go out and actively look for it. It takes some nerve, but people who use the techniques presented in this chapter have proven that they do work. The techniques help you find better jobs in less time. And that's what job search should be all about, isn't it?

### AVOID THE TEMPTATION TO JUST SCAN THIS MATERIAL—DO THE ACTIVITIES

I know that you will resist doing the activities included here. But trust me, completing them is worthwhile. Those who do them will have a better sense of what they are good at, what they want to do, and how to go about doing it. They are likely to get more interviews and to present themselves better in those interviews.

Interestingly, you will—after reading this section and doing its activities—have spent more time planning your career than most people. You will know far more than the average job seeker about how to go about finding a job. Although you may want to know more, I hope that this is enough to get you started.

Although this book will teach you techniques to find a better job in less time, job seeking requires you to act, not just learn. So consider what you can do to put the techniques to work for you. Do the activities. Create a daily plan. Get more interviews. The sooner and harder you get to work on your job search, the shorter it is likely to be.

# Changing Jobs and Careers Is Often Healthy

Most of us were told from an early age that each career move must be up, involving more money, responsibility, and prestige. However, research indicates that people change careers for many other reasons as well.

In a survey conducted by the Gallup Organization for the National Occupational Information Coordinating Committee, 44 percent of the working adults surveyed expected to be in a different job within three years. Yet only 41 percent had a definite plan to follow in mapping out their careers.

Logical, ordered careers are found more often with increasing levels of education. For example, although 25 percent of high school dropouts took the only job available, this was true for only 8 percent of those with at least some college. But you should not assume this means that such occupational stability is healthy. Many adult developmental psychologists believe occupational change is not only normal, but may even be necessary for sound adult growth and development.

**QUICK NOTE**

It is common, even normal, to reconsider occupational roles during your twenties, thirties, and forties, even in the absence of economic pressure to do so.

One viewpoint is that a healthy occupational change allows some previously undeveloped aspect of the self to emerge. The change may be as natural as from clerk to supervisor or as drastic as from professional musician to airline pilot. Although risk is always a factor when change is involved, reasonable risks are healthy and can raise self-esteem.

Whether you are seeking similar work in another setting or changing careers, you need a workable plan to find the right job. The rest of this chapter gives you the information you need to help you find a good job quickly.

# Seven Steps for a Quick and Successful Job Search

You can't just read about getting a job. The best way to get a job is to go out and get interviews! The best way to get interviews is to make a job out of getting a job. I have identified just seven things you need to do that make a big difference in your job search. The following sections cover each of these steps.

## SEVEN STEPS FOR A QUICK JOB SEARCH

1. Identify your skills.

2. Have a clear job objective.

3. Know where and how to look for job leads.

4. Spend at least 25 hours a week looking for a job—more if you're currently unemployed.

5. Get two interviews a day.

6. Do well in interviews.

7. Follow up on all contacts.

## *Step 1: Identify Your Skills*

An effective career plan requires that you know your skills. Chapters 5 and 6 cover the basics of how to identify your key skills. If you have not spent time on this issue, I strongly suggest that you do. It's very important for both planning your career and presenting yourself effectively throughout your job search.

Most job seekers cannot answer the question, "Why should I hire you?" The consequence of not being able to answer that question, as you might guess, is that your chances of getting a job offer are greatly reduced. Knowing your skills, therefore, gives you a distinct advantage in the job search as well as helps you write a more effective resume.

If you have not done the skills identification activities in chapters 5 and 6 or are not able to identify your key skills, review those chapters before you go on with your search for a job. Assuming that you have completed the activities in chapters 5 and 6, here are some reminder lists on your most important skills. Transfer your answers from those chapters to these lines.

## A Skills Review

**Your top five adaptive/self-management skills (from page 82)**

1. _____
2. _____
3. _____
4. _____
5. _____

**Your top five transferable skills (from page 85)**

1. _____
2. _____
3. _____
4. _____
5. _____

**Your top five job-related skills (from pages 102–103)**

1. _____
2. _____
3. _____
4. _____
5. _____

## *Step 2: Have a Clear Job Objective*

Having a clear job objective is not just an issue for your resume. I realize how difficult it can be to figure out the exact job you want; however, getting as close as you can is essential.

Too many people look for a job without having a good idea of exactly what they are looking for. Before you go out looking for "a" job, you need to first define exactly what it is you really want—"the" job. Most people think a job objective is the same as a job title, but it isn't. You need to consider other elements of what makes a job satisfying for you. Then, later, you can decide what that job is called and what industry it might be in.

Chapter 7 covers the basics of defining a clear job objective. That chapter also discusses the importance of considering your industry preferences. With that information, and additional study as needed, you should have a clearer sense of the job you want and the industry where you would like to work. So, if you don't have a clear job objective, I suggest you spend more time with chapter 7.

Here are a few points from chapter 7 to summarize the elements to consider in your ideal job. Transfer your answers from that chapter to these lines.

### Your Ideal Job

**What skills do you want to use? (from page 124)**

1. _____

2. _____

3. _____

4. _____

5. _____

**What special knowledge would you like to use in your ideal job? (from page 124)**

_____

_____

_____

**What types of people do you like to work with or for? (from pages 124–125)**

_____

_____

_____

**What type of work environment do you prefer? (from page 125)**

_____

_____

_____

**Where do you want your next job to be located? (from page 125)**

_____

_____

_____

*(continued)*

(continued)

**How much money do you hope to make in your next job? (from page 126)**

_____

**How much responsibility are you willing to accept? (from page 126)**

_____

_____

_____

**What things are important or have meaning to you? (from page 127)**

_____

_____

_____

**Describe your ideal job (from pages 127–128):**

_____

_____

_____

# Step 3: Know Where and How to Look for Job Leads

One survey found that about 85 percent of all employers don't advertise their job openings. They hire people they know, people who find out about the jobs through word of mouth, or people who happen to be in the right place at the right time. Although the Internet has changed how some employers find people, getting a solid lead is still too often a matter of "luck." But the good news is that, by using the right techniques, you can learn to increase your "luck" in finding job openings.

## Traditional Job Search Methods Are Not Very Effective

Most job seekers don't know how ineffective some traditional job hunting techniques tend to be. For example, the chart in figure 15.1 shows that fewer than 15 percent of all job seekers get jobs from reading the want ads.

**FIGURE 15.1: HOW PEOPLE FIND JOBS.**

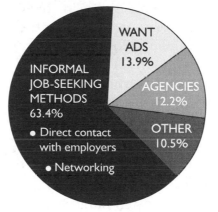

Here is more detail on the effectiveness of seven of the most popular traditional job search methods:

- **Help wanted ads:** Less than 15 percent of all people get their jobs through the newspaper want ads. Everyone who reads the paper knows about these openings, so competition for advertised jobs is fierce. You can get want ads through the Internet for most metropolitan newspapers—but so can everyone else. (Position advertisements on Internet job boards are discussed separately in chapter 16.) Still, some people get jobs through ads, so go ahead and apply. Just be sure to spend most of your time using more effective methods.

- **State employment services:** Each state has a network of local offices to administer unemployment compensation and provide job leads and other services. These services are provided without charge to you or employers. Names vary by state, so it may be called "Job Service," "Department of Labor," "Workforce Development," "Unemployment Office," "WorkOne," or another name.

Nationally, only about 5 percent of all job seekers get their jobs here, and these organizations typically know of only one-tenth (or fewer) of the job openings in a region. Local openings are posted on a government-funded Internet site at www.jobcentral.com/index.asp, where you can search by occupation and location anywhere in the country.

- **Private employment agencies:** Recent studies have found that staffing agencies work reasonably well for those who use them. But consider some cautions. For one thing, these agencies work best for entry-level positions or for those with specialized, in-demand skills. Most people who use a private agency usually find their jobs using some other source, making the success record of these businesses quite modest.

  Private agencies charge a fee as high as 20 percent of your annual salary to you or to the employer. Because of the high expense, you can require that you be referred only to interviews where the employer pays the fee. Keep in mind that most private agencies find job openings by calling employers, something you could do yourself.

### QUICK ALERT

Never work with a search firm or employment agency that charges you to get a job through them. Legitimate firms are paid only by the employer for whom they fill jobs. There should be no cost to you. (But don't confuse this advice with the fees you pay to private-practice career counselors or coaches; they provide coaching services for a fee and don't promise you a job.)

- **Temporary agencies:** These can be a source of quick but temporary jobs to bring in some income while you look for long-term employment. Temp jobs also give you experience in a variety of settings—something that can help you land full-time jobs later. More and more employers are also using these jobs as a way to evaluate workers for permanent jobs. So consider using these agencies if it makes sense, but continue an active search for a full-time job.

- **Sending out resumes:** One survey found that you would have to mail more than 500 unsolicited resumes to get one interview! Like other traditional approaches, use this method sparingly because the numbers are stacked against you.

  A better approach is to contact the person who might hire you, by phone or via e-mail, to set up an interview directly; then send a resume. If you insist on sending out unsolicited resumes, do this on weekends and evenings and save the "prime time" job-searching hours for more effective techniques.

- **Filling out applications:** Most employers use applications to screen people out. Larger organizations may require them, but remember that your task is to get an interview, not fill out an application. If you do complete applications, make them neat and error-free and do not include anything that could get you screened out. Never present something in a way an employer would see as a negative. For example, instead of saying you were "fired," say "position eliminated due to corporate downsizing." If the form asks for pay requirements, simply write in something like "flexible" instead of giving a specific number.

### QUICK TIP

If necessary, leave a problem question or section blank on an application, or write "Will explain in interview." This might help keep you from being screened out immediately. Sometimes it's easier to explain things in person.

- **Human resource departments:** Hardly anyone gets hired by interviewers in HR or personnel departments. Their job is to screen you and then refer the "best" applicants to the person who would supervise you. You may need to cooperate with the people in HR, but it is often better to talk directly to the person who is most likely to supervise you—even if no opening exists at the moment. And remember that many smaller organizations don't even have HR or personnel offices.

## The Two Job Search Methods That Work Best

About two-thirds of all people get their jobs using informal methods. These jobs are often not advertised and are part of the "hidden" job market. How can you find them?

There are two basic informal job search methods: networking with people you know (which I call warm contacts), and making direct contacts with an employer (which I call cold contacts). They are both based on the most important job search rule of all: **Don't wait until the job is open before contacting the employer!**

Most jobs are filled by someone the employer meets before the job is formally open. So the trick is to meet people who can hire you *before* a job is available. Instead of saying, "Do you have any jobs open?" say, "I realize you may not have any openings now, but I would still like to talk to you about the possibility of future openings.

### Develop a Network of Contacts in Five Easy Steps

One study found that about 40 percent of all people found their jobs through a lead provided by a friend, a relative, or an acquaintance. Developing new contacts is called "networking," and here's how it works:

1. **Make lists of people you know.** Develop a list of anyone with whom you are friendly; then make a separate list of all your relatives. These two lists alone often add up to 25 to 100 people or more. Next, think of other groups with whom you have something in common, such as former coworkers or classmates; members of your social or sports groups; members of your professional association; former employers; and members of your religious group. You may not know many of these people personally, but most will help you if you ask them.

2. **Contact the people on your lists in a systematic way.** Each of these people is a contact for you. Obviously, some lists and some people on those lists will be more helpful than others, but almost any one of them could help you find a job lead.

3. **Present yourself well.** Begin with your friends and relatives. Call or e-mail them and tell them you are looking for a job and need their help. Be as clear as possible about what you are looking for

and what skills and qualifications you have. Look at the sample phone script later in this chapter for presentation ideas.

4. **Ask them for leads.** It's possible that they will know of a job opening that is just right for you. If so, get the details and get right on it! More likely, however, they will not, so here are three questions you should ask:

   - **Do you know of any openings for a person with my skills?** If the answer is no (which it usually is), ask the next question.

   - **Do you know of someone else who might know of such an opening?** If your contact does, get that name and ask for another one. If he or she doesn't, ask the next question.

   - **Do you know of anyone who might know of someone else who might?** Another good way to ask this is "Do you know someone who knows lots of people?" If all else fails, this will usually get you a name.

5. **Contact these referrals and ask them the same questions.** For each original contact, you can extend your network of acquaintances by hundreds of people. Eventually, one of these people will hire you or refer you to someone who will. If you use networking thoroughly, it may be the only job search technique you need.

## QUICK TIP

If you're worried that you don't know enough people to network effectively, concentrate on going to group events where you'll have a large pool of people from which to develop contacts, rather than just meeting people one by one. Attend professional association meetings, lectures, classes, social functions, and anywhere that you can meet a lot of folks.

Networking is about much more than asking people if they know of any job openings. The answer is likely to be no, so that question doesn't get you far. Instead, look at networking as a way to build relationships with people who know other people, who may know other people who know of jobs. Networking is also about getting advice about your search and insight into the organizations you're trying to break into.

## QUICK TIP

An easy way to find networking contacts you might have lost track of is to join an online networking site such as LinkedIn (www.linkedin.com) to search for their names on the site. If they are also a member (and millions of people now are), you will find out where they work now and be able to connect with them online. Then you can easily see who's in their networks and can ask them to help you connect with others.

**FIGURE 15.2: HOW REFERRALS CAN EXPAND YOUR NETWORK.**

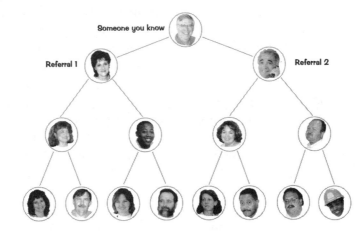

If you ask each referral for two names and follow through, your network will soon look like this:

### *Use Cold Contacts—Contact Employers Directly*

It takes more courage, but contacting an employer directly is a variation on the networking idea and a very effective job search technique. I call these cold contacts because you don't know or have an existing connection with the employers. Following are two basic techniques for making cold contacts.

- **Use the Yellow Pages to find potential employers.** Online sites like www.yellowpages.com and others allow you to find potential employers anywhere, but the print version is best if you're looking for a local job. You can begin by looking at the index and asking for each entry, "Would an organization of this kind need a person with my skills?" If the answer is "yes," then that type of organization or business is a possible target. You can also rate "yes" entries based on your interest, writing an "A" next to those that seem very interesting, a "B" next to those you are not sure of, and a "C" next to those that don't seem interesting at all.

  Next, select a type of organization that got a "yes" response (such as "hotels") and turn to the section of the Yellow Pages where they are listed. Then call the organizations and ask to speak to the person who is most likely to hire or supervise you. A sample telephone script is included later in this section to give you ideas about what to say.

  The Internet provides a variety of ways to do the same thing in a different way. For example, Yellow Pages listings are available online for any geographic area of the country. And many businesses have Web sites where you can get information and apply for job openings. There are also databases of companies that you can search to develop "hit lists." Several of these databases are listed in chapter 16.

- **Drop in without an appointment.** Although building security has become increasingly tight in some locations, you can sometimes simply walk into many potential employers' organizations and ask to speak to the person in charge. This is particularly effective in small businesses, but it works surprisingly well in larger ones, too. Remember, you want an interview even if there are no openings now. If your timing is inconvenient, ask for a better time to come back for an interview.

- **Use the phone to get job leads.** Once you have created your JIST Card (see chapter 14), it's easy to create a telephone contact script based on it. Adapt the basic script to call people you know or your Yellow Pages leads. Select Yellow Pages index categories that might use a person with your skills and get the numbers of specific organizations in that category. Once you get to the person who is most likely to supervise you, present your phone script.

Although it doesn't work every time, most people, with practice, can get one or more interviews in an hour by making these cold calls. Here is a sample phone script based on a JIST Card:

*Hello, my name is Pam Nykanen. I'm interested in a position in hotel management. I have four years of experience in sales, catering, and accounting with a 300-room hotel. I also have an associate degree in Hotel Management, plus one year of experience with the Bradey Culinary Institute. During my employment, I helped double revenues from meetings and conferences and increased bar revenues by 46 percent. I have good problem-solving skills and am good with people. I am also well organized, hardworking, and detail oriented. When may I come in for an interview?*

Although this example assumes that you are calling someone you don't know, the script can be easily modified for presentation to warm contacts, including referrals. Using the script for making cold calls takes courage, but it works for most people.

## MOST JOBS ARE WITH SMALL EMPLOYERS

About 70 percent of all people work in small businesses—those with 250 or fewer employees. While the largest corporations have reduced the number of employees, small businesses have been creating as many as 80 percent of the new jobs over the past decade.

Smaller organizations are where most of the job search action is. Many opportunities exist to obtain training and promotions in smaller organizations, too. Many do not even have HR departments, so nontraditional job search techniques are particularly effective with these companies.

## *Step 4: Spend 25 Hours or More a Week Looking for a Job*

On the average, job seekers spend fewer than 15 hours a week looking for work. The average length of unemployment varies from three or more months, with some being out of work far longer (older workers and higher earners are two groups who take longer). There is a clear connection between how long it takes to find a job and the number of hours spent looking on a daily and weekly basis.

The more time you spend on your job search each week, the less time you are likely to remain unemployed. Of course, using more effective job search methods also helps. Those who follow my advice have proven, over and over, that they get jobs in less than half the average time; and they often get better jobs, too. Time management is the key.

**QUICK ALERT**

Of course, if you are currently employed and looking for a better job, you would spend less than 25 hours a week looking—but the principles remain the same.

If you are unemployed and looking for a full-time job, you should look for a job on a full-time basis. It just makes sense, although many do not do so because of discouragement, lack of good techniques, and lack of structure. Most job seekers have no idea what they are going to do next Thursday—they don't have a plan. The most important thing is to decide how many hours you can commit to your job search, and stay with it. If you are unemployed, you should spend a minimum of 25 hours a week on solid job search activities with no goofing around, and even more is better. The following worksheet walks you through a simple but effective process to help you organize your job search schedule.

# Structure Your Job Search Like a Job

**1.  Decide how many hours you will spend a week looking for work.**

Write here how many hours you are willing to spend each week looking for a job:

_____

**2.  Decide which days and times you will look for work.**

Answering the following questions requires you to have a schedule and a plan, just as you had when you were working.

Which days of the week will you spend looking for a job? _____

_____

How many hours will you look each day?  _____

At what time will you begin and end your job search on each of these days? _____

**3.  Create a specific daily schedule.**

A specific daily job search schedule is very important because most job seekers find it hard to stay productive each day. You already know which job search methods are most effective, and you should plan on spending most of your time using those methods.

The sample daily schedule that follows has been very effective for people who have used it, and it will give you ideas for your own. Although you are welcome to create your daily schedule however you like, I urge you to consider one similar to this one because it works.

| | |
|---|---|
| 7–8 a.m. | Get up, shower, dress, eat breakfast. |
| 8–8:15 a.m. | Organize work space; review schedule for interviews or follow-ups; update schedule. |
| 8:15–9 a.m. | Review old leads for follow-up; develop new leads (want ads, Internet, networking lists, and so on). |
| 9–10 a.m. | Make networking or direct employer phone calls or Internet contacts; set up meetings and interviews. |
| 10–10:15 a.m. | Take a break! |
| 10:15–11 a.m. | Make more new calls and Internet contacts. |

| | |
|---|---|
| 11–12 p.m. | Make follow-up calls and e-mails as needed. |
| 12–1 p.m. | Lunch break. |
| 1–5 p.m. | Go on interviews and networking meetings; make cold contacts in the field; conduct research for upcoming interviews. |
| 5–8 p.m. | Attend networking events. |

4.  **Get a schedule book and write down your job search schedule.**

    This is important: If you are not accustomed to using a daily schedule book or planner, promise yourself that you will get a good one today. Choose one that allows plenty of space for each day's plan on an hourly basis, plus room for daily "to-do" listings. Write in your daily schedule in advance; then add interviews as they come. Get used to carrying it with you and using it!

**QUICK TIP**

If a schedule book sounds a little too "old school" for you, you can manage your schedule with an electronic device, such as a BlackBerry or mobile phone, or with a calendar program on your PC. But if you're on a budget, you can pick up a spiral-bound organizer at an office-supply store for less than $10.

## Step 5: Get Two Interviews a Day

The average job seeker gets about five interviews a month—fewer than two interviews a week. Yet many job seekers using the techniques I suggest routinely get two interviews a day. But to accomplish this, you must first redefine what an interview is.

### THE NEW DEFINITION OF AN INTERVIEW

An interview is any face-to-face contact with a person who has the authority to hire or supervise someone with your skills. The person may or may not have an opening at the time.

With this definition, it is *much* easier to get interviews. You can now interview with all kinds of potential employers, not just those who have job openings. Many job seekers use the Yellow Pages to get two interviews with just one hour of calls by using the telephone contact script discussed earlier. Others drop in on a potential employer and ask for an unscheduled interview—and they get one. And getting names of others to contact from those you know—networking—is quite effective if you persist.

Getting two interviews a day equals 10 a week and 40 a month. That's 800 percent more interviews than the average job seeker gets. Who do you think will get a job offer quicker? So set out each day to get at least two interviews. It's quite possible to do, now that you know how.

## Step 6: Do Well in Interviews

No matter how you get an interview, once you're there, you will have to create a good impression

- Even if your resume is one of the 10 best ever written.

- Even if you have the best of credentials.

- Even if you really want the job.

**QUICK TIP**

One study indicated that, of those who made it as far as the interview (many others were screened out before then), about 40 percent created a bad first impression, mostly based on their dress and grooming. First impressions count, and if you make a bad one, your chances of getting a job offer rapidly decrease to about zero.

The following sections give advice for making a good impression in job interviews.

### Dress for Success

Although there is more to making a good first impression than your dress and grooming, this is fortunately something that you can control. So, for this reason, I have created the following rule:

**FARR'S DRESS AND GROOMING RULE:**
Dress the way you think the boss is most likely to dress—only neater.

Dress for success. If necessary, ask someone who dresses well to help you select an interview outfit. Pay close attention to your grooming, too.

## How to Answer Tough Interview Questions

Interviews are where the job search action happens. You have to get them; then you have to do well in them. If you have done your homework, you will seek out interviews for jobs that will maximize your skills. That's a good start, but your ability to communicate your skills in the interview makes an enormous difference.

This is where, according to employer surveys, most job seekers have problems. A large percentage of job seekers don't effectively communicate the skills they have to do the job, and they answer one or more "problem" questions poorly. Trust me, this is a big problem. If you leave the interview without having answered one or more problem questions effectively, your odds of getting a job offer are greatly decreased.

Although thousands of problem interview questions are possible, here are just 10 that, if you can plan how to answer them well, will prepare you for most interviews.

**TOP 10 PROBLEM QUESTIONS**

1. Why don't you tell me about yourself?
2. Why should I hire you?
3. What are your major strengths?
4. What are your major weaknesses?
5. What sort of pay do you expect to receive?
6. How does your previous experience relate to the jobs we have here?
7. What are your plans for the future?

(continued)

(continued)

8.  What will your former employer (or references) say about you?

9.  Why are you looking for this type of position, and why here?

10.  Why don't you tell me about your personal situation?

I don't have the space here to give thorough answers to all of these questions, and there are potentially hundreds of additional questions you might be asked. Instead, let me suggest several techniques I have developed that you can use to answer almost any interview question.

## A TRADITIONAL INTERVIEW IS NOT A FRIENDLY EXCHANGE

In a traditional interview situation, there is a job opening, and you are one of several (or one of a hundred) applicants. In this setting, the employer's task is to eliminate all but one applicant.

Assuming that you got as far as an interview, the interviewer's questions are designed to elicit information that can be used to screen you out. If you are wise, you know that your task is to avoid getting screened out. It's not an open and honest interaction, is it? This illustrates yet another advantage of nontraditional job search techniques: the ability to talk to an employer before an opening exists. This eliminates the stress of a traditional interview. Employers are not trying to screen you out, and you are not trying to keep them from finding out the bad stuff about you.

## The Three-Step Process for Answering Interview Questions

I know this might seem too simple, but the Three-Step Process is easy to remember. Its simplicity allows you to evaluate a question and create a good answer. The technique is based on sound principles and has worked for thousands of people.

1.  **Understand what is really being asked.**

    Most questions are really designed to find out about your self-management skills and personality. Although they are rarely this blunt, the employer's real questions are often directed at finding out the following:

- Can I depend on you?

- Are you easy to get along with?

- Are you a good worker?

- Do you have the experience and training to do the job if we hire you?

- Are you likely to stay on the job for a reasonable period of time and be productive?

Ultimately, if the employer is not convinced that you will stay and be a good worker, it won't matter if you have the best credentials. He or she won't hire you.

2. **Answer the question briefly, in a non-damaging way.**

   Acknowledge the facts, but present them as an advantage rather than a disadvantage.

   Many interview questions encourage you to provide negative information. The classic is the "What are your major weaknesses?" question that I included in my top 10 problem questions list. Obviously, this is a trick question, and many people are not prepared for it. A good response might be to mention something that is not all that damaging, such as "I have been told that I am a perfectionist, sometimes not delegating as effectively as I might." But your answer is not complete until you do the last step.

3. **Answer the real concern by presenting your related skills.**

   Base your answer on the key skills that you have identified and that are needed in this job. Give examples to support your skills statements. For example, an employer might say to a recent graduate, "We were looking for someone with more experience in this field. Why should we consider you?" Here is one possible answer: "I'm sure there are people who have more experience, but I do have more than six years of work experience, including three years of advanced training and hands-on experience using the latest methods and techniques. Because my training is recent, I am open to new ideas and am used to working hard and learning quickly."

In the example I presented in Step 2 (about your need to delegate more effectively), a good skills statement might be "I have been working on this problem and have learned to be more willing to let my staff do things, making sure that they have good training and supervision. I've found that their performance improves, and it frees me up to do other things."

Whatever your situation, learn to use it to your advantage. It is essential to communicate your skills during an interview, and the Three-Step Process gives you a technique that can dramatically improve your responses. It works!

## Step 7: Follow Up on All Contacts

People who follow up with potential employers and with others in their network get jobs faster than those who do not. This is another principle that seems too simple to be so important, but it is true.

### FOUR RULES FOR EFFECTIVE FOLLOW-UP

1. Send a thank-you note to every person who helps you in your job search.

2. Send the thank-you note within 24 hours of speaking with the person.

3. Enclose JIST Cards with thank-you notes and all other correspondence.

4. Develop a system to keep following up with good contacts.

### Thank-You Notes Make a Difference

Within 24 hours of the interview, send a thank-you note or e-mail to each person you spoke with. This gives you a great advantage over all the competing job seekers who don't take time to do this. Thank-you notes can be handwritten or typed on quality paper and matching envelopes or e-mailed. Keep your note simple, neat, and errorless. Following is a sample.

**FIGURE 15.3: SAMPLE THANK-YOU NOTE.**

April 16, 20XX                                          2234 Riverwood Ave.
                                                       Philadelphia, PA 17963

Ms. Sandra Kijek
Henderson & Associates, Inc.
1801 Washington Blvd., Suite 1201
Philadelphia, PA 17963

Dear Ms. Kijek:

Thank you for sharing your time with me so generously today. I really appreciated
seeing your state-of-the-art computer equipment.

Your advice has already proved helpful. I have an appointment to meet with Mr.
Robert Hopper on Friday as you anticipated.

Please consider referring me to others if you think of someone else who might need
a person with my skills.

Sincerely,

William Richardson

See chapter 14 for more examples of thank-you notes and letters.

## Use Job Lead Cards to Organize Your Contacts

Use a simple 3-×-5–inch card to keep essential information about
each person in your network. Buy a 3-×-5–inch card file box and tabs
for each day of the month. File the cards under the date you want to
contact the person, and the rest is easy. I've found that staying in
touch with a good contact every other week can pay off big.

### QUICK TIP

You can take advantage of technology to help you manage your job search.
A contact-management program such as ACT! enables you to create electronic "cards" for each contact and integrate them into your weekly schedule.
You might also create a spreadsheet with a program such as Microsoft Excel
where you log your activity and keep details on each person and organization. Even better, the JibberJobber Web site (www.jibberjobber.com) provides online tools for tracking your contacts and managing your job search.

Here's a sample card to give you ideas for creating your own if you use the index card method.

**FIGURE 15.4: SAMPLE JOB LEAD CARD.**

ORGANIZATION: _Mutual Health Insurance_

CONTACT PERSON: _Anna Tomey_   PHONE: _317-355-0216_

SOURCE OF LEAD: _Aunt Ruth_

NOTES: _4/10 Called. Anna on vacation. Call back 4/15. 4/15 Interview set 4/20 at 1:30. 4/20 Anna showed me around. They use the same computers we used in school! (Friendly people.) Sent thank-you note and JIST Card, call back 5/1. 5/1 Second interview 5/8 at 9 a.m.!_

# The Quick Job Search Review

Here are a few thoughts to keep in mind as you go forward with your job search:

- Approach your job search as if it were a job itself.
- Get organized and spend at least 25 hours per week actively looking.
- Know your skills and have a clear job objective.
- Get lots of interviews, including exploratory interviews through networking.
- Have a good answer to the question "Why should I hire you?"
- Follow up on all the leads you generate and send out lots of thank-you notes and JIST Cards.
- Pay attention to all the details; then be yourself in the interview.

Remember that employers are people, too. They will hire someone who they feel will do the job well, be reliable, and fit easily into the work environment.

- When you want the job, tell the employer that you want the job and why.
- Believe in yourself and ask people to help you.

It's that simple.

# CHAPTER 16

# Quick Tips for Using the Internet in Your Job Search

Now that you've gotten an overview of the quickest and most efficient job search methods, this chapter focuses on the Internet as one of those job search tools.

This chapter assumes you know how to use the Internet. If the Internet and World Wide Web are new to you, I recommend *Best Career and Education Web Sites* by Anne Wolfinger. This book covers the basics of how the Internet works, plus provides information on using it for career planning and job seeking.

Career and job hunting resources are all over the Internet. Telling you all that it contains relevant to your search is just not possible. My objective is not to cover all there is to know about career resources on the Web. Instead, I want to help you make the most of this powerful tool in your search and avoid some of the common pitfalls.

## The Internet as a Tool for Your Job Search

You probably use the Internet every day. But is it a good place for job seeking? Yes and no.

I say yes because people do get jobs through contacts they've made on the Internet, and the numbers that do are increasing. The Internet is another tool to use in your search for a good job. But you should also know that the Internet has its limitations.

## *The Dangers of Online Job Hunting*

Although the Internet has worked for many in finding job leads, far more people have been disappointed. Online job hunting can seem like the greatest thing since sliced bread in that it's so easy. You zap your resume out into cyberspace and sit back while it does all the work for you—24 hours a day if you post the resume in a database rather than just applying to jobs one at a time. It's true that the Internet has made job searching much easier in a lot of ways, but using it is often not as effective as you might hope.

### QUICK ALERT

Never give your Social Security number out on the Internet. The only exception is when you're applying for federal jobs through USAJOBS or directly with a government agency, in which case your SSN is required as part of your application. Even so, recent security breaches have left those numbers vulnerable to identity thieves.

### It Makes You Too Passive

Many job seekers assume they can simply put resumes in Internet resume databases and employers will line up to hire them. It sometimes happens this way, but not often. This is the same negative experience that people have when mailing lots of unsolicited resumes to human resource offices—a hopeful but mostly ineffective, shot-in-the-dark approach that has been around since long before computers.

### There's a Huge Amount of Competition

Many Web sites have thousands of job seekers posting resumes and applying for jobs every day. Monster.com, for example, has more than 16 million resumes in its database. So you have huge amounts of competition. The odds of your resume being the one that gets looked at are slim. You have to make sure your resume has the right keywords (as discussed in chapter 4) and then hope for the best.

## A Threat to Your Personal Security

A major downside to online job hunting is the potential for personal security breaches, ranging from the annoying, as in unwanted spam mail, to the highly invasive, such as identity theft. Many job seekers opt for leaving their phone number and address off of their electronic resume—using only their e-mail address—to minimize the chances that criminals can track down their Social Security number or other personal data.

### PHISHING AND SPOOFING

A warning from the U.S. Office of Personnel Management's Web site regarding fraudulent e-mails:

"Spam e-mail is such a common occurrence, you may think you know what to look for. But there are two types of e-mail scams that can be more difficult to identify, and that can be especially harmful if you fail to notice the warning signs: phishing and spoofing. Both practices concern fraudulent e-mail where the 'from' address has been forged to make it appear as if it came from somewhere, or someone, other than the actual source.

"Phishing e-mails are used to fraudulently obtain personal identification and account information. They can also be used to lure the recipient into downloading malicious spyware or malware programs. The message will often suggest there are issues with the recipient's account that require immediate attention. A link will also be provided to a spoof Web site where the recipient will be asked to provide personal/account information or download malicious software.

"Spoof e-mails often include a fraudulent offer of employment and/or the invitation to serve as a go-between for payment processing or money transfers. In most cases, the sender uses a program to auto-generate an e-mail list using random e-mail addresses. Like with phishing e-mails, the sender's address is often disguised."

## There Are Many Ways to Use the Internet in Your Job Search

Job seeking on the Internet involves more than simply visiting job boards and posting your resume in resume banks. The job seekers who got the jobs at the TV station used the Internet in an active way.

And they combined a number of methods, both Internet and more conventional ones (such as going to the interview), to get the jobs.

Don't forget that in addition to posting your resume or browsing jobs, you can use the Internet in other ways in your job search such as research, networking, and identifying employers to contact directly. Here are some of the ways the Internet can help you in your job search:

- **Employer Web sites:** Many employers have Web sites that include substantial information plus a list of job openings. Some sites allow you to interact with staff online or via e-mail to get answers to questions about working there.

- **Information:** You can search for information on a specific employer or industry, get job descriptions that list skills and requirements to emphasize in interviews (and on your resume), find career counseling and job search advice, and look up almost anything else you need related to your job search.

- **E-mail:** Most employers accept resumes via e-mail, and many will correspond with you this way. Many resume database sites will send you e-mail notices of newly added jobs that meet your criteria.

- **Specialty sites:** People in the TV industry have specialized associations and magazines, and the same is true of other fields. Your task is to find the Web sites that specialize in the jobs that interest you. Many have job postings, useful information, and access to people in the know. Also, many geographic-specific sites for cities and towns list local openings. A simple keyword search using a search engine like Google.com or Yahoo.com can broaden your search.

- **Blogs:** Millions of people are writing articles every day for their own blogs (short for "web logs"). Many of these blogs can give you an idea of what it's like to work in a particular field or company, or can even pass along job leads. You can search for relevant blogs at http://blogsearch.google.com.

- **Networking:** Online networking sites such as LinkedIn, ecademy, and Ryze enable you to build your network and leverage it to find job opportunities.

### QUICK TIP

Save time in your search by typing your search information directly into your Web browser's address bar. You may be led to just what you're looking for without having to go through a search engine.

- **Newsgroups:** Thousands of newsgroups specialize in topics of interest to their respective users and provide excellent networking opportunities. Some are for members of specific organizations, like accountants in a given city. Others are open to those interested in specialty topics. Newsgroups can be a good source of local or field-specific contacts who may be able to give you job leads. Some newsgroups list job openings. To learn more about newsgroups and how to find them, visit www.learnthenet.com, or http://groups.google.com.

The sites listed later in this chapter will help you find additional Internet resources. I encourage you to be creative in using these and other tools to conduct an active job search.

# Eight Quick Tips to Increase Your Job Search Effectiveness on the Internet

You could get lucky putting your resume on the Internet and waiting for an employer to contact you. It does happen. But being passive on the Internet is often about as effective as using other passive job search methods, which is not very effective at all.

You can do far more on the Internet than simply posting your resume in one or more resume databases. The list of Internet sites later in this chapter gives you job search sites to visit, but here are some brief points to use in preparing:

1. **Be as specific as possible in the job you seek.** This is important in using any job search method, and even more so in using the

Internet. The Internet is so enormous in its reach that looking for a nonspecific job is simply not an appropriate task. So do your career planning homework—reviewing chapters 5, 6, and 7 again, if needed—and be focused in what you are seeking.

2. **Keep your expectations reasonable.** The people who have the most success on the Internet are those who best understand its limitations. For example, those with technical skills that are in short supply will have more employers looking for these skills and more success on the Internet. Keep in mind that many listed jobs are already filled by the time you see them and that thousands may apply to those that sound particularly attractive.

3. **Consider your willingness to move.** If you don't want to move, or are willing to move only to certain locations, restrict your job search to geographic areas that meet your criteria. Many Internet databases enable you to view only those jobs that match your geographic preferences.

4. **Seek out relevant sites.** Simply getting your resume listed on several Internet sites is often not enough. Many employers do not use these sites, or they use one but not another. Many professional associations post job openings on their sites or list other sites that would be of interest to that profession. Check out the resources available to people in the industries or occupations that interest you.

5. **Find specific employer sites.** Most employers have their own Internet sites that list job openings, allow you to apply online, and even provide access to staff who can answer your questions.

6. **Use informal chat rooms or request help.** Many Web sites have interactive chat rooms or allow you to post a message on their online bulletin boards for others to respond to on the board, or privately by e-mail. These methods allow you to meet potential employers or others in your field that can provide the advice or leads you seek.

7. **Use the listings of large Internet browsers or service providers.** While thousands of career-related Internet sites exist, some are better than others. Many sites listed later in this chapter provide links to other recommended sites. Large service

providers such as America Online (www.aol.com) and MSN (www.msn.com) offer career-related information and job listings on their sites and links to other sites. Most larger search engines give links to recommended career-related sites and can be quite useful.

8. **Don't get ripped off online.** Because the Internet has few regulations, crooks use it as a way to take money from trusting souls. Remember that anyone can set up a site, even if the person does not provide a legitimate service. So be careful before you pay money for anything on the Internet. A general rule is that if it sounds too good to be true, it probably is. For example, if a site "guarantees" that it will find you a job or charges high fees, I recommend that you look elsewhere.

# The Most Useful Internet Sites

Thousands of career and job-related sites are on the Internet, and more are added every day. You can waste an enormous amount of time finding what you need. So, to help you save time, I have listed sites here that are among the most helpful. Since many of these sites provide links to other sites, I've listed only a few of the better sites in each category. You can find links to many other sites by starting with these. Among many other resources, JIST Publishing's site at www.jist.com has free career and job search information as well as links to other sites. Note that Web sites sometimes change addresses or shut down, so one or more of the sites mentioned here may not be valid in the future.

**QUICK NOTE**

Some of these listings come from *Best Career and Education Web Sites* (JIST Publishing) by Anne Wolfinger. The book provides more details on each site than I could provide here, as well as on many other sites, organized into useful categories. But these will give you good places to begin.

## Sites with the Best Links to Other Career and Job Search Sites

These sites describe and provide Internet links to other career-related sites. For example, some provide lists of sites by type of job, by employer name, by region, or by other useful criteria.

- **Career Resource Center (www.careers.org):** Provides more than 7,500 links to sites listing job openings at businesses, on job banks, and other resources.

- **CareerOneStop (www.careeronestop.org):** Based on the Department of Labor's vision for America's Labor Market Information System, this site is a gateway to some of the best job listings and free career information sites on the Internet.

- **Job-Hunt (www.job-hunt.org):** More than 9,000 links to carefully selected career resources and employers by state.

- **JobWeb (www.jobweb.com):** Maintained by the National Association of Colleges and Employers. This site is aimed at new college graduates.

- **Quintessential Careers (www.quintcareers.com):** An outstanding site with a huge number of resources and helpful links on all career planning and job hunting topics.

- **The Riley Guide (www.rileyguide.com):** One of the first comprehensive career sites on the Web and still considered by many to be one of the best.

## Best Resume Banks and Sites Listing Job Openings

These Web sites provide listings of job openings and allow you to add your resume for employers to look at. All allow you to look up job openings in a variety of useful ways including by location, job type, and other criteria. Most get their fees from employers and don't charge job seekers. These sites often provide features such as resume and job search advice, e-mail notification to you of new job entries that meet your criteria, and more.

**QUICK TIP**

If you want to save some time, instead of visiting each job bank, you can go to an aggregator such as Simply Hired (www.simplyhired.com), which searches thousands of sites and brings you the results from all of them at the same time.

- **Best Jobs in the USA Today (www.bestjobsusa.com):** Features career-related articles and employer-listed jobs.

- **CareerBuilder (www.careerbuilder.com):** Generally considered to be one of the top three Internet job destinations (along with Monster and Yahoo! HotJobs). Includes more than 1.5 million openings. CareerBuilder partners with more than 150 newspapers across the country, as well as MSN and AOL.

- **CareerSite (www.careersite.com):** Includes a large network of professional resume writers in addition to the usual job listing service.

- **Employment Guide (www.employmentguide.com):** An easy to use, good all-purpose site.

- **ExecuNet (www.execunet.com):** Lists job openings for top-level managers and executives and offers networking opportunities.

- **JobBank USA (www.jobbankusa.com):** Established in 1995, this is one of the more reliable, comprehensive sites.

- **Job Central National Labor Exchange (www.jobcentral.com/index.asp):** A service of DirectEmployers Association, a nonprofit consortium of leading U.S. corporations, in alliance with the National Association of State Workforce Agencies (NASWA). This replacement for America's Job Bank lists openings from all 50 state employment services, plus gives employer-maintained listings and other services.

- **Monster (www.monster.com):** One of the biggest, with lots of features, including browsing or keyword searches of the job database, employer profiles, career fair listings, and career information. Also has a great online networking feature, Monster Networking.

- **TrueCareers (www.truecareers.com):** A resume-posting and job search site for degreed professionals.

- **USAJOBS (www.usajobs.com):** The primary source for federal government jobs and employment information, run by the U.S. Office of Personnel Management.

- **Yahoo! Hot Jobs (http://hotjobs.yahoo.com):** One of the "big three." A full-featured site well worth a visit.

## Best Sites for Occupational Information

These sites provide solid information on the skills, training, work environment, pay, and other important information on all major jobs. Use this to emphasize your most relevant skills and experiences in your resume or prepare for an interview by knowing in advance what skills and other characteristics are most important to an employer. You can also use these sites to identify many jobs that require your skills but that you might otherwise overlook in your job search.

- **Occupational Outlook Handbook (www.bls.gov/oco):** This is the primary source for detailed information on the top 280 jobs in the U.S. economy, held by more than 80 percent of the workforce.

- **O*NET Online (http://online.onetcenter.org/):** Also funded by the U.S. Department of Labor, this site provides descriptions for the 1,100 or so major jobs the government tracks, with sorts by skills required and other criteria.

## Best Sites for Recent Grads or Students

Many good sites exist for students and recent graduates, and here are a few of the best. They provide information, links to other sites, and listings of internships and job openings.

- Campus Career Center (www.campuscareercenter.com)

- College Grad Job Hunter (www.collegegrad.com)

- CollegeJournal (http://college.wsj.com)

- JobWeb (www.jobweb.com)

- MonsterTrak (www.monstertrak.monster.com)

## Best Sites for College, Training, and Financial Aid Information

Many excellent sites provide information on education and training options. Some of the sites here link you to school sites packed with specific information about their programs.

- **College Board** (www.collegeboard.org): Information about the SAT and other standardized college admissions tests.

- **FastWeb** (www.fastweb.com): Matches student profiles with more than 1.3 million financial aid awards.

- **FinAid** (www.finaid.org): A site sponsored by the National Association of Student Financial Aid Administrators.

- **National Association of Colleges and Employers (NACE)** (www.jobweb.org): A collaboration between college career centers and major employers.

- **Peterson's Education Center** (www.petersons.com): Information on colleges, financial aid, internships, and more.

- **U.S. Department of Education's Financial Aid site** (www.fafsa.ed.gov): Allows you to look up and submit applications for various government financial aid programs.

- **U.S. News Education** (www.usnews.com/usnews/edu/ eduhome.htm): Includes school rankings, "best education buys," career tips, financial aid information, and links to other sites.

# Closing Thoughts: Remember Your Main Purpose

You could spend years browsing the Internet's career-related sites. Some people, in fact, have made a career of doing this—and writing books about it. But your task is to get interviews and job offers, not hang around working on your resume, or browsing the Internet, or whatever.

So, please, use the Internet in your search for a new job but be active, not passive. Use other job search methods, too. Spend time every week and every day on the job search. And keep the faith.

One other thing: The Internet is open 24 hours a day, so keep your daytime hours open for contacting employers directly and use the Internet at night and on weekends.

© JIST Publishing

# APPENDIX A

## Sample Job Description from the *Occupational Outlook Handbook*

The *Occupational Outlook Handbook (OOH)* is an important source of information about many jobs. Updated every two years by the U.S. Department of Labor, it provides helpful descriptions for about 280 jobs. These jobs are the most popular ones in our economy and about 88 percent of all people work in one of them.

Included here is the content from one job listed in the *OOH* as an example. I selected the description for school teachers because most people are familiar with this job. As you read the description for school teachers, understand that one or more similar descriptions are in the *OOH* for jobs that will interest you.

The *OOH* descriptions can be very helpful in a variety of ways. For example, as you read a description, you can circle key skills the job requires. This will help you to know which skills you should emphasize in your resume and in interviews. If you are interviewing for a job, reviewing the description in advance can help you to do a much better job in the interview.

Another way to use these descriptions is to look up past jobs to identify skills you needed for them. In many cases, those same or similar skills will be needed in the job you want now. You can cite your previous jobs to support your having the skills needed in the new job. For example, you will find that a school teacher needs to keep up with computer skills, which is a requirement in many other jobs.

As you review the sample description, note that it provides other important information such as salary ranges, education or training required, related jobs, and other details that can help you make career decisions as well as look for a job. Although the descriptions don't change much between editions, data on salaries and growth projections are typically several years old before they are published, so look for the most recent edition of the book.

**QUICK NOTE**

I feel strongly about the value of the *OOH* and encourage you to use it routinely throughout your job search. The book version is available in most libraries and bookstores, or from www.jist.com.

To help you use the *OOH* most efficiently to find information about jobs that interest you, I have added boxes that list the many job-related questions you will find answers to in each section.

# Sample *OOH* Job Description: Teachers— Preschool, Kindergarten, Elementary, Middle, and Secondary

## Significant Points

**QUESTIONS ANSWERED IN THIS SECTION:**
- What are the most important things to know about this job?

Public school teachers must have at least a bachelor's degree, complete an approved teacher education program, and be licensed.

Many States offer alternative licensing programs to attract people into teaching, especially for hard-to-fill positions.

Excellent job opportunities are expected as retirements, especially among secondary school teachers, outweigh slowing enrollment growth; opportunities will vary by geographic area and subject taught.

# Nature of the Work

**QUESTIONS ANSWERED IN THIS SECTION:**

- What is this job like?

- What would I do on a daily basis in this job?

- What tools and equipment would I use on this job?

- How closely would I be supervised on this job?

- What are some alternative titles for this job?

- What are some of the specialties within this job?

Teachers act as facilitators or coaches, using interactive discussions and "hands-on" approaches to help students learn and apply concepts in subjects such as science, mathematics, or English. They utilize "props" or "manipulatives" to help children understand abstract concepts, solve problems, and develop critical thought processes. For example, they teach the concepts of numbers or of addition and subtraction by playing board games. As the children get older, the teachers use more sophisticated materials, such as science apparatus, cameras, or computers.

To encourage collaboration in solving problems, students are increasingly working in groups to discuss and solve problems together. Preparing students for the future workforce is a major stimulus generating changes in education. To be prepared, students must be able to interact with others, adapt to new technology, and think through problems logically. Teachers provide the tools and the environment for their students to develop these skills.

Preschool, kindergarten, and elementary school teachers play a vital role in the development of children. What children learn and experience during their early years can shape their views of themselves and the world and can affect their later success or failure in school, work, and their personal lives. Preschool, kindergarten, and elementary school teachers introduce children to mathematics, language, science, and social studies. They use games, music, artwork, films, books, computers, and other tools to teach basic skills.

Preschool children learn mainly through play and interactive activities. *Preschool teachers* capitalize on children's play to further language and vocabulary development (using storytelling, rhyming games, and acting games), improve social skills (having the children work together to build a neighborhood in a sandbox), and introduce scientific and mathematical concepts (showing the children how to balance and count blocks when building a bridge or how to mix colors when painting). Thus, a less structured approach, including small-group lessons, one-on-one instruction, and learning through creative activities such as art, dance, and music, is adopted to teach preschool children. Play and hands-on teaching also are used by *kindergarten teachers*, but academics begin to take priority in kindergarten classrooms. Letter recognition, phonics, numbers, and awareness of nature and science, introduced at the preschool level, are taught primarily in kindergarten.

Most *elementary school teachers* instruct one class of children in several subjects. In some schools, two or more teachers work as a team and are jointly responsible for a group of students in at least one subject. In other schools, a teacher may teach one special subject—usually music, art, reading, science, arithmetic, or physical education—to a number of classes. A small but growing number of teachers instruct multilevel classrooms, with students at several different learning levels.

*Middle school teachers* and *secondary school teachers* help students delve more deeply into subjects introduced in elementary school and expose them to more information about the world. Middle and secondary school teachers specialize in a specific subject, such as English, Spanish, mathematics, history, or biology. They also can teach subjects that are career oriented. *Vocational education teachers*, also referred to as career and technical or career-technology teachers, instruct and train students to work in a wide variety of fields, such as healthcare, business, auto repair, communications, and, increasingly, technology. They often teach courses that are in high demand by area employers, who may provide input into the curriculum and offer internships to students. Many vocational teachers play an active role in building and overseeing these partnerships. Additional responsibilities of middle and secondary school teachers may include career guidance and job placement, as well as follow-ups with students after graduation. (Special education teachers—who instruct elementary and secondary school students who have a variety of disabilities—are discussed separately in this section of the *Handbook*.)

Computers play an integral role in the education teachers provide. Resources such as educational software and the Internet expose students to a vast range of experiences and promote interactive learning. Through the Internet, students can communicate with other students anywhere in the world, allowing them to share experiences and differing viewpoints. Students also use the Internet for individual research projects and to gather information. Computers are used in other classroom activities as well, from solving math problems to learning English as a second language. Teachers also may use computers to record grades and perform other administrative and clerical duties. They must continually update their skills so that they can instruct and use the latest technology in the classroom.

Teachers often work with students from varied ethnic, racial, and religious backgrounds. With growing minority populations in most parts of the country, it is important for teachers to work effectively with a diverse student population. Accordingly, some schools offer training to help teachers enhance their awareness and understanding of different cultures. Teachers may also include multicultural programming in their lesson plans, to address the needs of all students, regardless of their cultural background.

Teachers design classroom presentations to meet students' needs and abilities. They also work with students individually. Teachers plan, evaluate, and assign lessons; prepare, administer, and grade tests; listen to oral presentations; and maintain classroom discipline. They observe and evaluate a student's performance and potential and increasingly are asked to use new assessment methods. For example, teachers may examine a portfolio of a student's artwork or writing in order to judge the student's overall progress. They then can provide additional assistance in areas in which a student needs help. Teachers also grade papers, prepare report cards, and meet with parents and school staff to discuss a student's academic progress or personal problems.

In addition to conducting classroom activities, teachers oversee study halls and homerooms, supervise extracurricular activities, and accompany students on field trips. They may identify students with physical or mental problems and refer the students to the proper authorities. Secondary school teachers occasionally assist students in choosing courses, colleges, and careers. Teachers also participate in education conferences and workshops.

In recent years, site-based management, which allows teachers and parents to participate actively in management decisions regarding school operations, has gained popularity. In many schools, teachers are increasingly involved in making decisions regarding the budget, personnel, textbooks, curriculum design, and teaching methods.

# Working Conditions

## QUESTIONS ANSWERED IN THIS SECTION:

- What are the typical working hours for this job?

- What is the workplace environment for this job?

- What physical activities does this job require?

- How likely am I to be injured in this job?

- What special equipment would I need to know how to operate?

- How much travel does this job require?

Seeing students develop new skills and gain an appreciation of knowledge and learning can be very rewarding. However, teaching may be frustrating when one is dealing with unmotivated or disrespectful students. Occasionally, teachers must cope with unruly behavior and violence in the schools. Teachers may experience stress in dealing with large classes, heavy workloads, or old schools that are run down and lack many modern amenities. Accountability standards also may increase stress levels, with teachers expected to produce students who are able to exhibit satisfactory performance on standardized tests in core subjects. Many teachers, particularly in public schools, are also frustrated by the lack of control they have over what they are required to teach.

Teachers in private schools generally enjoy smaller class sizes and more control over establishing the curriculum and setting standards for performance and discipline. Their students also tend to be more motivated, since private schools can be selective in their admissions processes.

Teachers are sometimes isolated from their colleagues because they work alone in a classroom of students. However, some schools allow teachers to work in teams and with mentors to enhance their professional development.

Including school duties performed outside the classroom, many teachers work more than 40 hours a week. Part-time schedules are more common among preschool and kindergarten teachers. Although some school districts have gone to all-day kindergartens, most kindergarten teachers still teach two kindergarten classes a day. Most teachers work the traditional 10-month school year with a 2-month vacation during the summer. During the vacation break, those on the 10-month schedule may teach in summer sessions, take other jobs, travel, or pursue personal interests. Many enroll in college courses or workshops to continue their education. Teachers in districts with a year-round schedule typically work 8 weeks, are on vacation for 1 week, and have a 5-week midwinter break. Preschool teachers working in day care settings often work year round.

Most States have tenure laws that prevent public school teachers from being fired without just cause and due process. Teachers may obtain tenure after they have satisfactorily completed a probationary period of teaching, normally 3 years. Tenure does not absolutely guarantee a job, but it does provide some security.

# Training, Other Qualifications, and Advancement

## QUESTIONS ANSWERED IN THIS SECTION:

- What training and education do employers prefer for this job?

- How long will it take to train for this job?

- What are the possibilities for advancement on this job?

- What skills, aptitudes, and personal characteristics do I need in order to do this job?

- What certification and licensing does this job require?

- What opportunities for continuing education does this job provide?

All 50 States and the District of Columbia require public school teachers to be licensed. Licensure is not required for teachers in private schools in most States. Usually licensure is granted by the State Board of Education or a licensure advisory committee. Teachers may be licensed to teach the early childhood grades (usually preschool through grade 3); the elementary grades (grades 1 through 6 or 8); the middle grades (grades 5 through 8); a secondary-education subject area (usually grades 7 through 12); or a special subject, such as reading or music (usually grades kindergarten through 12).

Requirements for regular licenses to teach kindergarten through grade 12 vary by State. However, all States require general education teachers to have a bachelor's degree and to have completed an approved teacher training program with a prescribed number of subject and education credits, as well as supervised practice teaching. Some States also require technology training and the attainment of a minimum grade point average. A number of States require that teachers obtain a master's degree in education within a specified period after they begin teaching.

Almost all States require applicants for a teacher's license to be tested for competency in basic skills, such as reading and writing, and in teaching. Almost all also require the teacher to exhibit proficiency in his or her subject. Many school systems are presently moving toward implementing performance-based systems for licensure, which usually require a teacher to demonstrate satisfactory teaching performance over an extended period in order to obtain a provisional license, in addition to passing an examination in their subject. Most States require continuing education for renewal of the teacher's license. Many States have reciprocity agreements that make it easier for teachers licensed in one State to become licensed in another.

Many States also offer alternative licensure programs for teachers who have a bachelor's degree in the subject they will teach, but who lack the necessary education courses required for a regular license. Many of these alternative licensure programs are designed to ease shortages of teachers of certain subjects, such as mathematics and science. Other programs provide teachers for urban and rural schools that have difficulty filling positions with teachers from traditional licensure programs. Alternative licensure programs are intended to attract people into teaching who do not fulfill traditional licensing standards, including recent college graduates who did not complete education programs and those changing from another career to teaching. In some programs, individuals begin teaching quickly under provisional licensure. After working under the close supervision of experienced educators for 1 or 2 years while taking education courses outside school hours, they receive regular licensure if they have progressed satisfactorily. In other programs, college graduates who do not meet licensure requirements take only those courses that they lack and then become licensed. This approach may take 1 or 2 semesters of full-time study. States may issue emergency licenses to individuals who do not meet the requirements for a regular license when schools cannot attract enough qualified teachers to fill positions. Teachers who need to be licensed may enter programs that grant a master's degree in education, as well as a license.

In many States, vocational teachers have many of the same requirements for teaching as their academic counterparts. However, because knowledge and experience in a particular field are important criteria for the job, some States will license vocational education teachers without a bachelor's degree, provided they can demonstrate expertise in their field. A minimum number of hours in education courses may also be required.

Licensing requirements for preschool teachers also vary by State. Requirements for public preschool teachers are generally more stringent than those for private preschool teachers. Some States require a bachelor's degree in early childhood education, while others require an associate's degree, and still others require certification by a nationally recognized authority. The Child Development Associate (CDA) credential, the most common type of certification, requires a mix of classroom training and experience working with children, along with an independent assessment of an individual's competence.

Private schools are generally exempt from meeting State licensing standards. For secondary school teacher jobs, they prefer candidates who have a bachelor's degree in the subject they intend to teach, or in childhood education for elementary school teachers. They seek candidates among recent college graduates as well as from those who have established careers in other fields. Private schools associated with religious institutions also desire candidates who share the values that are important to the institution.

In some cases, teachers of kindergarten through high school may attain professional certification in order to demonstrate competency beyond that required for a license. The National Board for Professional Teaching Standards offers a voluntary national certification. To become nationally accredited, experienced teachers must prove their aptitude by compiling a portfolio showing their work in the classroom and by passing a written assessment and evaluation of their teaching knowledge. Currently, teachers may become certified in a variety of areas, on the basis of the age of the students and, in some cases, the subject taught. For example, teachers may obtain a certificate for teaching English language arts to early adolescents (aged 11 to 15), or they may become certified as early childhood generalists. All States recognize national certification, and many States and school districts provide special benefits to teachers holding such certification. Benefits typically include higher salaries and reimbursement for continuing education and certification fees. In addition, many States allow nationally certified teachers to carry a license from one State to another.

The National Council for Accreditation of Teacher Education currently accredits teacher education programs across the United States. Graduation from an accredited program is not necessary to become a teacher, but it does make it easier to fulfill licensure requirements. Generally, 4-year colleges require students to wait until their sophomore year before applying for admission to teacher education programs. Traditional education programs for kindergarten and elementary school teachers include courses—designed specifically for those preparing to teach—in mathematics, physical science, social science, music, art, and literature, as well as prescribed professional education courses, such as philosophy of education, psychology of learning, and teaching methods. Aspiring secondary school teachers most often major in the subject they plan to teach while also taking a program of study in teacher preparation. Teacher education programs are now required to include classes in the use of computers and other technologies in order to maintain their accreditation. Most programs require students to perform a student-teaching internship.

Many States now offer professional development schools—partnerships between universities and elementary or secondary schools. Students enter these 1-year programs after completion of their bachelor's degree. Professional development schools merge theory with practice and allow the student to experience a year of teaching firsthand, under professional guidance.

In addition to being knowledgeable in their subject, teachers must have the ability to communicate, inspire trust and confidence, and motivate students, as well as understand the students' educational and emotional needs. Teachers must be able to recognize and respond to individual and cultural differences in students and employ different teaching methods that will result in higher student achievement. They should be organized, dependable, patient, and creative. Teachers also must be able to work cooperatively and communicate effectively with other teachers, support staff, parents, and members of the community.

With additional preparation, teachers may move into positions as school librarians, reading specialists, instructional coordinators, or guidance counselors. Teachers may become administrators or supervisors, although the number of these positions is limited and competition can be intense. In some systems, highly qualified, experienced teachers can become senior or mentor teachers, with higher pay and additional responsibilities. They guide and assist less experienced teachers while keeping most of their own teaching responsibilities. Preschool teachers usually work their way up from assistant teacher, to teacher, to lead teacher—who may be responsible for the instruction of several classes—and, finally, to director of the center. Preschool teachers with a bachelor's degree frequently are qualified to teach kindergarten through grade 3 as well. Teaching at these higher grades often results in higher pay.

# Employment

## QUESTIONS ANSWERED IN THIS SECTION:

- How many jobs are there in this occupation?
- What industries are the jobs in?
- What percentage of workers in this job are self-employed?
- How many people in this job work part-time?
- In what geographic locations are the jobs?

Preschool, kindergarten, elementary school, middle school, and secondary school teachers, except special education, held about 3.8 million jobs in 2004. Of the teachers in those jobs, about 1.5 million are elementary school teachers, 1.1 million are secondary school teachers, 628,000 are middle school teachers, 431,000 are preschool teachers, and 171,000 are kindergarten teachers. The majority work in local government educational services. About 10 percent work for private schools. Preschool teachers, except special education, are most often employed in child daycare services (61 percent), religious organizations (12 percent), local government educational services (9 percent), and private educational services (7 percent). Employment of teachers is geographically distributed much the same as the population.

# Job Outlook

## QUESTIONS ANSWERED IN THIS SECTION:

- Will there be more jobs available in this career in the future, or fewer?
- What factors are likely to influence the number of available jobs in this field?

Job opportunities for teachers over the next 10 years will vary from good to excellent, depending on the locality, grade level, and subject taught. Most job openings will result from the need to replace the large number of teachers who are expected to retire over the 2004-14 period. Also, many beginning teachers decide to leave teaching after a year or two—especially those employed in poor, urban schools—creating additional job openings for teachers. Shortages of qualified teachers will likely continue, resulting in competition among some localities, with schools luring teachers from other States and districts with bonuses and higher pay.

Through 2014, overall student enrollments in elementary, middle, and secondary schools—a key factor in the demand for teachers—are expected to rise more slowly than in the past as children of the baby boom generation leave the school system. This will cause employment to grow as fast as the average for teachers from kindergarten through the secondary grades. Projected enrollments will vary by region. Fast-growing States in the West—particularly California, Idaho, Hawaii, Alaska, Utah, and New Mexico—will experience the largest enrollment increases. Enrollments in the South will increase at a more modest rate than in recent years, while those in the Northeast and Midwest are expected to hold relatively steady or decline. Teachers who are geographically mobile and who obtain licensure in more than one subject should have a distinct advantage in finding a job.

The job market for teachers also continues to vary by school location and by subject taught. Job prospects should be better in inner cities and rural areas than in suburban districts. Many inner cities—often characterized by overcrowded, ill-equipped schools and higher-than-average poverty rates—and rural areas—characterized by their remote location and relatively low salaries—have difficulty attracting and retaining enough teachers. Currently, many school districts have difficulty hiring qualified teachers in some subject areas—most often mathematics, science (especially chemistry and physics), bilingual education, and foreign languages. Increasing enrollments of minorities, coupled with a shortage of minority teachers, should cause efforts to recruit minority teachers to intensify. Also, the number of non-English-speaking students will continue to grow, creating demand for bilingual teachers and for those who teach English as a second language. Specialties that have an adequate number of qualified teachers include general elementary education, physical education, and social studies. Qualified vocational teachers also are currently in demand in a variety of fields at both the middle school and secondary school levels.

The number of teachers employed is dependent as well on State and local expenditures for education and on the enactment of legislation to increase the quality and scope of public education. At the Federal level, there has been a large increase in funding for education, particularly for the hiring of qualified teachers in lower income areas. Also, some States are instituting programs to improve early childhood education, such as offering full day kindergarten and universal preschool. These last two programs, along with projected higher enrollment growth for preschool age children, will create many new jobs for preschool teachers, which are expected to grow much faster than the average for all occupations.

The supply of teachers is expected to increase in response to reports of improved job prospects, better pay, more teacher involvement in school policy, and greater public interest in education. In recent years, the total number of bachelor's and master's degrees granted in education has increased steadily. Because of a shortage of teachers in certain locations, and in anticipation of the loss of a number of teachers to retirement, many States have implemented policies that will encourage more students to become teachers. In addition, more teachers may be drawn from a reserve pool of career changers, substitute teachers, and teachers completing alternative certification programs.

# Earnings

Median annual earnings of kindergarten, elementary, middle, and secondary school teachers ranged from $41,400 to $45,920 in May 2004; the lowest 10 percent earned $26,730 to $31,180; the top 10 percent earned $66,240 to $71,370. Median earnings for preschool teachers were $20,980.

According to the American Federation of Teachers, beginning teachers with a bachelor's degree earned an average of $31,704 in the 2003-04 school year. The estimated average salary of all public elementary and secondary school teachers in the 2003-04 school year was $46,597. Private school teachers generally earn less than public school teachers, but may be given other benefits, such as free or subsidized housing.

In 2004, more than half of all elementary, middle, and secondary school teachers belonged to unions—mainly the American Federation of Teachers and the National Education Association—that bargain with school systems over wages, hours, and other terms and conditions of employment. Fewer preschool and kindergarten teachers were union members—about 17 percent in 2004.

Teachers can boost their salary in a number of ways. In some schools, teachers receive extra pay for coaching sports and working with students in extracurricular activities. Getting a master's degree or national certification often results in a raise in pay, as does acting as a mentor. Some teachers earn extra income during the summer by teaching summer school or performing other jobs in the school system.

# Related Occupations

Preschool, kindergarten, elementary school, middle school, and secondary school teaching requires a variety of skills and aptitudes, including a talent for working with children; organizational, administrative, and recordkeeping abilities; research and communication skills; the power to influence, motivate, and train others; patience; and creativity. Workers in other occupations requiring some of these aptitudes include teachers—postsecondary; counselors; teacher assistants; education administrators; librarians; childcare workers; public relations specialists; social workers; and athletes, coaches, umpires, and related workers.

# Sources of Additional Information

## QUESTIONS ANSWERED IN THIS SECTION:

- Where can I learn more about this job on the Internet?

- What are some of the professional associations for people employed in this job?

**Disclaimer:**

Links to non-BLS Internet sites are provided for your convenience and do not constitute an endorsement.

Information on licensure or certification requirements and approved teacher training institutions is available from local school systems and State departments of education.

Information on the teaching profession and on how to become a teacher can be obtained from:

Recruiting New Teachers, Inc., 385 Concord Ave., Suite 103, Belmont, MA 02478.

Information on teachers' unions and education-related issues may be obtained from the following sources:

American Federation of Teachers, 555 New Jersey Ave. NW., Washington, DC 20001.

National Education Association, 1201 16th St. NW., Washington, DC 20036.

A list of institutions with accredited teacher education programs can be obtained from:

National Council for Accreditation of Teacher Education, 2010 Massachusetts Ave. NW., Suite 500, Washington, DC 20036-1023. Internet: http://www.ncate.org

Information on alternative certification programs can be obtained from:

National Center for Alternative Certification, 1901 Pennsylvania Ave NW, Suite 201, Washington, DC 20006. Internet: http://www.teach-now.org

For information on vocational education and vocational education teachers, contact:

Association for Career and Technical Education, 1410 King St., Alexandria, VA 22314. Internet: http://www.acteonline.org

For information on careers in educating children and issues affecting preschool teachers, contact either of the following organizations:

National Association for the Education of Young Children, 1509 16th St. NW., Washington, DC 20036. Internet: http://www.naeyc.org

Council for Professional Recognition, 2460 16th St. NW., Washington, DC 20009-3575. Internet: http://www.cdacouncil.org

# APPENDIX B

# How to Contact the Professional Resume Writers Who Contributed to This Book

The following professional resume writers contributed resumes to this book. I acknowledge with appreciation their well-written examples.

**Tammy W. Chisholm, CPRW**
MBA Resumes/Advanced Career Marketing
P.O. Box 2403
Mechanicsville, VA 23116
Phone: (804) 878-9296
Fax: (320) 306-1752
E-mail: twchisholm@advancedcareermarketing.com
www.advancedcareermarketing.com

**Kristin Coleman**
Coleman Career Services
Poughkeepsie, NY 12603
Phone: (845) 452-8274
E-mail: Kristin@colemancareerservices.com

**Denyse Cowling, CPC, RPR, CIS**
Career Intelligence Inc.
548 Hurd Ave.
Burlington, ON L7S 1T1
Canada
Phone: (905) 333-8283
Toll-free: (866) 909-0128
E-mail: dcowlings@cogeco.ca
www.careerintelligence.ca

**Jean Cummings, CPRW, CPBS, CEIP, M.A.T.**
A Resume For Today
123 Minot Rd.
Concord, MA 01742
Phone: (978) 254-5472
E-mail: jc@yesresumes.com
www.aResumeForToday.com

**Norine T. Dagliano, NCRW, CPRW, CFRW/CC**
ekm Inspirations
14 N. Potomac St., Ste. 200A
Hagerstown, MD 21740
Phone: (301) 766-2032
Fax: (301) 745-5700
E-mail:
    norine@ekminspirations.com
www.ekminspirations.com

**Becky J. Davis, CPRW**
20 Chamberlain Ave.
Brunswick, ME 04011
Phone: (207) 373-1117
E-mail: RezWriter@aol.com

**Donna Farrise**
President, Dynamic Resumes of Long
    Island, Inc.
300 Motor Pkwy., Ste. 200
Hauppauge, NY 11788
Phone: (631) 951-4120
Toll-free: (800) 528-6796 or
    (800) 951-5191
Fax: (631) 952-1817
E-mail:
    donna@dynamicresumes.com
www.dynamicresumes.com

**Dayna Feist, CPRW, CEIP, JCTC**
Gatehouse Business Services
265 Charlotte St.
Asheville, NC 28801
Phone: (828) 254-7893
Fax: (828) 254-7894
E-mail: dayna@bestjobever.com
www.bestjobever.com

**Terri Lynn Ferrara, CCMC**
Traverse City, MI

**Harold J. Flantzer**
Professional Career Resources/CFA
    Career Centre
8344 Lefferts Blvd., Ste. 2N
Kew Gardens, NY 11415
Phone: (212) 696-6494
Toll-free fax: (877) 848-3295
E-mail: ProCareers@att.net

**Gail Frank, NCRW, CPRW, JCTC, CEIP, MA**
Employment University
10409 Greendale Dr.
Tampa, FL 33626
Phone: (813) 926-1353
Fax: (813) 926-1092
E-mail:
    gailfrank@post.harvard.edu
www.employmentu.com

**Louise Garver, CPRW, CPBS, CEIP, CMP, CLBF, MCDP, JCTC**
Career Directions, LLC
P.O. Box 587
Broad Brook, CT 06016
Phone: (860) 623-9476
Fax: (860) 623-9473
E-mail: louisegarver@cox.net
www.careerdirectionsllc.com

**Wendy Gelberg, M.Ed., CPRW, IJCTC**
President, Gentle Job Search/
  Advantage Resumes
21 Hawthorn Ave.
Needham, MA 02492
Phone: (781) 444-0778
Fax: (781) 455-0778
E-mail: WGelberg@aol.com
www.gentlejobsearch.com

**Don Goodman, CCMC, CPRW**
About Jobs LLC
Offices in U.S. and Canada
Toll-free: (800) 909-0109
Toll-free fax: (877) 572-0991
E-mail:
  dgoodman@GotTheJob.com
www.GotTheJob.com

**Jill Grindle, CPRW**
Resume Inkstincts
Agawam, MA 01001
Phone (413) 789-6046
Fax: (203) 413-4376
E-mail:
  j.grindle@resumeinkstincts.com
www.rersumeinkstincts.com

**Susan Guarneri, NCCC, NCC, DCC, CPRW, CERW, CPBS, CCMC**
Guarneri Associates
6670 Crystal Lake Rd.
Three Lakes, WI 54562
Toll-free: (866) 881-4055
E-mail: susan@resume-magic.com
www.resume-magic.com
Skype: susan.guarneri

**Erika C. Harrigan, CPRW**
Success Partners
Somerset, NJ 08873
Phone: (732) 421-1221
E-mail: eharrigan@
  successpartnerservices.com
www.successpartnerservices.com

**Mary E. Hayward, CPRW, JCTC, CMBTI**
Career Options
18 Canoe Brook Rd., Apt. 17
Putney, VT 05346
Phone: (802) 387-3396
Fax: (802) 258-3252
E-mail: mary.hayward@sit.edu
www.gethiredresumes.com

**Maria E. Hebda, CCMC, CPRW**
Managing Executive, Career Solutions,
  LLC
Trenton, MI
Phone: (734) 676-9170
Fax: (734) 676-9487
E-mail:
  mhebda@writingresumes.com
www.certifiedresumewriters.com,
  www.certifiedcareercoaches.com,
  and www.writingresumes.com

**Gay Anne Himebaugh**
Seaview Résumé Solutions
2855 E. Coast Hwy., Ste. 102
Corona del Mar, CA 92625
Phone: (949) 673-2400
Fax: (949) 673-2428
E-mail: resumes@
  seaviewsecretarial.com
www.seaviewsecretarialsolutions.com

**Erin Kennedy, CPRW**
Professional Resume Services
Lapeer, MI
Phone and fax: (866) 793-9224
E-mail:
    ekennedy@proreswriters.com
www.proreswriters.com

**Kathy Keshemberg, NCRW**
A Career Advantage
1210 George St.
Appleton, WI 54915
Phone: (920) 731-5167
Toll-free: (877) 731-5167
E-mail: kk@acareeradvantage.com
www.acareeradvantage.com

**Lorie Lebert, CPRW, IJCTC,
    CCMC**
THE LORIEL GROUP
P.O. Box 91
Brighton, MI 48116
Phone: (810) 229-6811
Toll-free: (800) 870-9059
E-mail: Lorie@ResumeROI.com
www.CoachingROI.com

**Abby M. Locke, MBA, CRW,
    CFRW, CRBAC, NCRW**
Premier Writing Solutions, LLC
Phone: (202) 635-2197
Toll-free fax: (866) 350-4220
E-mail: info@premierwriting.com
www.premierwriting.com

**Sharon McCormick, M.S., MCC,
    NCCC, NCC, CPRW**
Sharon McCormick Career &
    Vocational Consulting Services
5500 Fortunes Ridge Dr.,
    Unit 85C
Durham, NC 27713
Phone: (919) 424-1244
E-mail:
    smccormick003@nc.rr.com

**Melanie A. Noonan, CPS**
West Patterson, NJ

**Don Orlando, MBA, CPRW,
    JCTC, CCM, CCMC**
The McLean Group
640 S. McDonough St.
Montgomery, AL 36104
Phone: (334) 264-2020
Fax: (334) 264-9227
E-mail: yourcareercoach@
    charterinternet.com

**Judit E. Price, MS, IJCTC, CCM,
    CPRW**
Certified Brand Specialist
Berke and Price Associates
Skills for Career Success
6 Newtowne Way
Chelmsford, MA 01824
Phone: (978) 256-0482
www.careercampaign.com

**Ross Primack, CPRW, CEIP,
    GCDF**
Connecticut Dept. of Labor
200 Folly Brook Blvd.
Wethersfield, CT 06109-1114
Phone: (860) 263-6041
E-mail: ross.primack@ct.gov
www.ctdol.state.ct.us

**Laura Smith-Proulx, CPRW**
An Expert Resume
15400 W. 64th Ave., Ste. E9 #164
Arvada, CO 80007
Toll-free: (877) 258-3517
Toll-free fax: (866) 374-4428
E-mail:
info@anexpertresume.com
www.anexpertresume.com

**Michelle Mastruserio Reitz,**
**CPRW**
Printed Pages
3985 Race Rd., Ste. 6
Cincinnati, OH 45211
Phone: (513) 598-9100
Fax: (513) 598-9220
E-mail:
michelle@printedpages.com
www.printedpages.com

**Billie Ruth Sucher, MS, CTMS,**
**CTSB, JCTC**
Billie Ruth Sucher & Associates
7177 Hickman Rd., Ste. 10
Urbandale, IA 50322
Phone: (515) 276-0061
Fax: (515) 334-8076
E-mail: billie@billiesucher.com

**Brenda Thompson, MS, MBA,**
**CCMC**
TH and Associates
P.O. Box 1043
Bowie, MD 20718
Phone: (301) 266-1115
Fax: (301) 352-6135
E-mail: thworks@comcast.net
www.thworks.net

**Edward Turilli, MA**
AccuWriter Resume, Writing, & Career
Services
100 Ochre Point Ave.
North Kingstown, RI, and Bonita
Springs, FL
Phone: (401) 268-3020
E-mail: edtur@cox.net
www.resumes4-u.com and
www.careers4-u.com

**James Walker, MS**
Counselor, ACAP Center
Bldg. 210, Rm. 006, Custer Ave.
Ft. Riley, KS 66442
Phone: (785) 239-2278
Fax: (785) 239-2251
E-mail: jwalker8199@yahoo.com

**Jeremy Worthington, CARW**
Buckeye Resumes
2092 Atterbury Ave.
Columbus, OH 43229
Phone: (614) 861-6606
Fax (614) 737-6166
E-mail:
jeremy@buckeyeresumes.com
www.buckeyeresumes.com

**Daisy Wright, CDP**
Lead Career Coach and Author
The Wright Career Solution
Brampton, ON, L6Z 4V6
Canada
Phone: (905) 840-7039
E-mail: careercoach@
thewrightcareer.com
www.thewrightcareer.com

## Professional Associations for Resume Writers and Career Counselors

Contact these organizations directly or see their Web sites for recommendations of resume writers in your area.

### Career Directors International

Phone: (321) 752-0442
Toll-free: (888) 867-7972
E-mail: info@careerdirectors.com
Web site: www.careerdirectors.com

### Career Management Alliance

A Division of Kennedy Information, Inc.
1 Phoenix Mill Lane, Fl. 3
Peterborough, NH 03458
Phone: (603) 924-0900, ext. 617
Fax: (603) 924-4034
Web site: www.careermanagementalliance.com

### National Résumé Writers' Association

www.nrwaweb.com

### Professional Association of Résumé Writers & Career Coaches

1388 Brightwaters Blvd., NE
St. Petersburg, FL 33704
Phone: (727) 821-2274
Toll-free: (800) 822-7279
Fax: (727) 894-1277
E-mail: PARWhq@aol.com
Web site: www.parw.com

# Index

*150 Best Jobs for Your Skills,* 86

## A

accomplishments, resumes, 8–9, 26–27, 176
accounting resume samples, 268–269
ACT!, 361
action statements, cover letters, 294
action words, resumes, 8–9, 24
adaptive skills, 78, 80–82
Adaptive Skills Checklist, 81–82
addresses
    alternative, 149–150
    chronological resumes, 20
    cover letters, 293
age discrimination, 134–135, 142–143
appearance, resumes, 9
applications, job searches, 347
armed forces, job opportunities, 115
Association of Online Resume and Career
    Professionals (AORCP) Web site, 155
audience, cover letters, 292

## B

basic skills, 42–43
basics, resumes, 6–10
    accomplishments, stressing, 8–9, 176
    action words, 8–9, 24
    appearance, 9
    length, 6–7
    paper, 10
    "perfect", 10
    printing quality, 9–10
    proofreading, 8
    writing yourself, 9
Beatty, Richard, 338
*Best Career and Education Web Sites,* 371
Best Jobs in the USA Today Web site, 373
*Best Resumes for College Students and New Grads,*
    139
Blogger, 71
blogs, 70–71, 73
bracket of responsibility, objectives, 129
brevity and clarity, resumes, 175
business managers and executives resume samples,
    185–189, 226–227

## C

Campus Career Center Web site, 374
CareerBuilder Web site, 373
career changers resume samples, 228–231
career changes, 138, 339
Career Directors International (CDI) Web site, 155,
    394
*Career Guide to Industries,* 122
Career Management Alliance (The Alliance) Web
    site, 155–156, 394
CareerOneStop Web site, 372
career planning, 106–123, 337–338. *See also*
    objectives
    *Career Guide to Industries,* 122
    *Guide for Occupational Exploration (GOE),*
        118–121
        interest areas, 118–119
        work groups, 119–121
    industry choices, 121–123
    Occupational Information Network
        (O*NET), 115–118
    *Occupational Outlook Handbook,* 107–115
        job descriptions, 108
        job lists, 109–115
        job targets, identifying, 108
        salary information, 108
        skills needed, identifying, 107–108
        transferable skills, identifying, 108
    related occupations, 106–107
career portfolios, online, 71–74
Career Professionals of Canada Web site, 155
Career Resources Center Web site, 372
CareerSite Web site, 373
children, resume problem, 144
Chisholm, Tammy W., 389
chronological resumes, 11, 15–36, 157–158
    address, 20
    business, management and executives, and
        finance samples, 185–189
    education and training, 23–24, 158
    education samples, 220–224
    e-mail addresses, 20–21
    final drafts, 29
    heading, 19

healthcare and medical samples, 190–195
hospitality and culinary samples, 196–199
IT and engineering samples, 200–204
mechanical and skilled trades sample, 209–210
media, information, and communications samples, 211–212
modifications, 158
name, 19
objectives, 21–23
   adding, 158
   samples, 23
personal information, 27–28
phone numbers, 20–21
professional organizations, 26–27
recognition and awards, 27
references, 28
sales (including retail) and marketing samples, 213–219
samples, 16–18
sections, 19–28
skills, emphasizing, 158
strengths, emphasizing, 158
students and new graduates with limited work experience samples, 205–208
work experience, 24–26
   accomplishments, 26–27
   dates, 25
   duties, 26
   employers, 25
   job titles, 25
clerical and administrative resume samples, 232–235
closings, cover letters, 294
cold contacts, 351–352
Coleman, Kristin, 389
College Board Web site, 375
College Grad Job Hunter Web site, 374
CollegeJournal Web site, 374
combination resumes, 11, 50–60, 159
   career changer, older, 52–54
   JIST card sample, 50–51
   lack of experience, 53, 55–56, 59–60
   white space and brief copy, 55, 57–58
Comprehensive Resume Worksheet, 162–173
computer skills, 79
confidentiality, 19
Construction Trades and Related Workers job list, 113–114
copies, resumes, 180

counselors, 156, 394
cover letters, 291–314
   action statements, 294
   address, 293
   appearance, 293–294
   audience, 292
   closings, 294
   errors, 293
   experiences, 294
   opening, 294
   personal contacts, 294–300
      no interview scheduled, 295, 300
      post-interview, 295, 299
      pre-interview, no specific job, 295, 298
      pre-interview, specific job, 295, 297
      samples, 296–300
   personalization, 293
   quick tips, 292–294
   recipients, 292
   salutation, 293
   samples, 304–314
      career changer, 314
      no interview scheduled, 300, 304, 306–307, 309–312
      post-interview, 299
      pre-interview, no specific job, 298, 305
      pre-interview, specific job, 297, 308
      want ad response, 313
   skills, 294
   unknown recipients, 301–303
   unsolicited resumes, 303
   want ad response, 302
Cowling, Denyse, 389
creative resumes, 12, 159–160
creativity, skills resumes, 40
criminal record, resume problem, 145–146
Cummings, Jean, 390
curriculum vitae, 5, 27, 160–161. See also resumes
CV, see curriculum vitae

## D

Dagliano, Norine T., 390
dates, work experience, 25
Davis, Becky J., 390
design tips, resumes, 177–180
   copies, number of, 180
   edit for appearance, 179
   envelopes, 179

fonts, 178
graphics, 179
length, 178
paper, 179
photocopies, 180
professional writers, 177
readability, 177–178
small print, 178
*Dictionary of Occupational Titles,* 109
*Directory of Professional Resume Writers,* 154
Disability, resume problem, 144
DisabilityInfo.gov, 144
Dixson, Kirsten, 69–74
*Don't Send a Resume,* 4
drafts, 176
dress for success, interviews, 356–357
duties, work experience, 26

## E

editing, resumes, 46, 179
education and training resume samples, 23–24, 236
Education and Training Worksheet, 88–91
education, resume problem, 142
education resume samples, 220–224, 270–271
Eight Quick Questions to Help You Define Your Ideal Job Worksheet, 123–128
electronic resumes, 61–74
    accounting samples, 268–269
    adopting existing resumes, 66–67
    education samples, 270–271
    employer Web sites, 62–63
    executive samples, 272–274
    human resources, 275–277
    information technology samples, 278
    keywords, 67–69
        search technology, 67–68
        selection, 68–69
    length, 66
    manufacturing samples, 279–281
    public administration samples, 282–284
    sales samples, 285–287
    samples, 267–287
    text-only sample, 63–66
e-mail addresses
    chronological resumes, 20–21
    resume problem, 149
    thank-you letters, 319
e-mail attachments, 332

employer-desired skills, 86
employers, work experience, 25
employer Web sites, 62–63
employment agencies, 346
Employment Guide Web site, 373
employment proposals, 5. *See also* resumes
enclosures, 160, 332
*Enhanced Occupational Outlook Handbook,* 109
entrepreneurs resume samples, 237
envelopes, 179
errors, cover letters, 293
ExecuNet Web site, 373
executive resume samples, 272–274
experience, resume problem, 140
experiences, cover letters, 294
experts, resumes, 6
*EZ Occupational Outlook Handbook,* 115

## F

family status, resume problem, 144
Farming, Fishing, and Forestry Occupations job list, 113
Farrise, Donna, 390
Farr's Dress and Grooming Rule, 357
FastWeb Web site, 375
Feist, Dayna, 390
Ferrara, Terri Lynn, 390
FinAid Web site, 375
final drafts
    chronological resumes, 29
    skills resumes, 46
finance and accounting resume samples, 238–239
fired, resume problem, 137
flags (self-sticking notes), 332–333
Flantzer, Harold J., 390
follow-up, 14, 360–362
follow-up letters, 332
fonts, resumes, 178
Fox, Jeffrey, 4
Frank, Gail, 390

## G

*Gallery of Best Resumes,* 10
gaps in work history, resume problem, 136
Garver, Louise, 390
Gelberg, Wendy, 391
Goodman, Don, 391
graphics, resumes, 179
Grindle, Jill, 391

Guarneri, Susan, 391
*Guide for Occupational Exploration (GOE)*, 118–121.
    *See also New Guide for Occupational Exploration*
        interest areas, 118–119
        work groups, 119–121

## H

handwritten thank-you letters, 319
Harrigan, Erika C., 391
Harris polls, 70
Hayward, Mary E., 391
heading, chronological resumes, 19
healthcare and medical resume samples, 190–195
healthcare, medical, and veterinary resume
    samples, 240–241
Hebda, Maria E., 391
Himebaugh, Gay Anne, 391
history, unrelated to objective, 138
HomeFair's Salary Calculator, 108
honesty, resumes, 7, 174–175
hospitality and culinary resume samples, 196–199
hospitality resume samples, 242
human resources, job searches, 347
human resources resume samples, 275–277

## I

industry choices, 121–123
information, collecting and documenting, 87–103,
    161–173
        Comprehensive Resume Worksheet,
            162–173
        Education and Training Worksheet, 88–91
        filling out forms, 87–88
        Other Life Experiences Worksheet, 101–102
        Work and Volunteer History Worksheet,
            92–100
        Your Most Important Accomplishments and
            Skills to Tell an Employer Worksheet,
            102–103
information technology resume samples, 278
Installation, Maintenance, and Repair Occupations
    job list, 114
Instant Resume Worksheet, 30–36
International Association of Career Coaches Web
    site, 156
Internet job searches, 69–74, 365–376
        blogs, 70–71, 73, 368
        career portfolios, 71–74
        college, training, and financial aid Web
            sites, 375

dangers, 366–367
effectiveness, 369–371
e-mail, 368
employer Web sites, 368
information, 368
networking, 369
newsgroups, 369
occupational information, 374
online identity, 70
phishing and spoofing, 367
resume banks, 372–374
search engines, 70
security, 367
specialty sites, 368
students or recent grads, 374–375
Web sites, best links, 372
interviews
    dress for success, 356–357
    follow-up, 14
    negatives, handling, 134
    number per day, 14, 355–356
    questions
        answering process, 358–360
        problematic, 357–358
    skills, 138
    successful, 14
    traditional, 358
IT and engineering resume samples, 200–204,
    243–245

## J

JibberJobber Web site, 361
JIST Cards, 47–49, 326–331
    career changer, 47
    combination resume sample, 50–54
    defined, 47
    e-mail signature lines, 327
    format, 326–327
    job search helpers, 318
    lack of work experience, 53, 55–56, 59–60
    paper, 327
    post-interview, 317
    pre-interview, 316
    results, 326
    samples, 328–331
        chemist, 329
        electronics installer, 330
        hotel manager, 331
        manager, 332
        office worker, 328

systems analyst, 329
warehouse manager, 330
thank-you letters, 320
uses, 327
white space and brief copy, 55, 57–58
JIST Web site, 85
JobBank USA Web site, 373
Job Central National Labor Exchange Web site, 373
job descriptions, skills resumes, 42
Job-Hunt Web site, 372
job lead cards, 361–362
job objectives, *see* objectives
The Job Objective Worksheet, 130–131
job-related skills, 79, 85–86
job searches
advice, 337–338
applications, 347
best methods, 348–352
cold contacts, 351–352
employment agencies, 346
follow-up, 14, 360–362
human resources, 347
impressions, 356–360
Internet, 69–74
interviews per day, 14, 355–356
job lead cards, 361–362
leads, 344–352
networking, 348–350
objectives, clearly defined, 342–344
quick review, 362–363
resumes, 347
skills, identifying, 340–341
small employers, 352
state employment services, 345–346
techniques, 13
temporary agencies, 346
thank-you letters, 318, 322
time spent, 13–14, 353–355
tips, 13–14
tools, 4–5
want ads, 345
*Job Search Magic*, 338
job-specific skills, 43
job titles
objectives, 129
work experience, 25
JobWeb Web site, 372, 375

**K**

Kennedy, Erin, 392
Keshemberg, Kathy, 392
key skill proofs, 44–46
key skills lists, 42–43
keywords, electronic resumes, 67–69
search technology, 67–68
selection, 68–69
Kursmark, Louise, 139

**L**

lack of education, 142
lack of experience, 140
JIST Cards, 53, 55–56, 59–60
skills resume, 38–40
Lathrop, Richard, 59
leads, job searches, 344–352
Lebert, Lorie, 392
length
electronic resumes, 66
limits, 178
thank-you letters, 319–320
traditional resumes, 6–7
letters. *See also* thank-you letters
unsolicited, 334
Locke, Abby M., 392

**M**

Management and Business and Financial Operations Occupations job list, 109–110
manufacturing resume samples, 279–281
McCormick, Sharon, 392
mechanical and skilled trades resume samples, 209–210, 246–251
media, arts, information, and communications resume samples, 211–212, 252–255
Microsoft Excel, 361
Microsoft Word, 301
military-to-civilian transitions resume samples, 256–258
military work experience, 25
MonsterTrak Web site, 375
Monster Web site, 373
moved recently, resume problem, 141

**N**

name, chronological resumes, 19
National Association of Colleges and Employers (NACE) Web site, 375

national origin, resume problem, 141
National Résumé Writers' Association Web site, 155, 394
need for resumes, 4–5
negative references, 145
negatives, resume, 133–135, 137
networking, 348–350, 369
*New Guide for Occupational Exploration,* 118. *See also Guide for Occupational Exploration*
newsgroups, 369
*Next-Day Job Interview,* 138
Noble, David, 10
no degree/no college resume samples, 259–260
Noonan, Melanie A., 392
numbers, resumes, 175

## O

objectives, 13, 21–23, 40–41
    defining, 123–128
    Eight Quick Questions to Help You Define Your Ideal Job Worksheet, 123–128
    finalizing, 131–132
    heading, 41
    The Job Objective Worksheet, 130–131
    job searches, 342–344
    need for resumes, 105–106
    samples, 23
    supporting, 175
    unsure about, 141
    writing, 128–130
        bracket of responsibility, 129
        job titles, 129
        skills, important, 129–130
        specifics, 130
Occupational Information Network (O*NET), 115–118
*Occupational Outlook Handbook (OOH),* 26, 69, 107–115
    job descriptions, 108
    job lists, 109–115
    job targets, identifying, 108
    salary information, 108
    sample job description, 377–387
    skills needed, identifying, 107–108
    transferable skills, identifying, 108
    Web site, 374
Office and Administrative Support Occupations job list, 112–113
older workers, resume problem, 143

*150 Best Jobs for Your Skills,* 86
One-Stop career centers Web site, 156
*O*NET Dictionary of Occupational Titles,* 69, 116
O*NET Online Web site, 374
online identities, 70
online job searches, 69–74
    blogs, 70–71, 73, 368
    career portfolios, 71–74
    college, training, and financial aid Web sites, 375
    dangers, 366–367
    effectiveness, 369–371
    e-mail, 368
    employer Web sites, 368
    information, 368
    networking, 369
    newsgroups, 369
    occupational information, 374
    online identity, 70
    phishing and spoofing, 367
    resume banks, 372–374
    search engines, 70
    security, 367
    specialty sites, 368
    students or recent grads, 374–375
    Web sites, best links, 372
opening, cover letters, 294
Orlando, Don, 392
Other Life Experiences Worksheet, 101–102
out of work, resume problem, 136–137
overqualified, resume problem, 140–141

## P

paper
    resumes, 10, 179
    thank-you letters, 319
"perfect" resumes, 10, 13
personal contacts, cover letters, 294–300
    no interview scheduled, 295, 300
    post-interview, 295, 299
    pre-interview, no specific job, 295, 298
    pre-interview, specific job, 295, 297
    samples, 296–300
personal information
    chronological resumes, 27–28
    resume problem, 150
personality traits, 78–79
personalization, cover letters, 293
Peterson's Education Center Web site, 375

phishing and spoofing, 367
phone messages, 20–21
    resume problem, 147–148
phone numbers
    chronological resumes, 20–21
    resume problem, 147–148
photocopies, 180
photographs, resume problem, 150–151
physical limitations, resume problem, 144
portfolios, 160
Price, Judit E., 392
Primack, Ross, 392
print and photocopy shops, 156–157
printing quality, resumes, 9–10
problems
    addresses, alternative, 149–150
    age discrimination, 134–135
    changing careers, 138
    children, 144
    criminal record, 145–146
    disability, 144
    e-mail addresses, 149
    family status, 144
    fired, 137
    gaps in work history, 136
    handling, 135–136
    hiding in skills resumes, 38
    history, unrelated to objective, 138
    interviews, 134
    lack of education, 142
    lack of experience, 53, 55–56, 59–60, 140
    moved recently, 141
    national origin, 141
    negative references, 145
    negatives, 133–135, 137
    objective, unsure about, 141
    older workers, 143
    out of work, 136–137
    overqualified, 140–141
    personal information, 150
    phone numbers and messages, 147–148
    photographs, 150–151
    physical limitations, 144
    race, 141
    recent graduates, 139
    references, 151
    religion, 141
    "Resume" header, 147
    sensitive subjects, 134–135
    youth, 142

Production Occupations job list, 114–115
Professional and Related Occupations job list,
    110–112
Professional Association of Résumé Writers &
    Career Coaches (PARW/CC) Web site, 155, 394
professional organizations, chronological resumes,
    26–27
professional profiles, 5. *See also* resumes
proofreading, resumes, 8, 46, 176
public administration resume samples, 282–284
Purdue University's College of Liberal Arts Web
    site, 161

## Q

qualifications briefs, 5, 59–60. *See also* resumes
questions
    answering process, 358–360
    problematic, 357–358
Quintessential Careers Web site, 372

## R

race, resume problem, 141
readability, resumes, 177–178
recent graduates, resume problem, 139
recipients, cover letters, 292
recognition and awards, chronological resumes, 27
references
    chronological resumes, 28
    letters, 333–334
    lists, 333
    negative, 145
    resume problem, 151
Reitz, Michelle Mastruserio, 393
religion, resume problem, 141
ResTrust, 141
*Résumé Magic*, 63
resumes
    basics, 6–10
        accomplishments, stressing, 8–9
        action words, 8–9
        appearance, 9
        length, 6–7
        paper, 10
        "perfect", 10
        printing quality, 9–10
        proofreading, 8
        writing yourself, 9
    brevity and clarity, 175
    chronological, 11, 15–36, 157–158
    combination, 11, 159

creative, 12, 159–160
defined, 3–4
design tips, 177–180
drafts, 176
electronic, 61–74
experts, 6
header, resume problem, 147
honesty, 7, 174–175
job search tools, 4–5
names used, 5
need for, 4–5
numbers, 175
objectives, 105–106, 175
"perfect", 10, 13
proofreading, 176
quick tips, 3–14
requirement, 4
sensitive subjects, 134–135
skills, or functional, 11, 37–49, 159
structured communications, 5
text-only, 66–67
    text-only sample, 63–66
*The Resume Solution,* 55
resume writers, 154–155, 177, 394
The Riley Guide Web site, 372

## S

Salary.com Web site, 108
sales (including retail) and marketing resume
    samples, 213–219
Sales and Related Occupations job list, 112
sales resume samples, 261–262, 285–287
salutation
    cover letters, 293
    thank-you letters, 319
search engines, 70
self-sticking notes, 332–333
sensitive subjects, resume problem, 134–135
Service Occupations job list, 112
signature, thank-you letters, 320
Simply Hired Web site, 373
skills, 13, 77–86, 176
    adaptive, 78, 80–82
    computer, 79
    cover letters, 294
    employer-desired, 86
    identifying, 79–85
    job-related, 79, 85–86
    job searches, 340–341
    objectives, 129–130

personality traits, 78–79
transferable, 79, 82–85
skills, or functional, resumes, 11, 37–49, 159
    business managers and executives samples,
        226–227
    career changers samples, 228–231
    clerical and administrative samples,
        232–235
    creativity, 40
    editing, 46
    education and training samples, 236
    entrepreneurs samples, 237
    final drafts, 46
    finance and accounting samples, 238–239
    healthcare, medical, and veterinary samples,
        240–241
    hiding problems, 38
    hospitality resume samples, 242
    IT, engineering samples, 243–245
    job descriptions, 42
    lack of work experience, 38–40
    mechanical and skilled trades, technology
        samples, 246–251
    media, arts, and communications samples,
        252–255
    military-to-civilian transitions samples,
        256–258
    no degree/no college samples, 259–260
    objectives, 40–41
    proofreading, 46
    sales samples, 261–262
    samples, 38–40, 47–60
        career changer, 47–49
        lack of work experience, 38–40
    sections, 40
    skills section, 41–46
        headings, 41
        job-specific skills, 43
        key skill proofs, 44–46
        key skills lists, 42–43
        transferable skills, 44
    students and new graduates samples,
        263–265
A Skills Review Worksheet, 341
skills section, skills resumes, 41–46
    headings, 41
    job-specific skills, 43
    key skill proofs, 44–46
    key skills lists, 42–43
    transferable skills, 44

Skills Triad, 78
small employers, 352
small print, resumes, 178
Smith-Proulx, Laura, 393
state employment services, 345–346
sticky notes, 332–333
structured communications, resumes, 5
Structure Your Job Search Like a Job Worksheet, 354–355
students and new graduates resume samples, 205–208, 263–265
Sucher, Billie Ruth, 393
Swanson, David, 55

**T**

temporary agencies, 346
text-only resumes, 66–67
thank-you letters, 315–325, 360–361
  e-mail, 319
  handwritten, 319
  JIST Cards, 320
  job search helpers, 318, 322
  length, 319–320
  paper, 319
  post-interviews, 317–318
  pre-interviews, 316
  quick tips, 319–320
  salutation, 319
  samples, 321–325
  signature, 320
  timing, 320
Thompson, Brenda, 393
Three Good Worker Traits Worksheet, 80
timing, thank-you letters, 320
traditional questions, 358
transferable skills, 42–44, 79, 82–85
Transferable Skills Checklist, 83–84
Transportation and Material Moving Occupations job list, 115
TrueCareers Web site, 374
Turilli, Edward, 393
TypePad, 71

**U**

*The Ultimate Job Search,* 338
unknown recipients, cover letters, 301–303
unsolicited letters, 334
unsolicited resumes, cover letters, 303
USAJOBS Web site, 374

U.S. Department of Education's Financial Aid Web site, 375
U.S. News Education Web site, 375

**V**

*The Very Quick Job Search,* 338
volunteer work, 25

**W**

Walker, James, 393
want ad response, cover letters, 302
want ads, 345
Weblogs, *see* blogs
Web sites
  Association of Online Resume and Career Professionals (AORCP), 155
  best career-related links, 372
  Best Jobs in the USA Today, 373
  Brandego, 74
  Campus Career Center, 374
  CareerBuilder, 373
  Career Directors International (CDI), 155
  Career Management Alliance (The Alliance), 155–156
  CareerOneStop, 372
  Career Professionals of Canada, 155
  Career Resource Center, 372
  CareerSite, 373
  College Board, 375
  College Grad Job Hunter, 374
  CollegeJournal, 374
  college, training, and financial aid Web sites, 375
  DisabilityInfo.gov, 144
  employer, 62–63
  Employment Guide, 373
  ExecuNet, 373
  FastWeb, 375
  FinAid, 375
  HireVue, 151
  HomeFair's Salary Calculator, 108
  International Association of Career Coaches, 156
  InterviewStream, 151
  JibberJobber, 361
  JIST.com, 85
  JobBank USA, 373
  Job Central National Labor Exchange, 373
  Job-Hunt, 372

JobWeb, 372, 375
Learn the Net, 369
Monster, 373
MonsterTrak, 375
National Association of Colleges and
    Employers (NACE), 375
National Résumé Writers' Association, 155
*Occupational Outlook Handbook,* 109, 374
One-Stop career centers, 156
O*NET, 117, 374
Peterson's Education Center, 375
Professional Association of Résumé Writers
    & Career Coaches (PARW/CC), 155
Purdue University's College of Liberal Arts,
    161
Quintessential Careers, 372
ResTrust, 141
resume banks, 372–374
The Riley Guide, 372
Salary.com, 108
Simply Hired, 373
students or recent grads, 374–375
TrueCareers, 374
USAJOBS, 374
U.S. Department of Education's Financial
    Aid, 375
U.S. News Education, 375
WorkBlast, 151
Yahoo! HotJobs, 374
Whitcomb, Susan Britton, 63, 338
*Who's Hiring Who,* 59
Wolfinger, Anne, 371
Work and Volunteer History Worksheet, 92–100
work experience, chronological resumes, 24–26
    accomplishments, 26–27
    dates, 25
    duties, 26
    employers, 25
    job titles, 25
worksheets
    Adaptive Skills Checklist, 81–82
    Comprehensive Resume, 162–173
    Education and Training, 88–91
    Eight Quick Questions to Help You Define
        Your Ideal Job, 123–128
    Instant Resume, 30–36
    The Job Objective, 130–131
    Other Life Experiences, 101–102
    A Skills Review, 341
    Structure Your Job Search Like a Job,
        354–355
    Three Good Worker Traits, 80
    Transferable Skills Checklist, 83–84
    Work and Volunteer History, 92–100
    Your Ideal Job, 342–344
    Your Most Important Accomplishments and
        Skills to Tell an Employer, 102–103
    Your Top Five Transferable Skills, 85
    Your Top Three Adaptive Skills, 82
Worthington, Jeremy, 393
Wright, Daisy, 393
writing as yourself, resumes, 9, 173–174

# X–Z

Yahoo! HotJobs Web site, 374
Your Ideal Job Worksheet, 342–344
Your Most Important Accomplishments and Skills
    to Tell an Employer Worksheet, 102–103
Your Top Five Transferable Skills Worksheet, 85
Your Top Three Adaptive Skills Worksheet, 82
youth, resume problem, 142